The Political Economy of Monetary Solidarity

The Political Economy of Monetary Solidarity

Understanding the Euro Experiment

Waltraud Schelkle

OXFORD
UNIVERSITY PRESS

OXFORD
UNIVERSITY PRESS

Great Clarendon Street, Oxford, OX2 6DP,
United Kingdom

Oxford University Press is a department of the University of Oxford.
It furthers the University's objective of excellence in research, scholarship, and education by publishing worldwide. Oxford is a registered trade mark of Oxford University Press in the UK and in certain other countries

First Edition published in 2017

Published in the United States of America by Oxford University Press
198 Madison Avenue, New York, NY 10016, United States of America

British Library Cataloguing in Publication Data
Data available

Library of Congress Control Number: 2016954937

ISBN 978–0–19–871793–5

Cover Image: ©Sofya Goncharuk/Shutterstock

Acknowledgments

One of the greatest pleasures of writing a book is to experience how many colleagues, students, and friends are out there, generously spending time and effort on what will pass as somebody else's work. I am deeply grateful to them all.

None has been a more dedicated friend than Deborah Mabbett (Birkbeck) who read the book script twice and worked tirelessly to improve its language and argument. Zbigniew Truchlewski (Central European University, Budapest) planted the idea of this book in my mind several years ago and then organized a workshop at Central European University at which the entire script was discussed; I am immensely grateful for extensive written comments by Achim Kemmerling, Akos Mate, Antonio Leite, Alfredo Hernandez Sanchez, Imre Szabo, and above all Zbig himself. Peter Hall (Harvard) has several times given me his extremely insightful comments, notwithstanding the fact that so many people make demands on his time. Alison Johnston (Oregon State) engaged, as usual, in an intense and cheerful discussion of our different crisis interpretations. Chloé Touzet (Oxford) wrote perceptive comments on two chapters; so did Christa van Wijnbergen (Utrecht), as always constructive and most helpful. Even before it had started, Anke Hassel (Hertie School of Governance) gave me encouraging comments on my book project.

Colleagues and friends spent considerable time giving me constructive feedback: Suzanne Berger (MIT), Richard Bronk (LSE), Sebastian Dullien (Berlin), Peter Gourevitch (Brown), Randall Henning (American University), Abby Innes (LSE), Erik Jones (Johns Hopkins), Mareike Kleine (LSE), Ellen Meade (Federal Reserve Bank), David Moss (Harvard), Constanzo Ranci (Milan), Vivien Schmidt (Boston), and Stefanie Walter (Zürich). I also benefited from questions and comments by seminar participants at Central European University Budapest, at the European Central Bank (ECB), Center for European Studies at Harvard, the Hertie School of Governance, the University of Uppsala, the University of Zürich, and, last but not least, at my home institution, the European Institute at London School of Economics. Its directors, the late Maurice Fraser, Sara Hobolt, and Kevin Featherstone, have been as supportive as one can wish for.

Staff at the ECB were very helpful in answering questions about TARGET (Ulrich Bindseil, Tobias Linzert, and Daniela Russo); so was the chief economist of the Bundesbank, Jens Ulbrich. Philippine Cour-Thimann, Johannes Lindner, and Bernhard Winkler were most stimulating interlocutors at the ECB.

Two anonymous referees provided straightforward and constructive comments which were gratefully received. Dominic Byatt from Oxford University Press was a prompt and encouraging editor in every exchange I had with him; the OUP editorial team was extremely efficient and pleasant to work with. Sean Deel (LSE) did an excellent job in putting together the Index.

Last but not least, I want to thank the Leverhulme Trust for funding a research fellowship in 2014–15 (RF-2014-710/7) that supported my sabbatical at the Minda de Gunzburg Center for European Studies at Harvard. It provided a most conducive research environment, pleasantly interrupted by the Visiting Scholars seminars convened by Arthur Goldhammer and the Political Economy faculty seminar led by Jeff Frieden at the Government department. Joaquin Almunia (Visiting Fellow Harvard and LSE, former Commissioner) and Hans-Helmut Kotz (Harvard, former Bundesbank) readily gave me the opportunity to ask them many questions.

My family went through a very difficult time while I was at Harvard and I will be forever grateful to my parents and my sister, in particular, that they wanted me to stay and continue my research rather than be with them.

Contents

List of Figures

List of Tables

List of Abbreviations

CEE	Central and Eastern Europe
EA	Euro Area
ECB	European Central Bank
EFSF	European Financial Stability Facility
EITC	Earned Income Tax Credit
ELA	Emergency Liquidity Assistance
EMU	Economic and Monetary Union
ERM	Exchange Rate Mechanism
ESCB	European System of Central Banks
ESM	European Stability Mechanism
EU	European Union
FDIC	Federal Deposit Insurance Corporation
FOMC	Federal Reserve Open Market Committee
GDP	gross domestic product
IMF	International Monetary Fund
LTRO	Long-Term Refinancing Operations
OCA	Optimal Currency Area
OECD	Organisation for Economic Co-operation and Development
OMT	Outright Monetary Transactions
REER	Real Effective Exchange Rate
RFC	Reconstruction Finance Corporation
S&L	Savings and Loans
SGP	Stability and Growth Pact
SMP	Securities Market Programme
SNAP	Supplementary Nutritional Assistance Program
SRM	Single Resolution Mechanism
SSM	Single Supervisory Mechanism
TANF	Temporary Assistance for Needy Families
TFEU	Treaty on the Functioning of the European Union

1

Introduction

Understanding the Euro Experiment

Monetary solidarity is not what many readers would spontaneously associate with the euro experiment. Deliberate or at least consciously tolerated risk sharing between members of a currency union—which is how monetary solidarity is defined here—is indeed an inconspicuous feature of the euro area (EA). It exists, yet the potential for mutually beneficial cooperation in this regard is not exploited. The first section deals with the puzzle of political economy that is driving the analysis in this book while the second section gives a general introduction to the economics that underpins this study. The chapter concludes with an overview of the book.

1.1 The Political-Economic Paradox of Diversity

Creating the European monetary union between an ever expanding number of diverse and unequal nation states is arguably one of the biggest social experiments in history (Stiglitz 2016: xiv). This study will show that if this experiment were to fail, it may not be because of diversity and inequality of its members—as is often argued—but because of the limited capacity to share and diversify risks. A diverse union brings with it large potential gains from risk diversification, but cooperation is needed to realize these gains. Collective action problems beset all policy cooperation, but they become more intractable as the parties become more heterogeneous (Snidal 1995: 62–7; Imbs and Mauro 2007: 26–30). Mistrust, misperception, and lack of information stand in the way of risk pooling. Different preferences and power asymmetries may also lead to conflict in setting the priorities for collective action. Some may want to internalize all externalities in a central budget; others will fear the excessive risk taking that comprehensive insurance may incentivize. All this leads to the paradox that the more diverse potential members are, the larger the potential economic gains from monetary union, yet the more difficult it may be to realize these gains politically.

This paradox of diversity is used here as a lens for understanding the EA, but it is relevant beyond Europe. Member states of the EA managed to form a monetary union, but then limited risk sharing very tightly. Observers noted early on that a minimum of fiscal risk sharing may be required to make a currency union stable enough to be mutually beneficial, and this is often seen as the major lesson of the financial crisis (Goodhart and Smith 1993; De Grauwe and Moesen 2009). The paradox of diversity can also explain why it took the United States (US) more than 150 years and innumerable financial crises before a viable monetary-fiscal constitution became acceptable to the members of the federation. That history was not an exercise in optimization but a trial-and-error process of finding economically stabilizing and politically acceptable ways of governing a single currency. Although not pursued here, the paradox also sheds light on why we see so little currency unification outside Europe. This is despite the fact that the euro experiment is closely observed in parts of Africa, Asia, and Latin America where policymakers and citizens see exchange rate volatility and balance-of-payments imbalances as a massive problem (Fritz and Metzger 2006; Kawai and Lombardi 2014).

Monetary solidarity is required to attenuate the tensions inherent in this paradox. Using a common currency or stabilizing exchange rates brings about some risk sharing, but monetary solidarity means more than this. It refers to institutions such as the cross-border payments system that comes with a single currency and replaces the need for foreign exchange reserves in a fixed exchange rate system. Its immediate purpose is to save transaction costs, but, in the financial crisis, it turned into effective insurance of trade against a sudden stop of capital flows. However, monetary solidarity is rarely the declared intention of monetary system design; rather, it is the outcome of institutional evolution. US history shows that the insurance function of the cross-border payments system can be called into question (Chapter 9). Other risk-sharing mechanisms that have developed in the EA, such as emergency funds and extraordinary monetary policies, have been openly contested. More often tolerated than deliberately created, the risk-sharing properties and solidaristic features of core EA institutions have to be demonstrated. This is the main task this book has set itself.

Most accounts see diversity and inequality among its members as the EA's most fundamental problem, especially after 2010. An early critic, the Harvard economist Martin Feldstein (2012), speaks for many when he states: "The euro should now be recognized as an experiment that failed. This failure . . . was not an accident or the result of bureaucratic mismanagement but rather the inevitable consequence of imposing a single currency on a very heterogeneous group of countries." Eminent scholars in economics, comparative political economy, and political science agreed on this point. They have identified most problematic forms of heterogeneity from the vantage point of their different disciplines. Economics highlights susceptibility to country-specific shocks for which exchange rate adjustments are needed (Krugman 2013: 444). Political economy proposes that countries have different growth models that cannot live with the same monetary policy (Hall 2014a; Scharpf 2011). Political scientists argue that democracies are based on an enshrined political consensus that is incompatible with prioritizing a stable currency (Jones 2013; Matthijs and Blyth 2015). All these scholars defend national diversity against what they perceive as the straitjacket of a single currency.

These verdicts see diversity as a problem for a monetary union. It would make the EA a deeply flawed project. Does this mean that the architects of monetary union were not aware of how diverse and unequal the applicants for union membership were? The Delors report that laid the groundwork for the European monetary union could not be clearer on this point:

> Even after attaining economic and monetary union, the Community would continue to consist of individual nations with differing economic, social, cultural and political characteristics. The existence and preservation of this plurality would require a degree of autonomy in economic decision-making to remain with individual member countries and a balance to be struck between national and Community competences. For this reason it would not be possible simply to follow the example of existing federal States; it would be necessary to develop an innovative and unique approach. (Committee 1989: para. 17)

Critical verdicts therefore rest on claims about how a mistaken economic venture has been undertaken by elites entranced with the political project of an ever closer union, or engaged in crude power play, or laboring under outright delusion. All of these claims can be traced in Feldstein's essay (2012).

European policymakers of quite varied ideological leanings and with different attitudes towards European integration undertook monetary integration conscious, not ignorant, of the differences between their countries.[1] Rather skeptical central bankers, not economically illiterate euro-federalists, were put in the driving seat for devising a strategy towards currency unification (Moravcsik 1998: 431–5; Dyson and Featherstone 1999: 342–50, 583). While Commission President Delors was a committed Europhile, he understood that he had to give a prominent role to central bankers with an institutional

[1] The evidence for this is overwhelming, as the magisterial studies by Moravcsik (1998) and Dyson and Featherstone (1999) show; see also Jones (2002: 1, 94–6) and Verdun (2000: 161–83) among others.

interest in preserving their national currencies, so as to assure the skeptics that the project would take diverse—and adverse—concerns into account.

The single currency was the endpoint of a long drawn-out process of experimenting with collective exchange rate stabilization and overcoming balance of payments constraints, beginning with the European Payments Union in the 1950s (Mourlon-Druol 2012: 22). These efforts gained much more prominence when the dollar standard became destabilizing after the late 1960s. They were then sustained by repeated banking and current-account crises in the wake of financial liberalization (Babecký et al. 2012), which made national administrations ready for ever closer forms of exchange rate-based policy coordination. The Delors report was explicit about this background (Committee 1989: paras 1–6). Eventually, exchange rate stabilization turned into the experiment of creating a supranational central bank to issue fiat money, without direct backing from any state fiscal authority (Goodhart 1998: 410; James 2012: 389).

This non-state money is an experiment in the specific sense that historically combined functions of macroeconomic policy were separated and assigned to different levels of governance: nominal income stabilization to the new supranational monetary authority, allocative efficiency, and growth to fiscal authorities and wage bargainers. The prevention of systemic financial panic was assigned to national supervisors even though the Single Market Programme promoted financial integration. This separation of powers and responsibilities is seen by many as evidence that the monetary union was built on a German model, as Kathleen McNamara (1998: 5–6) forcefully argued. The assignment was certainly not based on the theory of fiscal federalism as the old and a new vintage would understand it (Oates 2005) since the assignment gives fiscal stabilization hardly any role to play for the union as a whole. It entailed the minimum amount of integration deemed sufficient to get the benefits of a single hard currency: low inflation and low market interest rates. More would follow if necessary and desirable, in line with the norm of an "ever closer union." These promised benefits made a heterogeneous group of countries (or governments and stakeholders inside these countries) sign up to a monetary union. In so doing, they signed up to institutionalized policy cooperation among formally equal, sovereign nation states, to a degree that is unprecedented in history (Eichengreen 2008; Moravcsik 2012: 64).

1.1.1 *Diversity as Opportunity and as Challenge*

This study takes diversity and inequality among EA members not as a problem but as a social fact. Diversity and inequality will not disappear in some long-term convergence process, just as neither has disappeared in the US dollar area or even in an old centralized state like the United Kingdom. The critics of the

EA experiment rely on metrics like income differentials to claim that Texas and California or northern and southern England are more similar than Germany and France, or that Mississippi and Rhode Island, Scotland and Greater London are less unequal than Portugal and Estonia. But income differentials may not be the only relevant measure of diversity, and even if it were, it is not clear how small the difference has to be in order to be compatible with membership in a currency union. The differences that the following chapters will look at include sectoral specialization in agriculture and manufacturing (Chapter 4), high and low vulnerability to exchange rate instability and current-account crises (Chapter 5), high and low growth potential (Chapter 6), being an emigration or an immigration region (Chapter 8), and being more or less dependent on capital inflows (Chapter 9). In no case do I find that diversity on these metrics is an insurmountable obstacle to joining a currency union—it depends on the extent of risk sharing that the parties can politically agree to introduce.

This shifts the focus on problems and promises of interstate cooperation, away from a sole focus on economic adjustment mechanisms like price and wage flexibility. The literature on this is large and varied. For the political economy of monetary solidarity, Axelrod (1984), Keohane (1984), and the contributions to Keohane and Ostrom (1995) are highly relevant. This literature has explored the conditions under which different interests, power asymmetries, and varying time horizons facilitate or obstruct cooperation. The international relations strand around Robert Keohane has its origins in the realization that by the late 1970s, the post-war order had become less clearly dominated by US hegemony. There was then a fear of the breakdown of international cooperation between formally equal, sovereign nations: anarchy might follow the breakdown of hierarchy. But rather than looking for new power constellations, as the realist school around Stephen Krasner did, it asked for how and when institutions would evolve that make sustained cooperation in international relations possible (Drezner 2013: 282; Henning, 2017). In line with realists, these scholars explained the evolution or failure of these institutions with rational self-interest. A monetary union among formerly sovereign states can be seen as an international regime of interlinked institutions dealing with their collective action problems. Elinor Ostrom (1990) explored individuals' drive and capacity for self-organization. Like her colleagues from international relations, she challenged the need for a supreme power to counter the destructive tendencies of rational egoists in the realm of institutional economics.

One of the key questions is whether heterogeneity of members is useful for cooperation or undermines it (Snidal 1995). Different interests can be compatible, just as they are in market exchange, and institutions that can link different issues or lengthen the time horizon of members may be helpful to overcome obstacles of heterogeneity (Martin 1995). This literature can explain why the different interests of governments and their constituencies in low inflation and low interest rates were not satisfied by mere exchange rate cooperation (Section 5.1). The desire for exchange rate stability was widely shared within and across countries, albeit for divergent reasons: in some it means getting rid of pressures for depreciation and in others for appreciation.

Yet the preferences for an accommodating or constraining monetary policy may still cause insurmountable frictions and prevent currency unification. This can be due to opposition by organized labor and businesses in certain sectors that are well adjusted or advantaged by the status quo. This is an approach that Jeffry Frieden has developed over many years, Stefanie Walter more recently. Both have shown these domestic preferences to be relevant for determining exchange rate choices in US states, in Europe, and in Latin America (Frieden 2002, 2015a; Walter 2008). My study does not deny this when it takes a more aggregated view. On the contrary, it tries to make sense of the fact that in very different countries political and business elites, often with substantial popular support, aspired to have their country become a member of the common currency area. But it does not go into the detail of how domestic alliances shifted and a crucial coalition formed in favor of the euro experiment.

A general answer to how such a momentous shift was possible in very different countries can be gleaned from economics. It is the idea of insurance or, more generally, risk sharing: diversity of membership can be an opportunity for risk diversification (Imbs and Mauro 2007). More specifically, joining a heterogeneous union can help a member state to reduce, shift, and spread downside risks for national income, employment, and consumption. The risk of each member in the pool becomes smaller, the less common the national risks are. If national or regional risks do not all materialize at the same time, there will always be some that are lucky and can support the unlucky. This is the case of asynchronous business cycles, where economic paths are only weakly correlated. The risk of the overall pool can even be reduced if the fortune of one member is directly linked to the misfortune of another (negative correlation). A strengthening currency vis-à-vis the US dollar may be a boon for a region depending on oil imports as they get cheaper while a region depending on car exports to the US market finds it harder to sustain its business.

The benefits of risk sharing can also be reaped by enabling members to take more gainful risks without raising the potential damage to themselves. Greater economic specialization has been the route to higher income for individuals as well as geopolitical entities. But specialization is a form of risk taking and brings with it vulnerability: that technological advances and changes in taste make a particular skill or sector obsolete, or that a crucial ingredient becomes so scarce that it renders production unprofitable. If monetary union can diversify the risk of economic specialization, for instance by making cross-border financial investors share it, then this could benefit the risk pool as a whole as it raises potential aggregate growth (Obstfeld 1984: 1311).

Finally, the introduction of a single currency can spread risk more widely and even reduce it. To give three specific examples: first, the liquidity risk of assets denominated in one currency diminishes for each investor as the pool of these assets becomes larger. Second, the risk of running out of foreign exchange reserves is reduced as more trade with other member states is conducted in the same currency. Third, there is an immediate benefit in terms of a lower risk premium paid by firms, households, and the government in former soft-currency areas. Those in former hard-currency areas lose a general competitive advantage but this can be compensated for by more real exchange rate stability as well as expanding markets in the other member states.

1.1.2 *The Puzzle of Monetary Solidarity*

But risk sharing does not happen automatically. A single currency has to be introduced, maintained, and stabilized. If left to spontaneous market forces, monetary-financial integration can also lead to concentration and accumulation of risks or to shifting of risks onto those that are least able to bear them. Policies and markets have to be developed and maintained with a view to what they do to risks. Rules on financial innovation and competition, prudential supervision, and lending of last resort are relevant here, along with the upholding of commitments between governments. Each of these interventions may have a specific rationale and be done on their own merit rather than with a view to risk sharing at large (Jones 2012: 58).

A currency union is therefore not only about sharing pre-existing (exogenous) risks but also managing (endogenous) risks that emerge with integration. Especially in situations of crisis, this requires cooperation against the odds that members of the risk pool may resist certain manifestations of interdependence. Members may want to share some risks but not others, only catastrophic risks or only risks up to a certain limit. Pooling risks means greater interdependence: the bad luck of one member becomes a common concern, because the member may be entitled to compensation and because its bad luck can spill over more easily onto other members if financial systems have become more linked. Collective action is required to manage this interdependence to the mutual benefit of the members in the risk pool. What is in the rational interest of each member is not necessarily compatible with the common interest.

We should not assume that monetary solidarity in the sense of deliberate, accepted, or at least tolerated risk sharing is the primary intention of governments seeking gains from cooperation. There are many strong forces that militate against collective action in general and risk sharing in a monetary union in particular (Section 2.3). Fear of excessive risk taking by others is a much-cited concern; fear of increasing interdependence, being susceptible to the externalities of other members' woes, is at least a lingering issue. The inconvenience of having to honor a commitment when it is needed most is an underestimated obstacle to risk pooling although other commitment problems of governments were explicitly handled in the policy architecture of the union.

Reaping gains from cooperation fully would require hierarchy, a supranational or federal government that could act as a risk manager, just like governments do in and for markets. What makes an authority a government is that it has the legitimate powers to compel, to tax, and to print money (Moss 2002: 52). It can mandate social insurance where private offers are not forthcoming and thus extend risk sharing. It can regulate private offers to shift some or all risks onto those that are better able to bear them, for instance through limited liability from debtors (countries and their citizens or companies and their employees) to creditors. It can enlist future generations into the risk pool through public debt, pay-as-you-go schemes, and the issue of the legal tender, thus spreading the risk of default and vastly extending the commitment that the sharing of some risks requires.

When it is not individuals but states that have to be cajoled into risk sharing, authority is even more difficult to establish. Even in the US, the federal government can generally not force states to comply with its policies: instead it must incentivize them. The European Commission has not even the instrument of budgetary incentives and is for the time being more a fourth branch of government for transnational socio-economic regulation than a nascent federal government (Majone 1993).

There are many ways in which collective action may fail. Even so, many European governments have delegated away monetary policy, one of the signature policies of any sovereign state. Herein lies the puzzle. Historically, the US federation is an example of monetary risk sharing against the odds (Chapter 4): the US dollar area was founded with the introduction of the greenback just when the political union had broken up, during the bitter divisions between the states in the North and South. Many decades later, a federal budget, combined with a central bank and a federal deposit insurance and resolution authority, ended a financial history of banking crises not seen anywhere else in the Western hemisphere (Broz 1998: 5; see Chapter 4). The comparison with the US does not show that it has complete risk sharing and that the EA has none; rather it shows that it took a long time to find a less crisis-prone settlement in the US. Indeed, the sequence was not so different because US states were initially as reluctant to engage in collective action as are member states in the EA today. Centralized solutions were accepted only after all else had failed.

This study provides evidence for risk sharing and even monetary solidarity in the EA. The financial crisis demonstrated the power of the monetary channel of risk sharing: the sole government power that an EA institution has, the power to print money, has been used massively since 2007 to alleviate a devastating liquidity crisis in all member states. And despite all the mayhem, payments in euro have been processed between member states without any interruption. A currency union in Europe was first devised in the 1970s and the project repeatedly foundered (Verdun 2000). But when the union was finally created, it started with a larger membership than originally envisaged, pooling traditionally strong and traditionally weak currency areas. Membership kept on expanding even at the height of crisis, including the considerably poorer but fast-growing economies of the former Soviet Union, as three Baltic states joined between 2011 and 2015.

Avoiding the next crisis is and has been a prime instigator of monetary solidarity in Europe and the US, making risk sharing a by-product of crisis management that is preoccupied with shielding the lucky from the fall-out of crisis in unlucky countries. The power asymmetries that come to the fore in these situations make solidarity typically feel like tough love rather than tender care. A prime example of such tough love are the emergency funds created in the European Union (EU) after 2010 which combine historically unprecedented amounts of sovereign lending with very harsh and intrusive conditionality. The theory of collective action can explain why monetary solidarity is not necessarily a pretty sight.

1.1.3 *Overcoming Collective Action Problems*

The solution to the puzzle of monetary solidarity cannot be found in some pre-existing bond of European governments. Risk sharing as such has not been an explicit goal of monetary union while exchange rate stabilization was. The negotiations over the terms of the EA were protracted and extremely hard as the readers of Moravcsik (1998) and Dyson and Featherstone (1999) know. The maintenance of agreed institutions, like the Stability and Growth Pact, has been a struggle since its inception; the maintenance of the euro since 2010 led to acrimonious conflicts.[2] In line with the institutionalist literature around Keohane and Ostrom (1995), I assume that governments cooperate only if they see it as beneficial for their goals. This is not to deny that some decision makers act out of a real belief in European integration and a sense of historical responsibility. But I doubt that such beliefs can carry their constituencies with them when it comes to the more mundane task of creating and

[2] Batastin (2012) and Sandbu (2015) give particularly vivid accounts of the conflicts.

upholding institutions of monetary integration, such as new rules for budgetary discipline.

The *by-product theory of collective action* provides a solution to the puzzle of monetary solidarity and deliberate risk sharing even if it was not the primary intention of interstate cooperation. It draws on work by Lawrence Broz (1997, 1998) which shows, with painstaking historical evidence, how internationally active banks in New York managed to campaign effectively for the introduction of the Federal Reserve System.[3] They had a purely private interest in the creation of this system, but the system their initiative helped to create was a public good. The active private interests did not exhaust all the benefits. Similarly, we find that proponents of monetary integration have particular interests in stable exchange rates, low inflation, and low interest rates. But a stable currency is then a public good used by all citizens of that currency area and even beyond: some governments outside use it as a stability anchor, from Denmark to Bulgaria and Croatia.

This by-product theory can explain the creation of a common resource. Ostrom's work on "governing the commons" (Ostrom 1990) provides insights into its management once provided. Monitoring is needed to preserve a common resource because, unlike a pure public good, it can be exhausted. In a self-governing system, users monitor each other in the course of reaping their private benefits from the commons. In a similar vein, the use of a common currency in the collective (and diverse) interests of member states requires monitoring to prevent uses that diminish the quality of a currency: the tragedy of the commons. Again, a self-governing system is one where each member state has incentives and opportunities to monitor the others as a by-product of its own use of the common currency (Ostrom 1990: 19–20).

Some negotiators in the creation of the monetary union, notably from Germany, were quite explicit about their fear of a tragedy of the commons, even though they may not have used the term. The fear was specifically that other member states would overissue government bonds denominated in the common currency. This was considered as a moral hazard problem of a common currency: the larger capital market would absorb excessive debt issues of relatively small countries, yet if all do it, it will end up diminishing the quality of the currency, either through inflation or rising interest rates for all (Beetsma 2001: 28–9). The policy architecture of the Economic and Monetary Union (EMU) was thus built against this exploitation of a common resource as perceived by governments of hard-currency countries (Issing 2002; Chapter 5). This architecture was presented as an antidote to the deficit

[3] The concept of a by-product theory of collective action goes back to Mancur Olson (1971) who considered this to be a rather exceptional way for collective action to come about, compared to his "privileged group" theory. Section 2.2 contains more details on this.

bias of democracies generally and European countries specifically (Hallerberg 2004; Poterba and von Hagen 1999). However, the evidence on the political manipulation of budgets and economic policies generally is rather complex (Franzese 2002) and does not lend itself to quick fixes (Dubois 2016: 246–8). Moreover, underuse of the common resource can also be a problem, stifling growth.

Introducing and maintaining a common currency is beset with collective action problems. But a system with separate currencies is not free of collective action problems either. Before monetary union, member states other than Germany repeatedly experienced negative externalities from the Bundesbank's monetary policy (von Hagen 1989; Kenen 2000: 20). One aim of establishing a common currency was to rein these in or even eliminate them. The Bundesbank's setting of interest rates did not and arguably could not take all concerns of other member states in the pegged exchange rate system into account and so, inadvertently, pushed other members into interest rate moves that were not right for the cyclical state of their national economies. If they tried to use interest rates for domestic purposes, turmoil in financial markets ensued. In this light, we can see that the common currency did not mean sacrificing monetary sovereignty; instead, states sought to replace monetary dependence with a common monetary policy that was not exclusively geared to German conditions.

An important building block for the theory of monetary integration that this book develops is a systematic account of "political market failures" (Keohane 1984: 85). Sovereigns in international relations are confronted with coordination issues that are similar to those that market actors face in voluntary exchanges. If coordination is achieved, it must be because it is in each state's own interest, as there is no higher authority to enforce cooperation—the term "political market" highlights exactly the absence of hierarchy. Political science provides some clues on when we should expect such self-enforcing cooperation. Issue linkage can overcome different interests or interest intensities, repetition can overcome commitment and information problems, delegated monitoring can overcome free riding in coordination problems (Martin 1995: 76–7; Chapter 2).

The economic theory of the welfare state also provides insights into possible bases for solutions to political market failures (Barr 1992; Moss 2002: 39–52). Just as there is a range of policy options in which institutions providing insurance and redistribution reinforce the efficiency of the market economy, so can institutions that safeguard diversity give incentives for mutually beneficial cooperation (Snidal 1995: 62–7). Peter Baldwin's (1990) study of "the politics of social solidarity", from which the title of this book takes its cue, spells out its interest-based approach particularly clearly. He summarizes his historical comparison of US and Swedish welfare state developments thus: "Solidarity . . . has been the outcome of a generalized and reciprocal self-interest. Not ethics, but politics explain it" (Baldwin 1990: 299).

Risk sharing in a diverse monetary union provides rich empirical material with which to probe these insights. They support an approach to monetary solidarity which is essentially rationalist.[4] This approach is adopted here for several reasons. First, it is apt for a study in which the agents are governments, not individuals. Solidarity cannot be based on altruistic motives in a context where democratically elected governments have to agree on long-term commitments with other governments, each of them accountable to national parliaments and domestic public opinion, not to an imaginary European demos. The political system of democracy forces some degree of instrumental rationality upon politicians. Second, by assuming rationality and the pursuit of self-interest among relevant actors, the cards are stacked against finding solidarity. If we nonetheless find it, we will have more robust evidence than if extra-rational motivations like identification with fellow Europeans or feelings of belonging were invoked from the start.

Monetary solidarity here is a minimalist notion, not about the public's attitude towards the plight of individuals in other countries with which they share a currency. Such a substantive notion of solidarity is sensible when, for instance, the openness of welfare systems to migrants is the issue (Hall 2014b). In an intergovernmental setting, however, solidarity by stealth can be real solidarity and the only form to be had at the point of institution building.

1.2 The Economic Underpinning of Monetary Solidarity

Monetary integration is here understood to be a way of sharing risks between geopolitical entities, be it states within a confederation like the EU or within a federation like the US. The risks to be shared through monetary integration are typically related to financial instability. Sharing these risks can entail other forms of coordinated exchange rate stabilization short of currency unification, such as target zones (Miller et al. 1989; Schelkle 2001). Exchange rate instability became a preoccupation of policymakers after the breakdown of Bretton Woods since the early 1970s (Frankel 1996). When the domestic currency depreciates sharply, it raises the domestic currency value of foreign debt equally sharply, getting firms, households, and sovereigns with foreign debt into difficulties. Currency appreciation can also be damaging, potentially jeopardizing the financial robustness of internationally active banks, for

[4] Jones (2012: 58–9) is an interesting alternative account of solidarity between countries or governments, which follows different norms depending on the sphere of application: wartime alliances follow a different logic of solidarity than economic integration.

instance when their foreign debtors go bust, as well as impairing the competitiveness of export industries. Countries with exactly opposite motives, namely those exposed to depreciation and to appreciation pressures, have reason to seek some form of cooperation to stabilize their exchange rate. It was thought that most of these risks could be eliminated when exchange rates between major trading partners were abolished. But the previous balance-of-payments crises gave way to another form of crisis in the EA: negative feedback loops between domestic banks and their sovereigns (De Grauwe 2013: 26–7; Section 6.2).[5]

The prime source of exchange rate risk is that this crucial price of an economy is determined in asset markets, a view that had become consolidated in international economics textbooks by the mid-1980s (Frenkel and Mussa 1984). The theory of speculative currency attacks had just been triggered by Paul Krugman (1979) and became a lively research program for over two decades, moving ever further away from fundamental ("real") determinants toward modeling the speculative behavior in financial markets (Flood and Marion 1996). The gist of this literature is that nominal exchange rates tend to be more volatile than justified by changes in fundamentals (such as wages or consumer preferences) and can be over- or undervalued for what would be required for current-account balance. A common exchange rate spreads the volatility risks across the currency area and limits both movements and over- or undervaluation to other determinants of the real exchange rate (prices for labor and non-traded inputs, productivity). This eliminates competitive advantages or disadvantages that afflict individual firms by the mere fact that they are located in a particular currency area. Modern exchange rate economics therefore support the optimistic view that comparative advantages of firms would become more truthfully reflected in prices inside a monetary union. This view can be found in the major EMU study "One market, one money," prepared by the Directorate-General of Economic and Financial Affairs, on why a single currency would complement the Single Market (CEC 1990: 9): microeconomic efficiency, macroeconomic stability, and "equity as between countries and regions" would be fostered if exchange rates no longer disturbed or masked the underlying differences in national or regional competitiveness.

1.2.1 *Risks to Be Shared in Monetary Integration*

There can be many reasons why states may be able to share risks with other states to mutual advantage (Moss 2002: 14–15). There can be high and low risk tolerance and unequal risk-bearing capacities which enable those with higher

[5] There are authors, such as Sinn (2012), who claim that the EA crisis is a balance-of-payments crisis. But this is a misrepresentation in my view, to be discussed in detail in Chapter 9.

tolerance or capacity to offer insurance to others: funding national or international assistance in the case of devastating floods or seasonal storms is such a form of interstate insurance. Differential risk assessments and complementary portfolio balancing can be other reasons: thus we see sovereign wealth funds investing in other countries' economies. But these instances of interstate risk sharing are still somewhat exotic and ad hoc, and play a more important role in risk sharing between private actors.[6] Between states, diversification of risks is arguably the most relevant rationale. Diversification happens whenever independent and less than fully correlated risks are pooled, be it through (regulated) markets and/or public institutions, for instance a central bank.

Currency unification creates such a risk pool. Before joining, investors attached a price to the probability that, for example, Portuguese firms would experience payment difficulties due to a current-account crisis or that inflation would lead to a devaluation of the escudo. This made for higher interest rates and also short maturities of credit. Once the likelihood of payment difficulties is reduced—because Portuguese firms earn their export revenues and have to pay their wages and import bills to a large extent in the same currency—then credit can be extended at a lower risk premium and for longer maturities. The same holds for indebted sovereigns, especially if they were indebted in foreign currency. The probability of members' payments difficulties becomes to some extent averaged, the extent depending on the exact nature of the insurance arrangement. If there is little integration of financial markets, payments difficulties may still occur in members' banking systems: if Portuguese firms lose out in trade competition and financial markets suddenly lose faith in their ability to pay back their credits, Portuguese banks that largely extended these credits are likely to have problems accessing wholesale markets for liquidity. The risk of payments difficulties then depends on the willingness of the joint central bank to act resolutely as lender of last resort to these banks; but the central bank may refer banks under such strain back to the fiscal authority of a member state and ask them to bail out the affected banks instead.

Current-account imbalances (or indeed speculative runs fueled by herding behavior) in foreign exchange markets affect countries with both deficits and surpluses, that is those facing depreciation and appreciation pressures. But their self-insurance potential is very different. A currency area with a deficit and under depreciation pressure cannot produce the means of payment in which trading firms have to pay their bills and in which market actors want to hold their assets. The counterpart with appreciation pressure, by contrast, can

[6] Economies specializing as financial centers can cater to these other motivations for interstate risk sharing. But such services are still in their infancy, for reasons discussed in Shiller's book on missing macro markets (1993).

simply accumulate foreign exchange reserves. This means the central bank expresses a demand for foreign currency that lowers the upward pressure on its own currency. It can also reduce the interest rate to make capital inflows less attractive, although a low interest rate comes at the cost of inflationary potential.[7] While the creditor countries are apparently in an advantageous position, it remains the case that, if the debtor country can no longer pay, banks and export firms in the creditor country will lose out as well. The Bretton Woods institutions were created for such situations and are in the interest of both parties: debtors and creditors. The emergency funds (the European Stability Mechanism and its temporary predecessor) that the EA has created since 2010 follow the International Monetary Fund (IMF) model. These funds pool the risk of insolvency crises that affect entire states. A diversified banking system without a home bias and a system-wide bank resolution facility would be an alternative, as the financial history of the US shows (Chapter 4).

Country-specific shocks and asynchronous business cycles are the risks stressed by the mainstream economic theory of monetary integration (Degiannakis et al. 2014; see Section 1.2.4). Proponents argue that countries at different stages of the business cycle or experiencing idiosyncratic shocks may require different movements of the exchange rate, and therefore should not enter a monetary union. The risk-sharing perspective, by contrast, sees asynchronous cycles and different vulnerabilities to shocks as opportunities for mutually beneficial insurance: if not all member states experience abnormally high unemployment or lower than trend income at the same time, the lucky members can thus compensate the unlucky ones in a downturn. Such compensation does not require transfer payments: it can come about through trade and cross-border asset holdings; external demand can replace depressed domestic demand; financial returns on assets held abroad can substitute for depressed profitability at home.

This compensation would be less valuable if each member had effective monetary policy at its disposal. But very few governments in the world have it, and Europeans are no exception.[8] The lesson of the 1980s and 1990s was that efforts to operate monetary policy for domestic demand management brought excessive exchange rate volatility. When they stabilized their exchange rates through

[7] This inflationary potential can be sterilized to some extent, for instance by raising reserve requirements for domestic banks. This is how the Bundesbank managed to undervalue the D-Mark (prevent instant revaluation) and keep inflation in check, by amassing foreign exchange reserves. It has the advantage of hardening a currency while keeping the exchange rate favorable for exports, imitated today by the Chinese central bank. This undervaluation strategy raises some doubts as to whether the Bundesbank was so un-Keynesian as is often portrayed since this strategy clearly stimulated (foreign) demand for domestic products and kept interest rates low thanks to revaluation expectations (Riese 1989).

[8] The 1992–3 crisis of the European Monetary System revealed this brutally (Section 5.1.1).

the Exchange Rate Mechanism (ERM), they had to follow the Bundesbank's lead on interest rates (James 2012: 343). Monetary union means for such "satellite" currency areas that interest rates are set in line with demand conditions across the EA, rather than just for German conditions. This joint monetary policy is a form of insurance.

1.2.2 *Risk-Sharing Mechanisms*

Risk pooling or sharing between states can be achieved through various mechanisms. A "transfer union" is often the first mechanism that springs to the mind of commentators.[9] But it is typically not the most important form of risk sharing even in fiscal federations like the US (Henning and Kessler 2012: 10–14). States can rarely rely on international assistance to any significant degree and the effects on the economic and social fabric may not even be desirable. Within nation states, transfers appear more viable: one region may depend extensively and continuously on transfers from other regions, provided through the central budget. However, even within nations, long-term net transfers may trigger secessionist movements by the richer regions, as the Northern League in Italy and a referendum about Catalonia's independence in Spain illustrate.

Monetary policy, with its effects on interest rates and exchange rates, is a politically less salient transfer mechanism. Higher or lower interest rates imply a transfer between debtor and creditor countries, but since markets are the transmission mechanism, the distributive effects do not normally appear as first-order policy effects. There are in all economies firms and households that are debtors and others creditors, as well as sectors that are net exporters and others that are net importers. Such internal diversity creates stakeholders and opponents of interstate risk sharing through monetary policy, but it also makes the implied transfers less visible and unidirectional.

Another mechanism of risk sharing is regulatory intervention, such as the assurance of free trade or a migration regime that allows workers and their families to move, find work, and integrate into the welfare system of another member state (Chapter 8). These are the supranational counterparts of familiar devices of regulatory risk management at the national level, such as limited liability for firms or consumer bankruptcy law (Moss 2002). These devices allocate risks over the parties to a contract. When they are efficient, they shift risk onto the party that can more easily bear it or provide time and

[9] Some lawyers see European emergency funds already as a way into a transfer union because borrowing sovereigns may default that would then make these funds draw on the guarantor countries (Ruffert 2011: 1291–3). However, IMF lending before the EA crisis then also constituted a transfer union between guarantor and debtor countries while the IMF is more plausibly understood as an institution to prevent such transfers.

opportunity for adjustment. For instance, the assurance of open borders can allow a country to engage in export-led adjustment without being stopped by countries in which these exports lead to job losses. Similarly, the ability to migrate allows citizens to make a living and even to remit some of their earnings to a country of origin that may not be able to generate enough jobs in the short to medium term. The more entrenched such assurances are, the more these institutions resemble insurance rather than ad hoc risk sharing which may be revoked when it is needed most.

Finally, the literature that first explored systematically interstate risk sharing of output shocks stressed financial market channels.[10] Closer financial market integration fosters cross-border lending, borrowing, and shareholding. The cross-border owner of shares or stocks has a claim on the output of another country. If the domestic economy experiences a downturn, household consumption can be sustained by income from property rights in foreign firms. This may also concern future consumption, for instance if pension funds are invested in foreign shares and can thus achieve a better rate of return on the claims of their policy holders than if they were only invested in domestic shares. Cross-border lending may allow those who have fallen on hard times to get credit from a foreign bank in times when the lending capacity of domestic banks has been curtailed. All this of course works vice versa in an upswing: consumption may be somewhat dampened by lower property income from abroad, and domestic credit may be scarcer or more expensive because some credit is extended to other countries. In reality, most households benefit from the international diversification of property rights and credit access only indirectly, if at all (Balli et al. 2011). But, as already indicated, households may hold savings deposits, pensions, or insurance policies with internationally diversified financial firms. International diversification was thought to stabilize the returns on assets which these banks, funds, or insurers hold on behalf of savers.

1.2.3 *Monetary Solidarity as the Outcome of Institutional Evolution*

The outline of risk-sharing mechanisms above implies that a monetary union has three pillars: the joint currency, a common monetary policy, and integrated financial markets. In the EA, restrictions on risk sharing were placed on all three. The joint currency was deliberately divorced from fiscal backstops (Goodhart 1998: 410); monetary policy was legally restrained in its

[10] The contribution of various channels to risk sharing was first systematically explored by Asdrubali et al. (1996) for US states and Sørensen and Yosha (1998) for Organisation for Economic Co-operation and Development (OECD) countries. Chapter 3 contains a more detailed discussion with further references.

lender-of-last-resort role to sovereigns even in a systemic crisis (De Grauwe 2011); and restraining fiscal rules were implemented to counteract the temptations of a large market for euro-denominated government bonds (Kenen 2003). The potential for risk sharing was acknowledged, only to be suppressed. But the suppression was partial and has proved not to be sustainable.

This begs the question: why look for interstate risk sharing as a by-product of national bargains at all? Was the EA not deliberately made to minimize risk sharing between member states? Skeptics can point to the infamous no-bailout clause of Article 125 of the Treaty on the Functioning of the European Union. It states that no member state is under any obligation to assume the debt of another member state. This seemed categorically to exclude any fiscal risk sharing. Yet, the clause acknowledges the potential for risk sharing that comes with currency unification at the same time as it tries to exclude it. In practice, this exclusion could not be maintained: five countries have been bailed out with the help of emergency funds created since 2010.[11] When limits to risk sharing become self-defeating and are no longer in the interest of important veto players or a majority of members in the risk pool, the limiting arrangements are likely to be reformed.[12]

The result of the bailouts was monetary solidarity, in the sense of creating for the first time a permanent capacity for fiscal risk sharing if a member state government is in distress, in the guise of the European Stability Mechanism. This institution building was a by-product of every member state's attempts to protect its own public finances from the damage that would have resulted from a deepening of the recession and failing banks that held bonds of the distressed sovereigns (Sandbu 2015: 53–8). It was also a by-product of member states trying to protect domestic creditors with claims on the five countries that were bailed out. The no-bailout clause became defunct, surviving only as the option that a member state can, in principle, refrain from contributing to a bailout program for another. The newly created fiscal capacity has been deliberately limited and access is strictly conditional: recipients have to accept an intrusive and restrictive stabilization program. Yet the EA's bailout programs are more than state governments in the United States can hope for if in fiscal difficulty (Henning and Kessler 2012). The political economy of monetary solidarity seeks to explain such apparent anomalies.

One explanation for such anomalies is that supranational collective goods that emerge as the by-product of national interests are not necessarily well designed. Indeed, they may not be designed at all, and subsequently prove to be too limited or dysfunctional, especially if introduced under the strains of a

[11] In temporal order: Greece, Ireland, Portugal, Spain, and Cyprus.

[12] This has also been a repeated experience with fiscal surveillance (Heipertz and Verdun 2004: 120–4; Schelkle 2005, 2009).

crisis (Snidal 1995: 51, 68). Inequality among participating states means risk allocation may be perverse and regressive, shifting costs of adjustment onto politically and economically weaker members that are ill-equipped to bear them. Yet crises are also opportunities for joint action, spurred by a sense of emergency that forces the executive's hands (White, J. 2015: 95–8), however objectionable the process. In a union of democracies, there is a chance that apparent dysfunctionalities and blatant inequities get ironed out over time. Particularly aggrieved member states will register an upsurge in Euroskepticism that rings alarm bells throughout the union. And perverse risk allocation among interdependent political economies can have knock-on effects which damage those who are apparently the winners in the first round. Even so, we should not expect a continuous reform process towards an ever more functional union. If the by-product theory has traction, other limitations and dysfunctionalities are likely to be introduced with each reform.

There is thus no *finalité* in monetary integration. The resources institutional actors owe each other under particular conditions are often implied rather than fully spelled out. Solidarity emerges in the practice of maintaining the common resource and managing it for long-term use. "Governing the commons" (Ostrom 1990) requires collective action with each member having a stake in it. This is a precondition for enjoying the national benefit sustainably. But as the empirical work of Elinor Ostrom has also shown, such governance without hierarchy is precarious.

1.2.4 *The Non-Solution of Mainstream Economic Theory*

The mainstream economic theory of monetary integration provides no solution to the puzzle of why risk sharing happens, on the contrary, it makes it only more startling. Hence, US economists are particularly fond of telling their audiences why European monetary integration should not have happened, can't work, and won't last (Jonung and Drea 2009). The theoretical basis for their verdict is typically that the EA is not an optimal currency area (OCA). This is true, but no currency area in the world is. The two most important founders of OCA theory later revoked essential parts of their contributions (Mundell 1973, 2002: 145–6; Kenen 2000: 16–17). Mundell argued that a common currency can foster risk sharing through financial markets and, thanks to the development of the asset price theory of the exchange rate, he ceased to consider exchange rates to be stabilizing instruments of adjustment (De Grauwe 2006).

The line of argument in OCA theory, even in advanced formulations such as that of Farhi and Werning (2014), can be summarized as follows: with monetary integration, member states give up an effective exchange rate instrument, lock themselves into a rigid currency regime, presumably to save some transaction costs, and thus compound the difficulties created by wage and price stickiness. Because private wage and price setters do not internalize the effects of their decisions on macroeconomic stabilization, private markets provide inefficiently low insurance against country-specific shocks. A fiscal union then has to come to the rescue. This theory leaves readers wondering why governments wanted a monetary union in the first place, especially if they excluded fiscal integration. Politics, in the trivial form of integrationist sentiment, is invoked to fill the gap, even by the most brilliant minds (Farhi and Werning 2014: fn 1; Krugman 2013: 447).

There are three reasons why OCA theory is problematic as the basis for judging the suitability of a monetary union (Schelkle 2013a, 2015).

First, it was developed in the 1960s in order to analyze the tensions in the Bretton Woods system. The question it set out to tackle was the choice of exchange rate regime facing (developed) countries. In a famous conference volume dedicated to promoting OCA theory, Mundell illustrated the "practical significance" of OCA analysis thus: "Europe today has a choice as to what kind of currency area it is going to have; whether it is more important to develop a gold bloc in Europe, or to keep Europe's currencies pegged to the dollar and to remain part of an Atlantic currency area" (Mundell and Swoboda 1969: 111). The theory does not talk about essential issues, such as whether member states should unify monetary policy and possibly fiscal policies or foster financial market integration.

Second, OCA theory is based on an outdated theory of what determines (fixed and flexible) exchange rates. Indeed, soon after OCA theory was expounded, Mundell and other economists developed the theory of the exchange rate as an asset price. An asset price is formed based on expected returns on portfolios of assets; when expectations about the future change, it can change abruptly, and without regard to flows of payments for goods and services. Rather than giving national authorities a degree of freedom, having a national currency forces them to steer policies and invest resources to stabilize this important asset price, as a floating exchange rate is not governed by the needs of the material economy. The excessive volatility of exchange rates since the 1970s was experienced as very disruptive in many countries even though it was soon to be dwarfed by banking crises (Babecký et al. 2012: 9–10; Bordo et al. 2001: 56–7). This is crucial for understanding why monetary integration looked so attractive on purely economic grounds.

Third, OCA theory has a very narrow focus: it treats monetary integration as a one-off decision, and does not consider the effects of monetary policy institutions and financial market integration that accompany a currency union.[13]

[13] Farhi and Werning (2014: fn 1) cannot have the original contributions in mind when they claim that OCA theory takes the existence of a currency union as given. Paul De Grauwe's recent

Rather, the original theory was preoccupied with the effects of labor market integration and industrial specialization. It does not help us to understand the difficulties of maintaining a currency union in a financial crisis. This has not prevented a renaissance of the theory to explain the EA crisis which is why we return to it in Section 6.2.1.

There are complementary critiques of OCA theory. Iversen et al. (2016: 10.8–10.9) formulate a strong rebuttal based on the "Varieties of Capitalism" approach to comparative political economy: as argued above, Iversen et al. saw a mutually compatible economic interest in low interest rates and low inflation; but the EA institutions were determined by the interests of Northern coordinated market economies which wanted to protect their regulated, productively inflexible labor markets[14] against competitive devaluation from Southern mixed market economies. This is a creative critique of OCA theory by comparative political economists. But they accept two basic tenets of that theory: that labor markets are the crucial battleground for reaping the benefits of a monetary union and that exchange rates could be manipulated at will by Southern economies. The economic theory underlying the political economy of monetary solidarity suggests that financial markets decide whether all or only some will gain from currency unification, in line with the path-breaking work of De Grauwe (2015). And an effective exchange rate policy was beyond most countries' macroeconomic policy authorities. It requires either coordination of policies that only a few countries, for instance Sweden, manage to pull off; or it rests on a hard-earned reputation that even the UK could not always rely on in its post-war history.

The theory of Optimal Financial Areas by Erik Jones and Geoffrey Underhill (2014) is the most developed account of monetary integration that has financial markets, rather than the common currency, as its core. In contrast to the strand of OCA theory to be reviewed in Chapter 3, Jones and Underhill (2014) do not take risk sharing through financial markets as a given but analyze the infrastructure necessary to make it happen. This is akin to the "interfaces of risk sharing" that Section 3.3 develops and then applies in the following chapters. But it is largely a functional theory that is less interested in answering why not all of the necessary elements emerge (Jones and Underhill 2014: 3). This inherent incompleteness, the sub-optimality of the European financial area, is in my view crucial to understanding the euro experiment.

editions on the economics of monetary integration illustrate how far removed from the original OCA theory an up-to-date, standard-setting textbook on the subject has become (De Grauwe 2015).

[14] The inflexibility consists of long-term employment relationships (low labor mobility) that combine high employment protection with investment in a trained labor force; and collective wage restraint (low wage flexibility) to secure export markets at the cost of an underdeveloped domestic service economy. Hancké (2013) contains the most labor market focused explanation of national success and failure in the EA.

1.3 Overview

This study seeks to show that diversity of membership is a potential and actual source of mutual benefits from currency union. It makes this argument for the EA of nineteen countries (as of 2015),[15] a currency union of nation states without historical precedent (Eichengreen 2008). Readers with interests beyond the EU may well ask what this study can teach them. In other words: what is the European currency union a case of? And which diversities between member states matter for monetary integration?

The European monetary union is a particular institutionalization of risk sharing between member states; the US dollar area is another. In fact, even regions in the UK—easily one of the most centralized tax-transfer states in the OECD—can be analyzed in those terms: the governor of the Bank of England, Mark Carney (2015), compared risk sharing between regions in the UK with that between member states of the EA. He suggested that the UK was recovering from the crisis more quickly, first, because of deeper as well as less bank-based financial integration, and second because of fiscal integration, notably that the budget of the Scottish government was not as dependent on oil revenues as the Scottish economy.

The UK case is suggestive, but the US federation allows for a richer comparison with the EA. The semi-sovereignty of US states gives rise to collective action problems that are categorically similar to those that the EA constantly faces, given that its member states have parliaments with legislative authority to authorize budgets and judicial systems that apply both state and federal law. The economic literature on channels of risk sharing between states started with an investigation of the US that was then applied to the OECD, the EU, and later the EA. The ambition of the empirical chapters is to highlight how similar the policy issues are and have been historically, even though the two monetary unions tackle them very differently. They are not least "united in diversity" (Alber and Gilbert 2010) with each other but also among themselves. How the US turned its diversity into an opportunity for risk sharing—albeit not completely—is the guiding question for this comparison.

Chapters 2 and 3 provide the conceptual and empirical basis for a general account of the political economy of monetary solidarity in currency unions. Chapter 2 spells out the political market failures that collective action is up against and the by-product theory of public goods provision that can make such action happen despite resistance and obstacles. Once a monetary union is established, its governance can be analyzed in light of the collective action theory that Elinor Ostrom (1990) initiated, based on in-depth studies of how

[15] The EMU is often used synonymously for the EA but this is formally incorrect since the Economic Union refers to the Single or Internal Market to which all EU countries belong.

communities govern a common resource. Her work, and that of her many followers, examined the conditions that make prevention of a "tragedy of the commons" possible, an aspect that is completely absent from the mainstream theory of monetary integration, OCA theory. These insights from managing common pool resources were linked up with mainstream international relations and political economy by contributors to Keohane and Ostrom (1995). There have been very few and limited attempts, such as Hallerberg (2004) and Raudla (2010), at applying these insights to maintaining a currency union.

Chapter 3 reviews the empirical economic literature that has explored the benefits and the extent of interstate risk sharing. This literature is behind a cautious paradigm shift by EU institutions, as outlined in the EU's Five Presidents' report (Juncker et al. 2015), whereby the previous emphasis on discipline and convergence is combined with a new emphasis on risk sharing. This is a promising departure from OCA theory that sees diversity ("asymmetry") of members as an opportunity for risk sharing and establishes that, in normal times, monetary-financial integration leads to consumption smoothing of output shocks. But the relevance of this literature is limited, above all, by its assumption that financial markets are efficient in diversifying output volatility. Exploring the institutional prerequisites for financial markets to play this role, the chapter suggests that multiple interfaces of risk sharing between monetary, fiscal, and prudential authorities have to be in place. Any one channel (central banking, public budgets, resolution mechanisms by the financial industry) is too weak to insure interdependent financial systems and is overburdened with maintaining the integrity of a currency union on their own.

Before taking a close look at the institutional design and evolution of the EA, Chapter 4 turns to the historical evolution of macroeconomic risk sharing in the US. The US was the country with the highest frequency of financial crises in the developed world in the nineteenth and early twentieth century (Broz 1997: 5). The US example has often played a role in the debate between those who advocated a political union ahead of monetary union and vice versa, but we will see that neither can draw much evidence for their position from this example. The US dollar area exhibited high diversity in economic structures, particularly between the agricultural-rural South and West which were dependent on elastic seasonal credit, and the industrial-financial Northeast where the dominant interests were keen to get a hard currency that would be traded internationally. In the US monetary union, as in the EA, financial crises were the main drivers of reforms that overcame political resistance. The first national currency was introduced in the midst of the American Civil War, when the political union had broken up. The setting of priorities in collective action that such crises generated was, however, often contested and subject to frequent revision. US history also provides ample evidence that financial markets are rather unreliable channels of interstate risk sharing.

Diversity was an important motivation for founding the European monetary union. As emphasized above, the architects of the EA were fully aware of the fact that the newly created monetary union would include political economies with very different inflation records: traditional low-inflation countries such as Germany and the Netherlands, traditional high-inflation countries such as Italy and Spain, and many in between. To the extent that these differences were due to national monetary policies, the common currency would eliminate them. The policy architecture that was built was single-mindedly focused on stability-oriented monetary policy and prudent fiscal policy. In Chapter 5 I argue that this was meant to protect the commons of a currency providing low inflation and low interest rates. This goes against the reading that EMU followed an ordo- or neoliberal script. Furthermore, some risk sharing was built into the policy framework. For instance, the European Central Bank (ECB) did not differentiate between government bonds according to the national issuer when used as collateral in borrowing from the central bank; while this was done for narrow monetary policy reasons, it also constituted risk pooling that the ECB defended when criticized. At the same time, financial integration, instead of smoothing risks, expanded them. Cross-border capital flows financed catch-up growth but they also led to unprecedented macroeconomic imbalances. There was an intruder to the commons which was not well monitored, and this was cross-border banking.

Chapter 6 takes up the EA crisis that erupted in early 2010, following on from the earlier financial crisis and testing the policy framework to almost breaking point. Scholarly accounts of the European monetary union have been tested as well. In this chapter, the political economy of monetary solidarity is contrasted with two other diagnoses of why the EA has proven so vulnerable to turmoil, the theory of OCAs (Krugman 2013), and the comparative political economy of growth regimes, which has its roots in the Varieties of Capitalism literature (Hall 2012, 2014a; Iversen et al. 2016). The main argument against these competing diagnoses is that they cannot do justice to the diversity of crisis experiences in the five countries in need of support. The diagnosis implied by the political economy of monetary solidarity is that the unlucky few were singled out due to their financial vulnerabilities in an environment of self-fulfilling market panic. All experienced a negative feedback loop between bank and sovereign balance sheets, with enormous costs in terms of income and employment losses. The EA's limited risk-sharing institutions could not protect them against what was partly a common shock and partly endogenous financial instability, even though they received bailout funds that were multiples of ordinary IMF lending.

Since 2009, there have been frantic reforms to these institutions. Chapter 7 analyzes these with a view to whether and how they extended monetary solidarity. The findings are mixed. The first response to the sovereign debt phase of the international financial crisis was to extend and tighten the rules for fiscal risk prevention, although it took until mid-2016 before two member states, Portugal and Spain, were even considered for sanctions and let off the hook at the last minute (Eder 2016); France and Italy had received repeated exemptions under the new rules. At the same time, some fiscal capacity for risk sharing has been created, although support for distressed member states was extended only under the most stringent conditions. Behind this limited fiscal capacity, a contentious extension of the ECB's ability to lend indirectly to sovereigns was announced by Mario Draghi (2012). This proved sufficient to end the escalating crisis for the time being. The banking union showed a similar pattern: on the one hand, it made a big step forward in creating the world's biggest jurisdiction of harmonized banking supervision in terms of financial assets, with the ECB at its helm; yet at the same time fiscal backstops for bank resolution are minimal and a European deposit insurance scheme has not yet come to pass. This has left the ECB as the principal firefighter, although driven less by choice than by market panic. In this, it has proved to be rather effective, but it has been exposed to political challenges at every twist and turn.

Chapters 8 and 9 look at specific risk-sharing mechanisms which highlight other manifestations of diversity. Member states of both the US and the EA monetary unions have quite different income levels. One way to alleviate the risk of being born in a poor region is migration. Migration was one of the risk-sharing mechanisms that the mainstream theory of monetary integration highlighted, figuring prominently in Mundell's original analysis. There it was seen as a way to adjust to idiosyncratic regional shocks. Yet, even in the US, cyclical shocks have never been a major driver of migration flows, although lasting differences in economic opportunities are. Regulated and formally institutionalized rights to migrate can act as individual insurance. Chapter 8 argues that welfare states are not obstacles to but vehicles for social solidarity, making migration economically less regressive and politically more viable. But the analysis also raises doubts that what may work for individuals can contribute to risk sharing between regions. The conditions under which both the regions of origin and of destination will benefit from migration, either by lowering the volatility of an accelerated growth process or by trading off stability for higher growth, are quite specific and difficult to achieve.

Chapter 9 turns to consider institutions that insure against disruption to cross-border payments, specifically so-called "sudden stops." These arise when a crisis impedes the financial flows that allow countries to run current-account surpluses or deficits for long periods. They were familiar to the policymakers involved in negotiating the set-up of the EA, given that Germany's export surpluses and other member states' high deficits were a source of tension in efforts to stabilize exchange rates in the ERM. How is the risk of imbalances and the fall-out of financial instability shared in the EA? How can we explain that these risks are shared at all? Chapter 9 answers these questions by comparing the EA's cross-border payments system TARGET with the cross-border payments system ISA in the US. They performed very similarly during the extraordinary monetary times of 2008–13, replacing the interbank market on a truly impressive scale. But there was no US equivalent to the adversarial politicization that a platform for cross-border payments attracted in Germany and subsequently in the blogosphere.

Chapter 10 draws out the general conclusions. One question that may have occurred to readers is whether all forms of diversity are helpful for diversifying risks. Earlier chapters considered differences in inflation performance, in income levels and growth potential, as well as current-account balances. I argue that the principal obstacle to risk sharing does not come from any economic diversity but from the collective action required to make risk diversification happen. Heterogeneity or diversity of membership can hinder monetary solidarity but it can also provide incentives, in line with what an earlier political science literature hypothesized (Martin 1995; Snidal 1995). This leads on to policy implications. One issue is whether, over time, member states have to become more similar for the EA to function well; the other is whether ever closer integration with political union at the end is required. I argue that European monetary union should preserve diversity, for both political and economic reasons. Some fiscal capacity—and thus closer union in this sense—would help to prevent negative feedback loops between private and public debt. But fully fledged fiscal federalism has its own drawbacks. Above all, ever closer integration may undermine solidarity as it aggravates the real or perceived problems of moral hazard and interdependence. Finally, I discuss the implications of the EA being a monetary union of democracies but not a democratic union; this has consequences for the type of risk sharing that can be institutionally supported.

Ultimately, this attempt at understanding the experimental monetary union, to paraphrase Laffan et al. (1999), is motivated by a political concern that many citizens harbor when observing European integration with critical sympathy and a vested interest in its success. Forming a union was meant to ensure that open markets were governed collectively so that they would generate more wealth and distribute it more fairly than without such governance. The unity this requires promised to respect, value, and, indeed, preserve the diversity of public-sector and market institutions of its members. This "unity in diversity" norm was extended to the single currency: it was expected to end the asymmetric interest rate-setting power of the German Bundesbank, protect small open economies against the vagaries of volatile exchange rates, and thereby allow all members to develop according to their respective comparative advantages. The quest for unity in diversity is not just an example of the high-minded, yet empty rhetoric typical of official documents. It is a fundamental promise (Sandbu 2015: 270). In return, member states must accept constraints on their conduct of public affairs out of consideration for the effects on other members. The promise of unity in diversity is one side of the grand bargain that underpins the euro experiment.

Part I
Building Blocks

2

The Political Economy of Monetary Solidarity

The political economy of monetary solidarity is "political economy" in that it tries to explain why risk sharing in a union of diverse members is potentially advantageous but also rife with political conflict and economic strains, limiting the solidarity extended. Cooperation and conflict are two sides of the same coin (Keohane 1984: 51): in the absence of gains from cooperation, autarky could prevail and conflict would be avoided. This political economy approach has at its core collective action problems, which may concern outright failures to cooperate or tradeoffs between different possibilities and priorities in collective action.

The first section of this chapter explains the puzzle of rational cooperation. Why can it make sense for self-interested, instrumentally rational actors to cooperate with others even if there is no superior power that forces them to contribute to the common good? This was the question that a number of scholars asked after the breakdown of the US dollar standard of Bretton Woods, a breakdown that also spurred the first attempts at European monetary integration. The titles of two path-breaking books encapsulate the research program: Robert Axelrod's (1984) exploration of "the evolution of cooperation" and Robert Keohane's (1984) study of interstate cooperation "after hegemony." This research program can explain when, why, and how different and formally equal administrations would act collectively to cooperate in a currency union without a central government.

The following section specifies the theoretical framework that understands cooperation on risk sharing along the lines of Elinor Ostrom's work on "governing the commons" (Ostrom 1990). This conceptualization opened up a large space of inquiry between the polar opposites of anarchy and hierarchy that international relations scholars used to study (Snidal 1995: 51). A major challenge in adopting this conceptualization is to show that governing the commons with a diverse membership is possible. Ostrom (1990: 89, 210–18) thought that successful maintenance of a commons requires fairly homogenous users. "Governing the commons" is concerned with maintaining a common pool resource, it does not explain how the resource is mobilized in the first place. This is a major question in the case of a currency union which, after all, is not a natural finite resource like a piece of land that is used by the village community for grazing their cattle. The answer is found here in the "by-product theory of collective action" which traces the provision of a common good back to the selective incentives or special interests of those who produced it (Olson 1971: 132–5).

The third section spells out the four most important collective action problems facing parties that would like to cooperate in their own interest. Institutions may solve some problems but neglect others. For instance, the policy architecture of the EA emphasizes the prevention of moral hazard in the guise of fiscal profligacy at the cost of reduced insurance of member states against the spillovers of financial instability. There is a tension between the solutions to these two collective action problems (moral hazard and externalities). Prioritizing one over the other reveals underlying power constellations and keeps political contestation in a monetary union alive.

The chapter closes with a section on forms of risk sharing that are relevant for a political economy of account: whether it concerns redistribution or stabilization and risk sharing ex ante (insurance) or ex post (compensation). The hypothesis is that different combinations of these forms pose different problems for collective action.

2.1 The Puzzle of Rational Cooperation

How can we explain the cooperation between national democracies, especially when they are different and unequal? In democracies, the legitimation of government depends on winning domestic elections, and this is not necessarily facilitated by compromising with foreign governments. For cooperation, more resourceful countries have to give smaller or poorer countries, possibly with opposing views, a say in the conduct of their affairs; less resourceful countries have to allow others to meddle in their affairs with their consent. There is, of course, the empirical observation that international agreements and international organizations have mushroomed since the early 1980s (Drezner 2013: 284). Administrations seem to be ready to formulate cooperative plans, although compliance is more difficult. Inside and outside academia, many think that cooperative agreements between formally sovereign nations cannot endure or be effective. The bluff of "organized hypocrisy" that characterizes sovereign statehood (Krasner 2013: 352) must be called, sooner or later, if decision makers are rational. The more powerful nations will not let themselves be restrained forever, while smaller, weaker nations may free ride on the collective good provided by others so long as it is costly to punish their non-cooperation.

Two classic contributions to international political economy tried to solve this puzzle of rational cooperation. Against the background of diminishing US dominance, Axelrod (1984) and Keohane (1984) explained why cooperation and compliance with international commitments may prevail and even increase. The loss of hierarchy as a solution had led "realist" scholars and policymakers to expect a breakdown in cooperation and compliance. Both Axelrod and Keohane asked whether it is possible to explain interstate cooperation based on an instrumental notion of rationality, meaning a consistent and effective use of means to further one's self-interested (here: national) goals. The assumption of rationality is a methodological device to address the realist challenge and construct a robust argument about the possibility of international policy cooperation. It is not a substantive claim about the individual behavior of decision makers.

Axelrod (1984) undertook an experiment in which eminent scholars, many of them students of rational choice theory, were asked to find a robust strategy for surviving in a world of rational egoists. A non-cooperative strategy was expected to prevail and the only question was how smart each player had to be in order to outperform other egoists. But a simple tit-for-tat strategy beginning with cooperation, proposed by the mathematical psychologist Anatol Rapoport, was the most successful survival strategy. Axelrod (1984) then went on to show that this individually rational behavior can explain the social evolution of cooperation at the macro level. Computer simulations demonstrated that an individual player who cooperates and reciprocates can survive and prevail in most interactions with other rational strategies. While artificial, the setting is less unrealistic for the case of interstate cooperation than for interaction between individuals: in economic diplomacy generally and in the various Council formations of the EU specifically, entire teams of civil servants are engaged in repeated interactions for which they devise bargaining and retaliation strategies.

Keohane (1984: 78, 107) proposed that, even when they rationally pursue their national interest, governments still manage to commit to joint provision of international public goods, such as managed trade or more stable exchange rates, "after hegemony." In the benign version of Kindleberger (1973), hegemonic powers can solve the collective action problem of sovereign states, primarily by bribing them into cooperation and paying the lion's share of the cost of international public goods. Eichengreen's (1987) historical exploration of British and American hegemony suggested, however, that very rarely is hegemonic power so overwhelming that the hegemon can take decisions and implement them without the cooperation of second-tier nations. This has been the situation of Germany's "reluctant hegemony" (Bulmer and Paterson 2013) in the EA: its political leverage and its fiscal capacity are too small to stabilize the monetary union single handedly. Chapters 5–7 provide repeated examples where the German government either sought agreement with like-minded nations like the Netherlands and Finland before it took action, or struck deals with France in order to pre-empt lengthy negotiations at the EU level. Furthermore, even if the dominant power can muscle others into agreement, compliance with the agreement can still be a problem. Fiscal surveillance is a case in point (see Section 2.2.1). This was also the experience of coordinated US dollar–DM–Yen stabilization as an alternative to European exchange rate stabilization, which was never very successful (Putnam and Henning 1989).

Keohane's "after-hegemony" setting is therefore still relevant in the present context: governments are aware of their interdependence in a world structured by sovereign statehood, and they pursue their national interest through rational cooperation. This setting is analogous to market exchange in the model of atomistic or monopolistic competition.[1] It is a particularly testing ground for the provision of public goods, given that standard economic theory proposes that competitive actors' incentives alone will not bring about a welfare-maximizing general equilibrium that produces the efficient amount of public goods. Keohane's approach does not exclude the possibility that additional "extra-rational motivations" for coordination are present, such as moral imperatives or benefits from mere participation, but it does not rely on these motivations (Hardin 1982: 101–24; Keohane 1984: 110–32).

In a similar vein, this study tries to explain manifestations of monetary solidarity in line with rational nationalism. If solidarity can be found even under this adverse behavioral assumption, it is more convincing than if "the creation, maintenance, and evolution of international regimes" such as a monetary union rests "on assumptions about the 'public interest' or the General Will" (Keohane 1984: 107). Obviously, extra-rational motivations can play a role, such as the commitment to lasting peace in Europe, a feeling of historical guilt on the part of Germany, or the attempt to establish a counterweight to the United States. But the finding of monetary solidarity should not rely on such arguments. They are idiosyncratic and cannot inform a general political–economic theory of monetary integration.

There are also substantive reasons for assuming rationality in the present context. Monetary integration, both the common currency and the particular institutions needed to make it viable, has been introduced partly to compensate

[1] It is presumably for this reason that the Axelrod–Keohane strand of international political economy is called neoliberal institutionalism (Drezner 2013: 282), but this is a rather confusing use of the term "neoliberal."

for perceived weaknesses and flaws of national democracies, notably their alleged inflation and deficit biases (Schelkle 2006: 680–2). This has earned the EA, just like the EU as a whole, the perennial charge of having a "democratic deficit."[2] While not a false accusation, it misses an important point: the democratic deficit is the flip side of the attempt to mend deficits of national democracy. It does so by committing elected governments to policies that can be rationally justified as in the common interest and hence are not easily changed by shifting national majorities or domestic special interests. In a union of mature democracies, national action is contested and constrained in several ways (Moravcsik 2002: 607–10). Governments must convince their partners of the validity of a position or line of action, but must also convince domestic constituencies that any agreement is in the national interest. There is thus a political process that makes the management of the union and domestic affairs subject to deliberations based on generalizable self-interested arguments. The rational framing of policy agendas is a signature of the EU, leaving the wider public somewhat cold.

The solution to the puzzle of rational cooperation must therefore lie in interest constellations at home and abroad as well as institutions that sustain incentives to cooperate. The latter relates the work on interstate cooperation to work on international organizations (Goldstein and Steinberg 2010). As the subtitle of Keohane (1984) indicates, "discord" rather than harmony is a reliable trigger for governments seeking agreements with other governments. The operation of the Franco-German axis is a case in point; the two administrations usually represent opposing views that are openly expressed. But they are also determined to find an agreement in which most other member states will find their position more or less represented. Franco-German discord can therefore help to reduce the number of negotiators and speed up decisions (Heipertz and Verdun 2004: 149; Schelkle 2012a). But the compromise also has to be institutionalized, to replace discretionary decision making by two member states with routines and procedures in which other member states have a say.

Rationality implies that key actors seek cooperation only if this is necessary for achieving the results they care about. Exchange rate stabilization was historically a prime example of such instrumental cooperation. Even the Bundesbank could not achieve stability in the D-Mark exchange rate without the cooperation of other countries. From its beginnings in the 1970s, cooperation on exchange rate stabilization and later on monetary policy became densely institutionalized. This institutional density is typically the result of tightening the commitment to cooperation, countering the tendency of rational actors to evade commitments opportunistically in response to changing incentives.

[2] See Moravcsik (2002) as well as Follesdal and Hix (2006) for a stimulating debate of the EU's democratic deficit. Chapter 10 reflects on this debate in Section 10.3.1.

The Bundesbank was accused of pursuing its stabilization goals without regard to other members in the ERM; Italian and French policymakers were accused of being not as resolute in price stabilization as a stable exchange rate grid would require. This conflict came to a head in 1992–3 when the rejection of the Maastricht Treaty in a Danish referendum triggered a major currency crisis (Section 5.1.1). It was thought at the time that it would spell the end of the monetary integration project. Instead, German governments (under conservative chancellors) insisted on strict fiscal rules in return for giving up monetary autonomy (Jacoby 2015: 198; Schelkle 2009).

Cooperation thus became deeply entrenched, which is an international trend beyond European integration (Drezner 2013: table 13.1; Henning, 2017 for the EA). The question then becomes one of institutional choice (Drezner 2013: 284). In the present context this question is: why are particular institutions of risk sharing created or strengthened but not others? Increasing complexity is likely to bring back the problem of asymmetric power that thick or dense institutions are meant to rein in: the stronger are likely to wield their power and prioritize the institutional devices that suit their interests best. Chapters 6 and 7 on the evolution of economic governance during the crisis can show that increasing complexity was indeed a feature of reforms, in particular in fiscal surveillance; and Germany was assertive, especially in the set-up of institutions outside the Treaty,[3] yet there was also considerable resistance and non-compliance that undermined German dominance subsequently.

Risk sharing is a possible rationale of European monetary integration, supported by economic research since around the 1990s. But a rationale is not necessarily a practice, enshrined in empirically observable institutions. Indeed, rationality of policymakers sometimes prevents the risk-sharing potential of a diverse union from being exploited fully. For instance, failure to provide a collective good is often due to the fact that the parties involved do not trust the other side's reliability or capacity to honor the agreement. This can have many causes, from personal trustworthiness of populist leaders to the weakness of support in a politically polarized democracy. Diversity is among those reasons: the sheer lack of familiarity with the ways other political economies work can create a residual mistrust that only obvious economic success, the endorsement by markets, can suppress. These many sources of skepticism or outright mistrust imply that we cannot conclude from a plausible, and even desirable, rationale for cooperation that it will become the outcome of rational action.[4]

[3] Bickerton et al. (2015) analyze such institutions outside the Treaty as manifestations of a "new intergovernmentalism."

[4] This is of course a point that historical institutionalism has emphasized (Hall and Taylor 1996: 941–2).

This qualification should make clear, finally, that this conceptualization of rational cooperation is not to be confounded with a public-choice view of the world in which policymakers' actions are derived from individual utility maximization. This would be a fallacy of composition because neither in politics nor in economics can we infer "macrobehavior" from "micromotives," as Thomas Schelling (1978) put it.[5] Schelling (1978) systematically explained why individually rational pursuits can lead to aggregate outcomes that are in nobody's rational interest (Hardin 1982: 1–3). Conversely, Axelrod (1984) analyzed in detail how a cooperative strategy fares if confronted with other, less cooperative strategies; the evolutionary success of the former was evidence for its rationality as "macrobehavior." The methodological assumption of rationality that this study adopts requires that monetary solidarity is compatible with the rationality of relevant actors. But this compatibility does not imply a rationally desirable, functionalist outcome because such outcomes are beyond any actor's control.

2.2 The By-Product Theory of Collective Action

Exchange rate management and even more the move to a single currency and integrated financial markets require sustained cooperation between administrations of formally sovereign nation states. Joining the European monetary union was and is voluntary, decided by democratically elected governments and not imposed by hegemonic or colonial rule. In fact, the only potentially hegemonic member state, Germany, had to be convinced to take part and then used its veto player position to get concessions, in line with its ideological leanings but also in order to appease domestic opposition. Even so, governments in other member states pressed on with monetary union. This coming together of member states with very different interests and positions as regards exchange rate management appears as a major puzzle today, given that almost every explanation of the EA crisis rests on the verdict that the union is too diverse to be able to function.[6] Three lines of argument are particularly relevant.

Proponents of an optimal currency area, including political economists such as Moravcsik (2012) and Scharpf (2015), see too little convergence on flexible labor and competitive product markets as a cause of the crisis. This

[5] Concluding directly from micro motives to macro behavior is a common fallacy in neoclassical (Walrasian) economics, as shown by Kirman (1989): well-behaved individual excess demand functions do not yield well-behaved excess demand functions in the aggregate. The mainstream economist's quest for micro foundations of all market behavior is therefore rather questionable.

[6] Exceptions include contributors to the edited volume of Caporaso and Rhodes (2016), notably Erik Jones and Randall Henning, as well as the remarkable book by Martin Sandbu (2015).

diagnosis has been challenged by scholars in the same tradition: even if labor and product markets are not fully flexible, asymmetric or asynchronous shocks to output could be absorbed by integrated and diversified financial markets, and possibly a central budget, shielding consumption from volatility (Chapter 3 and Section 6.2.1).

Scholars of different varieties of capitalism, by contrast, see incompatible growth regimes as the problem in a monetary union that favors the coordinated market economies of Northern Europe (Iversen et al. 2016; Hall 2014a; Hancké 2013). The difficulty with this explanation is, in short, that it must assume that some countries have consistent (non-inflationary, high-productivity) institutional regimes while others have inconsistent regimes from which only exchange rate adjustment can provide some relief. This is hard to reconcile with the underlying theory of institutional complementarities and also does not entirely square with the comparative evidence: Ireland, Spain, and Cyprus do not fit the diagnosis (Section 6.2.2).

The ideational school in comparative political economy is slightly different in its diagnosis in that it sees an ideologically driven uniformity imposed on a diversity of member states as the cause of the EA's malaise (Matthijs and Blyth 2015; Matthijs and McNamara 2015). The problem with this diagnosis is that it sees more uniformity than we should expect from its own underlying theory of varied norms and social practices resisting one market logic. It ignores flexibility in the EA framework which actually sustains varied norms and practices (Chapter 5).

This book starts from the principle and time-honored practice of insurance to argue that diversity of members provides an economic opportunity for diversifying risks (Imbs and Mauro 2007; Lewis 1996). For example, asynchronous business cycles allow a member's economy in a downturn to benefit from high demand in another member's economy that is in an upturn, without the distorting effect of exchange rate moves that follow a financial market logic. Or, to take the example that motivated European currency unification: it allows members to pool the risks of different potentials for growth and instability. The high growth potential of poorer economies, stymied by a high-risk premium, can be realized if they can benefit from the low interest rate that richer member states with low growth potential bestow on the union; this creates expanding markets for the latter and thus raises their own growth potential. The first step of the counter-argument is therefore that diversity as such cannot explain economic problems of a heterogeneous union.

This shifts the need for an explanation, second, to the question of why the potential for risk diversification is not realized. There is not much evidence that member states were aware of this potential when policymakers embarked on the road to Maastricht. What is clear is that exchange rate instability after the breakdown of Bretton Woods and the higher frequency of currency crises that came with financial liberalization were a main motivation for European monetary integration. The Delors report opens with statements to that effect (Committee 1989: paras 1 and 5), and later quantitative and qualitative research confirmed that currency instability was a major concern of policymakers. Instability occurred at a higher frequency after 1973 although it also became less severe (Bordo et al. 2001: 56–7; James 2012: 4, 12). In the ERM, governments were repeatedly drawn into acrimonious negotiations over parity adjustments and burden sharing as regards policy responses. Yet this is not evidence that they sought risk sharing through monetary integration. The evidence suggests that the governments involved wanted above all to get rid of exchange rate volatility as a source of economic instability and political humiliation (Section 5.1.1). The question therefore is how risk sharing emerges if it is not the prime intention of elected officials.

2.2.1 *Origins in the Logic of Collective Action*

Monetary solidarity—deliberate and institutionalized sharing of risks that can afflict members of a monetary union—is a collective action problem. Denominating payments and incomes, assets and liabilities in a single currency inherently creates a risk pool for liquidity shocks. A stable currency that delivers low interest rates by sharing liquidity risks also reduces the risks to insolvency that debtor-investors, but also creditors, incur. But explaining how risk sharing comes about runs into the problem of endless regress: "Institutions resolve collective action problems, but institutions themselves are public goods, meaning that their origins are subject to the same dilemmas they are meant to resolve" (Broz 1998: 231). The effort to create a stable currency came on the back of existing efforts to stabilize exchange rates. Government finances, wage bargains, and price setting of firms can all contribute to or obstruct the stability of a currency and exchange rates. There are substantial free-riding incentives: even those who do not contribute to stability cannot be excluded from the diffuse benefits of a hard currency—low interest rates, low inflation, high liquidity. Excessive public deficits by a few small member states, too high or too low collective wage agreements in a few sectors and regions, or indeed buoyant mortgage credit growth in a few regions previously starved of long-term household finance, are each not enough to jeopardize the stability of a currency. But cumulatively their effects may be fatal, and anticipating the free riding of some may undermine the willingness of all to cooperate.

The account of the logic of collective action developed by Mancur Olson (1971) provides at least two theories of how the various stakeholders of a single currency could overcome this problem (Broz 1998: 234–5). First, the benefits from the common currency may accrue disproportionately to some stakeholders, the "privileged group." They therefore go ahead and provide it, not concerned by the free riding of the rest. This model is hard to reconcile with the evidence in Moravcsik (1998) and Dyson and Featherstone (1999) of how the euro came about. Highly indebted and/or inflationary countries like Belgium and Italy had the greatest benefits to expect from low inflation and low interest rates. The enormous adjustments they made—a constitutional mechanism for debt reduction in Belgium, massive labor market reforms and tax hikes in Italy—revealed their preferences beyond doubt. But they were not in a position to bring about the common currency. By contrast, the German government was in a position to veto or endorse the common currency but it could not expect great benefits from giving up the D-Mark. Hence, the German government insisted on safeguards against free riding and on commitment to stability-oriented behavior to be proven in a drawn-out qualification process. It intended to limit risk sharing to the common central bank issuing the single currency. It is no wonder that Majone (2016: 218–20) sees a damning verdict on the Economic and Monetary Union in Olson's logic, but he takes only Olson's preferred "privileged group" approach into account.

The evidence provided by the historical accounts (and beyond) is more compatible with a second theory that explains collective action as a joint or by-product of private rent seeking (Olson 1971: 132–5). This applies when the distribution of benefits is not unequal enough to make a select group provide the collective good; the private benefits are dispersed but they cannot be enjoyed without providing the collective good. This fits the case of monetary solidarity fairly well: the benefits of a common currency are varied, public and private, supranational and national. The private and national benefits were central to Moravcsik's (1998: 381–6) liberal intergovernmentalist interpretation. Collignon and Schwarzer (2002) document the advocacy of organized transnational business interests, and there is also evidence that organized labor in export-oriented sectors was in favor so as to prevent competitive devaluations, an account that is supported by a functionalist rationale in Iversen et al. (2016). The motivations of political elites were presumably more idiosyncratic: French policymakers hoped to get on a more equal footing with Germany and the United States; Italians and Belgians used it as a reform lever for an unsustainable domestic political economy; modernist Europhile elites in Greece, Portugal, and Spain sought to stabilize the young democracies through catch-up growth. The overlap of these aspirations was the common currency. By default, it allowed risk sharing on liquidity shocks that would otherwise drive up national risk premia.

This theory of collective action generally and monetary solidarity specifically is decidedly not functionalist. Collective action problems may be "solved" as a by-product of private incentives, but the solutions are not necessarily well designed, given that the wider benefits from collective interest representation are not what motivated the production of the common good. This is a problem for continuing cooperation. Hardin (1982: 35) calls it "a perverse aspect" of the by-product theory that there is "only a tenuous connection between a group's interest and what the organization based on selective incentives does for that interest." In the present context, this means that while the EA members have a collective interest in risk sharing, the monetary union might cater to it only by accident or default, if at all. The theory does not lead us to expect sustained monetary solidarity even if it can explain why it may be a joint product with private/national benefits. This puts the onus on the researcher to show not only that the joint product exists but also how it has been institutionalized to ensure ongoing cooperation.

An example of risk sharing by default is the integration of government bond markets, supported by market forces and by a single monetary policy (Section 5.2.2). There was also "accidental" risk sharing on a grand and unexpected scale through the cross-border payments system TARGET, notably the risk of a sudden stop of capital flows but also the flight of deposits and even the catastrophic risk of a break-up of the EA (Section 9.2). For each of these (and other) examples, it has to be shown how risk sharing by default and by accident can become deliberate and morph into monetary solidarity. This is the case when the inherent capacity comes to the fore and is acknowledged, endorsed, or at least tolerated without fundamental change. Such transformation into monetary solidarity is not assured and there will also be plenty of examples in which the potential for risk sharing does not materialize. For instance, the Quantitative Easing (Asset Purchase) program of the ECB, which started in early 2015, officially confined risk sharing to the (smaller) share of bonds that were taken on the ECB's books, excluding those that national central banks held at their own risk (ECB 2016). Again, monetary solidarity was a side effect of crisis management, but in this case it was consciously limited.

This seems to support, once again, Monnet's famous dictum that "Europe will be forged in crises, and will be the sum of the solutions adopted for those crises."[7] This statement is often interpreted as evidence for functional spillover: when the need arises, it will be fulfilled with further steps of integration. But there may also be dysfunctional spillover (Schmidt 2015: 36–7). Risk sharing that is the outcome of crisis management is not necessarily the most functional solution; it may be the result of ad hoc measures that favor the powerful. This jeopardizes future compliance: uneven distributional consequences may make members resentful, and lead them to openly defy or silently neglect their obligations. The Fiscal Compact, a hardened stability and growth pact imposed on other member states at the height of the crisis in

[7] "L'Europe se fera dans les crises et elle sera la somme des solutions apportées à ces crises" (Monnet 1976).

2010–11, is a pertinent example—it has been obstructed, silently, even by the Commission (Section 7.2.1). In this, the Compact joins the litany of reforms to fiscal surveillance that made this annual policy process ever more complex but neither effective nor legitimate (Schelkle 2009): it is seen as a German obsession and a hypocritical one at that since German governments also had difficulties, before and in the monetary union, of meeting the fiscal rules themselves.

The prophecy of one of the fathers of European integration is therefore more appropriately called *Monnet's curse*. It is not fate, however; Parsons and Matthijs (2015) challenge the generality of its claim and argue that major steps in European integration were political choices and not foisted onto governments by crisis. In a union of democracies, it is unlikely that the institutional outcome of parochial power politics will stand; more sophisticated power politics will prevail, so long as it can command a minimum of loyalty and collaboration from others. The real test for monetary solidarity is therefore whether what has been introduced under extreme circumstances survives, and possibly adapts institutionally once there is a return to normal times.

2.2.2 *Governing a Commons*

Elinor Ostrom's (1990) work can be combined with the by-product theory of how common goods are created, to explain how the common good can be maintained. Her contribution to institutional economics and public administration was stimulated by the dismal prediction that when an exhaustible resource is collectively owned, it must inevitably lead to a tragedy of the commons (Hardin 1968). She challenged the public-choice view that only private ownership or central government control can deliver sustainable usage of resources (Bermeo 2010). In fact, Ostrom (1990: 95–6) saw monitoring others' use of a collectively owned resource as a by-product of using this resource, individually and collectively, in a sustainable manner. Successful governing of the commons means providing monitoring as a joint product which is self-enforcing because it is tied to the private benefit.

The notion of a common pool resource has been taken up by scholars working on budgetary institutions in European member states soon after the Stability Pact was devised (Hallerberg and von Hagen 1997). It has the following features.

- A common pool resource cannot exclude (excessive) users easily, and is in this respect similar to a public good and unlike a private or a club good.
- But the use of a common pool resource is rival, that is the resource is depletable and in this respect similar to a private good (Ostrom 1990: 32; Snidal 1995: 50).

- In contrast to club goods, the problem of depletion by users with legitimate access remains a collective action problem. The theory of clubs (Buchanan 1965) shows how they achieve optimal access to prevent congestion.

The two concepts of an exhaustible commons and a collective good meet in the theoretical possibility that a common property can end up being badly used, even though this is in nobody's rational interest. Collective action to monitor the use of the commons is thus of the essence or it will end in tragedy: depletion.

The policy architecture of the EA can be rationalized in terms of Ostrom's theory of governing a commons, but it requires some adaptation of the original context.[8] The common good to be preserved is a hard, stable currency, although there are different views about how to do this (McNamara 1998; Pisani-Ferry 2006). Overuse and depletion of the commons in this context would mean euro-denominated debt being issued excessively, although, again, how this excess is to be determined remains contested (Heipertz and Verdun 2004). Depletion could come in two guises: the central bank would have to come to the rescue of a large defaulting debtor, typically thought to be a government, or suppress the high real interest rate by issuing more euros than is compatible with price stability (Brunila et al. 2001; Issing 2002). The incentives are there: each government can reap the full benefit of each monetary unit issued while it bears only a fraction of the costs in terms of additional inflation or a rise in the risk premium for all. The governance framework put the central bank under strict prohibition of financing governments directly and imposed strict fiscal rules, with the Commission as the monitor. The monetary union is conspicuously set up to avoid the tragedy of a common currency.

A high quality of the currency, in the sense of an international medium of payment and a stable reference point for transactions, can be seen as the common property to be preserved. The quality of a currency is created and maintained in ways analogous to the quality of land and is in that sense akin to an exhaustible commons. The architects of the euro tried to achieve quality by establishing institutional safeguards. But these institutional safeguards have not withstood a systemic crisis: in fact, it can be argued that the safeguards were misleading in their focus on public debt and counterproductive in their restraint on the central bank, even under the most adverse of circumstances (Section 6.2.3).

The quality of a currency is ultimately judged in financial markets which makes the monitoring of the commons even more difficult. Anticipating market responses can mean keeping the money supply relatively scarce even

[8] See Raudla (2010) for a critical review of the literature on "budgetary commons."

if the economy is stagnating, or it can mean going for growth and expanding the money supply in line with expanding credit demand. This is a defining conflict in macroeconomic stabilization that also flared up time and again in US monetary-financial history (Bordo and Wheelock 2011: 8, 14–16; Chapter 4). Neoclassically minded economists, traditionally housed on the top floor of the Bundesbank and in the Dutch finance ministry, support tight money while the more Keynesian-minded economists, inhabiting the City of London and the French bureaucracy, advocate elastic credit. While the former fear overexpansion with inflationary consequences, the latter fear undue restraint with adverse effects on economic growth. In modern central banking, this conflict between tight money and elastic credit can be reconciled but there is still room for legitimate debate between hawks and doves. Ostrom (1990: 18) acknowledged this: "The herders can overestimate or underestimate the carrying capacity of the meadow."

The framing of EA governance as a potential tragedy of the commons leads monitors to look for free riding and exploitation of a common resource, despite legitimately different views on how to use and preserve the commons. The budgetary institutions literature, with its focus on the common resource pool problem, demonstrates this bias (Hallerberg et al. 2009: 3–5; for an extension to the ECB see Dinger et al. 2014). This is more down the line of Garrett Hardin (1968) than of Elinor Ostrom (1990). Economically sensible monitoring should ensure that excessive use of the common resource of money creation is restrained but also that sufficient use creates desirable welfare.

Chapter 6 on the EA crisis and Chapter 7 on the institutional reforms since the crisis argue that the risk-sharing capacity of the monetary union has been underexploited. This argument is not derived from some ideal of a "complete and genuine union," as two major EU reports put it (van Rompuy et al. 2012, Juncker et al. 2015), but from an understanding of what would be minimally required to resolve the current crisis, specifically by interrupting the negative feedback loop between the insolvency of banks and sovereigns. However, it has to be granted that the EA has managed to create and maintain a hard and stable currency. This has come at the cost of almost any other consideration, and particularly at the cost of more growth (Section 7.1). A stable currency was the interest of all members that signed up to the EA. But the actual institutional choices were more in the interest of some countries than others as many observers noted: in those of Germany above all but also the Benelux countries and Finland, as well as some Central and Eastern European countries where governments tend to be fiscally conservative. If geopolitical entities are of very different weight, diplomatic mobilization, the threat of retaliation, or feedback effects are unlikely to achieve collective action that, for instance, the creation of a joint debt instrument ("Eurobond") would require. Advancing monetary solidarity between unequal partners remains a challenge, especially if it relies on being produced as a by-product of other primary motivations.

Lisa Martin (2001) explored in detail how cooperation can be sustained under circumstances of heterogeneous membership. She argued that the EA as set up for normal times is characterized by two institutional features: "the facilitation of stable linkages across issues, and disproportionately large bargaining power of small states" (Martin 2001: 137). The stable linkages are provided by the overlap of the Single Market and the monetary union. Tightly administered programs like cohesion policy or the common agricultural policy provide another stable linkage: they provide compensation to less advanced countries and regions for having to keep their borders open to competitors. The disproportionate influence of smaller states is ensured by closing down opportunities for flexible integration and prevention of opt-outs (Martin 2001: 138–43). They can then exploit their veto power in the choice of institutions which requires unanimity, while ongoing bargaining when they are already roped in weakens their influence due to qualified majority voting. Proposals for more flexible integration that, for instance, a number of contributors to Chalmers et al. (2016a) propose, are likely to weaken the institutional position of smaller member states: they can be sidelined as their consent is not necessarily required while the more influential member states have, by definition, the means to garner support from loyal partners.

Another way to maintain the commons is with a dedicated, professional monitoring system. The European Commission can play a role in fostering common pool resources. The Commission is an institution of political entrepreneurship, meaning that it is set up to "find it in their private interest to work to provide collective benefits to relevant groups" (Hardin 1982: 35). More integration and delegated monitoring of the commons is the professional pursuit of EU officials, serving the organizational interest of the agency. Political entrepreneurship proceeds by seeking out the overlapping interests in member states' agendas. Traditionally, this was seen as a role of the Commission. It used to be quite effective in overcoming the joint decision trap of institutional choice that Fritz Scharpf formalized as a major problem of ongoing EU governance. As he later noted, the EU escaped this trap to an almost concerning degree, namely by what he called the supranational hierarchical mode of governance (Scharpf 2006: 851) that "exercise[s] policy-making functions without any involvement of politically accountable actors in the Council or the European Parliament." Interestingly, though, in the crisis since 2008, it has been the ECB rather than the Commission that has played the role of a political entrepreneur that urges governments to collective action (Schelkle 2014a). The central bank provided the collective benefit of keeping the financial system afloat and could thus preserve the infrastructure for its monetary policy. Yet, this firefighting left the ECB uncomfortably exposed to political criticism and contestation (Section 7.2.3).

2.3 Political Market Failures

Collective action failures between formally sovereign nation states are analytically similar to market failures (Keohane 1984: 85–100). Elected governments represent their constituencies and pursue their interests as they perceive them, with uncertain degrees of consideration for other governments in a similar position. Rationally and nationally pursued self-interest can obstruct mutually beneficial cooperation because the contracting parties cannot ascertain how well they can protect their interests (for example, because they lack well-defined property rights, relevant information, or do not trust the other's commitment). Political market failure is compounded by incomplete bargaining frameworks and endemic commitment problems in democracies, where the original contracting party is bound to change.

This political market failure approach has been accused of downplaying the distributive concerns that governments may have when they contemplate cooperation with others (Mearsheimer 2010: 402–5). The critics have a point. It is an implication of the rationality assumption: rational actors should be concerned about their absolute and not their relative gains when they consider joining or sustaining a cooperative arrangement. The realist alternative is succinctly formulated by Grieco (1988: 600), who first brought this point to wider attention: "states prefer that relative achievements of jointly produced gains not advantage partners, and their concerns about relative gains may constrain their willingness to cooperate." Concerns over the country's position in the fragile balance of powers, rather than material gain, may make or break cooperation. The inherent assumption of the original market failure conceptualization was, by contrast, that interstate cooperation makes the overall pie grow, and there is an incentive to cooperate so long as every country shares to some indeterminate degree in these gains. The distributive struggle is not completely neglected but each country is assumed to be less concerned with shares than with the absolute gains. Moreover, payoffs can comprise different kinds of economic gain, while realist scholarship requires payoffs to be measurable in the currency of power, by which the relative gain is estimated.

In subsequent formulations of rational cooperation between states, the uneven distribution of gains is seen as a potential lever for continuing cooperation. The point of issue linkages and package deals is exactly that negotiating governments ask for compensation in one area in return for concessions in another. Martin (2001: 135) recalls the request by new members of the EU in the late 1980s, led by Spain, to receive additional regional aid in return for their consent to the Maastricht Treaty on the Single Market and the monetary union. The Cohesion Fund was introduced on more generous terms than had been available before, and provided absolute gains for Greece, Ireland, Portugal, and Spain which had national incomes of 90 percent or less of the EU average at the time. The realist interpretation of this deal would suggest that it corrected for the relative advantage that the further opening of borders and the enlargement of the trade bloc handed to the old member states, then the Western European core. But material gains from regional aid for the public purse, trade gains for the private sector, and status gains in the international economic arena have very different valuations in the currency of power. It would seem more straightforward and politically intuitive to explain the case of interstate cooperation among diverse members as balancing different kinds of absolute economic gains.

Two types of economic and political market failures were the focus of attention in Keohane (1984: 85): externalities and asymmetric information. He thought that commitment problems could actually be solved more easily thanks to rational expectations, lowering of transaction costs, and repetition which all institution building involves (Keohane 1984: 100–9). This hypothesis for normal times, in which rules and routines are available, may be turned on its head under stress: commitments can be much more problematic if the insurance contract was implicit and is drawn upon for the first time; in fact, the fortunate may deny that they have a commitment. Recent contributions have also added the insight that behavioral problems of misperception prevent actors from pursuing their best self-interest, a point that Keohane (1984: 108) readily conceded.

Table 2.1 gives an overview of four types of political market failure and then takes off from the last column to give examples of collective action failures in monetary integration. Moss (2002: 36–49) and Barr (2012: 83–99) contain superb treatments of the various failures of private cooperation in and through markets that are here applied to sovereigns.[9]

2.3.1 *Externalities*

Externalities or spillovers are everywhere: the sheer fact of interdependence brings them about. For instance, the growth of one country uses up resources that cannot be enjoyed by others and the environmental damage done in recent centuries suggests that this resource depletion was not adequately priced. This allowed risks like pollution to be shifted onto other, notably less

[9] Readers may jump to Table 2.1 and return to it as a summary, but it may also be helpful as a dense preview.

Table 2.1. Overview of economic and political market failures

	What is the problem?	Why do markets (partially or completely) fail?	Why does interstate cooperation (partially or completely) fail?
Externalities	(a) interdependence that is not acknowledged (b) ill-defined property rights that allow risk shifting (c) feedback loops from responses to others' behavior that are destabilizing	True costs (negative externalities) or true benefits (positive externalities) are not reflected in prices and can therefore not be traded efficiently	Underprovision of public goods (positive externalities in consumption); overexploitation of resources (tragedy of the commons); regressive risk shifting on the weaker members
Asymmetric information	Raises aggregate risk in the pool: (a) adverse selection: hidden information about the true risk ex ante (b) moral hazard: hidden information about risk-taking behavior ex post	Good risks may withdraw from market or alleged bad risks may be discriminated against; underinsurance is the consequence in either case	Both problems raise aggregate risk in the pool which makes potential members unwilling to join or limit risk sharing for fear of interdependence
Lack of commitment	Dynamic inconsistency of behavior: promises of a course of action are not compatible with incentives in the future; leads to underinsurance	Private insurance of highly correlated current risks is not credible because insurer cannot promise to not default	Cooperation is not credible (a) because of government incentives or (b) because of dilemma of government responsiveness to domestic actors
Misperception	Behavior under uncertainty uses heuristic devices that are not compatible with instrumental rationality and subjective utility maximization; can be exploited	Systematic biases lead to over- or underinsurance; prudent insurance suppliers may be driven out by reckless providers; good risks among insurance seekers may withdraw from market	Mutually beneficial cooperation may be vulnerable to populist campaigns based on biased framing and misperceptions of other countries

Source: Own compilation, inspired by Moss (2002: 36–52)

developed countries, which did not benefit from the wealth that the pollution undoubtedly also generated. Herding behavior, creating market panics, is a leading example of an externality arising when, under uncertainty, the behavior of one actor triggers others to behave in a similar way, each trying to evade negative consequences if they do so in time but everybody aggravating the situation for themselves and others. This externality was at work in the EA crisis (and in financial instability in US history as well, as Section 4.2 shows repeatedly): a negative feedback loop evolves when banks face a funding shortage and need government support, this weakens public finances which lowers credit ratings and raises risk premia on government bonds, which then weakens the balance sheets of banks holding these bonds as supposedly safe assets, creating further funding problems (Brunnermeier and Sannikov 2013: 366–8; Farhi and Tirole 2014; Section 6.2.3).

Externalities can be positive as well as negative. Either way, rational governments, answerable for their policies to domestic parliaments and local media, have little reason to take the concerns of their neighbors into account. They will produce too little of the good externalities and too much of the bad. An example of a potential positive externality is counter-cyclical fiscal policies in the EA (Fitoussi et al. 1993; Schelkle 2012b: 141–4). In interdependent economies, rational nationalists can count on stimulus by other states to spill over into their economies, above all through their neighbors' increased demand for exports. Yet, if all choose to rely on expansionary measures of others, hoping to save the fiscal cost of a stimulus, too little active demand management is the result. As already mentioned, fear of the opposite, negative, externality prevailed at the time the EA architecture was built: that once in the common currency area, governments would incur excessive public debt. Their national bond issue would not drive up interest rates as much in an enlarged and unified bond market as in a smaller national market. Thus, "excessive" borrowers shift the cost in terms of rising interest rates partly on others. If these incentives work in several member states, overissue is the result, exhausting the commons of low interest rates and creditworthiness. The fear of this negative externality justified constraints on risk sharing in the form of fiscal rules, enshrined in the Stability and Growth Pact and later the Fiscal Compact.

Prior to the creation of the single currency, a negative externality notoriously arose from the Bundesbank's setting of interest rates (James 2012: 343). Whenever it let the D-Mark revalue against the US dollar, for instance to prevent an inflationary spillover from US monetary policy to the German economy, tensions arose in the ERM, which tried to maintain a grid of stable exchange rates between European member states. Capital outflows forced other European central banks to raise their interest rates so as to keep the parities intact. But higher interest costs for investment and the ensuing strength of their currencies against the US dollar depressed economic activity. The risks of US monetary policy, as perceived by Germany's central bank, were thus shifted onto weaker currency areas.

The market solution that Ronald Coase (1960) famously proposed, namely to establish and enforce property rights that give agents incentives to internalize these effects, is not easy to replicate in a Hobbesian world of sovereign nations. At the international level, there is no hierarchical power equivalent to a state vis-à-vis its citizens, which could effectively police a system of property rights. Moreover, governments are not unitary actors but consist of authorities with their own remits monitored by and responsive to different audiences.

A further issue is that independent and proud agents pursue their institutional interests, even defying cooperative agreements between governments because they see it as part of their mandate to stand up to elected governments. This was the case of the Bundesbank in the past. For instance, Giavazzi and Giovannini (1987) and von Hagen (1989) discuss the evidence that the German central bank observed only the letter but not the spirit of the intergovernmental agreement that central banks should intervene symmetrically in the ERM. This obligation required it to support central banks under devaluation pressure by selling D-Marks and buying the other currency. Yet after each such intervention, the Bundesbank was quick to undo this monetary expansion through domestic credit restraint ("sterilization"), thus renewing the pressure. Majone (2001) gives reasons why the Bundesbank's behavior may be interpreted as the behavior of a trustee faithful to its perceived mandate, rather than overreach ("drift") of an agent. Even so, the Bundesbank is a noteworthy example of a non-majoritarian national authority that could not or would not internalize externalities that the elected principal, the German government, had agreed to cooperate on under the Basel-Nyborg accord in September 1987. This behavior by the Bundesbank was a relevant motivation for other member states to seek currency unification.

2.3.2 *Asymmetric Information*

Information that is unevenly distributed between two parties is devastating to the efficiency and even the emergence of cooperation, especially if both are rationally aware of this asymmetry. To take the example of insurance as a particular form of cooperation: the party that wants to offload risks knows more about their existing risk factors (adverse selection) and future risk-taking behavior (moral hazard) than the other party that might assume this risk against an insurance premium. The insuring party knows that the potential for adverse selection and moral hazard exists, and if it cannot find remedies may refrain from offering insurance or entering a mutual insurance scheme, even though there is room for an insurance arrangement that would be beneficial for both.

A more specific example relevant to monetary integration is again the role of fiscal behavior. Every mature democracy in Europe has encountered the difficulty of keeping strict budget constraints: traditional hard-currency countries like Germany, the Netherlands, and Finland included. Member states struggled to meet the fiscal indicators for entering the monetary union. The European Commission, in charge of adjudicating the process, had a veritable fight on its hands, as James Savage (2005) meticulously and entertainingly documented. But only the Greek administration had systematically falsified data about its public finances at the point of EA entry, which was revealed by a report of the Commission's statistical agency soon afterwards (Eurostat 2004). This was a clear case of adverse selection—it raised the aggregate risk of the pool and thus reduced the insurance potential of the common currency. Successive Greek administrations continued to run higher deficits and accumulate more debt than allowed under the EA's fiscal rules. This can be seen as an instance of moral hazard, additional risk taking under the cover of insurance, if one believes that, if Greece had remained outside the EA, Greek governments would have mended their fiscal ways.

Given the prominence of this interpretation, it is important to keep in mind that moral hazard is not an easy to establish claim about purposeful risk taking, shifting the downside onto others. Less purposeful action may have been the reason: not active risk taking but continued lack of control is an equally plausible explanation. After all, Greek governments' action of running higher than declared deficits was barely hidden. Eurostat (2010: ch.3) kept on informing the Council that the Greek data could not be trusted but the Council, as well as credit-rating agencies and other professional investors, ignored this publicly available information. This can be interpreted as an endorsement of risk taking that may be actually beneficial for everybody since it pays off in high growth and expanding markets. Or all sides were complicit in risk taking, in which case there was no risk shifting by Greek authorities onto others involved. The implication of this diagnosis is that the default risk that all sides tolerated before 2009 should have been shared by both sides, public debtor and private creditor, when it materialized. This is the view of Sandbu (2015: 48–79), among many others.

There are solutions to adverse selection (hidden information) and moral hazard (hidden action), respectively. Adverse selection can be guarded against by gathering information prior to offering insurance. The Maastricht process asked candidates to live over two electoral cycles in a low-inflation environment without changing the exchange rate so as to reveal whether the candidate's political economy could sustain a regime that ensures a hard currency. Moral hazard can be addressed by exclusions and co-payments. The no-bailout clause of Article 123 of the Treaty on the Functioning of the EU (TFEU) was meant to exclude insurance in the case of public overindebtedness. The refusal to introduce any joint fiscal capacity was an exclusion intended to curb risk taking, meaning that member states would be on their own if they got themselves into fiscal difficulty. The systemic financial crisis from 2008 onwards made this strict limitation of fiscal risk sharing untenable. Hence, the no-bailout clause was reinterpreted, emergency funds were created and the ECB intervened in secondary government bond markets. Critics suggested that this would lead to moral hazard in the future, but countries made substantial co-payments. They endured severe recessions subsequent to the bond market panic, and were subject to the detailed prescriptions (conditionality) in the bailout programs. Both types of co-payment can be expected to curb excessive risk taking because those seeking insurance bear some (in this case most) of the costs. The insurance given consisted largely of a protracted phase of low interest rates that was a cost to taxpayers and savers in guarantor countries.

2.3.3 *Lack of Commitment*

Commitment problems arise when promises are not aligned with future incentives so that the promises are not credible. A particularly influential version of the commitment problem, formulated by Kydland and Prescott (1977), sees it arising when rational egoists have the ability to manipulate their constraints. For instance, policy authorities have an incentive to manipulate inflation expectations by announcing stabilizing monetary policy and subsequently reneging in order to achieve higher employment. However, if others are equally rational and anticipate this incentive to break a commitment, those behaving inconsistently will not get away with it—their promises are simply not credible. The unsuccessfully promising party then faces a worse inflation–unemployment tradeoff than if it had been able to keep its promise, so it has an incentive to enter hard commitments and thus make its promise credible. A commitment is hard if rational egoists can no longer manipulate their constraint.

This is in short how Giavazzi and Pagano (1988) rationalized the repeated attempts of Italian governments to stay in the ERM, and by extension, adopt the euro. This explained why a government would so visibly commit to a hard currency which it could apparently not maintain without a straitjacket. Giving up the currency meant that Italian governments lost the ability to manipulate inflation expectations and then engineer surprise inflation or devaluation. This diagnosis of the commitment problem implied that it was Italian governments that created inflation for their own electoral reasons. Faced with the consequences of structural high inflation, they changed their ways and tied their hands.

It is arguable, however, that the authorities were merely weak and accommodated inflationary pressures, while distributive conflicts between social partners were the underlying cause of the price–wage spiral. If so, the Italian authorities' behavior is consistent with the more general interpretation and solution of the commitment problem that Elster (1979) proposed. The incarnation of this attitude towards commitments is the mythical figure Ulysses who ties himself to the mast while passing the seductive Sirens. Commitments here are rational ways of dealing with anticipated irrational future behavior, like addiction or harmful opportunism. Thus, polities give themselves constitutions that lay down fundamental rules that can only be changed with supermajorities. This interpretation of the commitment problem suggests that joining the EA meant for Italian governments that they could retain their ability to respond to social conflicts over income distribution (listen to the Sirens) but (tied to the mast) exclude the response of weakening the currency through inflation. In this light, the Italian elites' desire to make their country a member of the EA was a way out of "the dilemma of government responsiveness" (Rodrik and Zeckhauser 1988). It addressed the commitment problem of weak and prudent, not hyperactive and profligate, governments. Joining a monetary union enabled them to stick to their promise and not help out private actors who had predictably brought losses on themselves and the economy at large. Intransigent social partners, reckless banks, and overambitious home buyers spring to mind.

This points to a more general caveat: breaking promises may be the consequence of rationally pursued self-interest, but it can also be due to inherent weakness. Before joining the monetary union, the government of a small open economy with some foreign exchange debt could simply not guarantee that it would never default, because a currency crisis can lead to an overshooting exchange rate depreciation that wrecks the economy and the budget. After joining the EA, governments had to enter an extremely restrictive set of commitments: they do not share public liabilities, the central bank is not allowed to buy government bonds directly even under the most extreme systemic crisis while a transnational framework for prudential regulation promoted that banks hold large quantities of government debt (Pisani-Ferry 2012). An administration that sticks to its promise to honor overbearing commitments (paying back debt to foreigners or shouldering the cost of bank bailouts nationally) may be voted out of office before it can deliver on the promise. Taking the weakness of administrations into account suggests that sovereign commitments have to be handled flexibly: there must be contingencies under which commitments are suspended or they will be broken and blame wrongly attributed. The trick is to make this flexibility credible (Lohmann 2003).

Risk sharing poses a specific commitment problem: after a contingency has arisen and affects some members of the pool but not others, the fortunate have incentives to renege on their promise to share the pain. The Greek sovereign debt crisis allowed the creditor countries to refuse the existence of a commitment as the no-bailout clause had excluded this risk from coverage. This was more difficult to maintain in the case of the Irish and Spanish banking crises. The involvement of cross-border banks in the overextension of credit to countries that needed bailouts raised the question of whether more losses should have been borne by those banks—and possibly their sovereigns if they chose to prop up their banks. Sandbu (2015: 165–73) argues that this sharing of losses (through debtor default) would have been in the enlightened self-interest of the parties. This is true but a more general commitment problem of a monetary union lies underneath. Given uncertainty, not every contingency can be specified in advance, hence commitments may be implicit until an unknown unknown materializes. The promotion of financial integration through a common currency can be seen as having created a commitment for all members to insure each other if integrated markets fail systematically.

Another standard—and sometimes justified—excuse for the fortunate is to blame moral hazard on the part of the unfortunate for their bad luck and deny them compensation. In private insurance, there is recourse to courts when an insurer does not want to pay out, but between sovereigns such situations are difficult to adjudicate. The Commission could in principle play that role but its authority rests on the trust it can command on both sides. In the case of bailout programs, analyzed in Section 6.1, we observe the curious coincidence of harsh conditionality—as if high co-payments had to be extracted for past moral hazard on the part of distressed countries—and at the same time record bailout funding—as if the guarantors acknowledged the need.

2.3.4 *Misperception*

Under this heading, Moss (2002: 40–5) groups a whole set of systematic biases in the perception and understanding of risks that lead to over or under-insurance. The benchmark is insurance in line with rationality as understood by subjective-expected-utility theory. But it can be rational for people to use heuristic devices to deal with situations of subjective or objective uncertainty, that is when the probability distribution itself is unknown.[10] Two psychologists, Daniel Kahneman and the late Amos Tversky (1979), demonstrated that some of these heuristics show systematic bias. Framing is one example: depending on whether the same issue is framed as saving lives or accepting deaths, interviewees react with inconsistent risk preferences, risk averse in one case and risk loving in the other. "Availability" also produces biases: striking or recent news gets undue attention when assessing risks. Individuals tend to be irrational when it comes to low probability events like eccentric accidents or natural disasters—they either overestimate or ignore at their peril how likely it is. There is finally the optimistic bias that the average driver considers himself to be less prone to accidents than the average driver.

All this sounds familiar from our own life experience. But it is not straightforward to draw conclusions from this research for international cooperation between institutional actors. This is not to deny that politicians, just like everybody else, are susceptible to irrational decisions, especially under pressure. But in mature democracies, summit conclusions and leaders' pronouncements

[10] Especially since the standard model of economic choice under uncertainty has itself rather absurd implications. See Rabin and Thaler (2001) on the modeling of risk aversion.

are politics, not policy. Before a resolution becomes a policy intervention, it has to pass many checks and balances in the legislature, the bureaucracy, and the media. The two-level game of politics in international relations adds another check on domestic politics (Putnam 1988): the case for domestic measures has to convince other governments and a supranational administration. International integration should actually reduce misperceptions that stem from a narrow national framing of issues. Hence, it would amount to a fallacy of composition, taking the part for the whole, if these insights of behavioral economics were used to "explain" the limited rationality of certain policies with the psychology of decision makers (Hardin 1982: 1–3).

Perception problems of individuals can explain, however, why policies that are of mutual benefit cannot be implemented. The media, especially when they take pride in being the voice of the common people, are susceptible to the same misperceptions as their readers and listeners, and sometimes seem to heighten or exploit those misperceptions. Idiosyncratic stories about some well-off Greek pensioners crowded out the evidence that Greece had one of the highest old-age poverty rates in the OECD even before the crisis. This made it hard for any guarantor government to get a bailout program approved by its parliament that did not contain cuts in Greek pensions.[11] The crisis in all Southern European countries and Ireland came to be framed as a crisis of public debt rather than as one of private debt and credit; panic in national segments of the euro government bond market dominated perceptions and defined the crisis. This predisposed the Council of Economic and Finance Ministers to tighten the fiscal surveillance framework; although Greece could have been sanctioned under the old rules while Ireland, Spain, and Cyprus did not primarily have a fiscal crisis, Portugal was a borderline case (Section 6.1).

As indicated, the institutional checks and balances of democracy, the rule of law, and international relations can be a solution to perception problems. Both impose the norms of rational discourse that require policies to be justified outside the context of scandal and outrage, and call for a basis beyond parochial and ill-informed concerns. Yet it is unlikely that rational discourse can trump popular misperceptions. This makes hypocrisy an inherent element of modern politics and policymaking (Runciman 2008: 195–6). The French and German governments' ways of coping with the financial crisis in 2008–10 are cases in point (Schelkle 2012a): the rhetoric of crisis management satisfied popular expectations in each country, invoking a strong state in France and the responsibilities of markets in Germany, while the measures adopted were the polar opposites. The French government implemented a minimal stimulus program, mindful of its budgetary situation, while the

[11] The stories were particularly promoted by the tabloid *Bild-Zeitung* in Germany, which published them as part of its campaign against any bailout package for Greece.

German coalition government went for a large aggregate stimulus program that satisfied well-represented economic interests, such as the car industry.

To sum up: the four types of political market failures expand perspectives on the collective action problem of managing a common currency provided by political theory (Ostrom 1990: 2–7). The political market failure approach is in contrast to three models most used in political theory: the tragedy of the commons, the prisoner's dilemma, and the privileged group theory of the logic of collective action (Olson 1971). All have the problem of free riding on others' efforts at their foundation. But this seems to be too narrow a base for understanding collective action problems among geopolitical entities (states). For a start, there is a modest number of state parties, whereas free riding is more likely to be endemic when there is a large number of individuals with preoccupations other than collective action, rationally avoiding the costs of engagement. Furthermore, institutional actors, such as bureaucracies and policymaking organizations like central banks, are set up to act in the state's interest. Free riding on other states may occur but is only one reason why they do not cooperate. The following chapters try to substantiate this claim.

2.4 Forms of Risk Sharing

Distributional considerations are important for distinguishing forms of interstate risk sharing. But the focus on relative versus absolute gains that characterizes the international relations literature (Mearsheimer 2010) is less relevant in this context. Rational cooperation on sharing risks is prone to different collective action failures depending on whether they primarily stabilize or primarily redistribute, and whether they do so either through insurance ex ante or compensation ex post (Moss 2002: 18–19).

A case of pure stabilization through insurance would be a multilateral fund to stabilize income in recessions. It provides stabilization insofar as it aims only to reduce the volatility of member states' national income, and not to adjust relative levels over time. It provides insurance because members of the fund agree on the rule for risk sharing ex ante, that is before the situation arises. Contributions might also be paid into a fund beforehand, but this is not crucial here: prior agreement on rules can suffice to achieve ex ante risk sharing. The EA typically organizes insurance through regulatory means, most recently through a bail-in rule for all government bonds which will make private creditors share the cost of future debt restructuring. Capital markets can perform income and consumption smoothing as well, with an internationally diversified portfolio, assembled prior to the shock, acting as insurance. But the process requires that the citizens of the country affected own shares in other member states. This has not happened on a grand scale, even though Robert Shiller (1993) worked out the technicalities of such macro markets some time ago.

Stabilizing insurance should theoretically be the form of risk sharing we find most often. Even members with different income levels would benefit from smoothing volatility, and it should be possible to devise and agree rules ex ante that ensure that each can expect some benefit out of the scheme. But the pure stabilization scheme that the Commission was asked to devise in the early 1990s was ditched by the Council as soon as it was published (Italianer and Vanheukelen 1993; Goodhart 2011). Problems of information asymmetry were a crucial obstacle.

A scheme of redistribution reduces the dispersion of expected outcomes, for instance by raising the national income of poorer member states through transfers. It can also be an ex ante arrangement ("social insurance") if the rules under which a member of the scheme receives redistributive transfers are formally defined beforehand. The EU's regional policy is of this nature, stipulating that member states or regions below the EU average income (90 percent or 75 percent) can receive transfers. Because it is redistributive, richer member states may not be keen on such a scheme, but the ex ante specification of rules leaves open the possibility that they may at some point benefit from it as well. For instance, eligibility may be defined on a regional basis so that poor regions in rich member states can receive funds. Again, the EU often provides such redistribution through regulatory means: the regulation of free movement is a redistributive insurance scheme for individuals that the EU sustains by granting social citizenship to EU migrants and their families (Chapter 8). Such redistributive schemes typically have to be mandatory, because otherwise those who expect to be net payers may opt out; it follows that the commitment is typically part of a bigger deal, in this case the four freedoms of the Single Market.

Insurance can be distinguished from compensation, which is risk sharing ex post. The failure to establish rules before a calamity occurs is an obstacle to collective action. To the fortunate members, the quest for compensation by an unfortunate member appears as a cost of interdependence (externality) which was not agreed. Nonetheless, stabilizing compensation may be agreed by structuring it as a loan rather than a transfer. In theory, international credit markets can perform this interstate risk sharing, but their pro-cyclical tendencies mean that they are likely to impose more onerous terms and make a return to normalcy more difficult than if official lending is arranged. The five countries whose government bonds were sold off by market investors, driving prices for these bonds down and bond yields up,[12] could not get credit to

[12] In its simplest form, a bond is a promise to pay a fixed amount of interest p.a. (for instance €5k) on its nominal face value (for simplicity €100k), which the bond issuer promises to pay back at

Table 2.2. Configurations of interstate risk sharing

Risk sharing	Arranged ex ante	Arranged ex post
To smooth volatility of expected outcome	*Stabilizing insurance* (cross-border payments system, Chapter 9)	*Credit (stabilizing compensation)* (central bank lending of last resort, Chapter 7)
To change level of expected outcome	*Social insurance* (migration as a social right, Chapter 8)	*Transfer (ad hoc compensation)* (debt write-off for member states, Chapter 6)

tide them over the financial crisis; on the contrary, it would have accelerated their ruin if they had not received official loans to cover their budget deficits. The first Greek bailout program treated the government's debt largely as a matter for stabilizing compensation, as if the country merely had to overcome a temporary shock. The debt write-down in the second bailout acknowledged that a transfer was needed, which was imposed on the private sector, however; only the third bailout program has included official transfers in the disguise of grant elements to the official loans (interest-free phase, interest rate well below market rate, long maturity). As the programs moved from credit to transfer, the negotiations became ever more acrimonious: the need for ad hoc compensation suggests that there was not full information and probably some hidden action on the part of the needy involved.

Table 2.2 summarizes these distinctions. In parentheses, I list examples of risk sharing in the EA that will be discussed in later chapters. An example of stabilizing insurance is the cross-border systems for processing payments in euros (TARGET) which is outlined and compared with the US payments system (ISA) in Chapter 9. Redistribution through social insurance is exemplified by the rules governing intra-US and intra-EU labor mobility, discussed in Chapter 8. Stabilizing compensation can be illustrated with the extraordinary measures adopted by the ECB in Chapter 6. Finally, an example of the difficult case of ad hoc compensation is hard to come by, for the reasons indicated. The provision of sovereign bailouts, specifically inconspicuous grant elements in the restructuring of Greek debt, is the only example this study has come across, briefly discussed in Chapter 6.

Moving from the economics of risk sharing to political economy, it is important to note that there is an irreducibly constructive element in the classifications of Table 2.2. The three Greek bailout programs just mentioned are a case in point. Economists tend to take risks as categorically given, for instance an output or demand shock, and ask which mode of risk sharing would be most effective in tackling a particular risk. This is a perfectly valid

a defined future date. So if the price of the bond falls below this face value (from €100k to €80k), the fixed interest payment (€5k) means a rising yield (5/80 = 6.25 percent, up from 5/100 = 5 percent).

research question that is of great interest to public policy. But it inevitably has a blind spot. The mode of risk sharing can also determine what kind of risk something is: bad luck, bad behavior, or manifest disadvantage.

These modes construct communities of risk that can explain how extensive and robust mutual support is going to be in the presence of political market failures (Atkinson 1999: 83–91; Baldwin 1990: 12–14). For instance, it is well established in the comparative political economy of welfare states that arrangements constructed as insurance tend to be politically more robust and generous than those constructed as assistance. Social insurance has elements of both. The stress on insurance enlists citizens into a community of fate (shared risk), whereby the unlucky receive transfers from a common fund. The stress on social (assistance), by contrast, provides for transfers from the non-poor to the poor, while seeking to avoid a clear separation of the paying and receiving communities.

We can see similar possibilities for construction in the way that risk sharing between geopolitical entities is viewed. Stabilizing insurance treats the risk of low income or low growth as bad luck, a deviation from trend, and takes those in need of support into a "community of fate" with the lucky non-poor members. The bad luck could be intense competition affecting economic sectors in which a member state's firms were specialized. One way of providing social insurance is a common interest rate policy that takes the growth concerns of the unfortunate member state into account. The fortunate members would "contribute" to insurance by putting up with interest rates lower than is appropriate for their economies, or by having investments go abroad instead of creating these jobs at home. Their willingness to accommodate another member will depend on whether they can see a common currency as potentially benefiting their less fortunate future self, when their economies might be stagnating.

Cohesion policy for the late entrants into the EU is an example of a scheme which is framed analogously to social assistance. Those countries with less than 90 percent of EU average income get transfers, while those with above-average income are generally net contributors. Regional funds have been available for some time, but cohesion funding was specifically developed to compensate member states for the possible job losses in the wake of the Single Market Programme and the adoption of the euro (Moravcsik 1998: 446). At the time, it was part of a package deal for opening borders to superior competitors; a way of overcoming resistance to cooperation in the sense of Martin (1995, 2001). Over time, when the quid pro quo of open borders is no longer negotiable, the aspect of charitable risk sharing comes to dominate perceptions of these transfers. Altruism or simply compliance with treaty obligations can sustain such charity. But it is not solidarity in the sense used here—Baldwin's political notion of "generalized and reciprocal self-interest."

Political economists (and economists) tend to consider these motives to be less robust, keeping distributive conflict visible and salient. It is telling that the cohesion countries earned the acronym PIGS, insinuating that the funding they received was not development assistance to make them more resilient against the risks of the Single Market but a form of pork-barrel politics. Risk sharing in the form of assistance rather than insurance creates perceptions of one-sided support that is hard to sustain between states.

The modes of risk sharing listed in Table 2.2 are taken up in different chapters. Stabilizing insurance, expected to be the most robust form of rational cooperation, is the topic of the last chapter (9) before the conclusions. Social insurance provided through the regulation of economic migration in the EU is the theme of Chapter 8. It is, in terms of political robustness, on a par with stabilizing compensation that is delegated to an independent, specialized body, here: the central bank. Stabilization through lending programs was the most prominent mode of risk sharing during the crisis and is analyzed in Chapter 7. Finally, Chapter 6 on the crisis deals briefly with ad hoc compensation, which the theoretical approach adopted here sees as an exceptional form of risk sharing, exercised only under extreme duress.

3

Economic Risk Sharing between States

The political economy theory of monetary integration based on risk sharing has two elements: the rationalist-institutionalist scholarship on interstate cooperation, outlined in Chapter 2, and institutional economics under uncertainty, which is the topic of this chapter. The paradox of diversity suggests that one needs to consider both: the more diverse the membership of a risk pool, the higher the potential economic benefits from risk sharing but also the greater the political obstacles to exploiting these benefits.

Institutional economics under uncertainty takes its departure from the work of Kenneth Arrow (1963), George Akerlof (1970), and Joseph Stiglitz (1969). Almost any economic activity can be framed as risk taking and risk sharing. This takes seriously that economic activity happens in time and typically extends into a more or less uncertain future. Akerlof (1970) famously showed that car dealers can be understood as providing insurance against the risk of picking a lemon when buying a used car. This type of analysis has been extended to all walks of economic life. A large part of what any financial institution does, be it the stock market, an investment company, or a bank,[1] is to provide risk-sharing opportunities to capitalist firms: they can diversify the vagaries of business by shifting risk partly onto investors and creditors. The firm in turn can also be seen as an insurance provider to workers in that it pays a steady wage income in return for the worker contributing to a higher but volatile income stream for firm owners (Ellul et al. 2015). This "risk management turn" of economics highlights the importance of institutions other than the price mechanism. The analysis reveals the hidden risk-sharing arrangements of economic life for which Akerlof's used car dealer and the extensive study of David Moss (2002) provide striking examples.

[1] Diamond and Dybvig (1983) is the path-breaking article that interprets banks as insurers for saving households. Moss (2002: ch.3) shows how limited liability evolved as a risk-sharing device in US history that allowed firms to take much more risk.

The first section explains where benefits from risk sharing come from if members are similar except for the different timing of random shocks. The underlying law of large numbers is a benchmark against which the economic benefits from pooling risks of a *finite* number of *fundamentally different* members can be seen more clearly. The law underpins the economic literature on risk sharing through monetary-financial integration, which is reviewed in the second section. But it is the third section that expands the framework of "channels" to "interfaces" of risk sharing in light of theoretical advances in the economic literature since the financial crisis of 2007–8. The last section summarizes the difference between the risk-sharing literature that was a promising take-off from the theory of OCAs and the economics underpinning the political economy of monetary solidarity: financial markets can no longer be taken as channels of risk sharing but are themselves a source of risk that can destabilize entire economies.

3.1 The Idea of Risk Diversification

Risk diversification exploits the statistical property that "the variance of a sum of shocks is lower, the lower the covariance among the individual components" (Belke and Gros 2009: 46). In other words, the volatility of a risk pool is lower, the more idiosyncratic (or "asymmetric") the volatility of its members is. Member or individual component here can mean assets in a portfolio or the gross domestic product (GDP) of each state in a monetary union. The shocks to members have to be independent and exogenous, in other words not generated by the risk pooling itself. The covariance between individual shocks can also be negative, meaning that when one member has an upswing in fortunes, the other tends to experience a downturn. Low and even negative covariance means, in terms of randomness, diversity of membership.

The law of large numbers draws out the implications of this property and can serve as a benchmark for illustrating the difference between the economics and the political economy of risk sharing. Discovered by Jacob Bernoulli in the early eighteenth century, it says that what may be individually risky (high variance) or indeed uncertain (unknown variance) can be turned into a certain average by appropriate risk pooling. It can be illustrated by adapting an example given by Moss (2002: 28–9). Let's assume that every member state in a monetary union experiences on average a year-long recession every five years that costs each about 5 percent of national income in that year. This means that each has a 20 percent probability of a recession each year and an average loss of 1 percent of annual national income.

If the political elites of two member states are particularly averse to such sharp recessions, they can agree to operate a bilateral stabilization fund that allows them to share their losses when the economy is in a downturn. There are three possible outcomes: both are in recession (4 percent probability), only one is in recession (32 percent probability), or none is in recession (64 percent probability).[2] But only in four out of 100 years will the recession be as sharp as before (5 percent loss in one year) and in thirty-two out of 100 years the income loss will be halved, either because the member is in recession and receives an insurance pay-out or because the member is not in recession but has to pay out to the other. So the aggregate risk has not been reduced but the national risk has: by just sharing their risk of a recession with one other state has reduced the likelihood for each that they will experience a severe downturn from one year in five to one year in twenty-five.

As more member states participate in the scheme, this variance drops further and further. If there were an infinite number of members, all risk could be eliminated. By paying the insurance premium of 1 percent out of which all recessions could be covered, each member state would have a slightly lower annual income than it would have in the good years in a world without insurance, yet each member's income would be completely stable. In other words, the risk of a recession has been completely diversified away, by exploiting the fact that members' recessions were not completely synchronized, and turned into an entirely predictable cost of insurance. This premium is a measure of risk aversion, the sure amount of income foregone in return for a perfectly smooth income flow.

How does this calculation change if we modify and apply the calculus to the heterogeneous European Union before and after the launch of the euro? Let's assume the same asynchronous business cycle pattern, but first within the old "D-Mark zone" of the ERM. A representative country would then be faced with a 32 percent probability that the German interest rate was not right for its cyclical situation. This is the probability that only the other member state or only the German economy were in recession, so Germany's neighbor either experienced a sharper recession or a worsening of its current-account balance with Germany.

- If the representative member state was in recession but Germany was not, there was no decrease in the interest rate; hence, the recession was deeper, lasted longer, or had to be fought with other means. If the authorities had tried to defy the Bundesbank's dominance and lowered interest rates regardless, it would have triggered devaluation pressures that sooner or

[2] Four percent probability for both being in recession is obtained by multiplying the probabilities for recessions (20 percent times 20 percent); the calculation is similar for neither being in recession (80 percent times 80 percent equals 64 percent) and for only one in recession (20 percent times 80 percent plus 80 percent times 20 percent equals 32 percent).

later would force it to raise interest rates in order to arrest the possible adverse effects on debt and trade payments.

- If only Germany was in a recession, the neighbor had to lower the interest rate with an overheating domestic economy as the likely result; if it did not follow Germany's lead, a relatively higher interest rate would lead to capital inflows, stimulating the economy, real or nominal revaluation pressures, and make any current-account deficit vis-à-vis Germany worse, in a situation where it was probably already worsening as German firms exported more to compensate for weak domestic demand.

Risk pooling without a common currency would have required the German central bank to take the effect on its neighbor into account and operate a monetary policy that is a (weighted) average of what is appropriate for the state of the German cycle and the neighbor's cycle. This is not inconceivable but it calls for an implausible degree of consideration for the other, as well as investments in data collection and forecasts for another economy.

Currency unification means, above all, a joint central bank which would do exactly that: its monetary stance would try to target the average with its interest rate or exchange rate policy. This averaging is equivalent to an insurance that compensates the unlucky (Germany or its neighbor) out of the contributions that both (all) members made. Obviously, this simple averaging rule for monetary policy becomes more difficult if member states are of different size, of different economic and political strength, have more or less deep cyclical fluctuations, etc. But it does not take away the fact that neighbors could expect more consideration for the state of their economy than from a dominant national central bank.

There are other important aspects in which the illustration of the law of large numbers differs from the situation of the European and other monetary unions. The first observation is that the business cycle was no longer an independent shock for any member state other than Germany—the German business cycle was a source of endogenous risk that originated from capital and goods markets integration with Germany, in particular the fact that their currencies had a different standing in financial markets. Moreover, currency unions are formed between relatively small numbers of geopolitical entities. There are still benefits from risk sharing but asymptotically perfect stability, as predicted by the law of large numbers, is not possible. Last but not least, members are not similarly sized and their sources of economic instability are different. These differences can make risk diversification even more attractive, however, because it is then more likely that risks are negatively correlated and the overall risk of the pool can be lowered.

How can states share risks to their citizens' income and consumption that stem from volatile output? This is the question that a rich empirical literature, starting with Asdrubali et al. (1996) and Sørensen and Yosha (1998), answers. While the traditional theory of monetary integration sees idiosyncratic ("asymmetric") shocks as a problem, this literature sees country-specific shocks as an opportunity for risk sharing. The term "risk sharing" is used in this literature to mean "the deliberate pooling of consumption risks" among individuals in different countries (Baxter 2012: 390).[3] Two types of shocks are not covered by this focus on idiosyncratic shocks: first, shocks that are common in their effect and hence cannot be shared among members (although they can be shared with future generations through public debt); second, common shocks that are different in their effect and can be shared but are symptoms of "fundamental differences" among members (Cesa-Bianchi et al. 2016: 4).

This last type of shock raises the political-economic paradox of diversity in its purest form: the common shock shows that the risk pool is economically a "community of fate" but the varied effects make solidarity hard to sustain politically. The financial crisis of 2007–8 was arguably such a common shock that differed in its impact on member states' economies and public finances enormously and became politically disintegrating (Section 6.2.3). It should be noted from the outset that this paradox cannot be grasped by this literature. However, country-specific shocks test solidarity among members as well and so it is worth looking how far certain country groupings have got in terms of sharing the risks from output shocks.

3.2 Sharing the Risk of Output Shocks between States

The negotiations about a monetary union in Europe led scholars to take a closer look at the US dollar area, to see how much the federal budget and financial and labor market integration contributed to the stabilization of US states. Ground-breaking work on specific risk-sharing channels included Sala-i-Martin and Sachs (1991) on the tax-transfer system, Barro and Sala-i-Martin (1991) on labor migration, and Atkeson and Bayoumi (1993) on capital markets. Bent Sørensen, the late Oved Yosha, and their various co-authors developed a methodology that allowed the contribution of multiple channels of risk sharing to be quantified. The idea that states might share risks was inspired by a literature on the efficiency of financial markets in trading risks so that firms can specialize profitably.[4] Geographic and industrial specialization makes producers vulnerable to idiosyncratic shocks; in theory, risk-averse

[3] It exploits the law of large numbers of consumers in a general equilibrium setting and applies it to countries, a step taken by Obstfeld (1984).

[4] See Kalemli-Ozcan et al. (2001: 107–12) for an excellent overview of the early literature that includes Helpman and Razin (1978) on trade and industry specialization under uncertainty and Obstfeld (1994) on gains from risk taking in integrating financial markets.

investors could protect themselves by holding a representative portfolio of assets that consists of claims on the output of all members in the risk pool (Imbs and Mauro 2007: 4).

This line of research provided a robust motivation for European monetary integration: diversity was not a problem but an opportunity, and membership beyond the core EU of the original six seemed to be a viable proposition. This literature was taken up recently by leading figures in the EU: the economic risk-sharing literature provides the underpinning for the so-called "Four Presidents" and "Five Presidents" reports (van Rompuy et al. 2012; Juncker et al. 2015). These contain ambitious and authoritative plans for "completing Europe's economic and monetary union." However, there are some problems with the established economic risk-sharing analysis. Its proponents put forward rather optimistic hypotheses about the effects of financial market integration on risk sharing, whereas the evidence, not least the experience of the financial crisis, suggests that such optimism is unwarranted.

The section first outlines the main channels which the economic risk-sharing literature has identified as enabling states (nations or regions) to share risks to the livelihood of their citizens. Second, it summarizes the evidence on how much groups of states share the risk from output shocks and how much the different channels contribute. The answers vary widely, depending on the methodology and the data sets used. The following section turns to the limitations of these findings. Most studies are confined to looking at the risk of a region-specific shock to output (so-called "supply shocks"), such as bad weather or a sudden oil price increase. I will show that shifting the focus to demand shocks and financial instability suggests that monetary integration is more problematic, but at the same time more promising, than implied by the economic theory of risk sharing.

3.2.1 *What Are the Main Channels of Risk Sharing between States?*

Economic risks that can be shared between states arise in the form of involuntary fluctuations of income, employment, and consumption of their citizens. The output of firms is instrumental to this, as it represents the value added in production and most people earn their income by being employed in firms producing this output. But the volatility of output as such is not a concern for welfare economists: taking risks is in the nature of capitalist businesses and they strive to get a reward for this. From a welfare economic perspective, the important question is how the effect of an output shock can be prevented from spilling over into a shock to income, employment, and consumption. The path-breaking idea of Asdrubali et al. (1996) and Sørensen and Yosha (1998) was to take the differences between output and income on the one hand, and income and consumption on the other, to identify possible buffers and estimate how much of the initial shock to output these buffers absorbed. So if a drop in output of 2 percent corresponds to a drop in consumption of only 1 percent, this is interpreted as a shock absorption of 50 percent. The analysis then seeks to find out through which channels this shock absorption has been achieved (Dullien 2014: 59).

This is a specific understanding of stabilization, a point to which we return. But two crucial implications of this methodology can already be noted. First of all, consumption must be less volatile than output or one would have doubts about the assumed causality from output shock to consumption volatility. And second, there must not be other relevant sources that affect consumption volatility directly, otherwise we could not attribute the difference between the variance in output and in consumption to the shock absorbers.

The shock absorbers, or more formally, the channels of risk sharing, can be inferred from national and regional accounts which give us several identities (≡ denoting that they hold by accounting convention or definition). The last of the aggregates in each equation is the shock absorber. For instance in equation (1), it is net international factor income that can prevent the shock to output from fully translating into a shock to gross income by moving in the opposite direction: when output falls due to a negative shock, factor income should rise in relative importance, thereby absorbing (some of) the shock.[5]

1. output (GDP) ≡ gross income (GNI)—net international factor income;
2. gross income (GNI) ≡ disposable income (DNI) + net fiscal transfers;
3. disposable income (DNI) ≡ consumption (C) + net savings.

Net international (or interregional) factor income consists of all the profit, interest, rent, and labor income that nationals earn abroad (for US studies: in another US state) minus profit, interest, rent, and salaries that foreigners earn from claims on the domestic economy. This is the interstate risk-sharing channel which this literature identifies with the insurance that capital markets provide. As domestically generated income takes a hit when there is an idiosyncratic output shock, the stream of income from claims on other countries' output can compensate for the shortfall. If the net factor income is negative, this means that foreigners hold net claims on domestic output, and stabilization occurs because profit income derived from domestic output falls and less has to be paid to capital owners abroad. In addition to this

[5] GDP in these studies is measured as output or gross value added in production. GNI/DNI stands for gross/disposable national income, respectively. *Gross* here means that capital depreciation has not been deducted. Sørensen and Yosha (1998) filter out capital depreciation as a source of risk sharing. But capital depreciation is subject to strict accounting rules that do not necessarily respond to business cycles and other shocks. Not surprisingly, they find that capital depreciation is destabilizing in the sense of not shock absorbing, as it stays fairly constant while output fluctuates.

capital markets channel, there may also be a labor component of net factor income, comprising remittances from cross-border workers. Many studies ignore this element, on the grounds that in advanced economies remittances are typically negligible relative to income from cross-border holdings of stocks and shares.

Because the focus is on interstate rather than intergenerational risk sharing, *net fiscal transfers* do not include the government's own budget deficits or surpluses. The relevant cross-border fiscal transfers are either the funds received from other governments or international organizations minus funds paid to them. Advanced countries are typically net payers and receive transfers only in an emergency. In the EU, quite a few members are net recipients of international transfers due to regional funds and agricultural policy. However, because these transfers are based on structural indicators and do not generally respond to cyclical supply shocks, they do not contribute to risk sharing as understood and measured in these studies. In an intranational context, net fiscal transfers are the difference between federal transfers that states receive and federal taxes they pay into the central budget, and these are often sensitive to output shocks. Net transfers from the central budget were once thought to be a potent source of interstate risk sharing within a federation. As state output goes down, states pay less income tax due to waning employment and receive more transfers, notably unemployment benefits, if insurance is federal. In turn, states where the economy is growing fast pay more income tax and receive lower benefit payments.

Net savings is the income not spent by households and, in most of these studies, by corporations (retained profit). This is intertemporal risk sharing that the literature identifies with credit markets whereby households save with and borrow from banks. Credit markets allow households to maintain a steady level of consumption by saving and dis-saving. But one should note that the evidence suggests that credit markets do not work in a stabilizing way. Household credit is pro-cyclical: households borrow more in good times, while when they need credit most, banks are unwilling to lend. Furthermore, most credit risk sharing is not interstate; rather, it brings about shifts between present and future consumption within the domestic economy. However, there may be an interstate element to credit-based risk sharing, particularly when the banking system is partly foreign-owned. Within a federation, cross-state bank ownership can be an important risk-sharing channel between states. In an international context, internationally diversified banking systems share risk, as in Central and Eastern Europe where national banking systems are largely in foreign ownership (Epstein 2014).

Risk sharing through *trade and, more generally, the current account* presents interesting and complex issues. In the standard accounts of interstate risk sharing, the current account is amalgamated with the credit market channel.

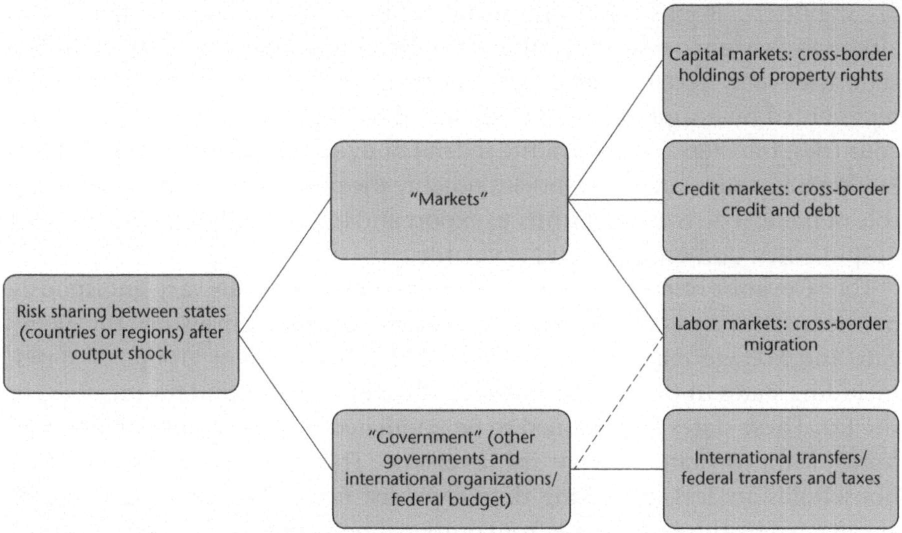

Figure 3.1. The main channels of risk sharing between states in the economic literature
Source: own elaboration of Asdrubali et al. (1996) and Sørensen and Yosha (1998)

This reflects the supply-side orientation of the literature. As I discuss further below, once demand shocks are considered the potential stabilizing role of trade is greatly enhanced. Flood et al. (2012) suggest that the output-stabilizing role of trade and technology transfer trump other channels of interstate risk sharing. In their view, trade affects output directly by alleviating bottlenecks and providing an outlet when domestic demand is low. It can, in principle, be isolated as the part of net savings that matches the current-account balance. But with a few exceptions, such as Mélitz and Zumer (1999), hardly any author explored this information.

Figure 3.1 summarizes the channels for sharing risks to consumption from output volatility that the literature identifies through national accounts data. This is the major methodological contribution of Asdrubali et al. (1996) and Sørensen and Yosha (1998): instead of testing how much countries or country groupings deviate from full risk sharing, they identify how much certain channels contribute to incomplete risk sharing (Kalemli-Ozcan et al. 2004: 5). They distinguish between markets and government as providers of shock absorbers. Markets allow risk sharing between states if citizens from one state can receive income from property (shares or stocks) they hold in other countries, directly or indirectly. They can also get credit or extend credit to other states if their banking system is internationally diversified and lends or borrows abroad. Citizens can also migrate and get a (better) job in another state. This migration channel may also trigger government expenditure and tax stabilizers, as jobs come with social entitlements in mature welfare states although they go to migrants rather than their home state (see Chapter 5). The state itself may receive transfers/social benefits from other states, typically represented by a supranational body like the World Bank or the EU; within countries, transfers come from the federal budget. Not shown in Figure 3.1 is any stabilization of demand shocks, notably the potentially output-stabilizing role of trade, which enables firms to export and import and thus smooth their output when domestic demand is volatile.

The relevance of each of these risk-sharing channels can vary enormously between states and between citizens. The methodology measures the aggregate and average relevance of these channels for different groups of states, including states in the United States, in the OECD world, and for members of the EU. These states are assumed to be populated by a "representative household" with constant relative risk aversion. This assumption ensures that households are less risk taking than capitalist firms. But not all households are affected by the average risk from output shocks: they have distinct income risks (Nichols and Rehm 2014). Furthermore, households have unequal access to credit and capital markets, whether directly or indirectly, for example through internationally diversified pension funds. These distributional questions are ignored in analyses based on a representative household. In practice, market channels are liable to be regressive in their distributional effects, with wealthier households better placed to diversify their risks. State channels may be more egalitarian in their distributive effects.

This economic literature touches on relevant political economy issues, but does not address them systematically. Some of the stabilization channels share risks ex ante, others only ex post (Table 2.1). Economists stress that the distinction affects what kind of shock can be shared. Ex ante risk sharing or *insurance* can help with permanent shocks. An example of a permanent downside risk that countries presumably would like to share is structural joblessness, which may be due to deindustrialization or technical progress. Capital markets provide such insurance if households manage to acquire property rights before the risk materializes. Once it has materialized, undiversified households will inevitably suffer losses. Credit markets are unlikely to help in the case of a permanent negative shock because banks are unlikely to keep on lending to an economy which has an impaired earnings capacity on the same terms. By contrast, they can help with transitory shocks, such as business cycle fluctuations or unusually bad weather, although, as noted above, it is an open question whether banks actually do lend in this stabilizing way. Becker and Hoffmann (2006) and Artis and Hoffmann (2008) find evidence for the economic relevance of the distinction between permanent and transitory shocks: differences in the predictability and persistence of shocks determine how effective capital and credit markets are as shock absorbers.

3.2.2 *How Much Do Various Channels Contribute to Risk Sharing?*

The studies reviewed in this chapter identify the extent of risk sharing by finding out how much of a shock to output (GDP) is absorbed through each of the following channels: cross-border factor income flows (identified with capital markets), savings and borrowing (credit markets), and fiscal transfers from outside the state (government). Consumption should be affected as little as possible if the three risk-sharing channels work. The literature has typically taken per capita growth rates or first differences (changes in levels) for estimating the volatility of output, income, and consumption. This takes out trend growth which is obviously not a volatility that one needs to compensate or insure against.[6]

The procedure uses the statistical relationship that the variance of output can be decomposed into the covariance of output with its constituent parts: output and national income, output and disposable income, and output and consumption.[7] Standardizing these covariances gives us the coefficients of covariance, usually expressed as percentages. One can then exploit a useful constraint, namely that the sum of these coefficients and the unsmoothed residual must add to 1 or 100 percent. In other words, it must be possible to decompose a shock to output into the components of cross-border factor flows, net international transfers/budget transfers, net savings, and a residual. Each component can be negative or positive. When the three national income components move in the "right" direction, there is effective shock absorption and the residual, which is the remaining covariance between output and consumption, will be small.

As noted above, international factor income could include both capital and labor income, but many studies look only at the capital channel. Labor migration used to be a relevant shock absorber for the US, as Barro and Sala-i-Martin (1991) established and Asdrubali et al. (1996: 1102–3) confirmed. However, even in the US, cross-border labor income reduced the spillover of a state's output shock to income by less than 3 percent. Since the 1980s, labor mobility in the US has been in secular decline and now contributes even less to interstate risk sharing (Molloy et al. 2014). Between OECD countries, cross-border labor income is irrelevant for risk sharing (Balli et al. 2011: 531–3), although the crisis may have changed that for the EU (see Chapter 8). This goes directly against the high hopes that the proponents of OCA theory still

[6] Becker and Hoffmann (2006) use ratios to income instead of per capita growth rates and have a principled argument on why de-trended levels are better suited than growth rates. Other scholars who have experimented with both seem not to have found much difference.

[7] The standard articles give good accounts of their procedure and the variations in econometric techniques they use. A Bank of England working paper was particularly helpful in this regard (Labhard and Sawicki 2006: 12–14). More critical assessments can be found in Baxter (2012) and the contributions of Mélitz and his co-authors (see below and Section 3.2.3).

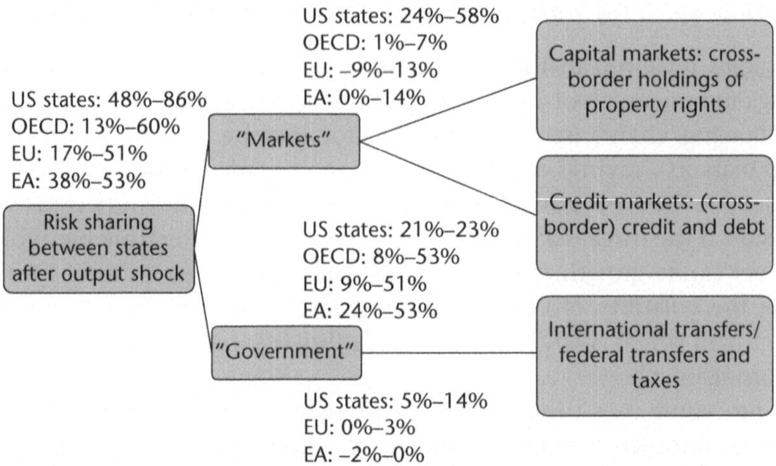

Figure 3.2. Range of empirical estimates for three risk-sharing channels
Source: see notes to Table 3.1A in the appendix

harbor for labor mobility acting as an adjustment mechanism for asymmetric (idiosyncratic) shocks in Europe (Krugman 2013: 441–2). Even if it were an important adjustment mechanism for individuals, it is far from clear that the economic effect on member states helps adjustment: the inherent selection bias of age and initiative, often also of education, makes it very likely that the region hit by a shock loses capacity for recovery while the better-off destinations gain.

Figure 3.2 shows Figure 3.1 with the range of estimates from seven comparable studies. More detail can be found in Table 3.1A in the appendix to this chapter.

The estimates vary widely and are sensitive to the time span covered, the selection of states within each group, and the quality of data sets. But there is consensus that consumption is nowhere completely shielded from output shocks, not even among US states. The estimate of the unsmoothed part ranges from 9 percent to 39 percent for the US.[8] Among OECD countries, between 36 percent and 80 percent of output shocks spill over into consumption volatility. Consumption here includes the volatility of government consumption, as its contribution to risk sharing cannot be assessed by a methodology measuring interstate risk sharing. The unsmoothed part is between 53 percent and 77 percent in the EU (before the 2004 enlargement and without Luxembourg), while it is between 51 percent and 61 percent in the EA.

[8] Del Negro (2002) disputes that there is any interstate risk sharing in the US and argues that the estimates of Asdrubali et al. (1996) have not taken into account measurement error of output which is a serious problem in regional accounts. Del Negro also notes that their sample is restricted to nineteen states only. I could not find any other author with such a fundamental critique.

The high-end estimates of uncompensated risks are from the study by Mélitz and Zumer (1999), suggesting a distinct lack of shock absorption through transactions among OECD and EU countries. They estimate the unsmoothed part of an output shock to consumption directly, instead of determining it as a residual. Mélitz and Zumer (1999) argued that the procedure of taking the residual as the uncompensated part of risk sharing is misleading if preference shocks occur, that is shocks to consumption that are not caused by output shocks. A low covariance of output and consumption growth may be due to direct shocks to consumption that occur independently of output shocks. If so, the extent of risk sharing is overestimated. More generally and importantly, there can be other shocks to consumption than those from output via income. Notably, financial market integration can destabilize consumption through asset price booms and busts (Christev and Mélitz 2011: 29). We come back to this point below in the context of a critique of the narrow focus of this literature on output shocks, but for now it is worth noting that the exclusion of demand shocks means that this approach tends to overestimate market channels and underestimate state channels of risk sharing (Dullien 2014: 59–60).

A big difference between intracountry and international risk sharing is that capital markets and private insurance play hardly any role for the latter, whereas they dominate within countries, particularly in the US. This is disappointing evidence for the expected effects and benefits of financial globalization (Kose et al. 2009). The bulk of risk sharing among OECD and EU countries comes from intertemporal smoothing, that is net savings or lending to and borrowing from domestic banks (Sørensen and Yosha 1998: 231–2). Mélitz and Zumer (1999: 175), who identify international net credit separately through current-account (im)balances, come to a similar conclusion.[9] Capital markets have provided only a small share of intertemporal and interstate risk sharing. The high imbalances of the 2000s, in the EU but also the OECD, increased the size of capital flows, but the effect on smoothing of consumption and income is questionable: capital markets may very well have destabilized both.

As noted above, fiscal transfers in an international context refer only to transfers between countries and not intertemporal smoothing through surpluses and deficits. Their relevance is minimal and they can even be destabilizing, indicated by the minus sign on international transfers for the EA, which

[9] This can be done by measuring the covariance of income (GNI) and domestic absorption, that is the sum of private and public consumption and investment—the difference in variance must be due to the current account and the international credit that goes with it.

typically do not vary with the business cycle. EU regional funds were quite substantial for Greece, Ireland, Portugal, and regions in Spain (the so-called Cohesion countries). But these funds are not designed to smooth cyclical fluctuations; they are supposed to respond to longer-term development needs and to support catching up (Bayoumi and Masson 1996: 319).

3.2.3 *Does Monetary Integration Lead to More Financial Risk Sharing?*

Research on what is driving changes in these estimates over time had barely started when it was rudely interrupted by the North Atlantic financial crisis in 2007–8. This means there is only a short period of "normal times" within which one might see whether monetary integration had a measurable effect on risk sharing. The comparison between varying samples of OECD countries, EU countries, and EA members do seem to show a "Euro effect." Interstate risk sharing through capital markets is higher between EA member states than between EU members in all recent studies that take account of it.

The most recent estimate by Kalemli-Ozcan et al. (2014: table 2) shows that for the member states most affected by the EA crisis (Greece, Ireland, Italy, Portugal, and Spain), capital markets contributed 12 percent to consumption smoothing of an output shock between 1990 and 2007. This is similar to what earlier estimates had shown the US federal budget to do for the states. The contribution of capital markets was, however, not significantly different from zero for the rest of the EU in its formation before Eastern enlargement. Support for a euro effect on increasing risk sharing also comes from Gerlach and Hoffmann (2008), who find that consumption volatility has decreased more than output and income volatility. Through pair-wise comparisons between member and non-member countries, they establish that improved risk sharing between EA member states can account for this apparent consumption smoothing, especially of more permanent shocks. This study goes against the received wisdom that international risk sharing can be at best about transitory (business cycle) shocks but is non-existent for permanent shocks. They suggest that policy convergence and deeper financial integration are responsible for their finding.

Christev and Mélitz (2011: 27–9) find that European currency unification has contributed to both capital market integration and consumption smoothing. These authors go specifically against the interpretation of Artis and Hoffmann (2008), similar to Gerlach and Hoffmann (2008) that capital market integration as such leads to consumption smoothing. Christev and Mélitz (2011) reconcile the finding that there is a euro effect on risk sharing but not from capital market smoothing by arguing that a monetary union could make more goods tradable. This leads to a shift from non-traded to traded goods in consumption, both of which makes consumption growth less dependent on the ups and downs of domestic output. Their interpretation is echoed by Flood et al. (2012) and Baxter (2012) who attribute lower output volatility and increased synchronization of business cycles to the rise in trade and technology transfer.

The comprehensive studies of Kose et al. (2003, 2007) do not directly speak to the question of a euro effect and how to interpret it. But they add another caveat about whether financial integration leads to increasing consumption risk sharing over time. First of all, they suggest that a well-known anomaly still holds, even for advanced ("industrial") economies (Kose et al. 2007: figure 3): output is more highly correlated across countries than consumption while the opposite should be the case if there is consumption risk sharing. They also find that, for emerging markets, international financial integration actually increases consumption volatility while this subsides with further development. The authors interpret this as evidence for the relevance of domestic institutional development of the financial system.

Taken together, these pre-crisis studies suggest that the notion of stabilization implied by the literature on interstate risk sharing through financial markets and monetary integration is too narrow to contribute much to our understanding of monetary solidarity in the euro area. Financial market integration is supposed to reduce the transmission of output volatility into consumption volatility in a straightforward way. However, monetary and financial integration may unsettle domestic credit and savings intermediation, thus destabilizing both output and consumption independently. If trade is a stabilizing force, the Single Market may have had a stabilizing influence on the euro area, rather than monetary integration per se.

3.2.4 *What Have We Learnt?*

Notwithstanding its limitations, the economic risk-sharing literature and the empirical research it stimulated has been path breaking for a new coherent way of thinking about monetary integration. Diversity, or as this literature calls it, asymmetry, can then be seen as the outcome of profitable specialization, facilitated by enhanced opportunities for risk sharing. "[A]symmetry of output (GDP) may not be important for the members of the EU if there is substantial risk-sharing between the members of the union" (Kalemli-Ozcan et al. 2004: 3). The literature also takes into account that the risk profile may change: output volatility, understood as country-specific ("asymmetric") shocks, may increase due to the chance for more industrial specialization, while income or consumption absolute and relative volatility may be reduced, thanks to improved risk sharing through financial markets.

This literature also breaks new ground by seeing markets as shock absorbers. While certainly guilty of an optimistic bias regarding financial markets, this perspective cannot be ignored by political economists as it has proved to have policy relevance. It underpins the latest EU policy initiative to create a capital market union (Véron 2015). For instance, Hoffmann and Sørensen (2012), two principal contributors to this literature, argue against contemporary proponents of a fiscal union to complete the EA: they claim that getting on with capital market integration would be a much more effective way of sharing risks between members. While the economics underpinning the political economy approach here disagrees with the notion that capital markets are a substitute for fiscal union, the argument has to be taken seriously. Analytically, it highlights the importance of identifying all relevant risk-sharing channels, not only those provided by governments.

But institutional economics can tell us that market integration is as much a policy choice as the introduction of a joint budget. Risk-sharing channels are not forces of nature: they are constructed and shaped through government intervention and cooperation across borders. It is then only a small further step for political economists to consider whether market channels may have political advantages that commend them to member states struggling to overcome their collective action problems. Regulating markets and providing an infrastructure for their stable and reliable operation for business and their customers could have as a side effect more robust ways of spreading risks to income, employment, and consumption between states. For better or worse, rightly or wrongly, market integration is often perceived as requiring less cooperation between governments. Establishing the validity of this claim is important for understanding the political economy of monetary solidarity.

One well-researched area is asymmetry in the sense of asynchronous business cycles. The risk-sharing literature, in the theoretical tradition of real business cycles,[10] expects that business cycles become less synchronized in response to productivity shocks because financial flows go to where rates of return are highest (Cesa-Bianchi et al. 2016: 2–3). This does not matter as long as cross-border ownership of assets leads to less idiosyncratic volatility of income (and by implication consumption), so that even those with a negative shock can participate in efficient capital allocation (Kalemli-Ozcan et al. 2004: 13). Greater deviations of member state outputs from average growth could thus still lead to greater income smoothing while overall output would increase, thanks to pro-cyclical capital movements. This is what Kalemli-Ozcan et al. (2004)

[10] Real business cycles theory says that economic cycles are an efficient way for economies to adjust to real shocks: they are like ripples in water when a stone is thrown into a lake. Hence, it refutes the need for counter-cyclical intervention that Keynesian economics recommends to smooth such fluctuations. A standard reference is Backus et al. (1992) which tackles the puzzle that, empirically, output fluctuations are more closely correlated across countries than consumption fluctuations while theoretically it should be the other way round.

find for the US while in the EU, to their great surprise, they find idiosyncratic income volatility—the deviation of state-level income growth from average EU income growth—is larger than idiosyncratic output volatility. This can only be the case if international factor income, between OECD countries largely from income on assets held abroad, is more volatile than output (Kalemli-Ozcan et al. 2004: 20). The authors hypothesize that financial investments that are not used to hedge against domestic output risks are to blame. A move from portfolio investments to more direct foreign investment would supposedly remedy this.

But Cesa-Bianchi et al. (2016) take issue with this interpretation, repeated in later and related work of Sebnem Kalemli-Ozcan and co-authors. These authors suggest that less synchronized business cycles (more idiosyncratic output growth) can also be due to inefficient financial markets that respond to common shocks when countries are different. The differences between economies may lead to more or less tight credit constraints that have a perverse effect: where such constraints become binding when a negative country-specific shock hits the economy, capital may be repatriated to alleviate these constraints. The shock to the domestic economy is then also transmitted to other countries and business cycles in output become more synchronized. This challenges the underlying view of Kalemli-Ozcan et al. (2004) that more integrated markets in the US are more efficient markets: credit constraints may simply be homogenously distributed across firms and sectors. Their study develops a methodology that allows them to distinguish between these two underlying causes—country-specific shocks in similar countries or common shocks on different economies—and find that the latter is more prevalent. Capital flows that alleviate domestic credit constraints lead to more cyclical synchronization among eighteen OECD economies than one would expect from efficient risk sharing—this could be the EU case in Kalemli-Ozcan et al. (2004). Common shocks that have different effects on member state economies lead to pro-cyclical capital flows that make business cycles less synchronized—this could be the US case in Kalemli-Ozcan et al. (2004). While the jury is still out on these matters, it is important to note at this stage that financial contagion can lead to "asymmetry" of a monetary union, heterogeneity would be endogenous to more financial interlinkages rather than a structural characteristic. This is an important consideration since the EA crisis (Section 6.2.3).

But where does the high pre-crisis idiosyncrasy in European national incomes come from? The focus on output shocks in the original methodology systematically underestimates stabilization by the non-market channel (Dullien 2014). Debates on stabilization of the EA revolve around the demand side: "Here, one usually wants to know how much of an initial drop in some component of aggregate demand is actually counteracted by existing institutions or certain policies, and by how much GDP actually contracts" (Dullien 2014: 59). Risk sharing would be found when a change in *expected* private investment, consumption, and external demand is prevented from translating fully into a change in output. Stabilizing intervention can work directly, but also through second-round effects. For instance, if a rise in imports occurs that reduces demand for domestic firms' output, unemployment insurance would have a first-round stabilizing effect on consumption, and a second-round effect in preventing a fall in consumption leading to a further decrease in output (Dullien 2014: 59–60).

Yet, the extent to which this is the case varies widely within Europe. Research on automatic stabilizers, built into national and federal tax-transfer systems, gives us an idea of how much demand and income volatility is absorbed by government channels within states. A comparison by Dolls et al. (2009, 2010), which has quickly become a standard reference, uses micro-simulations of shocks in nineteen EU states and the US federation (in aggregate). The simulations are based on models of statutory tax-transfer systems in Europe (EUROMOD) and in the US (TAXSIM). They identify the operation of automatic stabilizers as intended by the legislator, without the effect of discretionary policies or behavioral changes on the part of households. Dolls et al. (2010: 3–4, 16, 31–2) take state income taxes and unemployment benefits into account and thus arrive at higher estimates for automatic stabilizers in the US than previous studies which have looked only at federal fiscal effects. Even so, they find that automatic stabilizers in the US compensate 32 percent of an income shock compared to an average of 38.5 percent in the EA. The comparison is even less favorable for an unemployment shock: the US tax-transfer system compensates only 34 percent of a fall in income caused by a rise in unemployment, whereas 48.5 percent is compensated on average in the EA. However, there is wide variation among member states. Estimates range from 53 percent of an income shock that is absorbed by taxes and transfers in Belgium to only 28 percent in Spain and from 62 percent of an unemployment shock in Germany to 31 percent in Italy. It is very likely that there is substantial variation between US states as well, since state income taxes and unemployment benefits vary widely (see Chapter 8 for the latter).

In sum, in Europe's mature welfare states there is substantial stabilization of demand shocks, which is typically not cross-border and works through taxes and transfers. But the shock-absorption capacity of welfare states varies. And public risk sharing has so far little equivalence between states even though common shocks may originate in internationally integrated markets and affect countries differently (Ces-Bianchi et al. 2016: 19, 29). This gave rise to the idea of cross-border unemployment insurance to replicate domestic stabilization mechanisms (Dullien 2014; Italianer and Vanheukelen 1993). The banking union of the EA can also be seen in this light (Section 7.2.3).

3.3 From Channels to Interfaces of Risk Sharing

With hindsight, it is obvious that the growth and integration of financial markets created volatility. This does not exclude that they shared and smoothed the volatility of the real economy at the same time, for instance, output of credit-constrained firms while consumption became more idiosyncratic thanks to differences in welfare states and in household credit. Even so, this means that a lot of risk is endogenous, generated by financial integration itself, rather than originating in a source outside the financial system (Brunnermeier and Sannikov 2013: 333). In fact, the diversity of member states, as indicated by asynchronous business cycles, may be reinforced, if not created, by cross-border financial flows (Cesa-Bianchi et al. 2016).

The single currency proved to be a tremendous driver of financial integration, accompanied as it was by a common monetary policy, harmonized financial regulation, and, last but not least, a deep government bond market with no exchange rate risk (Obstfeld 2013). Furthermore, it is now evident that stabilizing monetary policy can increase market tolerance of risk and give rise to a "volatility paradox" (Brunnermeier and Sannikov 2013: 342, 352): the more successful monetary and fiscal policies are in underwriting the risks that financial institutions take, the more risks market actors may take. This fosters the growth of banks as well as their cross-border integration, one feeding on the other. The bigger institutions of private finance get, the less able is a national fiscal authority to underwrite the risks of runs on their deposits or of their bankruptcy, not least to prevent the losses of small savers (Obstfeld 2013: 11–12, 55). The central bank with its deep pockets then has to be called upon to underpin the system as lender of last resort.

If risk is largely endogenous, the framing of risk sharing as operating through "channels" is untenable. The terminology of "channels" implies that each risk-sharing mechanism is independent of the others. By contrast, the volatility paradox implies that stabilization in one channel leads to more risk taking through another. This financial market risk taking relies ultimately on fiscal and monetary capacities of stabilization. As is more fully explained in Chapter 6, a negative feedback loop between deteriorating bank balance sheets and deteriorating public finances may ensue that calls for a central bank's direct lending of last resort to governments (De Grauwe 2011). But central banks also need fiscal backing if they are to take credit risk on their balance sheets: the ECB was quite explicit on this and requested that member states create an emergency fund before they engage in a bond-buying program (Barber 2010).

The financial crisis and its aftermath have highlighted this set of interdependencies or interfaces between the "channels," but there are others which Table 3.1 summarizes. On the diagonal (entries 1, 5, and 9), the table

Table 3.1. Channels and issues arising at interfaces of risk sharing

	Monetary policy	Fiscal policy	Supervised financial markets
Fiat money	1 Price stability: Independent central banks targeting goods price and wage inflation Oversight of payments system	2 (Fiscal backstops; variable fiscal multipliers)	3 (Monetary-financial transmission)
Public finance	4 (Negative feedback loops)	5 Debt sustainability/ employment stabilization: fiscal rules and surveillance leaving capacity for structural reform; automatic stabilizers	6 (Negative feedback loops)
Private finance	7 (Monetary-financial transmission)	8 (Fiscal backstops; variable fiscal multipliers)	9 Financial stability: independent prudential regulation Self-insurance through deposit guarantees and resolution funds (Basel consensus)

Source: own elaboration

describes the standard policy assignments that underpin the risk-sharing literature. The diagonal describes a way of assigning instruments to policy objectives or targets that became firmly institutionalized in the 1990s. Monetary policy is assigned to target inflation generated by wage and price setting, focusing on income flows rather than asset prices. Effective transmission of counter-cyclical monetary policy smooths aggregate demand, and central banks oversee the payments system to ensure a smooth transmission of interest rate signals to the economy (Obstfeld 2013: 28). Fiscal policy contributes to stabilization automatically, through the operation of the tax and benefit system which pools risks across individuals. Financial regulation or self-regulation and supervision is meant to ensure that risks are allocated among shareholders or borrowers and lenders efficiently.

The consensus that financial, monetary, and fiscal stability should be guaranteed by separate institutions extended the long-standing idea that economic policy problems can be made tractable by ensuring that there are as many instruments as targets (Tinbergen 1952). Institutionalizing the assignments reflected economists' distrust of political discretion in policymaking. Hence the support for independent central banks, independent financial supervisors, and fiscal authorities bound by economically sensible rules (Goodhart and Schoenmaker 1995; Schelkle 2012b: 35–41). In Chapter 5,

I argue that politicians and policymakers accepted this approach and reduced their discretion in this way to solve collective action problems. Delegation to independent agencies, rules, and the threat of punishment are one way of overcoming multiple veto points in areas such as macroeconomic stabilization, where quick decisions are required or compliance is essential (Tsebelis 2002: 187–206, 248–82).

Political support for the consensus in favor of government self-restraint cannot simply be explained by a hegemonic economic discourse. There was always criticism of this consensus, not only from the heterodox corner but also from macroeconomists with research interests in monetary policy and financial markets (e.g. Buiter et al. 1993; Goodhart and Smith 1993; Tobin 1990). One of the key ideas in more recent macroeconomic critiques is that the consensus fails to recognize policy interactions and interdependencies that make policy assignments unstable.[11] Financial markets, public budgets, and, crucially, central banking are not autonomous and isolated mechanisms for pooling risks, once the task of achieving financial stability is taken into account. These cross-effects have become apparent since the financial crisis and have proved to have particular relevance for the euro area.

3.3.1 *Negative Feedback Loops*

A prime example of interdependence between monetary, fiscal, and financial policies is the *negative feedback loop*, which affects the interfaces of private and public finance (entries 4 and 6 in Table 3.1). Also termed the "doom" or "diabolic" loop, it describes the problem that governments must stand behind the banking system, providing funds for recapitalization in a crisis. However, this destabilizes their own finances, and can produce a sovereign debt crisis, weakening banks further if they hold sovereign debt as capital (Modyi and Sandri 2012; Farhi and Tirole 2014). In its simplest form, the negative feedback loop is a consequence of the disproportionate size of financial institutions relative to national budgets, as Obstfeld (2013: 9) stresses:

> When fiscal resources are limited relative to the potential problems at hand, however, and the option of unlimited money financing is unavailable, the credibility of government support becomes questionable. The credibility deficit, in turn, makes the financial system more fragile, thereby raising the probability of a crisis requiring official intervention. This further weakens the sovereign's market borrowing terms, which in turn further undermines private-sector financial stability, and so on.

[11] See Acharya et al. (2009), Brunnermeier et al. (2009), Brunnermeier and Sannikov (2013: 334, 361), Leeper and Nason (2015: 3, 45), and Obstfeld (2013: 25) for a critical re-evaluation of this conventional view in light of the financial crises since 2007.

Monetary financing of the sovereign may be able to stop a liquidity problem escalating into endemic insolvency, provided a currency crisis can be avoided (entry 4 in Table 3.1; De Grauwe 2011). The negative feedback loop thus engages all three elements of monetary solidarity: the central bank maintaining the integrity of the money market, fiscal authorities trying to contain spillovers from domestic instability, and integrated financial markets that can both absorb and shift risks. This is a considerable difficulty for collective action as it touches on the pre-crisis consensus on central bank independence and the taboo of monetizing public debt.

3.3.2 *Fiscal Backstops*

The macroeconomic literature recognizes now that systemic banking crises and effective lending of last resort by the central bank require *fiscal backstops* (Sims 2012: 222; Leeper and Nason 2015: 46).[12] While a government requires monetary backing to escape the negative feedback loop, monetary authorities require fiscal backing to contain and manage their role as lender of last resort to the financial system. They need governments to recapitalize and resolve banks, protecting in particular small savers from losses (entry 8 in Table 3.1). This fiscal support contains the risk that the central bank's provision of liquidity support postpones the resolution of solvency problems and perpetuates moral hazard among bankers. A central bank also may be reluctant for institutional reasons to take on risky assets in the course of providing liquidity support. Such measures may make the reversal of lax monetary policies more difficult, since default on assets will use up a central bank's loss-absorbing capital.[13] While the central bank cannot become insolvent as it can create more interest-bearing reserves without physical limit, this can aggravate inflationary pressures and is also likely to lead to devaluation of the currency. A currency that is printed only to give a lifeline to moribund banks is not attractive to hold. For all these reasons, the potential or actual assumption of solvency risks by the fiscal authorities is required (entry 2 in Table 3.1). They can give this backing directly or indirectly, by underwriting deposit guarantees, or establishing resolution funds that are financed by contributions from insured institutions themselves. These types of measure relieve the central bank from having to lend to banks on the borderline of insolvency.

[12] The Five Presidents' report on "completing Europe's [EMU]" acknowledges this: "In the short term, this risk-sharing [of asymmetric shocks] can be achieved through integrated financial and capital markets (private risk sharing) combined with the necessary common backstops, i.e. a last resort financial safety net, to the Banking Union" (Juncker et al. 2015: 4). But nowhere does the report acknowledge that shocks may be endogenous to financial integration.

[13] The loss-absorbing capital of the ECB amounts to €10.8 billion since December 2010 (ECB website "Capital subscription").

Acknowledging that central banks need direct or indirect fiscal backing amounts to the recognition that fiat money—that has no commodity as an external constraint to limit its issue—is "state money" as Goodhart (1998) put it. He criticized OCA theory for missing this political economy foundation of modern money. However, as he also noted, the architects of the EA have deliberately excluded such fiscal backing of the ECB. Member states do hold shares in the central bank's loss-absorbing capital, however, and could be called upon if the ECB was forced to take solvency risks on its books. Moreover, the European System of Central Banks is a rudimentary fiscal risk pool to the extent that central banks can absorb national bank bailouts of EA-wide significance through their earnings on the money issue (seignorage), which is revenue to the participating governments (Pauly 2009: fn 3).

3.3.3 *Monetary-Financial Transmission*

The transmission of monetary policy (entries 3 and 7 in Table 3.1) has come under renewed scrutiny as it has become clear that a low interest rate environment can boost the economy by allowing more risk taking by investors, but also can encourage collectively excessive risk taking (Borio and Zhu 2012: 242–4). Risk taking by households seems particularly susceptible to destabilizing dynamics: low interest rates make financing homeownership cheap and raise the present value of the security for mortgage credit, giving rise to a feedback loop of rising credit and rising housing values (Brunnermeier and Sannikov 2013: 341). It is unlikely that there was no sense among policymakers in the EU, or indeed the US, that something like this was happening before the financial crisis, but the institutionalized assignment of instruments to targets may have contributed to the failure to respond.

Another problem of monetary transmission is that monetary policy, by changing (the term structure of) interest rates and thus the relative prices of assets, also generates wealth effects. It is now recognized that this *wealth redistribution* channel makes monetary policy akin to "social insurance" (Brunnermeier and Sannikov 2013: 333) in that it allocates risks to different agents differently and substitutes for missing private insurance markets, even when prices are flexible. For instance, a protracted phase of near zero interest rates gives banks time to recapitalize themselves out of high margins between their refinancing costs and what they can earn on asset investments. But this shifts the cost of recapitalization to insurers and pension funds, and ultimately to their policy holders. They will earn low returns on their less risky asset holdings while they do not benefit from the low refinancing rates offered by the central bank. This is redistribution from stronger financial sectors to the weaker banking sector. It occurs even though the banks have brought their weakness largely on themselves.

3.3.4 *Variable Fiscal Multipliers*

Finally, recent economic research has highlighted that *fiscal multipliers* (entries 2, 8 in Table 3.1) are not constant but depend on the stage of the business cycle (Auerbach and Gorodnichenko 2011; Corsetti et al. 2012). In a deep recession or a liquidity trap, when the central bank has already lowered interest rates towards the zero bound, fiscal spending—and cuts in spending—have a very strong effect on private demand and income. This means that any attempt to reduce the budget deficit, typically by cutting spending in line with falling tax revenue, will be very costly because it will cause a collapse of private economic activity. This was, of course, pointed out by Keynes (1936: ch.17), who focused on fiscal policy as he considered monetary policy to be ineffective under the conditions of the Great Depression, that is when pessimism of investors is so overwhelming that any monetary stimulus is neutralized by more money holding.

For governments to be able to act in a stabilizing way, they must be able to incur debt, but if there is a "flight to safety" among investors, some sovereigns will be unable to finance deficit spending. This is a primary reason why fiscal risk sharing among states is necessary. Fiscal risk sharing can take the form of government-to-government lending through emergency funds under conditions that do not switch off automatic stabilizers, or it can be achieved by joint liability for the debt issued so as to prevent pro-cyclical government bond market pressures for austerity. Discretionary stimulus in those member states with fiscal space will also benefit constrained economies if they have sufficiently close trade links: foreign demand can compensate for lack of domestic demand to some extent.

3.4 The Limitations of Financial Risk Sharing

The approach to risk sharing pioneered by Bent Sørensen and Oved Yosha is a useful antidote to the preoccupation with flexible labor markets—and the alleged requirement to converge on a liberal type of labor market—that is found in the theory of optimum currency areas. What we can take from this literature is, first, that monetary integration is indistinguishable from financial integration and, second, that the latter can be a major source of risk sharing through markets.

The review of the risk-sharing literature in the previous section highlighted two interrelated limitations: its theoretically and methodologically driven focus on output shocks and its emphasis on market channels of risk sharing, especially capital market integration. The possibility that financial integration might have directly destabilizing effects on consumption is excluded by assumption, with some notable exceptions (Huizinga and Zhu 2004, Kose et al. 2007, Mélitz and Zumer 1999). This optimism about financial integration reflected US experience during the "Great Moderation," when the regime of financial repression was lifted and a period of macroeconomic stability ensued. However, the volatility of household earnings and consumption did not go down during this period (Gottschalk and Moffitt 2009; Dynan 2010).

Financial market integration did promote output smoothing but it also helped individuals, collective investors, and even states to incur more risks. There were high returns to this risk taking but they ended up benefiting disproportionately the salaries of financial managers and not the incomes of their clients (Denk 2015). Furthermore, we know now that financial markets can easily break down as channels of risk sharing and contribute to the accumulation of excessive risks instead. Monetary-financial integration creates new risks, not least because it can give rise to both productive and unproductive risk taking. One therefore has to think more rigorously about a system of risk sharing, with various interfaces of its elements, and not merely let a methodology of national accounts determine what can be captured.

Even if financial markets were more efficient, it is unlikely that the promise of consumption smoothing would have ever created enough political momentum to make governments, business, and organized labor support the euro experiment. The risk-sharing literature fails to capture the political drivers of the single currency. This is an issue for political economists and not meant as a criticism of economists contributing to this literature. Decision makers and their advisors looked for other benefits as the historical accounts of Dyson and Featherstone (1999) and more recently James (2012) show. If credibly stability-oriented, a single currency holds the promise of higher investment through lower and more stable interest rates. These should result from the rise in liquidity of asset markets, the use of a common currency in trade with other member states, the assurance of freedom of capital inside a monetary union, and the presence of a lender of last resort to a deeper financial system.[14] Hence, we need a by-product theory of collective action on risk sharing and to show that risk sharing is an enduring feature underlying these more obvious benefits.

The EA, as originally conceived, preserved channels of risk sharing, largely by adhering to conventions about the assignment of instruments to targets: monetary policy to price stability, fiscal policy to growth through structural reform, prudent regulation to financial stability. But in particular the neat assignment of responsibilities for price and financial stability has proved untenable, empirically and theoretically. The new empirical fact is the

[14] This is further elaborated in Section 5.1.2.

increasing size of financial markets vis-à-vis each member state of the union. Institutional interfaces, such as fiscal backstops for bank resolution and for lending of last resort to banks, were deliberately left underdeveloped (Chapter 5). The emphasis, in central banks and finance ministries of countries as different as France, Germany, and Britain, was on reducing the risks to price stability (Verdun 2000: 162, 165).[15] Catch-up growth was soon triggered by historically low interest rates inside the EA. The potential for boom-bust cycles in some member states quickly materialized. A common shock, in the guise of the US subprime market crisis that made interbank markets freeze, unleashed a destructive dynamic that overwhelmed any single channel of risk sharing (Chapter 6). Reforms since 2009 have made the euro area more resilient and hesitantly more solidaristic; the analytical framework of interfaces sheds light on this but also shows the limitations that remain (Chapter 7).

The search for monetary solidarity in the EA in Chapters 5–7 is preceded by a discussion of US monetary-financial history. This provides some perspective on what is supposedly the example of a diverse union that works and should have been followed by the Europeans. In contrast to the euro experiment, the dollar experiment started with a fairly complete system of risk sharing, the Hamilton Plan, but no national currency. Yet, political forces in favor of devolution and unfettered growth in the states undid every element of the Plan within two decades. It took many financial crises and finally the Great Depression to shift the political balance in favor of a viable system which addressed the interfaces of risk sharing.

[15] Their success can be gleaned from the evolution of countries' risk-return tradeoffs (Section 7.1).

Appendix

Table 3.1A. Estimates of cross-border channels of consumption risk sharing

Risk-sharing channel	States and time span	Range of estimates[a]	Sources and comments
Capital markets (interstate: mostly profit, interest, and rent from cross-border capital ownership)	US states		
	(1964–90)	39%	ASY96 (table 1)
	(1963–90)	24%	MZ (table 3)
	(1960–96)	58%	BH (table 1)
	(1970–98)	45%	M (table 7, includes retained profits and capital depreciation)
	OECD countries		
	(1960–94)	5–7%	MZ (table 10)
	(1960–96)	1%	BH (table 1)
	(1970–99)	n.s.	M (table 2, not directly comparable with US)
	(1992–2000)LR	5%	BKOS (table 5, capital gains
	(2000–7)	7%	only, factor income flows n.s.)
	EU or EA* states[b]		
	(1960–94)	8–13%	MZ
	(1960–96)	5% and 6%*	BH
	(1971–93)	−9%	ASY98 (includes capital depreciation)
	(1970–99)	n.s. and 0%*	M
	(2000–7)	n.s. and 14%*	BKOS
	(1990–2007)	n.s. and 12%*	KOLS (EA consists of Greece, Ireland, Italy, Portugal, and Spain only)
Credit markets (intertemporal: household savings, government net lending, and retained profits)	US states		
	(1964–90)	23%	ASY96
	(1963–90)	24%	MZ
	(1960–96)	28%	BH
	(1970–98)	21%	M
	OECD countries		
	(1960–94)	1–5% and 8–13%	MZ (1–5% from current-account imbalances, 8–13% from savings)
	(1960–96)	36%	BH
	(1970–99)	50%	M (corporate and government saving)
	(1992–2000)	51%	BKOS
	(2000–7)	53%	
	EU or EA* states[b]		
	(1960–94)	1–2% and 9–13%	MZ (1–2% from current-account imbalances, 9–13% from savings)
	(1960–96)	42% and 43%*	BH
	(1971–93)	50%	ASY98
	(1970–99)	51% and 53%*	M (corporate and government saving)
	(2000–7)	45% and 24%*	BKOS
	(1990–7)	49% and 31%*	KOLS (EA consists of GIIPS only)

(*continued*)

Table 3.1A. Continued

Risk-sharing channel	States and time span	Range of estimates[a]	Sources and comments
Fiscal policy (international transfers/fiscal transfers and stabilizers)	US states		
	(1964–90)	13%	ASY (unemployment insurance attributed to federal budget)
	(1963–90)	13%	MZ
	(1960–96)	5%	BH
	(1970–98)	14%	M
	OECD countries		
	(1970–99)	n.s.	M
	EU or EA* states[b]		
	(1971–93)	3%	ASY98
	(1970–99)	n.s. and −2%*	M
	(1990–2007)	n.s. and n.s.*	KOLS
Unsmoothed share of output shock	US states		
	(1964–90)	25%	ASY96
	(1963–90)	39%	MZ (directly estimated, not as a residual)
	(1960–96)	9%	BH (own calculation)
	(1970–98)	20%	M
	OECD countries		
	(1960–94)	80%	MZ (directly estimated)
	(1960–96)	63%	BH (own calculation as residual)
	(1970–99)	59%	M
	(1992–2000)	41%	BKOS
	(2000–7)	36%	
	EU or EA* states[b]		
	(1960–94)	77%	MZ (directly estimated)
	(1960–96)	53% and 51%*	BH (own calculation as residual)
	(1971–93)	56%	ASY98
	(1970–99)	59% and 56%*	M
	(2000–7)	56%*	BKOS (6% count for capital gains which are not significant, however)
	(1990–2007)	53% and 61%*	KOLS (−7% and −5%* from capital depreciation)

Notes: a = figures give percentage share of output shock compensated; b = * marks EA estimate in contrast to estimates applying to the EU

Key to sources: ASY96 = Asdrubali et al. 1996; ASY98 = Arreaza et al. 1998; BH = Becker and Hoffmann 2006; BKOS = Balli et al. 2012; KOLS = Kalemli-Ozcan et al. 2014; M = Marinheiro 2003; MZ = Mélitz and Zumer 1999

Part II

Evolving Monetary Unions of Limited Risk Sharing

4

A Short History of Risk Sharing in the US Monetary Union

"History doesn't repeat itself, but it does rhyme," Mark Twain supposedly said.[1] The rich literature on US financial history provides insights of striking relevance for the EA today. This chapter reviews that history, not in order to derive "lessons" as some of the recent literature does (Gaspar 2015), but rather to show how the analytical framework presented in previous chapters illuminates issues of monetary union generally. Reviewing the US experience in the light of the EA crisis gives us a better understanding of the political-economic paradox of diversity. Needless to say, the collective action problems of markets and governments in the US are different from those in the EA, but the comparison shows corresponding patterns and functional problems of heterogeneous monetary unions.

The US repeatedly experienced severe financial instability up until the first half of the twentieth century, including negative feedback loops between banks and fiscal authorities in the states. Stability increased as risk sharing was extended. However, it remains limited in some striking ways. States and municipalities in the US can go bankrupt, and the no-bailout clause for states is more strictly enforced than it is in the EA (Henning and Kessler 2012). So some incompleteness remains and is indeed deliberate.

The debate over the wisdom or folly of European monetary union has often been fought between the "coronation theory," which proposes that a common currency is the pinnacle of political union, and the "leverage theory" that the adoption of a common currency can serve as a driver towards political union. Supporters of the coronation theory often cite the US case in support, but the first section shows that the relationship between political and

[1] See Frieden (2015b) which has inspired this chapter. Helleiner (2003) is a major comparative study of the evolution of currency unions, McNamara (2003) is a similar attempt at comparing political and monetary integration in nineteenth-century US to late twentieth-century Europe.

monetary integration did not follow this script. There is even some support for the leverage theory, but both suffer from an unduly simplistic understanding of political union, which is usually equated with fiscal union. Remarkably, the US had important elements of fiscal union before it had monetary union, and fiscal union was not enough to bring about monetary stability. More risk-sharing institutions, notably the establishment of a stable central bank, were needed. In the following discussion, the second section goes through the crisis-prone history of the contestation over monetary-financial institutions in the US, while the third section explains how the interfaces between fiat money, public and private finances were developed. The last section sums up what rhymes in US and EA history.

The building of a diverse US dollar area was marked by the inherent tension between proponents of easier local credit conditions and those who favored tight money to make the greenback a respectable international currency. This tension had a sectoral and a geographic dimension: the poorer, more rural, and more agricultural South and West depended for their well-being on elastic credit supply while the more urban, industrializing, and finance-dominated Northeast and Midwest wanted above all monetary stability.[2] The political-economic conflicts were extremely divisive and had the potential to destroy the young republic. But there is no irredeemable economic conflict between elastic credit and tight money, just as there is no irredeemable conflict between low interest rates and low inflation in the EA. How conflictual or compatible these different goals are depends on the risk-sharing arrangements in place.

4.1 The Relationship between Monetary and Political Integration

What was to become the United States started as a confederation of settler colonies, united primarily in their rejection of an overpowering central state. The contestation over the sequencing of steps towards integration, as we perceive them today, appeared as a political fight between devolutionists and federalists. The devolutionists insisted on political self-determination for the states and were primarily interested in economic integration through a common physical and legal infrastructure. Money was not part of this infrastructure. Defenders of states' rights prevented the US from getting a central

[2] Frieden (2015a: 50). See Ferguson (1962) on the origins of this division which was not there right from the start, at the Constitutional Convention. His extensive research suggests that questions of public finance mobilized a "Southern interest" as much if not more than the stance on slavery (Ferguson 1962: 451–3).

bank before 1913, although there were at least two predecessors which failed. A federal fiscal backstop for the financial system had to wait for the New Deal in 1935, although the central government had helped states and their banks in financial difficulties before. War was a vulnerability of the devolutionist position: its financial legacy was invariably high public debt and a monetary overhang that forced at least some states to seek bailouts from the federal government. Ambitious public infrastructure projects, which included the promotion of banks, tended to overstretch state finances as well. Regular boom-bust cycles triggered a series of institutional experiments with the interface between commercial finance, proto-central banks, and federal public finance. The federalists for their part recognized early on that if they relieved the states from their debt, they could extract in return some concessions regarding the centralization of policy competences. The proto-central banks tended to err on the side of tight monetary control, however, so as to prevent a run on reserves. This was resented by a coalition of economic sectors and political forces, both for its concentration of power over states and for what they perceived as sacrificing growth for overall stability.

The risk-sharing arrangements that eventually emerged in the twentieth century were not designed to provide an economically optimal solution; rather, arrangements responded to flaws revealed in the most recent boom-bust cycle. The burden of proof was typically on those who favored centralizing solutions. This is compatible with the interpretation that public goods production for the union was a by-product of selective incentives in the states. Integration had to meet concrete economic challenges if veto players in states were to permit minimal union building. Broz (1997, 1998), contributors to Eichengreen and Frieden (2001), and Frieden (2015a), broadly support this proposition while emphasizing the role of political contestation. Moss (2002) and Moss and Brennan (2001) see more intentionality in the emergence of public risk management. They stress, above all, the role of enlightened civil servants and policy entrepreneurs.

The late establishment of the central bank seems to support the coronation theory whereby monetary integration follows political union. But this interpretation can only be upheld by ignoring a succession of prior measures affecting money, banking, and public debt. There is some support for the leverage theory, particularly in the so-called Hamilton Plan of 1791, which envisaged the mutualization of public debt and the creation of a central bank that would issue a national currency in the modern sense. The intention to leverage ever closer political union was transparent, building on the first step that had already been taken with the constitution. But the Hamilton Plan was undone after less than three decades.

Today's national currency, the greenback, was introduced more than seventy years later, shortly after the political union had broken up with the secession of the Southern slave states. The greenback was the currency of the victorious North and became the national currency only once the agrarian South was militarily and politically defeated. While the Northern states could be seen as leveraging monetary integration, it certainly did not further ever closer union. This raises some doubts about the identity-generating qualities of a single currency that scholars like Helleiner (2003) and McNamara (2003: 9) claim. The common currency proved politically divisive because the Southern and Western states felt short-changed by the "golden fetters" of the monetary regime (Frieden 2015a: ch.2). At the same time, the United States remained an economy subject to more financial and monetary panic than most other advanced economies of the Western hemisphere (Broz 1997: 5). This ended after the New Deal introduced a federal deposit guarantee and resolution authority for the financial system, in the guise of the Federal Deposit Insurance Corporation (FDIC). Crucially, the simultaneous abandonment of the specie standard allowed the central bank to combine tight inflation control with elastic credit supply, although managing this remains a tension that keeps central bankers on their toes. Financial repression was also exercised, particularly by maintaining administered interest rates in retail banking.[3] The federal tax-transfer system developed only slowly, and the contribution of the welfare state to macroeconomic stabilization remained limited.

At first sight, there are parallels in the sequencing of monetary and political integration in the US and in Europe. The joint currency was introduced before a full-fledged fiscal union in the macroeconomic sense. However, a central bank was introduced quite some time after the country had been politically reunited. The common currency was meant to leverage closer political union on terms that suited the modern economy of the victorious North. This currency union remained financially unstable and politically divided for at least two decades. Economic-financial integration proceeded regardless. This rhymes insofar as monetary integration came into its own in the EU in the 2000s while the project of building a political union stalled (Hodson 2009). The common currency exercised a politically unifying effect only when other institutions came to underpin it and embed it in a *system* of macroeconomic stabilization. It took the United States about 150 years for this system to evolve, from Hamilton's Plan to the New Deal (Frieden 2015b).

While the evolution of the US federation did not follow the coronation approach, it also provides counter-evidence to the leverage view that a common currency furthers ever closer political union. The currency prolonged

[3] Financial repression "includes directed lending to government by captive domestic audiences (such as pension funds), explicit or implicit caps on interest rates, regulation of cross-border capital movements, and (generally) a tighter connection between government and banks" (Reinhart and Sbrancia 2011: abstract).

the divisions of the civil war into peacetime. Only once the political-economic conflict was settled politically did currency arrangements stop being so divisive. Boom-bust cycles still occurred, however. These stopped only once fiat money, tight financial regulation, and stabilizing interfaces of private and public finance had been created, mainly in the aftermath of the Great Depression.

4.2 The Emerging Interfaces of Money, Banking, and Federal Public Finances

The first attempt to establish a union was ratified by thirteen states in 1781, during the War of Independence. The "Articles of Confederation and Perpetual Union" established a "Continental Congress" as its (unelected) central government. It had no enforceable taxation rights (Ferguson 1962: 455). To pay suppliers and soldiers, the Congress issued debt that it had no means to repay. It also printed paper money, the Continental dollar, which depreciated during and after the war, surviving to this day in the expression "not worth a Continental" (Hall and Sargent 2014: 148). The unit of account was the Spanish dollar, a silver coin minted by the Spanish Empire. Against this background, the 1789 Constitution defined the bare minimum of what was needed for a functioning federation. It consisted of three Articles that laid down the principles of a federal government based on the separation of legislative, executive, and judicial powers, three Articles about the rights and responsibilities of the states in the federation, and one Article that established the ratification procedure. It was the foundation for a rudimentary political union. Citizens' rights, such as freedom of speech, came as an afterthought, in a set of Amendments of which the first ten later formed the Bill of Rights.

The sustainability of state public debt was a major concern from the beginning. The union of states emerged out of war and its devastating effect, not only on lives but also on public finances. The ongoing struggle to find sources of revenue created a fiscal-financial nexus that was repeatedly a source of negative feedback loops and financial panic. The evolution of a national banking system that slowly crowded out the state bank system was crucial to the reduction of this risk. But a lender of last resort was slow to emerge because the states resisted the centralization of monetary powers. The creation of a national central bank took until the early twentieth century, when a reasonably stable configuration of interfaces between public and private finance as well as fiat money was established, almost 150 years after the Hamilton Plan had envisioned such a complete system of macroeconomic risk sharing.

4.2.1 *Alexander Hamilton's Plan for Central Risk Pooling*

In 1781, as the War of Independence (1775–83) was still being fought, Alexander Hamilton wrote in a letter: "A national debt, if it is not excessive, will be to us a national blessing. It will be a powerful cement of our Union" (quoted in McNamara 2003: 10n). He reckoned that the joint liability of federal debt could become a visible symbol for the strength of the federation if the whole was more creditworthy than its parts. He was to become the first finance minister of the United States, under President George Washington, and he proceeded to act on his insight. He relieved the states from their war-related debt and made the nationalized debt a source of states' revenue for which they in turn agreed to a constitution which created considerable central powers.

The 1789 Constitution gave the federal government the power to tax as well as the sole right to issue coinage. Because of a lack of minting capacity, Hamilton authorized the circulation of the Spanish dollar as legal tender several times. Only in 1853 was this foreign currency replaced with the domestic silver coin.[4] The Constitution was silent about note issuance by the federal government. There was principled opposition to paper money in the constitutional assembly, which foreshadowed later conflicts between monetary conservatives at the federal level and expansionists in some states (Giannini 2011: 66; Hall and Sargent 2014: 155).

The states were expressly prohibited from taxing exports and imports and issuing paper money (Sylla et al. 1987). These provisions took away important sources of state revenue at a time when many states had accumulated more debt during the War of Independence than they could service in peacetime. While state representatives were ready to agree to expand the prerogatives of the federal government only if they were relieved of their debt, the federalists, in turn, were willing to concede this demand because they reckoned that the overindebtedness of some states jeopardized the credit of all (Henning and Kessler 2012: 6–8).

The first part of the debt plan relieved states from their debt by taking certificates of state-incurred debt and turning them into federal securities (Trescott 1955: 232). The second element of the so-called Funding Act of 1790 was to turn the debt of the Confederation into new federal issues. Federal debt had often been issued to pay soldiers and suppliers. They tended to sell it, and the states had thus come to hold about a third of outstanding federal debt. The interest on these federal bonds became for the first years of the union a considerable source of state revenue, on average a fifth of their income and for some up to half (Trescott 1955: 228, 245). The third part of the plan was to

[4] *Encyclopaedia Britannica*, Macropaedia article "Coins and Coinage." Legal tender means that being paid in money with this status cannot be refused even if a private contract stipulates something else (for instance, the delivery of a commodity).

settle state accounts with the intention of equalizing the per capita cost of the war effort. What was not considered under the Hamilton Plan was compensation of citizens who held Continentals, the defunct paper money. If the union had redeemed them at par value, it would have doubled the federal debt. In a later currency reform, these citizens received only a dollar in specie for every 100 Continentals (Hall and Sargent 2014: 153).

The federal government restructured state debt before it assumed it.[5] Holders of non-performing state and Confederation bonds were given a package of federal bonds worth a fraction of their face value. This exchange amounted to a sizeable haircut, but it was still well above market value, and also brought the resumption of interest payments on which the states were in arrears. After debt service resumed, the former state, now federal, bonds began to trade at only 10–20 percent under par while they had traded at a 60 percent discount of their face value. Federal and state governments got access to domestic and international financial markets again (Frieden 2015b). It is notable that the compensation of bondholders, many of whom were foreigners, was considerably more generous than the compensation of those who owned Continental dollars.

An integral part of Hamilton's Plan was the foundation of the First Bank of the United States, given a twenty-year charter in 1791 (McNamara 2003: 10). Like its model, the Bank of England, it was a privately owned proto-central bank. It issued the US dollar which was, however, not a national currency but only legal tender for fiscal purposes, that is for payments by and to the Treasury. A standard means of payment at the time were banknotes: states had got around the constitutional prohibition on creating money by chartering banks to issue money (Sylla et al. 1987: 392). These banknotes had to be redeemable into a reserve medium that the banks could not produce *ad libitum*, so as to prevent the excessive issue of banknotes. Prudential regulation required banks to hold reserve assets in a specified fraction of their banknote issue. The stipulated reserves varied over time, but typically consisted of specie, such as gold or silver, and legal tender: the dollars issued by the First Bank. The First Bank was meant to centralize the reserve holdings of state banks, allowing the financial system to hold fewer reserves in the aggregate without making any individual bank less safe. The law of large numbers suggests that the likelihood of all banks having to exchange their banknotes for reserves becomes smaller and smaller as more members join the risk pool.

[5] Restructuring of debt is, in contrast to simple debt write-off, not repudiating the repayment of obligations. Rather, it formally upholds the obligation but changes the terms and conditions such that the effective debt repayment is reduced. This can happen in a variety of ways that typically amount to either a lower interest rate or a longer repayment period. Debt restructuring and write-off converge if the interest rate approaches zero and maturity becomes infinite.

Given its size and the function of turning banknotes into specie (coins) if required, the First Bank soon assumed a much more important role than its power to issue legal tender for fiscal purposes would lead one to expect. By setting the terms on which it would exchange banknotes for specie, it could influence the state banks' credit supply (Giannini 2011: 67).

With hindsight, it is easy to recognize that the Hamilton Plan built, in one ingenious stroke, a more perfect union. Yet it was also highly controversial, for reasons that resonate with debates today (Frieden 2015b). Many resented the centralization of public debt management and banking in principle (McNamara 2003: 11). There was vocal opposition from agrarian states in particular, even when they themselves got debt relief, because they saw relief as disproportionately benefiting financial interests in urban areas and abroad (Ferguson 1962: 457–9). Handsome profits were made by speculators who had bought some of the wartime junk bonds for next to nothing (Trescott 1955: 131). Moreover, the proto-central bank restricted the supply of credit in order to establish a stable and creditworthy union, but this was seen in many states as holding back their growth.

In the long run, the restricted supply of credit proved destructive for Hamilton's reforms. The number of state banks was expanding rapidly. The fractional reserve system drove them into using the First Bank which in turn could restrict their expansion by controlling the creation of specie/coinage. This mobilized state governments who looked for ways to make up for the fiscal straitjacket they were put in when their power to tax foreign trade was clipped and seignorage from direct note issue eliminated. To compensate for this, governments founded or licensed ever more state-chartered banks, giving them the profitable privilege of note issue and in return taxing their capital or holding income-yielding shares in them. At least one fifth and in most states a third of ordinary revenue came from these state-chartered banks (Sylla et al. 1987: 400). Thus, a powerful constituency against the First Bank formed within the state bank system which prevented the renewal of its charter in 1811 (Giannini 2011: 68).

The Anglo-American War of 1812 finally undid much of Hamilton's attempt at restoring the creditworthiness of the public sector. Federal and state governments had to resort to issuing excessive debt again, at deep discounts which made financing the war effort a vast expense (Hall and Sargent 2014: 156–8). The first attempt at building a closer monetary union thus failed. The by-product of fiscal risk sharing was not an institutional equilibrium. Hamilton's Plan spread the risk of overindebtedness across the union of states, but it did not spread the risk of meeting the uncertain fiscal demands of growing economies: this was shifted one-sidedly onto the states. This, coupled with the tight credit policy of the First Bank, led to the demise of the rudimentary monetary union.

4.2.2 *Experimenting with Federalism and Free Banking*

When the Anglo-American War ended in 1815, history seemed to repeat itself. The federal government assumed states' debt (Henning and Kessler 2012: 10) and a Second Bank of the US was founded to deal with the financial mayhem. It exchanged the inflated banknote issue for specie, writing down debt in the process; as before, it issued a legal tender for fiscal purposes (Broz 1998: 239; Capie et al. 1994: 7). Its twenty-year charter (1816–36) coincided with an "era of internal improvement." States invested massively in physical and financial infrastructure. This raised their (domestic and foreign) debt to levels that were 50 percent above the debts they had incurred in the two wars before combined (Wallis et al. 2004: 1). The Second Bank, under its competent President Biddle, financed some of this infrastructure, thus acting as a development bank, not least to build constituencies in the states. But it also tried to rein in credit expansion with a view to external stability: whenever the dollar exchange rate fell, state banks were requested to convert their banknotes, thus contracting credit and generating demand for the dollar. This quest for stability put Biddle at loggerheads with President Andrew Jackson, known still today as the incarnation of populist conservatism. The President challenged the Bank's policies as an exercise of federal power, and rallied the states behind him in a "Bank War" that the central bank was bound to lose (Giannini 2011: 68–71). The charter of the Second Bank was not renewed.

What followed was a period of experimentation with state-sponsored financial innovation, as well as free (unchartered) entry into the market by note-issuing banks. These experiments were backed by those who favored devolution of powers and elastic credit (Helleiner 2003: 123–39). Free entry made the expanding union very crisis-prone. Some states sought their own remedies and introduced obligatory insurance for bank liabilities, New York being the front runner in 1829 (Moss and Brennan 2001: 148–51). This safety fund system, with some variations introduced in six states, insured mostly the banknote issue but also deposits, and combined therefore lender-of-last-resort and deposit guarantee functions (FDIC 1998: 3–12). Each fund was paid for by contributions from banks but the state guaranteed the bond issue to set up the fund. Insurance was the pretext for closer supervision, notably that banks had to hold specified assets as loss-absorbing capital. The inventor of this system, Joshua Forman, got the idea that banks should have mutual liability for each other's debt from Chinese merchants: "The case of our banks is very similar; they enjoy in common the exclusive right of making a paper currency for the people of the state, and by the same rule should in common be answerable for that paper" (quoted in FDIC 1998: 3). This insurance system worked reasonably well.

But competition from the free banking movement undermined the safety fund system, and sovereign debt crises in the states ruined it. Shortly after the charter of the Second Bank expired in 1836, a major borrowing spree started, ironically fueled by the redistribution of a federal budget surplus (Trescott 1955: 239–40; Wallis et al. 2004: 6). It ended with the sovereign default of eight states and a territory (Florida) in the early 1840s, while twelve other states got into serious fiscal difficulties, out of a total of twenty-eight states. Michigan's safety fund did not survive this crisis. A common factor was that the states continued investing heavily in transport networks and creating state "land banks" but a long drawn-out recession made these investments over-optimistic.[6] There was a divide between supposedly profligate and prudent states which made the union unwilling to bail out and assume the debt of defaulting states, for what would have been the third time in fifty years (Wibbels 2003: 498; Henning and Kessler 2012: 11).

Economic historians have put forward a variety of reasons why those who defaulted did so: was it corruption or cronyism between state officials and bank managers, incompetence of state bureaucracies in planning large infrastructure projects, or just the bad luck of an economic downturn beyond governments' control? In a widely cited study, Wallis et al. (2004: 10–11) review these explanations and find them wanting in their generality. Each explanation assumes that the US was one country rather than "an empire of different geographic and economic regions at different stages of economic development" (Wallis et al. 2004: 26). The only similarity in all cases was that governments invested in what they saw as their future tax base, promoting higher land prices and more intensive land use through public investment. Wallis et al. (2004) document that there was actually nothing corrupt or megalomaniac in these projections. But with the benefit of hindsight we can see that these policies set up a feedback loop that made them vulnerable to the slightest shock or disappointment of projections (English 1996: 261–2; Frieden 2015b).

The default of the Southwestern states in the early 1840s was due to a particular feedback loop that rhymes closely with the disastrous experience of Ireland and Spain 170 years later. The Southwestern states had invested heavily in land (or plantation) banks by issuing state bonds to them in return for a share in their capital stock. The banks were responsible for servicing this debt. The other investors were plantation owners who acquired capital stock by giving the banks mortgages on their land. These private investors could then borrow to buy more land (and slaves) to work the land. Initially, banks financed these mortgage loans by selling the state bonds given to them. In case of default, the holders of these state bonds had to take recourse to the securitized loans: the mortgages of private investors, the plantation owners.

[6] The latter was in particular the case in the Southwestern states, ironically because they wanted to make up for the closure of Second Bank branches which had financed considerable activity in the trans-Appalachian west (Wallis et al. 2004: 6).

This created the perfect conditions for a feedback mechanism between defaulting banks and states (Wallis et al. 2004). As long as lending boomed, land values rose, making banks even more willing to lend against this security. But inevitably some event would eventually cast doubt on the valuation.[7] As land prices adjusted to more pessimistic expectations, mortgage credit came to exceed the value of the underlying security. This put borrowers "under water" (holding negative equity) and led them to default on their mortgages. Their default created difficulties for the banks which needed cash flow to pay interest on their liabilities, the state-issued bonds. When the bondholders approached the state government, they were told that the bonds were secured by mortgages that had defaulted or seriously depreciated. Obviously, states could have reassumed these debts or acted as lenders of last resort, which Alabama did (Wallis et al. 2004: 16). But sovereign credit was itself dependent on revenue from property taxes which collapsed with the fall in land prices and defaults on mortgages (Wallis et al. 2004: table 7). Issuing new public debt was not possible at a reasonable yield. Four out of the five Southwestern states chose to repudiate the state debt by letting the land banks fail.[8]

Another type of feedback loop could be observed in the simultaneous experiment of free banking. A front runner was again the state of New York. Free banking was the polar opposite of diversifying risks through central pooling, as favored by Hamilton. The immediate political motivation of the free banking movement and the Free Banking Act of 1838 was a conservative-libertarian backlash against state chartering of banks: government control at any level was resented (Moss and Brennan 2001: 151, 155–60). The Act allowed banks to enter the market and issue banknotes freely as long as they fulfilled two conditions: every bank had to hold loss-absorbing capital of $100,000 and had to cover its note issue with high-grade bonds or low-risk mortgages to be held with the state's comptroller. The high-grade bonds could initially be federal or any state bond but the list of eligible reserve assets was later narrowed down, disqualifying the bonds of other states. This was the opposite of spreading risk, since note-issuing banks and their customers in the state were susceptible to similar risks. Free banking was probably meant to be a risk-reduction strategy imposed by regulation (Moss and Brennan 2001: 156). Yet free banking shifted risk onto the note holders. If the bonds backing the note issue became dubious, the banknotes lost in value and traded at a discount: "there were effectively state currencies—all called dollars, but trading at different values depending upon how much faith people had in the

[7] In 1840, the shock arose from credit tightening by the Bank of England, that led to a tightening of monetary conditions in the US (English 1996: 263).

[8] Two states (Arkansas and Louisiana) later repaid most of their debt, presumably in order to resume access to international credit markets at low cost. However, Florida and Mississippi never repaid and got access as well (English 1996: 263–5).

backing of the banknotes issued by the state's banks" (Frieden 2015b: n.p.). Free banking dissolved the monetary union and shifted risks onto those least able to bear them.[9]

The reserve requirement greatly restricted the elasticity of credit supply: "a little like trying to eliminate automobile accidents by reducing the speed limit to zero," in the apt analogy of Moss (2002: 91). The free banks invented a new financial instrument to get around the credit constraint: their innovation was checks to be drawn on deposits. Checks economized on the use of banknotes, which allowed banks to expand their lending. Bank deposits soared relative to the controlled stock of notes and specie.

Furthermore, the 100 percent reserve on banknotes could not prevent a devastating feedback if notes were not accepted as a means of payment. When a bank panic started in 1857 because a large life insurance company could not honor its obligations towards New York banks, several of them were unable to redeem the banknotes in specie. Their attempt to sell the high-grade bonds did not help either. The specie price of bonds was bound to fall when everybody rushed to liquidate bonds in order to get specie (Moss and Brennan 2001: 157). The value of the reserve then dropped below 100 percent. The fall in bond prices made it less likely that the states could bail out a bank without jeopardizing their own viability, which in turn exacerbated the run on banks. A number of free banks and three safety funds failed, creating a nationwide panic in the process (Moss and Brennan 2001: 160).

What the conservative backers of free banking had not appreciated was that such a self-fulfilling panic through "fire sales" can only be stopped by spreading the risk over a larger pool. This requires centralization, either by backing banknote issues with federal bonds (provided the federation can withstand the troubles of individual states), or by creating a central bank that can act as market maker with a non-profit motive and deep pockets, buying the bonds (or more generally the reserve asset) and thus stabilizing their price in legal tender. Neither happened. Instead, eleven states wrote debt restrictions into their constitutions which became the norm of balanced budget rules for all states (Wallis et al. 2004: 27; Kelemen and Teo 2014: fn 1). These rules amount to a no-bailout clause for the financial system and it is hardly surprising that the US economy experienced many more bank panics subsequently.

4.2.3 *Panicking towards the New Deal*

In 1861, the US political union broke up over the political-economic question of slavery. Seven Southern states responded to the election of the abolitionist

[9] Chapter 8 can explain why: there was no payments system based on irredeemable banknotes (fiat money) to assure the unity of the monetary union.

President Lincoln by seceding, with four more joining the Confederacy soon afterwards. The Northern states and the President refused to acknowledge a secession that was in contempt of a democratic election. The ensuing civil war lasted until 1865. It was the defining conflict of US history since it concerned two existential questions, which the Princeton historian James McPherson succinctly summarizes:

> whether the United States was to be a dissolvable confederation of sovereign states or an indivisible nation with a sovereign national government; and whether this nation, born of a declaration that all men were created with an equal right to liberty, would continue to exist as the largest slaveholding country in the world.
> (Macpherson 2014)

The first of these questions still resonates in Europe, given the possibility of Greece's exit from the monetary union. The modern guise of the second question concerns the compatibility between national democracy in member states and membership obligations enshrined in an international treaty such as the EU's or the federal Constitution.

It was during wartime that the core of a monetary and banking union was re-created. The core was the National Banking Act of 1863 (Bordo and Wheelock 2011: 5; McNamara 2003: 13), legislated by Congress without the representatives from the secessionist states. Its main purpose was the creation of a system of nationwide operating banks, parallel to the state banks. The Act installed an independent treasury as the sole issuer of national banknotes. As part of the Treasury, the Office of the Comptroller of the Currency was founded, both to supervise federally chartered (national) banks and "to replace the circulation of state notes with a single national currency" (Jickling and Murphy 2010: 15). National banks could issue notes only if these were fully backed by federal government securities; if banks were unable to redeem their notes into legal tender, these bonds would be sold and their proceeds used to acquire dollars. Not only did this "backing" create a larger and more diversified risk pool, the Treasury also guaranteed the notes in full, irrespective of the value of the bonds backing them. The note issues of state banks without a national charter, by contrast, were taxed at a prohibitive rate and fell out of use (FDIC 1998: 10–12).

The US dollar area began as a Northern monetary union; the national currency was imposed by the victors on the rest of the country when the war was won. In 1869, this was challenged in the Supreme Court, which initially declared the measure unconstitutional but soon reversed itself (with the aid of the appointment of two new justices) and affirmed "that the federal government was empowered to make a paper fiduciary currency a legal tender" (Hall and Sargent 2014: 149). The divisive political symbolism of the common currency and the underlying economic conflict resurfaced when, after bitter discussions, the United States rejoined the gold standard in 1879, restoring convertibility into gold at the pre-Civil War parity (Broz 1997: 60–1). The hope was that this would ensure price and exchange rate stability. Yet the regime change gave rise to a "free silver" movement campaigning for a bimetallic standard so as to ease credit conditions and counter the deflationary tendency imposed by the gold standard (Frieden 2015a: 68–77). Once again, this pitched the mainly agrarian states in the South against the more urbanized and industrialized states of the Northeast. Fights over the monetary regime "were the defining feature of national politics from the 1870s to 1896" (Broz 1997: 61; Frieden 2015b: 49–50). This ended in 1896 when William Bryant, the leader of the movement supporting a bimetallic standard, was defeated in the presidential election.

Periodic financial havoc eventually eroded the opposition to a central bank. Between the end of the Civil War and the beginning of the Great Depression in 1929, the US experienced a national banking crisis in 1873, 1884, 1890, 1893, 1907, and 1914.[10] The economic damage caused by the 1893 and the 1907 panics each amounted to an estimated 10 percent of real per capita income (Broz 1997: 166). The President and Congress remained lukewarm regarding the proposal of a Third Bank of the US, but a group of New York bankers set up a commission to advance the proposal, against opposition from bankers in Chicago, and managed to get a sympathetic hearing in relevant parliamentary committees (Bordo and Wheelock 2011: 8–13; Broz 1997: 140–59).

The main interest of these bankers was the internationalization of the US dollar. To compete with financial centers in Europe, they needed a money market with internationally acceptable instruments of trade finance, denominated in dollars, but also a deeper and more liquid domestic money market. A currency afflicted by permanent domestic banking panics would not be internationally acceptable and so a central bank was needed as market maker. The commercial interests of banks and export sectors became the decisive driver behind the introduction of a central bank with an effective monetary transmission mechanism, the discount window.[11] Developing a market for discountable money market instruments made the asset side of banks' balance sheets liquid: their investments could be recycled into further lending by using them as security for getting high-powered money from the central bank. The discount window also gave the central bank a channel through which it could affect domestic credit conditions and the exchange

[10] I am grateful to Andrew Walter (University of Melbourne) for making his database on US banking crises available to me. See also Chwieroth and Walter (2013).

[11] Cf Broz (1997: 36–43, 137–52) for a superb political economy analysis of the importance of the discount market and the role of a central bank in developing this market.

rate. This allowed two major sources of instability that afflicted the US economy to be contained: the strong seasonal fluctuations of domestic interest rates, and the drain on national funding whenever the Bank of England raised interest rates to prevent gold flows. The selective incentives of New York banks had initiated the provision of a public good. The Federal Reserve Bank came into existence in 1913, owing its name to the animosities that the term "central bank" or "the Third Bank of the United States" would have aroused among devolutionists.

The newly established Fed was not yet operational when the panic of 1914 started; this was quelled by the Treasury. There were no provisions for how the Fed should respond to a banking panic and act as a lender of last resort, apparently because legislators believed that they had created a safe banking system (Bordo and Wheelock 2011: 15). Its resources were also enhanced: there was finally an income tax to raise revenue, twenty years after the legislation for it had been passed. The legislation in 1894 was a triumph for the Progressive movement, which had lobbied the Democratic Party for a redistributive tax to replace tariffs (Steinmo 1993: 69–77). But the law was ruled unconstitutional by the Supreme Court and could come into effect only once the 16th Amendment allowed the federal government to levy direct taxes that were not apportioned among the states (Sbragia 2008: 251). This allowed not only redistribution from rich to poor individuals but also redistribution among states. The first income tax levied a 1 percent tax on incomes above $3,000 and 6 percent on income over $20,000, both catching only a small minority of rich citizens. In the First World War, the top rate rose in quick steps to 77 percent. The war effort justified these extraordinarily progressive rates (Scheve and Stasavage 2016). But overt redistribution also immediately engendered lobbying for exemptions, and the revenue from income taxes remained low. Only towards the later stages of the Second World War did the Roosevelt administration succeed in broadening the tax base and introducing modern income and corporation taxes that were, again, surprisingly progressive if low in volume (Steinmo 1993: 101–2). This laid the foundation for fiscal federalism; until then, "federal funds bulked large... [only... t]o particular states at particular times" (Trescott 1955: 245).

The Fed meanwhile focused on developing the discount market. The dollar rapidly became an internationally accepted currency, a success helped by the First World War which stimulated export markets and increased reliance on national banks (Broz 1998: 254–6). In domestic affairs, the Fed did not commend itself, but confirmed the worst expectations of the devolutionist camp. Between 1921 and 1929, an average of 600 banks failed per year, ten times as many as in the years before (FDIC 1998: 20). Most of them were small rural banks that defaulted together with their clients, farmers, whose businesses were the victims of difficult world market conditions after the war and unusual droughts (E. N. White 2015: 10). The Federal Reserve Board remained complacent, attributing the failure of these provincial banks to bad management even as bank runs spread. When the Great Depression finally erupted in systemic financial collapse, it notoriously failed to provide the liquidity that domestic banks desperately needed (Friedman and Schwartz 1963: 357–9).

There were various attempts to compensate for the Federal Reserve Board's inaction in the Depression. A textbook asymmetric output shock had hit the Southern agrarian economy. The immediate problem was not unemployment but farmers' insolvency, which threatened the regional banking system. The Federal Reserve Board in Washington, DC, following the policy paradigm of the day that suited its own political agenda, wanted to inflict deflation on the US economy so as to lower the price level and to demonstrate independence from the Treasury after the First World War (E. N. White 2015: 8, 15). This threatened the collapse of the regional economy in the South and the member banks of the Federal Reserve Bank of Atlanta. The Atlanta Fed used its limited policymaking powers and acted as lender of last resort to regional banks.[12] Faced with criticism and reluctance by other Federal Reserve Banks to lend their excess gold reserves, the governor reminded them that the collapse of the Atlanta District would ripple through the system and affect them all (E. N. White 2015: 23–4). The Cleveland Fed came reluctantly to the rescue after it realized that its district would lose one of its biggest markets for manufactured farm machinery; furthermore, the claims of dealers who had sold these products to farmers on credit would be written down (E. N. White 2015: 23–4).[13] Pressure from Congress helped and the Atlanta Fed was later exonerated by the Federal Reserve Board in DC.

There were other private initiatives to support the banks. The National Credit Corporation tried to step into the breach. It failed within weeks, but its appeal for federal assistance succeeded and a federal program, the Reconstruction Finance Corporation (RFC), provided about $900 million in loans to 4,000 banks in the first year of its operation (1932). But Congress forced the RFC to publish the names of the banks benefiting from its loan program at which point no bank wanted to seek assistance any more, for fear of the stigma of being seen in need of support (FDIC 1998: 22). Not for the last time did legislators fear voters' outrage about costly bank bailouts. They become

[12] Before the New Deal reforms, the twelve district banks of the Federal Reserve System were "semi-autonomous" in the conduct of monetary policy: they were responsible for holding gold reserves and supervising their member banks. They could set discount rates, subject to the approval of the board in Washington, DC (Bordo and Wheelock 2011; E. N. White 2015: 3, 12). Each Fed is owned by its member banks.

[13] The Sixth Federal Reserve District of Atlanta comprises Alabama, Florida, Georgia, and portions of Louisiana, Mississippi, and Tennessee; the Fourth District of Cleveland serves Ohio, western Pennsylvania, the northern panhandle of West Virginia, and eastern Kentucky.

conspicuously concerned about moral hazard, with the flip side that the externality of individual bank failure could do its disastrous work.

The Fed became a policymaking authority for the domestic economy only once the New Deal legislation created the Federal Reserve Open Market Committee (FOMC) in 1935. This placed open-market operations, that is the buying and selling of short-term government bonds for monetary policy purposes, under the authority of the Federal Reserve. President Roosevelt also recalled all gold and silver certificates, effectively abolishing the metallic standard. This allowed the Fed to operate a much more elastic credit policy; in fact, the Fed's obligation to buy Treasury bonds at an administered low interest rate created an inflationary potential that was only removed with the Treasury-Fed Accord in 1951, which affirmed the Fed's authority to pursue macroeconomic stability through monetary policy.[14]

A final innovation of the New Deal was deposit insurance, which also gave prudential supervision some bite. State insurance for deposits had already been introduced in eight, mostly agrarian, states between 1908 and 1920 (FDIC 1998: 12–17). But these state insurance schemes had all ceased to exist by 1930, unable to cope with the severity of the economic downturn in their states. As the Great Depression unfolded, more and more states declared bank moratoria. A temporary federal deposit guarantee allowed banks to reopen. But rumors that the newly elected Roosevelt administration would devalue the US dollar led to capital flight into foreign currency and gold. The conversion of dollars into gold was a particular drain on the Federal Reserve Bank of New York. In order to protect itself from this drain, the Reserve Bank of Chicago at one point refused to rediscount checks from New York at par (Eichengreen et al. 2014: 14–15; ch.9). A federal bank holiday declared by President Roosevelt prevented this from happening, thus preserving the monetary union. Nonetheless, by March 1933, the banking union had ceased to exist: "Visitors arriving in Washington to attend the presidential inauguration found notices in their hotel rooms that checks drawn on out-of-town banks would not be honored" (FDIC 1998: 23).

Congressional proposals for federal insurance, numbering about 150 since the late 1880s, finally became acceptable. In 1935, the FDIC was founded as part of the Glass-Steagall Act, best known for its separation of investment and commercial deposit-taking banking. The Roosevelt administration opposed the FDIC initially (FDIC 1998: 17, 25–7). Its capital was initially provided by the Treasury and the twelve district banks of the Federal Reserve System, but

[14] The precise wording, quoted in the history section of the Fed's website (<http://www.federalreservehistory.org/Events/DetailView/30>), is that the Treasury and the Fed "reached full accord with respect to debt management and monetary policies to be pursued in furthering their common purpose and to assure the successful financing of the government's requirements and, at the same time, to minimize monetization of the public debt."

over time the banks' contributions were to finance the insurance of their deposits. Banks with more than $1 million in deposits had to join the Federal Reserve System, a mandatory social insurance feature opposed by state-chartered banks (FDIC 1998: 36–7). Full insurance was provided for deposits of up to $2,500, paid for by a contribution charged as a flat-rate fraction of total deposits. This fee structure shifted the relative financing burden onto larger banks compared to earlier proposals that would have given discounts for the self-insurance potential of large deposit banks. The provision of deposit insurance was the pretext for doing a solvency check on each participating bank: a good number were recapitalized through the RFC.

From then on, the FDIC had resolution authority and also exerted continuous supervision. This competence was shared with state authorities and other federal authorities (Jickling and Murphy 2010: 15–18). The Office of the Comptroller of the Currency was responsible for supervising national banks, the Federal Reserve for bank-holding companies and state-chartered banks that were members of the Federal Reserve System, the Federal Savings and Loan Insurance Corporation supervised thrifts, and the National Credit Union Administration looked after credit unions as part of the Farm Credit Administration. The FDIC came to supervise most federally and state-chartered banks, however, because it insured their deposits. The fragmentation of banking supervision and the overlap of jurisdictions remained permanent features. This overlap did not create a system of double control by state and federal authorities; instead, it allowed banks to engage in regulatory forum shopping, with regulators competing for fee-paying regulatees (Provost 2010). This contributed to the accumulation of risks leading up to the financial crisis.

4.2.4 *The Fiscal Underpinning of the Great Society*

The Depression era was notable as much for the development of fiscal policy as for the monetary innovations outlined above. Both fiscal and monetary instruments played their part in the stability of the first three decades of the post-war years, when a national system of economic management became more fully developed (Skocpol 1995: 14–15; Steinmo 1993: 22–6). Social security and unemployment insurance, both introduced in 1936, are systems of insurance that contribute to security for individuals and macroeconomic stability. The post-war years saw the addition of a number of other programs, including the extension of social security to cover disability and the addition of a supplementary non-contributory scheme. Food stamps, pioneered late in the Depression, were revived and the building of the "Great Society" brought means-tested health-care benefits and other innovations as part of the War on Poverty. However, it is important not to overestimate the extent of fiscal union in the US. Post-war federalism thwarted efforts to develop a federal welfare state that could complement monetary policies in stabilizing the macroeconomy. Notably "[u]nemployment benefits and taxation became quite uneven across the states, and it remained difficult to pool risks of economic downturns on a national basis or to coordinate unemployment benefits with Keynesian demand management" (Skocpol 1995: 13; Weir and Skocpol 1985: 132–48).

The entry point for states' deconstruction of federal efforts was the financing side of the Great Society. Introducing a properly financed social security plan was the one big victory for the New Deal under Roosevelt. At the time, social security was heavily criticized for being financed by "regressive" contributions, more precisely a proportional payroll tax on employees and employers. But Roosevelt explained to one of his critics from the left why an insurance scheme was politically more robust: "We put those payroll contributions there so as to give the contributors a legal, moral, and political right to collect their pensions... With those taxes in there, no damn politician can ever scrap my social security program" (quoted in Steinmo 1993: 99) A contributory scheme projected the norm of insurance based on merit rather than the norm of redistribution based on need. Insurance contributions supported the only generous national social policy: pensions. Successive reforms made the program quite redistributive: benefits are not proportional to contributions and the supplemental scheme extends coverage to non-contributors (Piketty and Saez 2007: 9). By contrast, redistributive income taxes led to "loophole madness" (Steinmo 1993: 142, 166; Piketty and Saez 2007: 11–13) that kept the overall tax-raising capacity of the federal state at bay.[15] Unemployment insurance also came to suffer from fiscal competition. States wanted to retain a say in benefits for able-bodied adults of working age, and their demands were supported by reformers who wanted states to set the terms in these programs so as to keep costs low (Skocpol 1995: 217–24).

The minimalist welfare state of the US has often been explained by an anti-state and anti-welfare ideology. But the painstaking work of Theda Skocpol (1992) suggests that collective action problems in a federal state provide a better explanation. By 1910, states and municipalities supported an inclusive public education system and all three levels of government—local, state, and federal—supported generous benefits to the veterans of the Unionist army as well as their widows and children. The United States was "by contemporary international standards, a precocious social spending state!" (Skocpol 1995: 12). This revealed demand for social safety nets contradicts the ideological

[15] State and local taxes are regressive or proportional, depending on whether one assumes that the incidence of property taxes is on owners or renters. A third of all US tax revenue is raised at the local and state level. Of these non-federal taxes, about 25 percent comes from (progressive) individual and corporate income taxes; 30 percent from property taxes, and about 35 percent from (regressive) sales and excise taxes (Piketty and Saez 2007: 10).

explanation. But when it came to financing safety nets, democratic representation in the US electoral system was biased against risk pooling at the federal level. "The reality of American federalism is that US representatives fundamentally represent local constituencies, even while they are members of the national legislature. As a result, local and state governments have a national voice that is quite unavailable in more centralized countries like Britain and Sweden" (Steinmo 1993: 97). According to Sven Steinmo, two institutional features restrained taxation even in emergencies. First, the electoral system makes members of Congress more concerned about visible benefits for their local constituencies, at the cost of a consistent policy stance of the party. Second, the sub-committee system in Congress gives the legislature disproportionate power of initiative vis-à-vis the executive, giving every member of Congress a platform for tinkering with the tax code. Thus, taxes were apparently redistributive, supposedly paid disproportionately by a well-off minority, but this minority managed to lobby the members of sub-committees for exemptions.

4.2.5 *Deregulation and the Return of Financial Instability*

The dismal fiscal situation was one contributing factor behind the demise of the "Golden Age" of growth and welfare state expansion in the US. High public debt and monetary accommodation were the domestic sources of the dollar's declining international status. The change in the monetary regime after 1971 and the Fed's shift to money supply control in 1979 (the "Volcker shock") led to increased exchange rate and interest rate volatility. Interest rates on government bonds rose to double-digit levels.

This created a major problem for the savings and loan (S&L) institutions, or "thrifts." They originated in mutual saving associations for homeownership in the early nineteenth century and were therefore politically cherished retail banks. Their loan business was in residential mortgages, so they were locked into long-term fixed-rate assets. Because they were not allowed to pay market interest rates on deposits, they lost more and more savers when interest rates rose. Only low-income households with no access to other savings vehicles stayed with the thrifts, their small savings being eroded by inflation with no interest compensation. Ironically, this regressive effect motivated the first legislation to liberalize financial markets, the Depository Institutions Deregulation and Monetary Control Act of 1980, passed under Democratic President Carter. The restrictions on interest rates on household deposits were phased out and the distinction between savings institutions removed so that they could all enter the same markets for financial products. To make up for the losses they had already incurred, rendering many thrifts insolvent, capital requirements were lowered and they were allowed to enter riskier market segments with the Depository Institutions Act (Garn-St. Germain) of 1982 under the Reagan administration (Robinson 2013). Regulators and legislators had an incentive to exercise forbearance because the federal deposit insurance fund for S&Ls was de facto insolvent and many S&Ls had no access to the Federal Reserve System as the lender of last resort.

Regional recessions were the straw that broke the camel's back: the geographic concentration of investments and lending made the risk that hit the S&Ls uninsurable at the state level (Todd 1994: 9; FDIC 1998: 49). Real-estate prices, especially in Texas, fell massively and left mortgage borrowers insolvent. Many S&Ls were wiped out because the low value of the houses and condominiums did not even make it worthwhile to incur the transactions costs of marketing them for sale in severely depressed regions. The Financial Institutions Reform, Recovery and Enforcement Act of 1989 finally acknowledged the problem. A bad bank cum resolution fund restructured the sector, the insolvent deposit insurance fund for the sector was closed down, and federal insurance was from then on provided by the FDIC (FDIC 1998: 51–3).

Devastating as the S&L crisis was, a feedback loop from the S&L debacle onto state budgets was prevented. Since the 1950s, many states had sponsored the opening of private deposit insurance funds. Many failed in state-specific crises: first in Mississippi in 1976, then in Nebraska and California in 1983, Ohio and Maryland in 1985, Utah and Colorado in 1987, and finally in Rhode Island in 1991 (Todd 1994: 1).[16] Three of the biggest calamities, that could have wrecked the state easily, are compared by Todd (1994: 8–13). One way or another, each state got an indirect federal bailout. Rhode Island received a federal loan guarantee for a bond issue to restructure and recapitalize its S&L sector. The way out for S&Ls in Ohio was short-term liquidity assistance from the Federal Reserve Bank of Cleveland, aided by the governor's declaration of a bank holiday "that required all institutions insured by the failed private fund to close until they were either assured of receiving federal deposit insurance or sold or merged into a federally insured institution" (Todd 1994: 10). In Maryland, the Federal Reserve Bank of Richmond had to step into the breach and provide support to the S&Ls for more than four years. It bought time for the state government to compensate depositors out of the revenue from state-sponsored bond issues (Todd 1994: 12). But Ohio and Maryland relied too openly on offloading their problems unto the federal deposit insurance "without substantial injection of state funds" (Todd 1994: 3), acting in bad faith which Congress punished. Substantial amounts of state funds had to be used to restructure the sector.

[16] The sector's federal deposit insurance fund stopped accepting new claims by early 1989.

Other states were also affected: in Massachusetts, North Carolina, and Pennsylvania, the state deposit insurance funds asked member banks to apply for federal deposit insurance while they acted only as back-up insurers for deposit amounts that did not qualify. Texas experienced the biggest crisis, counting for more than half of all S&L losses. It was rescued in the so-called Southwest Plan, overseen by the FDIC, which guaranteed losses of up to $50 billion (GAO 1990).

Throughout the S&L crisis, the letter of the no-bailout norm for state budgets was honored in that the federal government did not assume state debt directly (Henning and Kessler 2012: 12). But there was still a federal safety net that prevented a feedback loop by assuring bond markets of a backstop should the state default.[17] A price was extracted for this support: state governments had to cut public goods provision and raise taxes.

4.3 The Political Economy of Monetary Solidarity in the US Dollar Area

Federal institution building in the US was not initiated by deliberate risk sharing in money and finance, but banking crisis after banking crisis reminded the authorities of the day that better risk management was needed. The process was not driven by continuous learning but by political contestation, discrediting of failed options and innovation under duress. There is one exception to this description: the first US finance minister, Alexander Hamilton, could be said to have had deliberate risk sharing in mind when he proposed his plans to create a reasonably functional monetary-fiscal banking union by 1790 (Frieden 2015b, Gaspar 2015). Yet his reforms unwound in conflicts of interest between state governments, rivalries among banks, and ideological battles over the concentration of federal power. It took more crises and failed experiments, with rising expectations on the part of electorates regarding the government's handling of crises (Chwieroth and Walter 2013), before a relatively robust federal risk pool was instated.

This risk pooling did not include what Hamilton had considered to be the strongest fiscal bond, namely joint liability for state debt and federal bailing out of states. Instead, it was the FDIC that came to stabilize state-chartered banks by providing a fiscal backstop independent of the budget, thereby interrupting the negative feedback loop from failing regional banks to

[17] As of 1999, the cost of the S&L crisis was estimated to amount to $153 billion, over 80 percent of which was borne by the US taxpayer and the rest by the thrift industry. Assets of about $519 billion were restructured and the number of federally insured thrift institutions halved between 1986 and 1995 (Curry and Shibut 2000: 26, 33).

state budgets.[18] But it took until the late 1980s before this crucial element of risk sharing in the US monetary union came to be firmly established. Fiscal federalism, with a devolved system of revenues and expenditures, contributed and still contributes little to financial stability. The federal budget is important for compensating the pro-cyclical tendency of state fiscal policies, a tendency induced by balanced budget rules, proudly enforced by state parliaments. In every crisis since the Great Depression, US states free rode on the stabilization efforts of Washington (Follette et al. 2008; Svec and Kondo 2012). That the federal government plays this critical role reflects the way that relations between states have evolved; a monetary system such as the EA which does not have robust political legitimation at the federal or supranational level must rely on a different approach to state-level fiscal policy to close off pro-cyclical tendencies.

There is more to be learned for the EA from other aspects of the political economy of the US monetary union. The eventual creation of monetary and fiscal safety nets has allowed for the creation of a regionally diversified financial system. It has proved possible to achieve monetary and financial stability without an unduly restrictive monetary policy, thereby reconciling the divergent interests of easy credit and strong money states. The boom-and-bust pattern of catch-up growth in regional economies that depended on commodity trade had to be made compatible with the more steady growth pattern of commerce and industry in well-off regions.

The US way to reconcile this diversity is a system of stabilization that combines elasticity of credit creation by the banking system with control of inflation by an operationally independent central bank, along with both fiscal and monetary arrangements to ensure financial stability. The system is a configuration of elements that depend for their effective operation on the functionality of the others. Such a system came about with the New Deal reforms. To see its interdependent stabilizing elements, it is helpful to go back to the analytical distinction of three interfaces as outlined in Chapter 3. These interfaces grasp the fact that risk-sharing channels operating autonomously are not sufficient and can, on the contrary, concentrate and accumulate risks. It shows how the differentiation of commercial banks, central banks, and federal public finances contributes to a system for sharing the risks of macroeconomic and financial instability, while highlighting the collective action problems among the constituent states that made the US federation of risk sharing take about 150 years to emerge.

[18] The FDIC is funded out of deposit insurance fees paid by insured banks and thrifts as well as interest earnings from its US Treasury holdings (FDIC 2014).

4.3.1 *The Interface of Public Finances and Banking*

The US started out with state-chartered banks that issued banknotes, with each state Treasury also acting as a monetary (licensing) authority. Banknotes soon served as the preferred means of payment since the coins issued by the federal Treasury were inconvenient and hoarded as a store of value, so not easy to get hold of. Note-issuing banks held specie and later state government bonds as reserves into which their banknotes had to be converted on demand of any banknote holder. While state sponsorship of banking enlarged states' fiscal capacity enormously and allowed them to play an important developmental role (McNamara 2003: 10), this overlap created a recurrent problem of what we now know as negative feedback ("doom" or "diabolic") loops.

Phasing out the issue of state banknotes after 1863 reduced the risk of credit-fueled bubbles which could ruin public finances and interrupt the payments system, with the negative spillovers onto other states that entailed. The creation of a national banking system (entry 6 in Table 4.1) was instrumental in this respect as it created competition to state banks and, with the heavy-handed help of the Office of the Comptroller of the Currency, crowded out the note issue of state banks. This was a victory of the monetary conservative states of the North and East over credit expansionists in the South and West, and was therefore not a political-institutional equilibrium. Nonetheless, it set in motion the regional diversification of the financial system that made the fate of banks less dependent on economic conditions, including public finances, in any one state.

Another link between public and private finances was state governments' sponsorship of development banks, providing them with start-up capital in the form of state bonds. Real-estate lending backed by bank capital consisting mainly of state bonds was a business model that made for devastating feedback loops. Public investment promoted borrowing on the basis of a security (land) the price of which responded positively to more borrowing. If the price of the security fell for some reason, the process went in reverse and bankrupted the borrower as well as the public purse.

This risk is present whenever banks are heavily invested in the bonds of a (state) government expected to help them in a crisis and are relatively large relative to a government's fiscal capacity, while diversification of the assets that banks hold as capital diminishes the risk. Diversification was an outcome of building a national banking system, including the creation of private insurance arrangements among banks. But the systemic crisis of the New Deal found the private solution wanting. The FDIC, acting both as a guarantor of deposits and as a resolution authority (entry 2 in Table 4.1) provided the answer. Its sustainability requires a federal government bond traded in a

Table 4.1. Evolving channels and interfaces of federal risk sharing in the US

	Monetary policy	Fiscal policy	Supervised financial markets
Fiat money	1 Price stability:	2 Demand stabilization and fiscal backstops:	3 Transmission of monetary policy signals:
	1935 Federal Reserve Open Market Committee	1914 first national income tax	1929 end of commodity standard
	1951 Accord	1935 Social Security Act 1935 FDIC	Creation of discount market, treasuries-focused monetary policy
Public finance	4 Monetary back-up to sovereign	5 Debt sustainability/ employment stabilization:	6 Government debt finance:
	1933/1935 Federal Reserve as lender of last resort		1863 National Banking System with federal government bonds as reserve
	No prohibition of monetary financing	1840s Balanced budget rules at state level 1914 National income tax (automatic stabilizer) at the federal level	
Private finance	7 Liquidity risk management:	8 Solvency risk management:	9 Financial stability:
	1913 Federal Reserve System with predecessors in 1791 and 1816 Unified payments system (ISA) 1863 National Banking Act creates national government bond market	1984–91 FDIC in S&L crisis, acting as deposit insurance and resolution authority	1935/1989 FDIC and prudential supervision of state-chartered banks, back-up for national bank supervision

Source: own elaboration

national sovereign bond market that pools fiscal risks of states. The FDIC holds these Treasury bonds as safe interest-earning assets.

In the S&L crisis of the 1980s to mid-1990s, one could see that federal insurance has a flip side (entry 8 in Table 4.1). It can be exploited by state administrations, to the extent that they can shift risk onto the FDIC. This presents the federal government with a dilemma of government responsiveness (Rodrik and Zeckhauser 1988): accepting the shifting of risks would set a bad example, on the one hand, but the externality causing further bank and state defaults could cripple the entire national economy, on the other. One way out of the dilemma is to give priority to stopping the externality of a feedback loop through lending of last resort to banks and/or the sovereign of the jurisdiction responsible for these banks (entry 4 in Table 4.1), first. Punishing the free riders by making the banks and state governments pay for the risks they took has to wait at this point. But political decision making does not necessarily facilitate this: the response to public outrage can be too tough in the sense of prioritizing costly punishment, or it can be too forgiving once the worst is over. The Fed became a lender of last resort only after it had failed miserably in the early 1930s; Bordo and Wheelock (2011: 27–33) discuss the complex reasons why this may have been the case, among them collective action failure of the various district banks of the Federal Reserve System. The Banking Acts of 1933 and 1935 marked the change, above all centralization of the Federal Reserve System and various extensions of the Fed's ability to lend in a situation of crisis (Bordo and Wheelock 2011: 33–4).

The EA has no counterpart to the FDIC. Its solution, when banks come under pressure, is first and foremost monetary: all banks have access to ECB liquidity. In the US, many state-chartered banks—more than half of all US banks and thrifts—are not members of the Federal Reserve System (FDIC 2014) and thus cannot borrow from the central bank. Lending of last resort by the central bank deals with the immediate problem, but leaves the resolution of failing banks to be funded by fiscally constrained member states.

4.3.2 *The Interface of Banking and Money*

In the early days of the US federation, money was indistinguishable from bank credit. Any liquidity crisis therefore also affected the payments system (entry 7 in Table 4.1). Asymmetric information and the absence of a lender of last resort easily triggered runs on banks when there were rumors about their viability. State authorities were prone to exacerbate each other's financial problems by declining to accept out-of-state banknotes. Under the gold standard, banknotes were supposedly backed by specie, but in a crisis they traded at a discount, further exacerbating the loss of confidence. Unchartered banks were therefore required to back their note issue 100 percent with reserve assets. But this eliminated credit creation by the banking system, and did not even ensure convertibility when reserves consisted mainly of domestic state bonds.

The "solution" pursued by the monetary authorities was to maintain strict quantitative control of money and credit supply, but restraint of credit heightened the tension between the North and East of the country, typically well represented by federal powers, against the poorer and socio-economically more backward Southern and Western states. In any case, ways were found to create credit despite apparently strict rules on money and banking. The adoption of fractional reserve banking allowed the movement from a commodity standard, based on gold, silver, or copper, to "a fiduciary standard, based on paper promises to pay... This allowed for a far more flexible money supply, since the volume of banknotes could now expand and contract with demand, even when the supply of precious metals remained fixed" (Moss 2002: 88–9).

For economies growing fast but also unevenly and in ups and downs, such elasticity was of the essence. The funds that the note issue generated could be lent out as credit, as long as the banknotes circulated. Banks were able to provide liquidity with which people could pay at the same time as they created credit with which the economy could generate more income. In fact, the banknote issue became "backed" by the credit business it generated: should it happen that more clients wanted to redeem notes into specie than the bank held in its vaults, the bank could recall loans and buy specie from other banks with excess reserves. Moss (2002: 89) calls it "a neat trick."

However, given asymmetric information, interbank transactions could easily fail before a national currency and a centralized Federal Reserve System ensured that a dollar issued in New York exchanged 1:1 for a dollar issued in Chicago. In a multi-currency system, state banks holding excess reserves of specie hesitated to sell specie against banknotes from banks that were experiencing high demand for specie from their clients. So banknotes were accepted only at a more or less steep discount. This inflicted a loss of purchasing power on all holders of the bank's note issue. This banknote-specific depreciation fed an entire "detector" business and generated significant transaction costs for the economy: "Discount rates were recorded on a regular basis in newspapers and specialized bank note reporters" (Moss 2002: 90). If the discount was steep enough, note holders were inclined to ask their banks for specie instead. The ensuing run on the bank could amount to the self-fulfilling prophecy that the bank was in trouble. Apart from this financial stability problem, there was also a macroeconomic issue: each bank issued notes with a view to its own demand and reserves but there was little control whether, collectively, banks had issued too many or too few banknotes for price stability, which ultimately depended on the (variable) collective willingness to hold the circulating stock of notes.

The crisis-prone microeconomics of markets was compounded by collective action problems inherent in devolved policymaking. State authorities often panicked as much as market actors. The problems of commitment and information asymmetry of single banks within a state are, if anything, worse between states. If the notes circulating in a state were in difficulty, they were easily declared unacceptable as a means of payment for cross-border transactions. This of course worsened the financial situation of banks and businesses from that state and became self-fulfilling. It was the equivalent of "liquidity ring fencing" by national financial supervisors in the EA (Section 6.2.3).

What the introduction of the Federal Reserve System did first was to differentiate money supply, and thus the payments system, from credit creation (entry 3 in Table 4.1). Central bank money, consisting of cash in circulation and bank reserves held with the monetary authority, was legal tender: nobody could refuse to be paid in the final means of payment. With the creation of a central bank, money still came largely into circulation through member banks drawing down their reserves or borrowing from the central bank against collateral in the discount market that the Fed developed. The discount market established the transmission mechanism by which the central bank could smooth seasonal interest rate fluctuations as well as cyclical pressures.

With a central bank, increased demand for liquidity, equivalent to demand for specie previously, did not force individual banks to recall loans. The relationship between cash that banks provided to their clients and the reserves they held, now with the central bank, could therefore be much more flexible.[19] The Fed thus assumed some of the liquidity risk that banks still carried, which arose when savers wanted to withdraw unexpectedly high amounts of cash from their deposit accounts.

How serious this remaining liquidity risk was for banks then depended on how ready the Fed was to give credit in situations where a member bank had run out of its reserves. From the late 1900s, central bankers adopted the so-called Bagehot rule, according to which central banks should lend freely at a penalty rate against good collateral (Bagehot 1882). The problem with this rule was that a severe downturn in a regional economy may quickly deplete the stock of good collateral as assets deteriorate. Furthermore, a penalty interest rate could accelerate the downturn (Grossman and Rockoff 2015). This problem was heightened in the US as there was a federal system for supplying money to the regional banking systems, so whether banks with liquidity problems should get credit at the discount window and on what terms required a collective decision. Eugene White's discussion of the depression of 1920–1 in agrarian states covered by the Federal Reserve District of Atlanta is a case in point: "The Atlanta minutes reveal that cooperation between Reserve banks was often grudging and hesitant" (E. N. White 2015: 21).

Regional fluctuations are a source of conflict for the central bank in a monetary union, as the single interest rate it establishes can be too high for some regions, too low for others. Alan Walters (1988) saw this as the fatal flaw of European monetary integration but the US example is equally pertinent. It took more than the setting up of a central bank in 1913 to overcome the collective action problem between the monetary authorities of states. Part of the problem was the gold standard: backing by specie reserves created inelasticity of money and credit supply because neither the private sector nor public authorities could generate specie on demand. Roosevelt's introduction of pure

[19] Readers familiar with the textbook concept of the credit multiplier will recognize that this implies rejecting its claim that credit creation of banks is a mechanical response to the injection or withdrawal of money (cash reserves) that makes them expand or contract credit (their earning assets) accordingly. In response to changes in the money supply, banks can vary the rates at which they attract more or less liquidity (Goodhart 1989: 137). It is exactly this elasticity that is the insurance benefit in normal times from the differentiation between money supply and credit production.

fiat money removed one potential source of virulent panic. New Deal reforms also removed the semi-autonomy of district banks and centralized monetary policymaking powers, with the Banking Acts in 1933 and 1935. In other words, the collective action problem was replaced by hierarchy.

The context of these reforms was of course the Great Depression. It revealed how interdependent the US regions had become. State and federal authorities were confronted with the existential question of whether to choose disintegration or centralization (McNamara 2003: 13). While the US under the New Deal was not a nation united to face adversity, there were no strong forces that would have benefited from a dissolution of the federation either. The result was a reasonably functional division of responsibilities: the money supply expanding and contracting with a view to the national business cycle and providing the reference for the elastic generation of credit by banks. This system financed high post-war growth with no major panic until the early 1980s when the end of financial repression unsettled the institutional equilibrium.

4.3.3 *The Interface of Money and Public Finances*

In the rudimentary states of the US, the printing of money was a way to raise public revenue, especially in wartime. This was a time-honored practice in pre-modern states but it also marked a limit of state power. Soldiers had to be forced to join armies if they knew they were paid in debased coins or worthless paper money, which did not exactly boost their morale and loyalty to the cause (Ferguson 1962: 454). Merchants and farmers who had to sell to the ruling class against such debased money were ruined over time, and with them the economy. Where means of force could not be used, as in international trade, the rulers had to pay in specie or foreign exchange they could not tinker with. The Continental dollar was a manifestation of the instrumental use of state money in wartime. But it remained an exception. States in the US federation were barred from the most egregious abuse of monetary power that authoritarian rulers in Old Europe had practiced over centuries.

The chartering of private note-issuing banks was favored as it prevented political opportunism in monetary affairs. But the absence of state money was one reason why the emerging US federation experienced in its short history more financial instability than any comparable economy at the time. Financial instability eased only once the US federation recognized that fiat money issued by a national central bank can enable a growing and heterogeneous economy to diversify its stability risks. If the collective interest in "the paper promise to pay" (Moss 2002: 88) can be institutionalized, it can bind the fiscal authorities to support the monetary system. The art of monetary institution building is to gain fiscal support while constraining governments' opportunities to instrumentalize the power to issue legal tender to solve their own financial problems.

In the US, this institutionalization took the form of a central bank that is "independent within government" (Board 2005: 3). It took some time before this institutionalized division of labor settled in. The process began with the establishment of the FOMC. Over time, the FOMC became the operationally independent policymaking authority in Washington, DC, ensuring that the Fed was no longer merely a clearing house for banks or the discount market maker for internationally active banks (Broz 1998). This implied a change in its policy orientation, away from preventing panics and speculative bubbles towards stabilizing the macroeconomy. The visible outcome of this was that the New York Fed was put into a subsidiary role over time (Hetzel 2013).

Macroeconomic stabilization did not preclude monetary financing of the government. The early decades after the Second World War were characterized by what Sargent and Wallace (1981) called "fiscal dominance." Until the Accord of 1951, the Fed had to buy both short- and long-term government bonds in open-market operations at low interest rates set by the Treasury.[20] This did not allow the FOMC to conduct an anti-inflationary monetary policy. The Accord determined that the Fed would buy only short-term government bonds (so-called Treasury bills) and leave the determination of interest rates for longer bond maturities to bond markets; the yield curve was supposed to act as market discipline on the federal budget policy (Hetzel 2013).[21] But market discipline did not work and the inflationary potential of fiscal dominance materialized; it even unsettled the dollar's international role.

A more assertive Fed policy awaited the political and economic developments of the 1980s. The monetarist policy introduced by Volcker led to much higher and more volatile interest rates. The Fed prioritized macroeconomic stability over financial stability with a policy that led directly to the S&L crisis. Now fiscal resources backed up monetary policy: the Fed did not have to bail out the S&Ls, but could leave the clearing up to state authorities and the FDIC.

Another interface of monetary and fiscal policy remained somewhat dysfunctional. Ideally, fiscal policy should contribute to stabilization, particularly in responding to region-specific shocks. But the minimal welfare state in the US contributed little to stabilization. Social security stabilized pensioner incomes but unemployment insurance was so tightly administered by states

[20] The interest rates set were 0.375 percent for short-term bonds and 2.5 percent for long-term bonds while inflation rates were 17.6 percent in 1946–7 and 21 percent by early 1951 (Romero 2013).

[21] This discipline was undermined by the US dollar's hegemonic position as European central banks shadowed the US inflation rate, with the notable exception of Germany. The ensuing current-account imbalances became a source of instability that unsettled the Bretton Woods regime (James 2012: 343).

that it was of limited value in this regard, while "welfare" (means-tested provision) can do very little for macroeconomic stabilization due to its low level and tight targeting.

4.3.4 *Comparative Political Economy*

The US federation of risk sharing emerged largely as a by-product of fighting financial instability, in a long drawn-out process of institutional experimentation. In contrast to the EA, a complete centralized solution was put forward at the beginning, which the fiscally starved states accepted to get rid of their war debt. But the Hamilton Plan unraveled in less than three decades due to strong ideological reservations against centralized power. Every subsequent attempt at restoring centralized monetary control was thwarted by the deep cleavage between Northeast and Southwest.

In the second half of the nineteenth century, risk pooling and diversification through a national currency and a national banking system addressed some sources of instability but created others by increasing economic interdependence. A case in point was the shock to the agrarian states covered by Federal Reserve District of Atlanta in the recession of 1920–1. It threatened to spill over into the District of Cleveland, with its manufacturing industries exporting to the agrarian economy. The problem became big enough that other Federal Reserve districts could eventually see the case for the Atlanta Fed's actions. The interdependence of creditor and debtor states made them aware of their common interest in stabilization. In the language of collective action theory: selective incentives on both sides made them cooperate and deliver lender-of-last-resort services to the Southern agrarian economy.

This historical example illustrates how such asymmetric shocks were accommodated within a heterogeneous currency union. The case can also be used to illustrate why flexible exchange rates between heterogeneous but interdependent states do not provide an easier solution. Had the badly hit Southern states in the District of Atlanta borrowed from the District of Cleveland in another currency, it is almost certain that currency markets would have forced a depreciation of the Atlanta dollar. This would have increased the Cleveland dollar debt of farmers in Atlanta who were already overstretched by the fall in price for their produce. The choice before the Cleveland Fed would have been the same: assist their colleagues from Atlanta or let the Cleveland District's claims be written off. Both Fed districts actually benefited from being members of a bigger currency area. They could draw on these bigger gold reserves and dollar liquidity should lenders and investors abandon them.

The Great Depression finally softened political resistance against financial and macroeconomic stabilization by the center. The outcome was monetary solidarity in the sense that the system of macrostabilization pooled more and more risk at the federal level after 150 years of experimentation and failure of devolved solutions. But risk sharing was and remains far from complete.

The most notable exception to federal risk pooling is the no-bailout norm for state debt, established in the early 1840s. The federal government refused to assume failing state bonds, after it had done so twice with no lasting signs of gratitude from the states. This norm has proved to be sustainable because the fiscal capacity of the states has been radically curtailed rather than maintained and pooled. Hamilton saw the assumption of state debt by the federal government as the "cement" of political union, but it was not used on the construction site of the US federation.

For decades the exercise of the no-bailout norm came at the price of financial panic, with feedback between bank default and a collapse of state finances. This is the clearest "rhyme" of history between the currency unions of the US and the EA. But, in the absence of an FDIC-like insurance mechanism for state banks, the EA states could not uphold their no-bailout rule. Default on sovereign bonds could have created havoc, given that nobody knew how many other toxic assets and non-performing loans were on banks' balance sheets. The US administration was on the phone when European heads of states negotiated, urging them to bail out Greece for the sake of international financial stability (Barber 2010). And just like their counterparts in the US before them, policymakers in the EA now seek to build a banking union that will maintain financial stability in the absence of a federal government. One of the foremost experts on European financial integration, Nicolas Véron (2015), calls this a "radical" experiment. It certainly is, but so was the creation of the US monetary union.

US monetary and financial history is as much under the spell of *Monnet's curse*—that union will be forged in crisis—as is the history of European monetary integration. It is arguably counter-evidence, not supporting evidence, for the idea that state building will eventually lay to rest fragmentation and factionalism, and lead to political identity and convergence on centralized standards (McNamara 2003: 6–8). Underlying conflicts remain intense. For Alberta Sbragia, an eminent scholar of American federalism and European integration, a "conflict between territorial and functional politics lies at the heart of the politics of federalism in the United States" (Sbragia 2008: 241). She argues that functional politics at the national level now tends to dominate territorial politics only because states and localities have become politically less well represented and neutralize each other through competition. Cooperation on macroeconomic stabilization seems to depend, above all, on the same party being in power at the national and the sub-national level (Rodden and Wibbels 2002: 523), but the political logic of checks and balances often leads voters to prefer different majorities at the two government levels. During the financial crisis of 2007–9, the national government, including the

Fed, was attacked for its overbearing tendencies even though it rescued the economy from its biggest crisis since the Great Depression (Schelkle 2012b; Mabbett and Schelkle 2016b).

The sequencing of financial-fiscal and monetary integration in the US differs from that of the EA. The US system evolved for a long time without a central bank issuing the ultimate means of payment (Helleiner 2003: 136–8). The federal budget came to pool risks of monetary and financial instability in states before the central bank did (Giannini 2011: 138; Moss 2002: 87). But this was not a viable assignment of responsibilities, since fiscal mechanisms work more slowly and are politically more contentious than monetary ones. Federal taxpayers' liability for the mishaps of some member states is immediate and transparent. Once modern central banking and the FDIC were in place, the federal budget could focus on income stabilization.

We should note, however, that fiscal policy in the US is still far from a complete and effective insurance mechanism. The negative effect of states on stabilization is well documented for the US, most recently by Follette et al. (2008) and Svec and Kondo (2012). They find that state and local budgets are "modestly procyclical." Balanced budget rules play a role in forcing state authorities to reduce expenditure in a recession, and they do not resist the temptation to expand in a boom. But since these rules have to be obeyed in most states with respect to budget forecasts, not actual data, sub-national governments have some leeway and can engage in limited counter-cyclical measures without projecting imbalances. Many state governments also have rainy day funds they can run down in bad times and fill up in good times. But neither fiscal technique seems to be used sufficiently to prevent the pro-cyclicality of sub-national budgets.

The widespread adoption of pro-cyclical discretionary measures to balance state budgets can be inferred from the study of Dolls et al. (2010: 31–2). Their estimates for the contribution of states to automatic stabilization in the US suggest that state income taxes could compensate about 5 percent of the 32 percent of an income shock and contribute 4 percent to the 34 percent compensation of an unemployment shock, but these in-built contributions do not materialize because states neutralize them under the pretext of balanced budget rules. The comparable figures for the EA are 38.5 percent of an income shock absorbed on average and 48.5 percent of an unemployment shock. Automatic stabilizing capacities vary enormously between member states, however. Even among Northern and Western European members, unemployment schemes absorb between 25 percent and 60 percent of a shock to employment; this absorption rate goes down to under 10 percent for Estonia, Greece, Italy, and Slovenia (Dolls et al. 2010: 13).

The European system started with much more developed state-level institutions, notably a clear differentiation between money and credit, developed financial regulation and supervision of national banks, and, above all, substantial tax-transfer systems with strong automatic stabilizers (Dolls et al. 2010). With more justification than US states in the nineteenth century, European governments could claim that the maintenance of monetary and financial stability did not require delegation of fiscal authority to the supranational/federal level in a union of diverse member states. This has proved illusory, however.

5

The System of Limited Risk Sharing in the Euro Area

The European monetary union has been portrayed, by one of the leading US scholars, as the less successful part of an unprecedented attempt at policy coordination: "Whatever the outcome of the crisis, the EU will remain without rival the most ambitious and successful example of voluntary international cooperation in world history" (Moravcsik 2012: 64). Another leading French scholar characterized the monetary union as "the last utopia of the 20th century" (Pisani-Ferry 2013: 19) Whether one loathes or admires the EA for this, these statements remind us of the enormity of the euro experiment. But governments of mature democracies, including their central bankers, are not usually guided by utopian visions, suggesting that we need a more prosaic account of why they signed up to monetary union and why they gave the union a particular institutional form.

The first section of this chapter offers an answer in two parts. First, I review the lessons drawn from the crisis of the ERM in 1992–3. Many observers saw this as the end of the monetary integration project, yet it proved to be a forceful driver for further integration. Second, the economic gains from monetary union are discussed. A diverse set of politically sovereign countries wanted to join the currency union for different but compatible reasons: to secure low inflation and low real interest rates. This section argues that the policy architecture of the EA institutionalized monetary solidarity as a by-product of the attempt to achieve these two goals. The final section summarizes why the European monetary union has such an ambiguous relationship to solidarity among its members, and how "the creation of a nonstate money" (Harold James 2012: 390) can be related to political integration.

5.1 Currency Unification against the Odds

Why did a diverse set of EU member states go from a managed exchange rate system to a common currency? The ERM, often referred to more generally as the European Monetary System, allowed countries with their own currencies to go in and out of a target zone of cross-exchange rate stability, as called for by national economic circumstances. But in 1992–3 some countries were forced out of the ERM, while others had to realign, and the boundaries of the target zone were temporarily widened. This was taken by contemporary observers to mean that opportunities for realignment could not be closed off permanently by adopting a single currency, but, reviewing the crisis with the benefit of hindsight, it provides a lens through which one can see the motives for monetary union.[1]

5.1.1 *The Trauma of the 1992–3 Crisis*

The trigger for turbulence in financial markets between September 1992 and August 1993 was the rejection of the Maastricht Treaty in a Danish referendum in June 1992 (Hobolt 2009: 162–76) and a near rejection by French voters soon afterwards, in September. This was taken as a sign of political resistance to restrictions on domestic policy discretion, including the constraint of maintaining a fixed exchange rate. The view of many economists at the time was that, if domestic wage-fixing institutions could not maintain competitiveness, countries should not give up the instrument of exchange rate adjustment.[2] Eichengreen and Wyplosz (1993: 60) summarize this view succinctly: "Exchange rate changes can avert these losses [in competitiveness] by altering many prices at once. This is the daylight savings time argument for exchange rate adjustments."

The break-up of the ERM in 1992 was preceded by five years of complete exchange rate stability. A textbook asymmetric shock hit the system in 1990 with German unification. At first, this provided a welcome demand stimulus for member states that were at the time largely in a recession. But the Bundesbank tried to nip in the bud the inflationary tendencies arising from monetary union with East Germany. The source of inflationary pressure was that the money supply was expanded by the political decision to transfer East German citizens' savings into deutschmarks at a favorable rate that gave these savings high purchasing power (Eichengreen and Wyplosz 1993: 75–9). By 1991, Germany had an investment boom while the rest of the ERM slipped back into recession (Branson 1993: 129). The German central bank called for parity realignment in the ERM that would have allowed it to ease interest rates, while others would have had to raise their interest rates (Deutsche Bundesbank 1991: 66; Eichengreen and Wyplosz 1993: 77–9, 110–13). Open disagreements on who

[1] See Sadeh and Verdun (2009) for a more general overview in light of integration theories.
[2] This view is also the basis of explanations of the euro area crisis by comparative political economists (Hall 2012; Hancké 2013: ch.4; Johnston 2016).

should adjust, Germany with inflation or other member states with devaluation, unsettled market observers further. The other member states might have hoped they could force the Bundesbank into a more expansionary policy, given that under a new ERM accord the central bank of a currency that appreciated was required to intervene in favor of members under depreciation pressures and extend credit to them automatically. The Banque de France actually lowered its short-term interest rate below the German rate in October 1991, hoping the Bundesbank would have to follow; when this did not occur and capital outflows increased, the French central bank had to raise interest rates abruptly (Eichengreen and Wyplosz 1993: 79n). On "Black Wednesday," September, 15, 1992, the British pound and the Italian lira were forced out of the ERM. In August 1993, the band of 2.25 percent around a central rate had to be widened to 15 percent because the French franc came again under severe pressure.

Economists at the time vehemently debated what caused the crisis. The diagnosis mattered enormously for the envisaged currency union, which had entered its first stage with the abolition of capital controls in 1990. Eichengreen and Wyplosz (1993) argued that the crisis was caused by a self-fulfilling speculative attack, Branson (1993) that ERM members' refusal to adjust to the fiscal shock of Germany's unification was to blame, while Dornbusch (1993) thought that accumulated losses of competitiveness vis-à-vis Germany had built up the pressure that then suddenly erupted. The short summary seems to be that different countries had different problems. Italy and to a lesser extent the UK and Spain had experienced real appreciation that made exports too expensive and imports too cheap for current-account balance; but the case was less clear for the others. Moreover, countries outside the ERM, Sweden and Finland in particular, experienced even worse currency, fiscal, and banking crises (Eichengreen and Wyplosz 1993: 64–5, 105–6).

Those who accepted the "daylight saving" argument for exchange rate adjustment had great difficulty understanding why governments would want to give up this instrument. Yet fixed exchange rate policies were widely pursued, even by countries that did not eventually join the EA. The Swedish government wanted to join but dropped the plan for lack of popular support in the late 1980s; it later endorsed a new plan to join the EA by 2006 with the full support of the central bank (Heikensten 2003), but could not carry the public with it in a referendum in 2003. Denmark was also excluded from EA membership as the result of its Maastricht referendum, but it subsequently maintained a firm peg to the central rate and later the euro. The UK was the exception to pegging, but there is little evidence that the floating exchange rate was seen by UK policymakers as beneficial to the real economy. It was far too volatile for this purpose.

One lesson that many European policymakers drew from the ERM crisis was that financial markets were unreliable and unfair judges of economic policies.

Governments had taken resolute steps towards adjustment, which was well under way by the time the attack hit them (Eichengreen and Wyplosz 1993: 69, 81). Italy retained an extremely high interest rate even after it was forced out of the ERM, contradicting speculation that there would be a policy change that would justify the attack ex post (Dornbusch 1993: 133). France had for quite some time better macroeconomic performance indicators—in terms of inflation and budget and current-account balances—than Germany in its post-unification upheaval. Only days before being attacked, the Spanish peseta was at the upper band of the exchange rate target, indicating appreciation pressures (Eichengreen and Wyplosz 1993: 80). But polls about the tight outcome of the French referendum dominated the news, leading exchange rate dealers to anticipate that member states would not be able to sustain policies that maintained the currency grid amidst high and rising unemployment (Eichengreen and Wyplosz 1993: 85–8). Hence the currencies of these member states suspected of incipient policy change were sold in order to realize capital gains when assets denominated in D-Mark or non-ERM currencies appreciated. By doing so, investors inadvertently strengthened the Bundesbank's hand.

To add insult to injury, the origin of the disturbance had been German unification. Germany had just been granted a swift and seamless EU enlargement, increasing its population size by a quarter, only to see the Bundesbank put massive adjustment pressure on cooperative neighbors. Currency markets in conjunction with a relentless central bank made politicians look hopeless and hapless. Even inside Germany, this was a political lose-lose situation: not for the first time, the finance minister seemed to be at the mercy of Bundesbank decisions.[3] The political fall-out was that resentment against Germany's dominance in the EU was openly expressed (Spiegel 1992).

Thus, far from putting governments off the single currency, the ERM crisis of 1992–3 built further political constituencies for it. For French elites in particular, the lesson was not missed: "The central fact of the [ERM] has been this: no single currency had an equal chance of appreciating and depreciating against the DM. Each was soft relative to the DM. That implied a significant bias in the foreign exchange market" (Dornbusch 1993: 132). However hard their policies tried to emulate and even surpass the German stance, foreign exchange markets had taken against the French franc.

The problem arguably ran deeper than the conservatism of German central bankers. The ERM crisis had driven home the point that exchange rate

[3] Moravcsik (1998: 394, 403–4) rightly notes that German chancellors of different ideological leanings had their problems with the Bundesbank's single-minded pursuit of low inflation, especially when this had apparently more costs in terms of sluggish domestic growth than benefits in terms of demand stimulus from buoyant exports ever since the 1980s.

cooperation suffered from a commitment problem that no obligation of symmetric intervention could solve (Eichengreen and Wyplosz 1993: 63, 111). It was simply not credible that the central bank of a strong currency area would support weak currency areas when intervention had to be unlimited in the absence of exchange rate adjustments and without capital controls. If a central bank gave up the right to choose whom to support, it would cease to be the issuer of a strong currency. This did not mean that the Bundesbank had no grasp of the political sensitivities. Throughout, the Bundesbank supported the Danish krona and the French franc, presumably because the upcoming referenda on the Maastricht Treaty showed fragile public support and the Bundesbank did not want to be accused of sabotage (Eichengreen and Wyplosz 1993: 112–13). Neither currency was devalued despite speculation against both. But it must still have been a humiliating experience to depend on the goodwill of a partner institution whose intransigence had made such goodwill necessary in the first place.

The ERM crisis had shown most governments how little monetary sovereignty they had. The alternative was not an effective exchange rate policy but exposure to unpredictable financial shocks and costly adjustment to the German lead. It was hoped that currency unification would solve the collective action problem of commitment to exchange rate cooperation when policy preferences and capacities are diverse. Governments were aware of this diversity. In fact, it motivated them to pursue currency unification against the odds that they would be punished at the ballot box. Germany and the Netherlands had little reason to unify their currencies, as there was little difference in outlook, neither had ever devalued in the ERM and the asymmetry of German leadership was not considered a problem. But even the Netherlands could see economic advantage in generalized monetary stability in Europe compared to the instability of an anchor currency (Maes and Verdun 2005: 339).

5.1.2 *Joining the Risk Pool of a Hard-Currency Area*

The ERM crisis not only demonstrated the political salience of exchange rate changes, but also the political and economic importance of interest rates. In a survey conducted by Eichengreen and Wyplosz (1993: tables 3 and 4), two thirds of exchange rate dealers mentioned high Bundesbank interest rates as the primary reason why they thought there would be a crisis. Furthermore, they recognized that central banks would not support a currency to the hilt if this meant maintaining high interest rates with a detrimental effect on the economy. Not just the level of interest rates but also their volatility presented problems. Both a high level and high volatility of the cost of debt make for shorter maturities which forces economic actors to be more short-termist.

High and volatile interest rates affect the economy through at least four channels that correspond to the sectors—firms, governments, households, financial sector—of an economy (Eichengreen and Wyplosz 1993: 101–7). The importance of these channels differs by country.

There is first the effect on economic activity: interest rates act like a tax on debt-financed investment projects. Even if financed out of retained profits, higher interest rates reduce the number of investment projects that appear profitable. The "interest tax" leaves less to equity investors, which may make them less inclined to innovate. A high interest rate also means that projects must pay off more quickly, so both the quantity and the quality of investment suffers and with it the employment that would be created. The corporate sector in some countries is more interest-sensitive than in others, because of higher debt levels and shorter maturities. Last but not least, higher interest rates leave less income to wage earners out of value added and this has a depressing effect on aggregate demand because wage earners tend to have a higher propensity to spend.

Second, interest rate payments on the outstanding stock of debt are also a major component in public expenditure. For example, Italy had a debt stock of around 100 percent of GDP, so a 1 percent rise in the average nominal yield of government bonds would raise government expenditure by more than 2 percent if the ratio of public expenditure to GDP is below 50 percent. Rising interest payments can push a sovereign into a debt trap where it has to raise debt in order to service the existing stock. This is all the more a risk given the depressing effect of high interest rates on economic activity which makes tax revenue decline. For high-debt countries like Italy and Belgium, this was an imminent threat.

Third, the biggest investment a household typically makes is the acquisition of a home and it is typically financed by a good share of debt. For countries with high rates of home ownership financed by flexible interest debt, a sharp rise in interest rates is a threat to households' well-being. Higher financing costs are a direct call on household income, and can also depress the property market and lead to a fall in house prices. If the loan to value ratio has been high, households may end up with negative equity when interest rates rise. In the late 1990s/early 2000s, variable interest rates for mortgages prevailed in the UK (an extreme case where fixed-rate periods were either non-existent or short), Finland, the Netherlands,[4] Ireland, Greece, Spain, and Portugal. However, Greece and Italy had very low shares of housing loans to households as percentage to GDP (10–12 percent), and in Ireland and Spain the ratio was modest at around 30 percent (ECB 2003: table 5.1).

[4] Mortgages in the Netherlands tend to be fixed rate, but their average duration is only ten years.

Finally, there are potential effects on banking. High interest rates for refinancing credit from the central bank or the money market tend to squeeze banks' margins, especially if the government leans on banks, as it did in France, not to pass on rising refinancing costs fully into lending costs. Banks are likely to become more risk averse because the depressing effect on economic activity and the likely fall in property prices make their non-performing loans go up. Thus the banking sector becomes less stable when interest rates rise. More generally, volatile interest rates make banks very fragile because, typically, they earn more flexible rates on their assets and pay less flexible ones on their liabilities. So a rapid decline in market interest rates, lowering their returns on assets while fixed interest rates on the savings products they offer stay high, depresses their earnings; a rapid rise in interest rates may lead to an outflow of deposits if banks do not pass on higher market rates, which can immediately raise their refinancing costs.

High interest rates thus affect different politically salient constituencies: investing businesses, indebted households, not least the Treasury. This applies to governments of soft- and hard-currency countries alike, although their worries may be a mirror image of each other: default of businesses in the one and non-performing loans of banks in the other. A high average level of interest rates usually goes hand in hand with high volatility that makes finance a tricky, highly speculative business for banks and their customers. Thus, preventing a sustained phase of high nominal and real interest rates was a common concern of all governments. The bet was that they would be more likely to achieve this by committing fully and visibly to the monetary union than by leaving the road to Maastricht, each fending for themselves.

Low inflation and low interest rates in the long run made commitment to a hard currency a viable proposition for very different countries, or more precisely: different constituencies and alliances in member states. Frieden (2002) and, more recently, Walter (2008) have been champions of this disaggregated view of monetary integration, systematically refuting the assumption that member states are unitary actors when they choose exchange rate arrangements. Disaggregation of interests helps to explain how diverse member states find common concerns which form the basis for political agreements. But while sectoral interests provide important support for political initiatives, they do not set the agenda. The sparse research that has looked closely into organized business lobbying for the euro does not provide strong evidence for a pivotal role (Collignon and Schwarzer 2002).

There is a widely held view that governments aspired to become Germany in economic policy terms, trying to emulate its model of low inflation and high export surpluses in the hope of the same success. The most sophisticated and intriguing explanation along those lines is that of Kathleen McNamara (1998: 65–71): she ascribes a crucial role to Germany in that its incarnation of the neoliberal-monetarist paradigm apparently proved to other European countries that the paradigm can produce stability and growth. My interpretation is that governments were fully aware of their hard-wired diversity and made no attempt to socially engineer their political economies in the German image. As already mentioned in Chapter 1, the Delors report acknowledged that "plurality" of nations in the Community would prevail (Committee 1989: para. 17). Nor did governments all fall for monetarism, although they were certainly in search of a workable paradigm that could replace Keynesian pump priming with its inflationary consequences (Hall 1989). There was never a full monetarist take-over in Europe. Monetarist thinking supported entirely flexible exchange rates and required governments to refrain from institutional or discretionary ways of influencing interest rates. It is more in line with the institutional choices we observe that governments saw advantages for stability and prosperity in a monetary arrangement that reduced risk premia and gave the labor market parties no pretext for inflationary price and wage setting.

But were governments fooling themselves as Martin Feldstein (2012) suggested? In the period of preparation to join the monetary union (1992–9), high long-term real interest rates (Figure 5.1) and volatility for the weaker members (Figure 5.2) persisted. One should note, however, that until 1993, in some cases 1995, there was no internationally binding definition of what long-term interest rates are.[5] No clear North–South divide in performance can

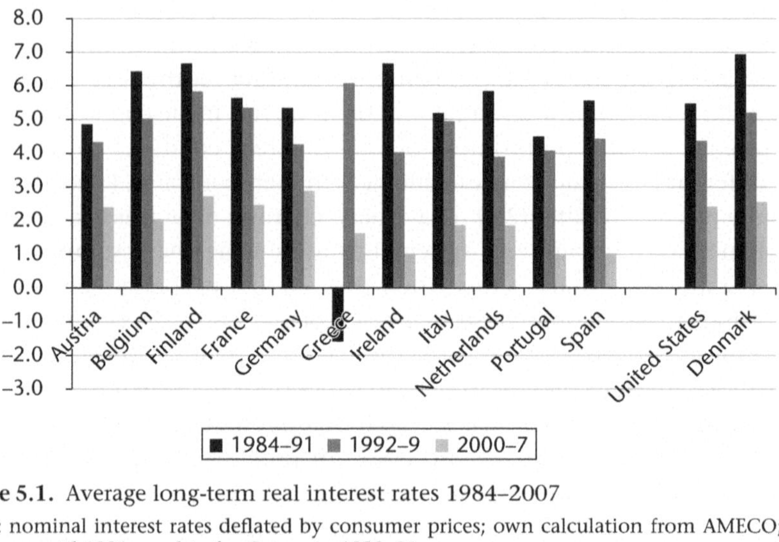

Figure 5.1. Average long-term real interest rates 1984–2007

Source: nominal interest rates deflated by consumer prices; own calculation from AMECO; West Germany until 1991, no data for Greece in 1989–91

[5] In Austria, a government bond of more than one year maturity was long-term. Since 1995, most countries take the central government ten-year bond as the benchmark for long-term rates,

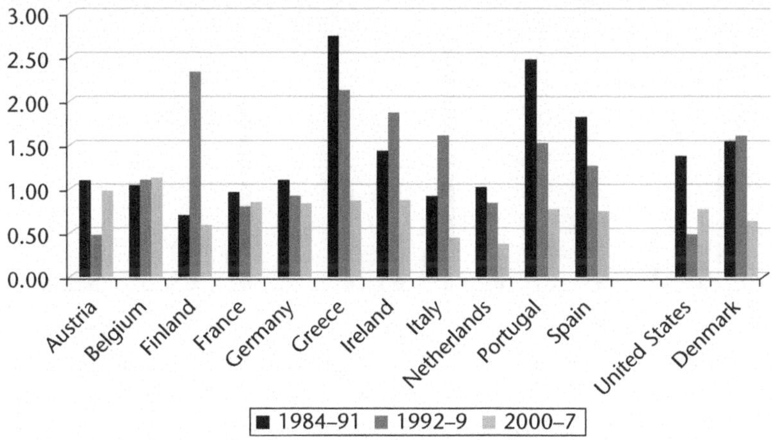

Figure 5.2. Volatility of long-term real interest rates 1984–2007
Source: own calculation from AMECO; West Germany until 1991, no data for Greece in 1989–91

be found during that period. For France and Italy, the Maastricht convergence process brought little impact on interest rate levels and, for Italy, some cost in volatility; only after monetary union did they share in the widespread decline in both. Greece moved from highly volatile, but overall negative, real interest rates towards slightly more stability but at very high positive levels; Spain and Portugal saw some easing of volatility. Interest rates remained high generally: the comparison with Denmark shows that even a highly developed and creditworthy country paid high real interest rates, admittedly because Denmark went through a difficult economic time in the 1980s.[6]

While the payoff on interest rates only materialized with monetary union, post-Maastricht commitments were matched by a strong decline in inflation outturns (Figure 5.3). There was a substantial and sustained change for the four Southern European countries in inflation performance. France is the country the inflation record of which resembles most closely that in non-EA countries shown for reference: the US and Denmark. In the 1990s, French policymakers were apparently engaged in "competitive disinflation" vis-à-vis Germany (Fitoussi et al. 1993: 17–30). After monetary union, cross-national variation in inflation rates was small but of course crucial for real interest rate outturns (Figure 5.4). Exceptionally low German inflation meant high real interest rates there, relative to Southern European countries and Ireland.

but for Greece, interest rates are available only for twelve months Treasury bonds issued by the central government (AMECO 2005: 102).

[6] Data on long-term interest rates for other economies outside the EA, in Central and Eastern Europe, but also Iceland or Turkey, are only available from the early to mid-2000s onwards.

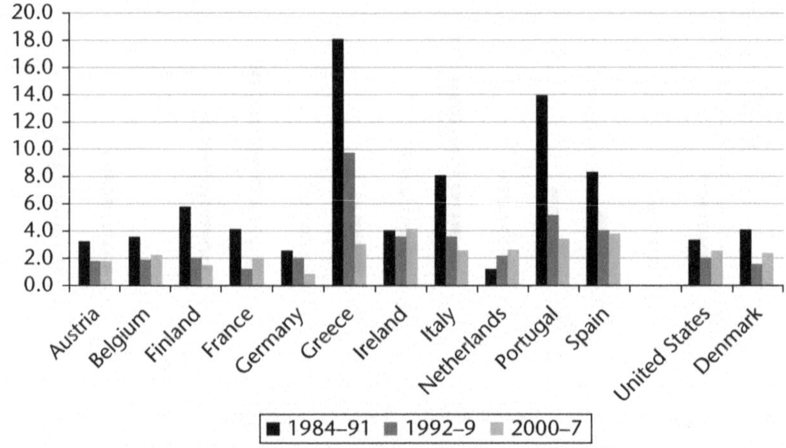

Figure 5.3. Average inflation rates 1984–2007, GDP deflator
Source: own calculation from AMECO; West Germany until 1991, no data for Greece in 1989–91

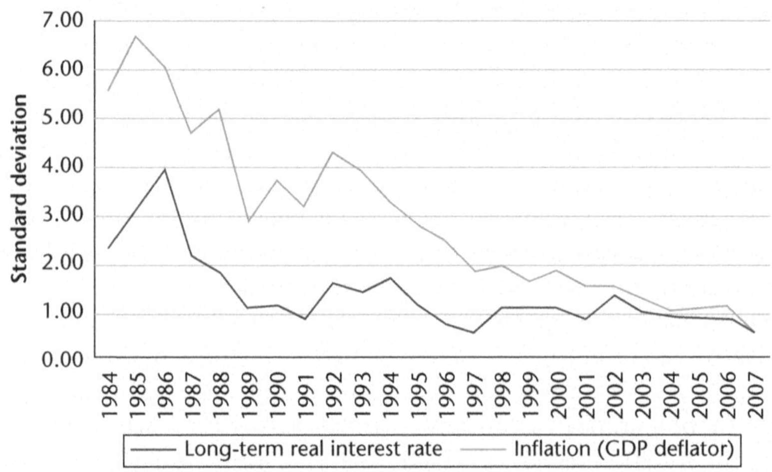

Figure 5.4. Convergence between EA-11 member states, 1984–2007
Source: own calculation from AMECO; West Germany until 1991, no data for Greece in 1989–91

Convergence between the prospective eleven EA members, measured in standard deviations from the mean, was considerably more pronounced for (flow[7]) inflation than for interest rates, as Figure 5.4 shows. Note that nominal interest rate convergence after monetary union means that variation in inflation and variation in real interest rates become equivalent.

[7] "Flow" inflation refers to consumer price inflation or the GDP deflator, by contrast with asset price inflation.

The remaining divergence between real interest rates came from the fact that the former hard-currency members tended to have lower inflation rates still than the former soft-currency members which drove real interest rates in different and unexpected directions. But the pattern is not uniform—Italy and Greece did not have inflation rates that were noticeably higher. It looked as if the two goals of low inflation and more stable low interest rates had been achieved.

5.2 The Interfaces of Money, Banking, and State Budgets

The move towards greater stability was achieved at the cost of some growth (Section 7.1), leading to criticism that the Maastricht process was a straitjacket on very different economies. A number of critics attribute this to the ideological hegemony of neo- or ordoliberalism (Blyth 2013; Schmidt and Thatcher 2013; Schäfer 2016). The emphasis on rule-based policymaking and active promotion of competitive markets is certainly compatible with an ideological interpretation (Amable 2010: 17). Ideas have usually their greatest influence when something new is to be tried out which does not yet have stakeholders, unlike the status quo to be overcome. But ideas can also be used strategically, to further one's interest through principled legitimation. Jabko (2006: 47–9 and *passim*) shows this in detail for the Delors Commission that became a champion of market integration, with market liberalization as the instrumental idea to win over supporters that were not per se interested in the centralization of European powers.

The first section argues that the straitjacket was the outcome of contestation over solutions to collective action problems, which the dominant country, Germany, justified in ideological terms. Subsequently, the EA countries built an extensive regulatory polity devoted to monitoring potential free riding, to managing spillovers, and to supervising commitments. That the practices embedded in this policy architecture were fiscally conservative is undeniable. But as the parties had to govern the commons, they arguably noticed that a neoliberal hands-off approach did not solve their collective action problems. It was, ironically, the supposedly neoliberal camp of member states around Germany (under Conservative administrations) that called for ever more detailed rules.

5.2.1 *The Set-Up of the Euro Area System*

The original architecture of the EA can be described like a building designed by Le Corbusier, a functionalist-modernist vision projected onto buildings and urban design (Pisani-Ferry 2013: 19). It separated the tasks of macroeconomic stabilization and assigned each to particular institutions (Cour-Thimann and Winkler 2013: 5–7). Price stabilization, understood as targeting a low inflation rate, was made the task of a supranational central bank that is singularly independent from governments. Sustainable financing of public goods and built-in counter-cyclical stabilization was assigned to national governments with no recourse to monetary financing or supranational bailout funds. And financial risk regulation and supervision was made the job of national authorities within a common and detailed legal framework that defined rights and responsibilities in home and host countries.

This functionalist assignment was the outcome of a political struggle, not the plan (Dyson and Featherstone 1999: 438–48). The struggle touched on profound constitutional questions. For instance, the ERM had been an agreement between central banks outside the EU framework—so should the policy architecture of the EA be an intergovernmentalist agreement, abandoning the usual Community method of integration? This was what the Dutch Presidency under Wim Kok proposed in autumn 1990. It implied that the adoption of the euro in stage III of the Maastricht process would be voluntary and taken by each government for itself. This was firmly rebuffed by the French administration and the German chancellor, although the German chief negotiator expressed sympathy for Kok's plan. France and Germany insisted on the Community method, whereby member states agreed on binding minimum harmonization that could be exceeded but not undercut at the national level. Decisions about EA membership were to be taken by the Council with unanimity.

There was also quite some controversy as to how the exchange rate regime would be decided. Should there be a managed parity with the US dollar or not, and should this be decided by the central bank autonomously, by the Council, or both together? Article 219 TFEU settles the issue in favor of overlapping competences in the sense that the Council can decide on an exchange rate regime that the ECB then has to implement, unless the central bank can argue that the price stability mandate would be jeopardized. This implies that the ECB could not be ordered to maintain a fixed peg to the US dollar if the Fed tolerates relatively high inflation. This overlap of competences was supported by the German government but opposed by the Bundesbank (Moravcsik 1998: 444–5).

The resulting constitution is marked by this compromise, at times tension, between national prerogatives and supranational regulation. The EA is institutionally intergovernmentalist, with the Council as the ultimate self-regulatory body, while the principles of integration conformed to the Community method. Member states are required to qualify for irreversible membership rather than having a choice, and commonly agreed rules have formal supremacy over national self-determination. However, the commonly agreed rules are often flexible in interpretation, with the Council having the final say.

The two shaded cells in the table represent the Maastricht pillars of monetary and fiscal policy, respectively. Monetary policy is assigned to ensure nominal stability, that is a low average rise in prices denominated in the euro; fiscal policy is supposed to stabilize national public finances for which there were supranational rules. Financial integration and stabilization (entry 9 in Table 5.1) was part of the Single Market Programme, institutionally separate from managing the common currency. The Financial Services Action Plan implemented a massive upward harmonization of regulatory standards, timed to occur alongside monetary union (Quaglia 2008, 2010).

The formal definition of the ECB's independence has been the subject of much discussion because it amounts to a radical innovation. International or supranational money had previously only been issued by hegemonic powers like the British Empire and the United States. But the ECB was divorced from nation state powers in an unprecedented way, to paraphrase Charles Goodhart (1998). Article 130(1) TFEU spells out the essence of the ECB's independence: "[N]either the European Central Bank, nor a national central bank, nor any member of their decision-making bodies shall seek or take instructions

Table 5.1. Channels and interfaces of risk sharing in the original EA

	Monetary policy	Fiscal policy	Supervised financial markets
Fiat money	1 Price stability: Independent central bank targeting goods price and wage inflation Oversight of payments system	2 Demand stabilization and fiscal backstops: (Automatic and discretionary demand stabilization as well as bank restructuring at national level)	3 Transmission of monetary policy signals: Collateral framework of the ECB
Public finance	4 Monetary back-up to sovereigns: Seignorage shared within Eurosystem Strict prohibition of debt monetization/ lender of last resort to sovereigns	5 Debt sustainability/ employment stabilization: Fiscal rules and surveillance leaving capacity for structural reform and national automatic stabilizers	6 Government debt finance: Identical zero risk weighting of government bonds for purposes of regulatory capital calculations (Basel Accord)
Private finance	7 Liquidity risk management: Compensation for lender of last resort to banks within Eurosystem Unified payments system (TARGET2) Discount policy to integrate sovereign bond market	8 Solvency risk management: National deposit guarantee schemes with minimum standards set in EU Directive (Bank resolution at national level)	9 Financial stability: Harmonized prudential regulation (Financial Services Action Plan) (Prudential supervision at national level)

Source: own elaboration; text in brackets denotes policies under national competences

from Union institutions, bodies, offices or agencies, from any government of a Member State or from any other body." Most observers see in this formal decision-making independence the long shadow of the Bundesbank's political influence on the negotiations for the monetary union. But this isolation from political influence was conferred on the European System of Central Banks (ESCB or Eurosystem) by the Delors Committee, to reassure skeptical central bankers throughout Europe, not only in the Bundesbank (Dyson and Featherstone 1999: 606–7).

The original provisions for fiscal policy (entry 5 in Table 5.1) are reminiscent of the first, most minimal, American confederation (Chapter 4). The EU has no direct taxation powers and no member state is obliged to bail out—that is assume or guarantee liabilities of—another member state. Coordination of fiscal policies between EA members must serve to ensure "budgetary discipline" (Article 136(1a) TFEU), based on the principle that all EU member states "shall avoid excessive government deficits" (Article 126(1) TFEU). The latter Article defined an elaborate set of steps and sanctions, for instance that the European Investment Bank may reconsider its lending if a government is a serial offender against the fiscal rules. An Excessive Deficit Procedure is defined in two Regulations and could be opened against all EU members, not just those in the EA. At the end of it, further sanctions could be applied to EA member states only. There is no equivalent to this elaborate system of fiscal surveillance in any fiscal federation. In the US, state legislatures enforce balanced budget rules: the federal government has no say.

However, the incarnation of fiscal discipline, the Stability and Growth Pact (SGP), was actually an afterthought to the negotiations. On the minds of leading experts were current-account imbalances and market instability due to capital flows (James 2012: 12, 196–7). The political negotiations left these issues unaddressed, and instead fastened onto the risks posed by unsustainable fiscal policies. In this narrow vision, instability must be caused by government failure.[8] This political economy diagnosis, advanced by two dominant member states, Germany and the Netherlands, but also by some Treasuries, not least the Italian, underpinned the peculiar macroeconomic institutions of the EA.

The fiscal provisions addressed the supposed moral hazard problem that, because the threats of higher risk premia and currency devaluation had been removed, governments would exploit the common currency by incurring

[8] There was also a preoccupation with wage settlements being incompatible with price stability but there was no policy process attached to it and so it had only the quality of OECD advice. Most importantly, wage developments in the EA overall could not be accused of jeopardizing price stability (Arpaia and Pichelmann 2007: 5–7), although reforms of wage-bargaining systems were justified on grounds of competitiveness.

excessive levels of debt. Fiscal risk sharing could only make this problem worse. In the world view of the German and Dutch hawks, there was no place for fiscal activism to achieve stability. All that was needed was fiscal restraint: this would ensure that the most problematic externalities would be reined in and the commitment to prudent policies enforced. Financial investors could possibly exercise some discipline through risk premia. While the Delors Committee was uncertain about the efficacy of market discipline (James 2012: 17, 248–9), the fiscal surveillance authorities in the Commission did not put much faith in it, especially after Italy's sovereign credit rating improved just as the government was found to run an "excessive" deficit (Buti et al. 2003: 14).

The two main pillars of the original architecture limited risk sharing to the provision of a stable currency, they were not concerned with pooling risks to macroeconomic stability (Schelkle 2005, 2006). These provisions specified fiscal rectitude and monetary soundness. Public debt would be reduced to sustainable levels (60 percent of GDP) and kept there by containing fiscal deficits (to 3 percent), while inflation would not be allowed to rise above 2 percent (the official ECB target).

5.2.2 *Elements of Risk Sharing before 2008*

Even though the original architecture limited risk sharing, it did provide some risk sharing. Official documents, such as the Commission report on the major costs and benefits of the European monetary union (Directorate-General 1990: 26) and the relevant summit conclusions, stressed the gains from currency stability, particularly in boosting growth in the long run. The following discussion shows how the negotiation and reregulation of the EA policy framework established the terms of an ex ante arranged risk pool. It amounted to—and was confined to—insurance against nominal instability. The discussion takes up first the safeguards against adverse selection and moral hazard, before turning to the insurance implicit in features of the ECB's constitution.

CONVERGENCE CRITERIA AGAINST ADVERSE SELECTION

The convergence criteria for EA membership had no foundation in mainstream economic theory (Buiter 2004). But they made sense as safeguards against adverse selection. To this very day, aspiring members must, in addition to meeting the fiscal criteria noted above, comply with provisions on inflation, interest rates, and exchange rates. Their inflation and long-term interest rates must not exceed a maximum margin above the average of the three lowest national rates in the EU (not the EA, and not merely the average), and they must have achieved a stable exchange rate, defined as not devaluing for two years beyond the limit set by the target zone of the ERM. In addition, they must have a national central bank that is independent from the government. All these criteria were meant to guarantee a membership for a low risk pool as regards "stable money."

The immediate motivation for German negotiators, in setting the fiscal conditions in particular, was to raise the bar for the accession of Italy, a big member state that was highly indebted (Dyson and Featherstone 1999: 532–3). The three stages of the Maastricht process meant that member states had to spend about two election periods qualifying for membership. This strengthened the position of technocrats in national administrations. After all, national administrations are not unitary actors. Italian governments have often been deeply divided between modernizers and traditionalists. During the lead up to accession, the Italian legislature abolished supposedly sacrosanct institutions of its political economy like wage indexing ("scala mobile") and the seniority bias in its pension system (Regini and Regalia 2013: 214–15).

It was received with great *Schadenfreude* that the German government struggled to meet the criteria and was itself caught in attempts to manipulate the fiscal indicators. A notorious example was the proposal of finance minister Theo Waigel to revalue Bundesbank gold reserves which were priced at historically low levels, sell the excess reserves and reduce public debt with the proceeds. But Bundesbank protests and Eurostat rulings thwarted this plan (Savage 2005: 123–6). The Bundesbank's case was purely political: the gold reserves were indeed undervalued but the German government would have lost the moral high ground if it were seen to be engaged in such maneuvers. It was obviously also a welcome opportunity for the Bundesbank to demonstrate its independence and presumably its displeasure with the introduction of the euro, to the great embarrassment of a Conservative finance minister.

FISCAL SURVEILLANCE AGAINST MORAL HAZARD

Fiscal surveillance was designed as a commitment technology for national executives (Schelkle 2006, 2007). The no-bailout clause and the SGP (entry 5 of Table 5.1) have always been explicitly justified as precautions against moral hazard which the insurance of a common currency may engender. The no-bailout clause of Article 125(1) TFEU reads:

> The Union ... [or a] Member State shall not be liable for or assume the commitments of central governments, regional, local or other public authorities, other bodies governed by public law, or public undertakings of another Member State, without prejudice to mutual financial guarantees for the joint execution of a specific project.

This is analogous to clauses in private health insurance contracts that exclude the coverage of injuries incurred in dangerous sports. Yet such exemptions from coverage cannot exclude similar injuries incurred in engaging in reasonably safe activities. Hence, the no-bailout clause is preceded by Article 122(2) TFEU:

> Where a Member State is in difficulties or is seriously threatened with severe difficulties caused by natural disasters or exceptional occurrences beyond its control, the Council, on a proposal from the Commission, may grant, under certain conditions, Union financial assistance to the Member State concerned. The President of the Council shall inform the European Parliament of the decision taken.

It was this Article that allowed the Council to help the Greek fiscal authorities in May 2010, based on interpreting the financial crisis of 2008–9 as an exceptional occurrence beyond the Greek government's control.

The fiscal rules were first drafted in 1995 by the German Treasury under the name of a "Stability Pact." This initiative reflected the Bundesbank's de facto veto position at this stage of integration, which had to be accommodated by some assurances (Moravcsik 1998: 304–404). After a major conflict with the French government under Lionel Jospin, "Growth" was added to the name (Dyson and Featherstone 1999: 426; 789–90), although this made hardly any difference in substance.

In its original formulation, key figures, including Germany's finance minister, thought that the fiscal rules could be kept simple to implement. Waigel favored a nominal rather than a cyclically adjusted deficit criterion, insisting that "3% is 3%." But, even in nominal terms, the general government deficit is an extremely complex statistic to calculate (Savage 2005: 62–5; Mabbett and Schelkle 2014: 14–19). The deficit measure of the SGP had not been produced by any member state before it was required by EU fiscal surveillance. It includes the consolidated balances of central, regional, and local governments as well as the balance of social security funds that often have their own financial accounts (so-called "para-fisci"). One cannot find this statistic for the United States.

Early on, the crucial deficit indicator was changed to a cyclically adjusted deficit indicator. This addressed the criticism that otherwise fiscal rules may force member states to pro-cyclical retrenchment. Cyclical adjustment filters out revenues and expenditures that are higher or lower because of the cyclical state of the economy, and calculates the budget balance that will be attained when the economy returns to trend or potential GDP. The cyclically adjusted or "structural" budget balance was seen as a measure for which governments can be held accountable, whereas the nominal measure is affected by economic circumstances beyond their control. A primary fiscal deficit, excluding interest payments, would be an even more meaningful measure of government discretion, as Olivier Blanchard (1990: 6–7, 11–12) argued early on in a study for the OECD. Interest rate payments on public debt accumulated over time are also not under the control of a present administration. Cyclical adjustment, particularly the calculation of trend GDP, is far from a straightforward procedure and different methods can lead to rather different estimates. The Commission has endeavored to monitor structural balances directly, and there has been a proliferation of indicators, notably of "age-related" spending categories and contingent liabilities from pensions (Schelkle 2009: 834). Commission officials at the operational level tended to shift attention from annual outturns and insisted on the importance of the medium-term objective of a cyclically balanced position, providing a justification for the postponement of enforcement action (Mabbett and Schelkle 2016a: 129).

The SGP became an evolving regime of inspections, with the threat of hard sanctions for excessive deficits (above 3 percent of GDP) but also the obligation to ensure a counter-cyclical stance over the cycle (the medium-term objective). The interest of veto players like the Bundesbank, vehemently opposed to the euro, had ironically the effect of giving more impetus to regulatory competences of the EU in fiscal policy. The outcome has been and still is institutionalized collective action on a grand scale (Hallerberg et al. 2009; Schelkle 2009). No such collective action of restraint was ever considered necessary in the Benelux monetary union between Belgium, with a debt-to-GDP ratio of over 100 percent, and Luxembourg, with a ratio of 10 percent that predated the EA (Wildasin 2002: 253). This suited the German administration also for domestic purposes because the alleged fiscal prudence of Germany is a grand myth, perpetuated by scholars who are actually quite critical of ordoliberalism; like most fiscal federations, it has a continuous struggle with hard budget constraints in a system of devolved budgetary policies (Rodden and Wibbels 2002: 501).

The exclusion of Parliament from adjudicating cases of excessive deficits or need for assistance indicates that member state executives intended to treat the Pact as governance of a commons, on which national democracies should feed sustainably. Consistent with Ostrom's monitoring theory, discussed in Chapter 2, the fiscal rules enshrined in the SGP leave it to peers in the Council to decide whether a user of the commons has indeed overexploited the collective good—there are no rules which would force member states to consider the underexploitation of their fiscal room for maneuver. The rules distinguish between bad luck, providing the case for insurance, and negligence, and interpret an "excessive deficit" or rising public debt as prima facie negligence not covered by the insurance of EA membership and thus possibly subject to a fine. The insurance consists in being able to finance an admissible deficit without sending alarming signals to markets or incurring a "risk premium" in the form of a sanction.

Deficits above 3 percent of GDP occurred from the start: Portugal was the first member state ever to break the then applicable fiscal rules in 2001.[9] But, as of mid-2016, no EA member state has ever been sanctioned under the Excessive Deficit Procedure. The dominant interpretation in the literature of why sanctions were never imposed is that every member state government anticipated sitting in the dock one day. They were "turkeys deciding on the menu for Christmas," refusing to police each other. In other words, the enforcement system itself suffers from moral hazard, this time in teams (Holmstrom 1982). It is equally plausible to argue, however, that the externality of overgrazing (debt and deficits defined as excessive) was not obvious to the monitors of the commons. Their incentives therefore favored retaining fiscal flexibility which is different from collusion and moral hazard. The envisaged sanctions made so little sense, imposing a fine on a country in fiscal difficulties only to aggravate these difficulties, that not even the most hard-nosed administrations advocated it when a case came before the Council. Given that this has happened over and over again, the most plausible rational argument is that the fiscal rules were meant to signal to each other that those above 3 percent deficit or 60 percent debt are in breach of a commitment; and while they may not be sanctioned, they cannot hope for leniency if public debt becomes a problem.

CENTRAL BANK INDEPENDENCE AND MUTUAL INSURANCE

The mandate of the ECB ensured that primacy was attached to achieving the collective good of low inflation (entry 1 of Table 5.1). Article 127(1) TFEU states:

> The primary objective of the European System of Central Banks . . . shall be to maintain price stability. Without prejudice to the objective of price stability, the ESCB shall support the general economic policies in the Union with a view to contributing to the achievement of the objectives of the Union.

Stability of employment and the exchange rate are thus subordinate even though they have been major national concerns driving attempts at monetary integration since the 1970s. Subordination of the employment goal was facilitated by a new economic consensus—to which ECB research has contributed significantly—that used the output gap for inflation targeting (Schelkle and Hassel 2013: 17). Too little employment would show up in disinflationary pressures, conversely approaching or exceeding full employment would result in inflation. Inflation targeting was therefore seen as a shorthand for

[9] The Excessive Deficit Procedures against member states are documented on the Commission website, http://ec.europa.eu/economy_finance/economic_governance/sgp/corrective_arm/index_en.htm (accessed October 31, 2015).

macroeconomic stabilization, with all the gains this would bring. But if monetary policy failed to have such beneficial side effects, there was little the central bank could and should do. It then came down to fiscal authorities to engage in reforms such as supply-side labor market policies (which central bankers often advocated).

Many commentators draw attention to the Germanic "ordoliberal" ideology that such a strong form of independence projects.[10] But despite the importance of Germany in the genesis of the European monetary union, the government did not seek institutional hegemony in running the ECB. From the start, the Governing Council was a comparatively egalitarian institution, at least against the benchmark of the US, where the president of the New York Fed has permanent representation on the Federal Open Market Committee while all other presidents of district Feds rotate. In the Governing Council of the ECB, there is no weighting of votes; the same formal voting power applies to Germany (representing almost 17 percent of the ECB's capital) and Malta (with 0.06 percent). As of January 2015, when Lithuania became the nineteenth member, the ECB could no longer postpone the introduction of the rotation system that the Treaty envisaged. The five biggest members (Germany, France, Italy, Spain, and the Netherlands) which hold together 57 percent of the ECB's capital have to take turns to abstain every five months; the remaining fourteen members representing 13 percent of the ECB's capital have eleven votes and must therefore abstain periodically for three months (ECB 2015a).[11] A simulation exercise with slightly different parameters by Bénassy-Quéré and Turkisch (2009) suggests that rotation makes little difference compared with monetary policy decisions taken by a unitary board or a system without rotation. In any case, the rotation system does not affect the constitutive principle of "one member, one vote" in the ECB's Governing Board, as the Council Decision (2003/223/EC: Preamble para (4)) establishing the system emphasized.

These governance principles are pertinent for an institution of mutual insurance. It is self-governed by a membership that consists of equals, deemed to ensure loyalty and ownership by each and all. Obviously, the voices of the German and French governors will be noted and publicly reported differently from those of the Maltese or Cypriot governors. But the contestation over extraordinary measures has also shown that the German Bundesbank can be outvoted (interview 2015). Officials representing the Bundesbank position, Axel Weber and Jürgen Stark, stepped down in protest against these measures

[10] Notably Blyth (2013: 13–14). Dullien and Guérot (2012) and Jacoby (2015) contain an update and outline very different ideological positions represented in Germany. See also Hien (2013) for a historically grounded account of the religious politics in post-war Germany in which ordoliberalism was on the Protestant side against a strong Catholic tradition of corporatism.

[11] The remainder, 30 percent of the capital, is subscribed by non-euro countries like the UK.

(Chapter 6) without doing any lasting damage to the reputation of the ECB as a competent policymaker. Jürgen Stark was officially the chief economist of the ECB but since he was not a particularly qualified economist, it was always clear to observers that he got his assignment to lend a hawkish appearance to the young institution. His resignation was meant to be a "wake-up call" but turned out to be the final curtain on a display of ordoliberalism. His doctrinaire and partisan voice was incompatible with the independence that the same doctrinaire voices had requested in return for the egalitarian set-up of a mutual institution.

The by-product theory of collective action can explain Germany's consent to a common central bank that gave the Bundesbank no privileged status, despite early attempts to establish it informally. Hierarchy, or in international relations, hegemony, can resolve collective action problems between states (Kindleberger 1973). But the country enjoying the privilege of shaping a hegemonic system in its image also comes under pressure to fulfil heavier obligations than those it dominates. This means in turn that if the hegemon is unwilling or incapable of bearing these obligations, it has a strong selective incentive to push for an egalitarian institution and promote cooperation (Eichengreen 1987). By restraining itself to equality among partners, a dominant government can refuse to bear a disproportionate burden. It can insist that all costs are shared proportionately. This was the essence of the German approach to crisis management.

COLLATERALIZED ECB LENDING AS SOCIAL INSURANCE

Lending against collateral is a universal central bank practice (Cheun et al. 2009: 9). Through its lending policy, the ECB can create a more or less inclusive risk pool for different assets (entries 3 and 7 of Table 5.1). It did this through its policies on accepting and discounting assets as collateral: it accepted the sovereign bonds of euro area member states and discounted them uniformly.[12] These bonds were not treated as one asset class by market investors before currency unification, but the ECB's collateral policy effectively made them one class and thus integrated these sovereign bond markets.

The statute of the Eurosystem only stipulates that lending to credit institutions and other market participants has to be "based on adequate collateral" (ESCB statute para 18(1)). The eligible securities are spelled out in the so-called collateral framework. The ECB's official aim in developing its collateral framework was to protect itself against losses should a borrowing institution fail to

[12] Collateral are assets that the central bank accepts as security, either for buying with a date set for banks to repurchase them ("repos") or simply when giving them credit ("secured or collateralized lending"). The duration of such lending used to be quite short, sometimes overnight but typically two weeks, and not more than three months.

honor its debt. Guarding against financial losses is not so much an economic necessity as a political imperative to signal competence and autonomy from financial pressures to lend (Bini-Smaghi 2011: sect.2). Central banks are generally under legal constraints to require collateral, and these constraints give the governments that hold their loss-absorbing capital an opportunity to review their actions (Cheun et al. 2009: 9n). This practice is not specific to the ECB but is a particularly sensitive issue for it, given the importance attached to its independence.

Until 2007, the ECB framework put all government bonds of a certain credit rating (at least A-) in its so-called Tier 1 of collateral it accepts (ECB 1999: 52–3). All EA government bonds were eligible. Tier 1 assets had to fulfil uniform criteria specified by the ECB while Tier 2 consisted of assets which were of particular importance to national financial markets and banking systems; the eligibility criteria were defined by national central banks and approved by the ECB. Only in 2007 did the ECB feel that financial integration had gone far enough to abolish the second tier of eligible collateral and impose uniform criteria. In comparison to major central banks, the ECB accepted the largest variety of collateral but it also stipulated a high credit standard, the equivalent of an A- rating, and applied high haircuts (Cheun et al. 2009: 9–10; ECB 2013a: 9-–11; Whelan 2014a: 8–9).

The ECB's collateral framework was criticized by Buiter and Sibert (2005: 3, 9–12) for treating all sovereign bonds in the EA as the same despite their very different default risks. They argued, first of all, that the ECB should not accept as collateral bonds issued by member state governments in breach of the SGP. Moreover, differences in default risks should be priced, which could be done by applying differential "haircuts": the discounts deducted from the market value of assets that are accepted as security (collateral) in repurchasing arrangements with banks or in determining loan amounts.[13] The collateral posted is marked to market daily and if prices go down the ECB (and other central banks) ask the counterparties (borrowing banks) to post additional collateral. The ECB applied different haircuts to different maturities of government bonds, because it argued that its haircuts price liquidity risk, not default risk. In the view of Buiter and Sibert (2005: 24), this amounted to treating the short-term default risk of all government bonds it accepted as uniformly equal to zero, equivalent to an implicit bailout guarantee. This practice also amounted to a low but significant subsidy of less creditworthy governments (Buiter and Sibert 2005: 14–21). Furthermore, because all bonds could be used to access ECB liquidity, the ECB's policy effectively suppressed

[13] It is analogous to the discount that is applied to the valuation of a house which underpins a mortgage loan. The ECB publishes which haircuts it applies to different categories of collateral on its website. See ECB (2014a) for comparative data on major central banks' collateral policies.

the market's evaluation of risk. This arguably led to too much interest rate convergence and undermined market discipline.

It was obviously much less politically sensitive for the ECB to stipulate high but uniform credit ratings (supplied by commercial agencies) than to engage in its own assessments of each member state's bonds. It is less obvious why the acceptance of collateral was not tied to the EU's fiscal surveillance framework, but there were interinstitutional obstacles. For the ECB to refuse to accept bonds from governments which were in breach of the SGP would have meant that the central bank was relying on the verdicts of the Commission and Council to determine its collateral policy. In turn, the ECB's "punishment" would have pre-empted the opening of an Excessive Deficit Procedure by the Commission. These institutional considerations are also aligned with an economic argument. It would create quite some instability in financial markets if the official notification of an excessive deficit rendered the bonds of a member state illiquid. The ECB would have generated strong market reactions and volatility if it had used its collateral policy as a disciplining instrument for fiscal policy.

The route chosen, of relying on credit ratings, meant that commercial rating agencies exercised authority over collateral policy, just as they influence governments' access to international capital markets. Accepting the verdicts of commercial agencies was politically less salient, until the financial crisis, and reinforced the ECB's independence from the Council. Before the crisis, credit rating agencies were more lenient disciplinarians than the SGP (Barta and Schelkle 2015). With hindsight, agencies like Moody's and Standard & Poor's priced risk too indiscriminately and favorably, looking at very few macroeconomic variables like inflation rates and budget deficits (Mosley 2003). This suited both sides: governments that were in search of non-inflationary sources of financing growth and social security; and market investors who, in a low yield environment, were looking for reasons to invest, not reasons to abstain from investing.

The ECB's general objective in treating highly rated sovereign debt instruments alike was to achieve integration of financial markets. Counterparties, meaning borrowing banks providing the collateral, could use the government bonds from different countries as perfect substitutes because their national central banks accepted them as collateral, following the so-called Correspondent Central Banking Model (Cheun et al. 2009: 12n). This gave banks an incentive to diversify their portfolios in terms of nationality of government bonds, and this was apparently effective. Cheun et al. (2009: 12n) report that "the use of collateral on a cross-border basis in credit operations with the Eurosystem increased from 12% in 1999 to more than 50% by 2006." Integration of financial markets was a goal of the ECB because it would make for a more uniform and predictable transmission of the ECB's interest rate policy.

In the absence of a single euro area government bond market, there was no obvious instrument for open-market operations (central banks generally use short-term Treasury bills). A portfolio of bonds had to be used, and this was not established until the launch of the Covered Bond Purchase Programme in July 2009 (Cheun et al. 2009: 11). Rather than using open-market operations, the ECB lent to banks (Cheun et al. 2009: 11).

The side effect of this policy of creating an integrated financial market was social insurance of sovereign default risk, as Buiter and Sibert (2005) sensed correctly and Brunnermeier and Sannikov (2013: 333) later rationalized for central banking more generally. This insurance was social rather than private because it was automatic (or mandatory) for all government bonds thus classified, while the uniform insurance premium (the "haircut") incorporated all members without regard to their riskiness. This assumes that Buiter and Sibert (2005) are correct to claim that financial markets would have imposed differentiated risk premia on sovereign bonds if the ECB had not treated them uniformly.[14] The policy of uniform treatment made perfect sense—from the ECB's point of view and even beyond this institutional perspective—given how politically sensitive and financially destabilizing differentiated treatment would have been. Social insurance is likely to have weakened market discipline, but how much of a problem this is depends on judgments about how responsive budget policies are to higher costs of debt finance and how efficient markets are in pricing risks. The ECB could argue that the member states had agreed on fiscal surveillance that was intended as a substitute for market discipline and it was for them to exercise self-governance.

LENDING OF LAST RESORT WITH A RESIDUAL FISCAL BACKSTOP

Lending of last resort to banks (entry 7 of Table 5.1) is not explicitly mandated in the Treaty or ECB Statute. There was no explicit financial stability mandate for the ECB apart from the obligation "to promote the smooth operation of the payments system" and to "contribute" to member states' conduct of prudential supervision (Article 130 TFEU). Even if there had been such a mandate, it would probably not have been high on the agenda (Toniolo and White 2015: 41–3). Before the financial crisis, all major central banks based their policy decisions on models that did not contain a financial sector in any meaningful way. This simplified the analysis considerably and the prevailing policy consensus did not suggest that it was necessary to include this complicating factor (Schelkle and Hassel 2013: 19). Much more attention was paid to labor markets and their inflationary role.

[14] This policy persisted during the crisis when bond market investors actually differentiated between default risks. See Whelan (2014a: 10–11) for a critical evaluation.

But, as just outlined, the ECB is autonomous in defining the terms of its lending policy, the quality of collateral it accepts, and the "haircut" it applies. Thus, in a liquidity crisis the ECB is able to lend against collateral of lower credit rating than in normal times (Schinasi and Teixeira 2006: 13). This is exactly what it did, engaging in "qualitative easing" by widening the set of eligible collateral earlier than any other major central bank (ECB 2013a: 14–15). It could thus reduce the risk that some banks which were illiquid would become insolvent. The ECB's lending of last resort spreads the remaining (diminished) solvency risk of the EA banking system to taxpayers in the EA.

Any losses the ECB incurs from its lending policy—or from other sources such as devaluation of foreign exchange reserves, for that matter—diminish the value of seignorage that EA Treasuries receive.[15] If the loss-absorbing capital of the ECB were wiped out in lending operations, it would have to be recapitalized by the subscribing governments.

The ESCB Statute (Article 32(4)) foresees that a national central bank can be indemnified by the system of central banks if it rescues a systemically important financial institution; the ECB, in turn, can be compensated for losses it incurs in the course of lending to banks that can ultimately not be rescued by asking for a share of the seignorage from each central bank (Article 33(2)). This is a somewhat curious provision because it implies a quasi-fiscal capacity for bank rescues within the Eurosystem, yet other policies point to rescues being a national fiscal responsibility.

Finally, banks can also ask for Emergency Liquidity Assistance (ELA) from national central banks in the ESCB. This is an overnight lending facility for which the national central bank can determine the collateral and for which national authorities are liable to bear the credit risk. This means that banks can receive credit from the national central bank against collateral that is not eligible under ECB rules (Whelan 2014a: 12). If the amount granted exceeds a certain value (€2 billion as of 2015), the Governing Council of the ECB must endorse it with qualified majority (ECB 2013b); the Council can also stop any ELA lending by a national central bank with a two-thirds majority if it concludes these operations "interfere" with the objectives of the Eurosystem. Before the crisis, this oversight was seen as a safeguard against inflationary liquidity provision by national central banks. Since the crisis, ELA lending has been suspected of serving as a way for member states to keep insolvent banks afloat and effectively shift risks onto European rather than national taxpayers,

[15] Seignorage is the surplus income that the Eurosystem earns from its issuance of fiat money, which results from the volume of money issued, the interest rate earned on it and the cost of printing and issuing this money (Vergote et al. 2010: 20). It is disbursed to the governments according to their share in paid-in capital of the ECB. Seignorage can be negative, for instance if a central bank makes huge losses on its foreign exchange reserve if the currency strongly appreciates and its interest earnings on the note issue are too low to compensate for it.

given that national Treasuries were themselves close to insolvency and would not be able to bear more losses (Obstfeld 2013: 33n). The ECB became extremely sensitive to this apparent moral hazard and engaged in some heavy-handed political interventions during the crisis, for instance setting the Irish and Cypriot government non-monetary conditions in return for continued access of banks to ELA (Whelan 2014a: 13–18). These interventions were a way for the ECB to limit the Eurosystem's assumption of credit risk and shift it back to the sovereign.

These ways to lend in the last resort in a system of central banks amount to a minimal or residual fiscal backstop. ELA is a way of roping in national fiscal authorities when the ECB regards banks' available collateral as inadequate. When the ECB does choose to lend and subsequently insolvency ensues, the compensatory mechanisms described above utilize the risk-pooling capacity of seignorage. In the event of a negative feedback loop between bank finances and public finances, last-resort lending can be used to interrupt the loop and spread the cost of bank failure to all Treasuries by having the central bank absorb the losses. Obviously, this is only a residual fiscal backstop as ECB seignorage is small relative to outstanding claims. But it is remarkable that existing legal provisions allow for monetary solidarity in lending of last resort, as a by-product of increasing the loss-absorbing capacity of any one member in the ESCB.[16]

5.2.3 *Exemptions from Monetary Solidarity*

The omissions in Table 5.1 are also telling as regards the scope of monetary solidarity before the crisis. Two are particularly conspicuous and were explicitly discussed before the euro arrived: financial supervision and joint fiscal liabilities.

The lack of EU-level financial supervision was spotted as a major shortcoming early on (entries 8 and 9 in Table 5.1, respectively). The Single Market Programme promoted cross-border financial transactions and the introduction of a common currency was supposed to give financial integration another boost. But there was no supervisory and fiscal infrastructure to support market integration. Governments ultimately could not agree on how to allocate fiscal costs should a cross-border bank require recapitalization, or should savers in such banks require compensation (Obstfeld 2013: 51; Schoenmaker and Siegmann 2014). Initially, mutual recognition took the place of harmonized supervision. Mutual recognition is the principle that what is lawfully

[16] A blog by Steele and Whittaker (2012) discusses more far-reaching proposals by economists as to whether the present value of seignorage should be used for central bank lending, able to absorb losses.

produced in one member state must be considered to be lawfully produced in any other member state. The license from one member state thus acts as a bank's "passport" to another member state. Host-country authorities rejected the mutual recognition principle, however. They did not trust that home-state supervisors would be able and willing to scrutinize bank branches abroad sufficiently closely. The way out was a program of upward harmonization under an accelerated legislative process which implemented the ambitious Financial Sector Action Plan (Posner 2007; Quaglia 2008).

Deposit guarantees and bank resolution procedures were also initially left to national provision. Deposit guarantees are typically financed or co-financed by fees from the financial industry. In a systemic crisis, the funds accumulated tend to be too low and governments have to bear the losses or give guarantees to bear them, in the hope of recovering some of the costs from the industry later.[17] The EU stipulated minimum standards in the 1994 Deposit Guarantee Schemes Directive (94/19/EC). It also had a say in bank resolution via state aid control that allowed Treasuries to release funds only once the Commission had approved such support (Schinasi and Teixeira 2006: 12–13; Mabbett and Schelkle 2014: 16–17). By the time the financial crisis broke, financial market regulation was actually quite densely regulated, leading to complaints about "red tape." But there was no pooling of resources in a cross-border deposit guarantee fund like the FDIC in the US, and no supranational backing for member states which had to step in and support their funds.

Overlapping competences also created uncertainty about who was responsible when an emergency arose. A Memorandum of Understanding was agreed between EU banking supervisors, central banks, and finance ministries in May 2005 regarding their roles and the rules of cooperation in the case of a systemic crisis (Schinasi and Teixeira 2006: 9), but cooperation inevitably came under strain in the financial crisis. National regulators belonged to hard-to-reconcile camps that blocked EU-level regulation, but this did not halt integration, which proceeded through other international fora such as the Basel Committee.[18] The Basel II framework allowed for extensive self-regulation of the industry: for instance some banks were allowed to use their own risk models to assess statutory capital requirements, subject only to inspection of the models applied.

Financial integration saw the regulatory polity in action, with the Commission trying to coordinate collective action with little fire power of its own. The thrust was financial integration rather than risk reduction and insurance. It

[17] An exhaustive overview of EU deposit guarantee schemes in place before the crisis can be found in JRC (2011: annex XXIV).

[18] See Quaglia (2010: 1010–11) for the two camps on financial regulation in the EU. Both Posner and Véron (2010) and Underhill and Zhang (2008) argued strongly that EU financial regulation was part of an international (OECD world) approach.

was politically convenient—and economically even justifiable—to treat financial supervision as part of the Single Market Programme rather than part of the governance structure of the EA. This was to some extent even necessary because one of the world's leading financial centers, the City of London, was part of the EU but stayed outside the EA.

The second exclusion from the policy architecture of the EA was direct fiscal risk sharing through joint public finances and monetization of public debt even under extreme circumstances (entries 2 and 4 in Table 5.1) In contrast to financial supervision, the exclusion of budgetary pooling was conscious and deliberate. Attempts to introduce some form of joint fiscal stabilization were categorically rejected by the usual suspects from Germany and the Netherlands, later joined by Finland. French counter-proposals were never pursued with much insistence. Pre-Maastricht proposals for a stabilization mechanism as effective as US fiscal federalism were worked out at the request of the Council by staff in the European Commission. Yet, these proposals were "turned down flat by the richer, Northern states at that time (1993), partly because they saw it as paving the way to a 'transfer union'" (Goodhart 2011).[19] The fear was moral hazard of fiscal authorities: they would have fewer incentives to stabilize their economies and engage in reforms to reduce structural unemployment. The proposed mechanism had actually addressed this fear because only a temporary rise, but not the level, of unemployment would give an entitlement to insurance, so as to leave incentives for combatting structural unemployment intact. Moreover, the stabilizing payment in addition to national unemployment insurance would have been paid only temporarily, for a year after the shock hit. But such finer details were lost in translation from a report of experts to a debate among governments.

It should be noted, however, that the stabilization of income flows, devised by Alexander Italianer and various advisors for the Commission in the early 1990s (European Economy 1993) and revived recently, for instance by Dullien (2014), would not have been able to deal with financial panic. As we have seen in Chapter 4, this requires an interface between monetary and fiscal policy, not a purely fiscal mechanism. In the US, this interface is represented by the FDIC, a deposit insurance and bank resolution authority, in normal times financed by the industry, its assets largely invested in the joint liability of US Treasury bonds and closely working with the lender of last resort, the Fed, in times of crisis.

[19] Charles Goodhart contributed to the 1993 exercise; the work on these proposals was presented in *European Economy* (1993: 415–538). See also Schelkle (2001: 306–13) and Dullien and Schwarzer (2007).

5.3 The Political Economy of Monetary Solidarity in the Euro Area

The analysis of the system of macrostabilization in the EA leads to observations that are not easy to reconcile with the hypothesis that ordoliberal hegemony prevailed. The negotiations on the initial set-up of EA institutions were indeed marked by Germany's dominant bargaining position, particularly in the emphasis on stability (Dyson and Featherstone 1999: 306–69). The SGP set the envelope for the admissible debt dynamic while the ECB's pursuit of an inflation target ensured that the monetary policy stance was restrictive. But several aspects of the institutional framework were consistent with a collective structure of governance in contrast to a hegemonic system. Membership was established in a fairly inclusive way, helped by the fact that the German gatekeeper also struggled with meeting the admission criteria. There were some surprisingly mutual aspects to the set-up of the monetary authority: voting in the ECB is egalitarian, the bank's collateralized refinancing policy pooled the risks of sovereign bonds issued by different member states, and the Eurosystem of national central banks can even engage in some residual fiscal risk sharing through seignorage.

These nascent interfaces between monetary, fiscal, and financial arrangements contradict the impression that the institutional framework for monetary union was all about avoiding risk sharing. Nor was the risk sharing that occurred entirely accidental, even if it was not the primary intention of the founders either. Decisions had to be made on how to apply the admission criteria; the egalitarian voting system in the ECB had to be explicitly agreed; the collateral policy had to be defended against critics. Compromises, not one dominant ideology, became enshrined in the institutions, and this allowed the ECB to operate more flexibly at the height of the crisis than many would have expected.

The debate about forming an economic and monetary union was officially all about creating an area of open and stable markets. Thus the defining conflict in macroeconomic stabilization, between those who benefit from easy credit conditions and those who benefit from tight money, was suppressed in public discourse, in favor of the latter. Bringing down inflation expectations was the economic policy priority of the times. Before monetary union, policymakers repeatedly had the experience that the satellite currency areas were forced to use the policy interest rate to go against domestic cyclical conditions, just in order to stabilize the exchange rate vis-à-vis the anchor currency, while allowing their currencies to float did not help macroeconomic management. In the aftermath of the crisis in 1992–3, supposed to bring a halt to monetary union, a large number of national administrations stayed the course. Subsequent macroeconomic developments showed the currency union to bring the benefits of both low inflation and low interest rates, as hoped for.

Against this background, it is much more comprehensible why national policymakers throughout the EU agreed to subject themselves to a policy framework in which the collective action problems to be tackled, moral hazard and fiscal externalities, were primarily defined by hard-currency countries. Financial markets rewarded former soft-currency countries with the same low costs of financing public and private investment. But, as Chapter 6 shows, this was a regime that had no way of dealing with unsustainable private debt that overwhelmed the bailing-out capacities of national fiscal authorities. The interfaces of risk sharing existed but were weakly developed. There was no protection against pro-cyclical market forces exposing former soft-currency countries to boom-and-bust cycles. This triggered another round of massive institution building. Even if the beginnings of the EA had been neo- or ordoliberal, this ideology did not help to govern the commons and could not be sustained.

The analysis of hidden forms of monetary solidarity alongside explicit limits on certain forms of risk sharing highlights the distinctive relationship between monetary and political integration. Governing the commons is different from the teleology of "ever closer union." This expression is used by commentators who envisage a sequential process of introducing economic, monetary, and political union. The "coronation theory" suggests that the collective decision procedures of a political union should be developed before monetary union because only these procedures can give legitimate authority for determining who should bear the risks once they materialize. The alternative "leverage theory" proposes that experience of the advantages of a monetary union will pave the way for political community building. The coronation theory was popular among German and Dutch policymakers, notably in the Bundesbank (Dyson and Featherstone 1999: 291; Maes and Verdun 2005: 339–40). The leverage theory is ascribed primarily to French and Belgian policymakers although a famous plan authored by two German Conservatives, Karl Lamers and Wolfgang Schäuble, also fitted this description (Hodson 2009: 511; Maes and Verdun 2005: 336).[20]

In light of the theory of interstate cooperation, we can see that the two concepts and political integration strategies indicate the different time horizons (or more technically: discount rates) of the negotiating parties. The hard-currency states, led by Germany and the Netherlands, adhered to a coronation

[20] The coronation theory is also known as an economist approach because of its emphasis on "real" economic and political integration coming first; the leverage theory is known as a monetarist approach because of its recommendation to introduce a common currency first (Torres 2007). These labels are rather confusing and therefore avoided here.

view of monetary union and were thus always happy to retreat to the waiting room until others conceded. They were in no haste to introduce the common currency, hence they could be in favor of this being the "organic" outcome of political integration. Patience gave them asymmetric bargaining power in selecting which collective action problems should be prioritized and hard-wired in the institutional solutions. The leverage concept was supported by those who were anxious to see the source of asymmetric shocks to their economies, Bundesbank policy, to be closed off for good.

Both views entail a conundrum. Coronation and leverage stipulate that a non-state money—or "money without politics" as Erik Jones (2002) put it—will either lead or follow political integration, understood as federal state building. Neither specifies the exact mechanisms that would make this happen (Hodson 2009: 510, 512). I suggest that there is no necessity for monetary union to stimulate political integration of the state-building kind. Instead monetary union brings with it a distinct form of political integration, understood as ongoing collective action. Governing a commons (Ostrom 1990), monitoring the risk pool of a common currency by its members, entails political integration as a process. For instance, fiscal surveillance in the EA is political integration, even though it was accompanied by resistance to fiscal risk sharing.

Political integration is typically thought of as either forming a (federal) nation state or identifying with (symbols of) a particular community. But states and their citizens also become politically integrated if they let themselves be governed by constraints that take other members' concerns into account. Political integration in this sense of the concept is a continuum and can go through periods of reversal. Power asymmetries and dominance by one nation over another are not excluded; after all, empires were also politically integrated. However, in the EU and in federations like the US, political integration happens through a horizontal (state-to-state) transfer of authority by states that are legally and normatively entitled to self-determination (Nicolaïdes 2013: 6). For this voluntary transfer of authority to occur, it is essential that respect for constraints is mutual. This is required not only to ensure reciprocity in the long run but also to provide the experience, especially among previously weaker members, that the flip side of constraints is protection and more room for maneuver thanks to the considerate behavior of others. This transfer can ultimately take the form of "demoicracy" in which different peoples "govern together but not as one" (Nicolaïdes 2013: 4; Cheneval and Schimmelfennig 2013).

Member states, their elected representatives, and the majority of voters who elect them certainly accept a lot of common governance. The influential work of Giandomenico Majone (1996) and his collaborators captured the nature of "governing together but not as one" and explained why member state sovereigns accept this. These scholars understood the EU as a regulatory state or polity. Developed in the heyday of the Single Market Programme, the regulatory state was characterized as "a fourth branch of government" for transnational economic regulation (Majone 1993a). The regulatory polity addresses collective action problems. In order to achieve gains for domestic firms and households, governments must agree on minimum standards and state authorities must internalize negative external effects of national practices, such as protectionism or excessive debt. The expansion of the regulatory polity can create centralized authority, reaching deeply into the fiscal accounting systems of national administrations and institutions regulating money and credit. But it is not state building in the sense of creating a political entity that attracts identification and allegiance from citizens (Mabbett and Schelkle 2009: 708–12; Genschel and Jachtenfuchs 2014).

The regulatory state form of political integration ties in with national tendencies to delegate policies to independent agencies (Moravcsik 2002: 606). Delegation can empower the executive and insulate public policies from the influence of powerful interest groups as well as from electoral pressures. This can be seen as generating a democratic deficit, an argument put most forcefully by Follesdal and Hix (2006). Yet this apparent deficit arises for the very reason that the regulatory polity addresses deficits of democracy: specifically, the tendency of national democracies to neglect the concerns of outsiders affected by their decisions, such as foreigners and future generations.

The European Court of Justice can be a powerful ally of the regulatory polity as will become obvious in Chapter 8. The drive for transparency, information, and accountability creates judicially enforceable rules. It gives organizations (and individuals through organizations) a venue to challenge their government. While such "Eurolegalism" (Kelemen 2011) has mostly been used for market integration, the intergovernmental Fiscal Compact of 2012 has, for the first time, enlisted the Court of Justice for the enforcement of fiscal rules. There is obviously an element of randomness and bias involved in judicial governance since those who are likely to litigate are those dissatisfied with the status quo, as Dan Kelemen's work shows in detail. Even so, accepting its verdicts, based on the supremacy of supranational law, is an expression of political integration.

The introduction and maintenance of the euro is part of political integration.[21] Monetary and political integration are not separate processes that can be instrumentally used to further each other. The monitoring of others' use of the commons was to some extent delegated to the Commission both because regulating budgets is a complex and time-consuming task and because

[21] This is also the overall thrust of Jabko (2006) who explores the strategic, and in this sense political, use of economic ideas about market integration and liberalization.

delegation could ensure a more equitable treatment of an unequal membership. Equitable treatment was a concern for good reason because some governments had more influence on establishing a regime of regulating budgets than others.

The attempt to "defiscalize" and thus apparently depoliticize macroeconomic stabilization had parallels in nation states in and outside the EA (Schelkle and Hassel 2013). The underlying idea was to separate monetary and fiscal policy so as to prevent monetization of public debt with its inflationary consequences and reassure financial markets. But under the influence of the hard-currency states and the Bundesbank, the result was an "unprecedented divorce" (Goodhart 1998: 410). This divorce further empowered liberalized financial markets, which were already in the ascendancy (Mügge 2010). They came to be even more sought after as a supposedly non-inflationary source of government finance (Abdelal 2007: ch.4).

As market actors did not respond to the verdict of the EU's fiscal surveillance, repeated violations of the Pact undermined the original disciplinarian rationale. The ECB could pursue a stability-oriented monetary policy even when the rules were broken. The rationale shifted away from externalities of interdependence to national deficit bias, the myopia supposedly inherent in democratic processes. But fiscal surveillance as an instrument to mend such perception problems of national democracies was politically divisive. It also served the perception that all instability is fiscal in origin. It was as if the users of the commons monitored each other very closely while they invited other users, namely financial investors, to come on the meadow. Only with hindsight would they realize that these visitors had a devastating effect on large patches of grass.

6

The Euro Area Crisis as a Stress Test for Monetary Solidarity

There is an abundant literature purporting to identify the "root causes of the Eurozone crisis." The notion of one crisis is convenient shorthand but also a distorting analytical construct (Jones 2015). As the first section of this chapter illustrates, the five member states in the eye of the storm had distinct and different reasons why they needed outside support.[1] This support was not only characterized by the extraordinary detail and strictness of the conditions attached to it but also by its historically unprecedented volume. We need to explain why this was called for even though countries were distressed for very different reasons.

The second section turns to explanations, the "root causes." The mainstream diagnosis is that the EA is not an OCA. A second account, based in comparative political economy, argues that the EA applies one monetary policy to incompatible growth regimes.[2] A common feature of these explanations is that they locate the EA crisis in the difficulties that some member states have in adjusting to shocks and/or operating under the constraints of a hard-currency area. Through the lens of the political economy of monetary solidarity, we can see that the crises in five member states were, with the exception of Greece, caused by incomplete risk sharing of a common shock. This common shock was partly the result of monetary-financial integration itself; it was not purely exogenous as the term "shock" strictly speaking implies.[3]

[1] Four countries received support from the EU and the IMF; the Spanish bank restructuring program was solely financed by the European Stability Mechanism.

[2] A third strong contender, that the EA is an expression of neoliberal hegemony which has put countries in a straitjacket of fiscal austerity, has been discussed in Chapter 5. Its explanation of the crisis also draws attention to incompatible growth regimes.

[3] The literature uses this term now somewhat loosely, for instance in Enderlein et al. (2012: paras 34–5), given that there is hardly ever a truly exogenous shock. Even the infamous oil-price shocks of the 1970s were a response to the inflation and exchange rate instability in advanced economies, creating more such instability.

What the countries in crisis have in common is a vicious cycle of (near) failing banks, a weakening economy, and overburdened fiscal authorities. Practically every member state could have been drawn into such a maelstrom but, instead of fostering solidarity, the selective market reaction and the enormity of the threat undermined it.

The final section concludes by reviewing briefly the plans for "completing" a "genuine" European monetary union as outlined in the Four and Five Presidents' reports (van Rompuy et al. 2012, Juncker et al. 2015). They are remarkable for their shift towards a risk-sharing paradigm, yet their vision also exhibits the flaws of the economic literature reviewed in Chapter 3: overconfidence in private (read: financial market) risk sharing and a supply-side focus on output instability. Moreover, the economic approach does not take the political constraints on fiscal risk sharing seriously. These constraints point to the adoption of different instruments if risk sharing is to be sustained.

6.1 The Puzzling Crisis and Its Costly Management

This section establishes what needs to be explained. There is first the empirical evidence that countries like Greece and Ireland got into difficulties for very different reasons. At the same time there are some resemblances between country experiences and none can be dismissed as an outlier. Financial assistance to distressed member states took the form of politically divisive conditionality combined with extremely high volumes of credit, in other words a combination of forms of support that seemed to maximize both its political and its economic costs.

6.1.1 *Multiple Crises in One*

We can use the program reports of the European Commission to illustrate just how different the crises in the five member states receiving assistance were and how differently they were perceived by those monitoring the adjustment effort in these countries.[4] Each country section describes first growth performance, then public and private domestic debt, and finally the external deficit and debt situation. They are listed in the order in which they received assistance (see Table 6.1).

[4] The program reports of all five countries have been published as Occasional Papers by the European Commission and are quoted as "European Economy [country]."

GREECE

In the decade before 2010, real GDP per capita in Greece increased on average twice as much as in the EA and, by 2009, the country's income was just 10 percent below the average of the currency union (European Economy Greece 2010: 3). This catching up was driven by a strong rise in public and private consumption as well as residential investment. In particular salaries in the public sector increased by more than GDP for at least a decade.

Strong growth performance had an ambiguous effect on fiscal indicators. The headline figure for the fiscal deficit was continuously above 3 percent but the debt-to-GDP ratio declined from 110 percent in 2000 to 95 percent in 2007—only to rise sharply when growth collapsed and deficits soared to double digits. Government debt absorbed 75 percent of all external financing that the Greek economy received, notably from Cypriot banks (European Economy Greece 2010: 6).

The fiscal problem trumped all others. In particular, it was the cause of financial stress for the banking system that was actually well capitalized before 2009. Financial stress came through three channels (European Economy Greece 2010: 7). First of all, rising yields on government bonds lowered the value of banks' assets, 8 percent of which consisted of claims on government. This reduced capital and resulted in losses to the extent that bonds were held in the trading book. Second, the lower asset value also reduced the value of collateral against which Greek banks could get liquidity from the ECB. This constraint materialized only during stalled negotiations of bailout programs, when the ECB excluded Greek banks from its lending, and this created uncertainty in bond markets. And lastly, exposure to sovereign risk crushed confidence in all Greek banks, causing withdrawal of foreign institutions and domestic savers from late 2009 onwards.

Private debt rose throughout the 2000s thanks to low interest rates and financial liberalization, but appeared relatively manageable at 120 percent of GDP by the end of 2011. The EA average was just about 10 percent lower (European Economy Cyprus 2013: 32). Private debt fueled significant house price increases. These imbalances were also a mirror image of extremely high current-account deficits, reaching 14 percent of GDP in 2008. External debt rose from 45 percent of GDP in 2000 to 100 percent in 2009. The real effective exchange rate (REER) was 10–20 percent overvalued in 2010, depending on the measure chosen (European Economy Greece 2010: 5).

In sum, a coherent interpretation of the Greek crisis seems to be the following: the economy suffered from an oversized and highly indebted public sector. This exacerbated the competitiveness problems of the private sector. Financial markets facilitated public profligacy in that both domestic and foreign banks held substantial amounts of government debt; the markets also put no constraints on Greece's rapidly accumulating high external debt.

IRELAND

The Irish economy grew very strongly from the early 1990s onwards. By the time the country became a member of the EA, it had a per capita income above the EU-15 average; relative per capita income peaked in 2006. This growth was driven by foreign direct investment attracted by low corporate taxes and light-touch regulation. An indicator of the extent of foreign investment and the corresponding claims on profits is that Ireland's GDP is 20 percent above gross national income (European Economy Ireland 2011: 8n). One implication of the presence of foreign investors was that the country shared its risk through capital markets quite extensively. Growth was accompanied by a rise in productivity and employment that spilled over from the trade to the non-trade sector. Continuous economic expansion was also fueled by massive investment in dwellings, reaching 14 percent of GDP in 2006, compared to a steady 6 percent in the EA-17 average (European Economy Ireland 2011: 7, fig. 4). By 2007, the construction sector had twice the share in the economy's value added as the EA average.

The fiscal situation was enviable until autumn 2008. Public debt was below 30 percent of GDP in 2005–6 and the budget balance in surplus throughout 2000–7. Given the overheating economy, fiscal policy was arguably not sufficiently counter-cyclical ("prudent"): the government was warned of this by the Ecofin Council in 2000 and 2007. This advice from the EU was not appreciated by a defiant administration, however. Revenues depended more and more on the housing boom, for instance through stamp duties and an income tax on holding gains. Property-related revenues rose from 8.4 percent in 2002 to 18 percent of revenues in 2006 (European Economy Ireland 2011: 15) and duly collapsed with the housing bust. Although the effect on the budget balance was counter-cyclical, it moved with the asset boom and bust rather than the business cycle in output and employment.

But the greatest vulnerability of Ireland's stellar performance was banking. Domestic credit expansion became frenetic: in 2004–6, household credit rose by 30 percent p.a. This expansion was highly concentrated in only five institutions. Apart from mortgage credit to households, credit was heavily skewed towards property development and construction (European Economy Ireland 2011: 9). Credit as a share of GDP rose from around 120 percent in 2002 to over 300 percent in 2009. The funding side was equally precarious. Only half of all loans were financed by deposits which made Irish banks very dependent on wholesale market funding. When markets froze, Irish banks had to rely on the Eurosystem, financing the equivalent of over 15 percent of bank liabilities by recourse to the ECB and overnight ELA from the Irish central bank (European Economy Ireland 2011: 9). Since losses on ELA are ultimately a national liability, this reinforced the fatal link between the banking system and sovereign finances. By July 2009, liquidity assistance from the Eurosystem was in the order of €130 billion, well above the volume of the first Greek bailout program and amounting to 77 percent of Ireland's 2009 GDP.

The current-account balance turned increasingly negative after 2004, due to strong wage growth and a strong euro. The latter was particularly significant for Ireland since the country had a high share of trade with the UK and the US (European Economy Ireland 2011: 8). REER appreciation (based on unit labor costs) vis-à-vis the rest of the EA was a mere 15 percent between 2000 and 2008 while appreciation vis-à-vis thirty-six other industrial countries was 40 percent. In terms of macroeconomic stability, this real appreciation and the cheaper imports it brought were, however, exactly what both Ireland with its overheating economy and the rest of the world with its savings glut needed.

In sum, Ireland is a case of an enormous boom-bust cycle that ended a very long stretch of uninterrupted expansion. The expansion turned one of the poorest countries in Europe into one of the richest. It had started before the introduction of the euro. Currency unification, with its further reassurance of diminished exchange rate instability that lowered risk premia, gave additional momentum to an already overheating economy. With hindsight, it is clear that fiscal policy was insufficiently restrictive. The government had a vested interest in the housing boom as it filled its coffers (and the pockets of corrupt government officials). It kept tax incentives for homeownership in place despite the manifest overexpansion of mortgage lending and house building.

PORTUGAL

Among the five EA members that needed external financial support, Portugal is the only country that stagnated throughout the decade before the crisis. Real income growth was around 1 percent per annum, about half the EA average. The economy maintained fairly high employment rates but at the cost of weak productivity growth. Potential output was on a downward path from the late 1990s onwards (European Economy Portugal 2011: 5). Wage growth had outstripped increases in labor productivity during the 1990s, in a boom anticipating accession to the EA. Portugal's difficult decade was predictable in that it was the only EU country that was to lose from Eastern enlargement: labor-intensive industries left it for the still cheaper production sites of the transition economies further east.

The government tried to soften the blow with an expansionary stance: Portugal was the first country to breach the SGP and it ran underlying deficits above the 3 percent threshold throughout the period before its crisis, partly covered by one-off deficit-reducing measures (European Economy Portugal 2011: 9). But since government debt started from a very low level, it stayed below the 60 percent ratio. Portugal's government debt was susceptible to contagion, however, since it was held largely by foreign investors, up to 75 percent in mid-2009.

The banking system did not have immediate problems because it ran a rather traditional business model, hence it was not exposed to toxic assets (European Economy Portugal 2011: 8–9). Nor was there a property bust. But the loan–deposit ratio of the national banking system was 1.6 and this became a critical vulnerability, after market funding froze and loans had to be refinanced. Banks had extended a lot of credit to the private sector. Debt stood at 250 percent of GDP by 2009, almost equally shared between households and non-financial firms.

Rising private and public debt was the mirror image of sustained current-account deficits; much debt was owed externally (European Economy Portugal 2011: 6–8). Portugal continuously registered between 6.5 and 10.5 percent net external borrowing between 2000 and 2008; external debt stood at 110 percent by 2010. Over 40 percent of foreign liabilities were in the form of deposits, a highly liquid form of debt which could easily be withdrawn. Easy external finance masked the structural problems of the economy: an export industry specialized in slow-growing sectors and catering to slow-growing EA markets, and a high-cost base due to a high share of uncompetitive state-owned enterprises.

To sum up, Portugal was a case of a somewhat backward economy which did not manage to upgrade when footloose industries left. It was not forced to adjust vigorously because plentiful finance was available for the ensuing imbalances. This does not mean that the government did not try to reform Portugal's labor markets and the welfare system—it did (Zartaloudis 2014). But it could not muster the political resolve for the big changes needed, especially in education where Portugal has been near the bottom of the league in the OECD world for a long time. Pressure for structural reforms was trumped by accommodating macroeconomic conditions.

SPAIN

Between 1997 and 2007, the Spanish economy experienced strong growth that translated into annual employment expansion of almost 4 percent (European Economy Spain 2012: 9). The unemployment rate more than halved to slightly over 8 percent in 2007. This was all the more impressive as the Spanish labor market absorbed a large cohort of baby boomers, rising female employment, and very high immigration, with the share of immigrants in the population rising from 2 percent in 1999 to 10 percent in 2007. Jobs were created in the wider economy, not only in construction and real-estate activities.

Similarly to Ireland, the growth model was "rich in taxes" because of the housing boom. From the early 2000s, the budget was balanced and went into surplus until 2007. Successive governments kept on spending on tax incentives for homeownership, as in Ireland. When the housing market collapsed, dragging the economy into a deep recession, deficits and debt exploded.

The driving force behind both the boom and its bias towards housing was the financial system. As long ago as 1995, the share of credit that went to housing and construction stood at almost 40 percent of all credit; by 2007, this had risen to 65 percent. During that time, credit for real-estate activity was rising at an annual rate of over 20 percent per annum, while consumer credit rose by 12 percent per annum. (European Economy Spain 2012: 9). The Spanish central bank was well aware of the unsustainability of this situation and imposed macroprudential policies on banks to rein them in (Alberola et al. 2011). But since foreign banks were ready to step into the breach and the measures were not popular with aspiring homeowners, the government urged the Banco de España to reduce these controls in the mid-2000s. There was also a deep division between internationally competitive, relatively sound, and well-regulated national banks on one hand, and regional savings banks prone to corruption, nepotism, and sheer incompetence on the other (European Economy Spain 2012: 17).

The current account was deep in deficit. Large capital inflows went more into investment than consumption, but investment consisted largely of construction and property dealing. Their expansionary effect drove up wages by an average of over 3 percent per annum. Labor productivity hardly increased (on average 0.4 percent) which is hardly surprising given the high employment growth. This meant that there was a sizeable real appreciation that drove the current account ever deeper into the red. In 2011, the year before Spain asked for a financial-sector assistance program, external debt stood at 165 percent of GDP.

In sum, Spain is a similar case to Ireland, in that the expansion of credit since the mid-1990s fueled a housing bubble both in asset markets and in the material economy. From this followed a benign yet fragile fiscal situation, impressive, if uneven, employment growth, a measurable rise in living standards, but also overvaluation of the real exchange rate. The big difference with Ireland was a much more severe external imbalance.

CYPRUS

A member of the EU since 2004 and of the EA since 2007, Cyprus experienced strong real GDP growth of 3 percent per annum between 2000 and 2009. The economy operated at full employment, with low inflation despite considerable wage increases which resulted in rising real per capita income. The country had developed a diversified and export-oriented services sector. High immigration helped to sustain this growth pattern.

Unsurprisingly, the fiscal situation was enviable. Public debt stood at 58 percent of GDP before the country's crisis in 2011–12. The budget balance had a turnaround, from −7 percent of GDP in 2003 to +3 percent in 2007. A small public sector employed extremely well-paid civil servants compared to the rest of the EU (European Economy Cyprus 2013: 27). The tax regime was very business-friendly and the country operated as a tax haven, indicated by a negative external income balance (European Economy Cyprus 2013: 19). And yet, by mid-2011, the government was unable to issue public debt at sustainable interest rates. Before it finally requested EU support in June 2012, the government tried to attract deposits from abroad, not least from well-off Russians with more or less reputable income sources. This attempt to organize inward capital flows on top of tax competition did little to make other member states sympathize with the plight of Cyprus.

Private debt was the highest in the EA, on a par with Ireland, and had reached 310 percent of GDP in 2011 (European Economy Cyprus 2013: 23, 32). Loans to the tune of 150 percent of GDP were directly related to housing, feeding an unsustainable boom. This exceedingly high domestic credit was fueled by foreign deposits which stood at more than 100 percent of GDP in 2008 and 2009. The size of the banking sector doubled between 2005 and 2009; its assets amounted to more than 800 percent of GDP in 2009 and still over 700 percent in 2012 (European Economy Cyprus 2013: 12). There was also high credit exposure to other banks which rendered the Cypriot financial system vulnerable to contagion. Bank regulation made investment in euro-denominated bonds attractive: thus Cypriot banks kept on investing heavily in Greek sovereign bonds when banks from other countries were shunning them.

The current account registered a high and rising deficit, which peaked at 15.6 percent of GDP in 2008. A persistently higher rise in wage costs than the EA average led to appreciation of the real exchange rate with trading partners over time. This was not only a source of vulnerability for the financial sector but also for the real economy.

In sum, Cyprus looked like a small highly successful economy. But financial exuberance turned this success into vulnerability and ultimately downfall. The rise in private debt and the housing boom invited disaster. Again, all the symptoms were present that characterized the cases of Ireland and Spain. The fiscal situation was stable although, with the benefit of hindsight, it is also clear that a more restrictive stance was called for. An enviable employment situation drew in high immigration, and the external imbalance deteriorated, mainly due to strong demand for imports, not weak export performance.

But the Cypriot crisis is also more than just a variation on the Irish and Spanish difficulties with private debt. The eventual trigger for crisis was Greece's sovereign default in 2011. The Cypriot banking system, spurred on by government regulation, had betted on a generous second bailout for Greece, buying Greek debt at a discounted price in the hope that it would rise after the second program. Instead, private holders were forced to write down debt to relieve the Greek government from part of its debt burden. The default of Greek bonds wiped out almost half of the Tier 1 capital of Cypriot banks within six months (European Economy Cyprus 2013: 14). It became clear that government finances would be overstretched by the unfolding banking crisis. This nexus between a foreign sovereign and domestic banks can explain why Greece was not allowed to default much earlier, in 2010. This was a point of contention between the EU and the IMF (Bastasin 2012: 149–52). The Cypriot banks' bet also bolstered those in major guarantor countries who saw moral hazard problems arising from the troika programs. This in turn prepared the ground for unrelenting conditionality and insistence on "bailing in," which extended to ordinary savers in Cyprus. In the first version of the program proposed by the Cypriot government to the troika and readily accepted by it, even insured depositors would have made losses. This was actually illegal under the EU Directive on deposit guarantees; the plan was later corrected but it remains a mystery why it had ever been adopted (Buiter et al. 2013: 6–7).

We can thus summarize: three out of five crises were private debt crises (in Cyprus, Ireland, and Spain) as in most countries outside the EA; there was a public debt crisis in Greece, and Portugal is a borderline case in which deindustrialization made the government compensate for the disappearance of jobs and low demand, resulting in a huge twin deficit (current account and public budget). The diversity of experiences in the countries that were in the eye of the storm, and the differences in political economies that underlie that diversity, presents a challenge for all explanations of the EA crisis. It is equally challenging to explain the form that crisis management took, as the next section indicates.

6.1.2 *Unprecedented Assistance in an Unprecedented Crisis*

Just as the EA showed signs of recovery in late 2009, the Greek government spooked markets and fellow governments in the Council with a sharp downward revision of its budget data. It was not the first time that this had happened when a new Greek administration came into office. But this time, the incoming Papandreou government received a robust rebuke by the Council of Economic and Finance Ministers (the Ecofin Council), which ordered a thorough investigation by Eurostat. This was duly delivered early in January 2010 (European Commission 2010).

This reaction and an unfortunate coincidence added to the market panic. Standard & Poor's had downgraded Greek bonds in light of the revised budgetary figures and, in an unrelated development, ECB President Trichet gave an interview in which he announced the phasing out of qualitative easing in light of improving economic data. As explained in Section 5.2.2, ECB collateral policies were highly influential on market actors' preferences for holding EA sovereign bonds. Banks proceeded to sell Greek bonds because they anticipated that they could no longer be posted as collateral with the ECB if standards were tightened. This was compounded by the response of pension funds and insurers to the Greek downgrade: they sold the bonds because regulation restricts their holding of risky assets. From then on until mid-2012, the EA was in a permanent state of battle with financial market instability while negotiating, reluctantly, a Greek bailout program. While the euro was never attacked, several member states needed financial assistance on a vast scale. Others, in particular Italy, came close and were rescued by exceptional monetary expansion. At times, this unfolding crisis threatened to break up the EA amidst social unrest and a decline in living standards rarely seen in peacetime.

By late 2015, five EA member states had received bailout funds. With the exception of Spain, these programs also included IMF credit. EU member states outside the EA, namely Hungary, Latvia, and Romania, also received assistance from intergovernmental support mechanisms. Table 6.1 reveals several remarkable features of emergency lending in the EU, not only in the EA. The acronyms indicate the complexity of multi-level emergency funding:[5]

- Balance of payments (BoP) assistance for non-EA countries, under the so-called *Medium-Term Financial Assistance Facility*, was available before 2008 and followed the logic of IMF programs, with the Council as the deciding body. It was also used for Hungary, however, where public finances were the immediate cause of trouble. Subsequent capital flight provided the cover for both the EU and the IMF to come in and prevent disorderly devaluation (Mabbett and Schelkle 2015: 515–16).
- The EFSM (*European Financial Stabilization Mechanism*) is a €60 billion fund that the European Commission can raise against the security of its budget. It was an innovation to give the Commission the right to issue bonds in capital markets. This facility can mobilize credit very fast and give time for negotiating the conditionality of other emergency funding.
- The EFSF (*European Financial Stability Facility*) was created alongside the EFSM in May 2010, with a lending capacity of €440 billion. This special purpose vehicle in Luxembourg was meant to be a temporary emergency

[5] The source of this information is the Commission homepage: "Financial assistance in EU member states" (URL: http://ec.europa.eu/economy_finance/assistance_eu_ms/index_en.htm, (accessed November 14, 2015).

fund only. It issued bonds that are guaranteed by the member states represented in the Ecofin Council according to their share in the paid-up capital of the ECB.

- The ESM (*European Stability Mechanism*) replaced the EFSF in October 2010, coming into effect two years later. It is a fund with its own legal status based on public law that has a lending capacity of €500 billion. The ESM can buy government debt from the issuing government (in the so-called primary market) as well as from bondholders (in the secondary market). It can also conduct programs designed solely to finance bank recapitalization, whereas the IMF can only do this as part of a country program. All lending must come with conditions on institutional reforms attached.

A first important observation can be drawn from the chronological listing of countries in Table 6.1. Non-EA countries needed to draw on emergency assistance more than a year before Greece. The economic downturn after September 2008 exposed them very quickly to currency attacks and balance of payments difficulties. Outside support was required despite the fact that these countries had actually accumulated less severe macroeconomic imbalances than Greece or Portugal (Mabbett and Schelkle 2015: 513–14). The delayed impact of the financial crisis on EA members was a mixed blessing, though. Imbalances accumulated for longer, making adjustment much harder. This raises the question whether EA member states should have used this grace period better and adjusted during that time. Quite a few governments in the Council took that position; the Slovakian government opted out of the rescue for Greece on these grounds. But international market conditions were exceptionally adverse for turning around the current-account balance to substitute for falling domestic demand, especially as all countries were seeking their way out of weak domestic demand. Moreover, the adjustments in the real economy were on their way, triggered by a credit crunch that was not causing an imminent threat of currency crises as in non-EA countries.

The sums involved were staggering, absolutely and compared to normal IMF programs (Barkbu et al. 2011; Pisani-Ferry et al. 2013). Before the crisis, the "Factsheet" on IMF quotas (as of September 24, 2015) explained that borrowing was limited to 200 percent of a member's quota annually and 600 percent cumulatively under the Stand-by and Extended Arrangements Facility. In the "Tequila Crisis" of 1994–5, Mexico initially drew on 300 percent of its quota, against great resistance from European Executive Directors. When the amount had to be expanded to an unheard-of 700 percent, IMF President Camdessus had to threaten to step down if support was not forthcoming (Boughton 2012: 470–2, 476–7). By contrast, European countries borrowed more than twenty times their quota (>2000 percent) in the case of Greece and Portugal and more than ten times as much in all other cases, non-EA countries included. This was

Table 6.1. Assistance programs for EA and non-EA countries in the EU, 2008–15

Country	Date of first program	Maximum amount	Specifics of the program
Hungary	November 2008 (request in October 2008)	€20.0 bn	Program covered 2009–10; EU BoP assistance €6.5 bn, IMF €12.5 bn, and World Bank €1 bn Maturity of debt up to 2016 1st program quitted early by government; request for 2nd program in November 2011 did not materialize
Latvia	January 2009 (request in November 2008)	€7.5 bn	Program covered 2009–12 (only €4.5 bn used); EU BoP assistance €3.1 bn, IMF €1.7 bn, Nordic countries €1.9 bn, World Bank €0.4 bn, European Bank for Reconstruction and Development, Czech Republic and Poland €0.4 bn Maturity of debt up to 2025
Romania	May 2009 (request in spring 2009)	€20.0 bn	Program covered 2009–11 (only €5 bn used); EU BoP assistance €5 bn, IMF €12.95 bn, World Bank €1 bn, EIB and European Bank for Reconstruction and Development €1bn Maturity of debt beyond 2018 Two more precautionary programs were not needed
Greece	May 2010 (request in April 2010)		Three programs: 2010–11 (planned -2013), 2012–14 (extended to June 2015), 2015–18
		€110.0 bn (-€2.7bn)	First: Bilateral Greek Loan Facility €80 bn (reduced by €2.7 bn due to withdrawal of Slovakia, Ireland, and Portugal), IMF €30 bn (€52.9 bn disbursed);
		€164.5 bn	Second: EFSF €144.7 bn, IMF €19.8 bn (€130.9 bn disbursed), plus default on private-sector bond holdings €197 bn;
		(€197 bn)	Third: ESM €86 bn Maturity of debt to be confirmed
		€86.0 bn	Various grant elements introduced in 2012 (no interest payments in the first ten years, interest proceeds from ECB bond buying returned)
Ireland	December 2010 (contrived request in November 2010)	€85.0 bn	Program covered 2010–13; EFSM €22.5 bn, EFSF €17.7 bn, UK €3.8 bn, Sweden 0.6 bn, Denmark €0.4 bn; IMF €22.5 bn; Irish Treasury and pension fund €17.5 bn; Maturity of debt until 2042
Portugal	May 2011 (request in April 2011)	€78.0 bn	Program covered 2011–14; EU/EFSM €26 bn, EFSF €26 bn, IMF €26 bn; Maturity of debt until 2029
Spain	July 2012	Up to €100.0 bn	Program covered July 2012–January 2014; ESM €41.3 bn used for bank recapitalization Maturity of debt until 2025
Cyprus	April–May 2013 (request in June 2012)	€10.0 bn	Program covered 2013–16; Up to €9 bn from ESM and up to €1 bn from IMF Maturity of debt up to 2031

Source: Eurostat data for GDP; own compilation as of November 13, 2015, from http://ec.europa.eu/economy_finance/assistance_eu_ms/intergovernmental_support/index_en.htm

legally possible because European countries received IMF credit from non-concessional facilities, i.e. at market-related interest rates without a pre-set cap on the amount. Pisani-Ferry et al. (2013: 29) show that European programs lasted considerably longer and had higher volumes than the average of all IMF programs.

The EA thus managed, via the IMF, to share the risks of the financial crisis with the rest of the world. The rest of the world, with the exception of North America and Oceania, is much poorer and hence this sharing generated considerable resentment among emerging powers. However, the seniority of IMF claims, exceeding those of EU public creditors and guarantors, does ensure that the rest of the world shares the risk only in the last resort. The EA could claim that the calamities of their member states threatened not only the currency union but the international financial system. This was the pretext for the IMF to extend its access limits on May 9, 2010: "access may be higher in exceptional circumstances."[6]

The EU added vast sums to this enormous IMF assistance. In the case of Hungary and Romania, the EU remained in a junior role, while intergovernmental emergency funding took center stage for EA countries and Latvia, amounting to a multiple of IMF assistance. The overall sums, expressed as a share of each country's 2007 GDP at market prices, amounted to:[7]

- 19 percent for Hungary, 20 percent for Latvia, and 4 percent for Romania (in the case of Latvia and Romania only disbursed credit);
- 115 percent for Greece (the disbursed credit of the first two programs plus committed sum of third program for a total of €289.6 billion);
- 43 percent for Ireland; 44 percent for Portugal; 3.8 percent for Spain (only the disbursed sum of €41 billion) and 57 percent for Cyprus.

Emergency funding through EU channels was calculated to cover fiscal shortfalls, including fiscal requirements of the banking system (for recapitalization), while IMF programs start from the need for capital flows in the presence of a current-account deficit (Pisani-Ferry et al. 2013: 15). Funds could also be given to finance current fiscal expenditure, for instance the arrears in government payments to suppliers that crippled the Greek economy. However, the bulk of Greek loans went to service financial debt, not to tide households or non-financial firms over their fall in income and demand, respectively.

[6] See IMF website "Factsheet: IMF Quotas," http://www.imf.org/external/np/exr/facts/quotas.htm (accessed November 14, 2015).

[7] Own calculations based on Eurostat data for national GDP and European Commission data for program volumes (see source for Table 6.1). See also Pisani-Ferry et al. (2013: 17 and 29–30).

The amount of international support given in the course of the EA crisis was unprecedented in the history of multilateral lending. The Greek programs broke the record for the largest sovereign bailout program ever (Pisani-Ferry et al. 2013: 39). To put this in perspective, the biggest single bank bailout ever was also performed around that time. In 2008, the UK government rescued the Royal Bank of Scotland. By late 2013, this had required cash outlays of £115 billion (€138 billion) according to HM Government (2014: para 3.14). This was more for just one bank than the first Greek program (only half of it disbursed) and more than the envelope of €100 billion for the entire Spanish banking system (only about 40 percent disbursed).

The comparatively cost-effective Spanish bank rescue indicates how risk pooling through the ECB and the ESM could work (Chislett 2014: 4–6). First of all, Spanish banks borrowed cheaply from the ECB and bought high-yielding sovereign bonds; their value increased massively after 2012. Moreover, the international financial assistance enabled the government to set up a bad bank, SAREB, that took over non-performing loans and illiquid real-estate assets in exchange for government-guaranteed SAREB bonds which the banks could use as collateral in borrowing from the ECB. Both measures amounted to financial engineering through the lender of last resort. The program was crucial to this extraordinary monetary risk pooling in that it gave the ECB fiscal cover in case the recovery of sovereign bonds had not materialized. The bad bank, SAREB, which had taken the uncertainty off banks' balance sheets, began to sell its bad assets in August 2013. Spain exited its ESM program in January 2014.

Financial support came with strong strings attached. The programs in which the EU was the senior partner and the ECB acted as a consultant, forming a "troika" with the IMF, involved intrusive structural conditionality. The IMF had abandoned this form of conditionality in 2002, at least in theory, after a thorough review in the early 2000s. It had found that the deep institutional reforms requested in return for credit were not complied with (IMF 2015). They were seen as externally imposed, tarnishing domestic reformers as subservient to outside imperialist forces. Participation in European rescue programs apparently made the IMF return to far-reaching and detailed conditionality. In a widely cited paper, Lütz and Kranke (2010: 11; 2014) talk of "the European rescue of the Washington Consensus." Barkbu et al. (2011: 13–18) and Griffiths and Todoulos (2014: 12–13) suggest, however, that ESM and IMF programs are not categorically different, notably because the IMF does not practice consistently what its earlier review recommended.[8]

[8] Section 7.2.2 comes back to this point.

The detail of conditionality is mind-boggling. One can discern a certain differentiation between the most urgent measures for specific cases: for instance, in Greece fiscal consolidation and a "comprehensive" pension reform took precedence, in Ireland and Cyprus it was the stabilization and "downsizing" of the financial sector. But the memorandums of understanding cover everything in every program because, of course, economies in crisis develop widespread imbalances. Conditions were sometimes highly specific, such as a €1 cut in the Irish minimum wage and "[f]urther [streamlining of] the Easter allowance to pensioners by limiting the benefit to pensioners with a monthly per household income of at most EUR 500" in Cyprus (European Economy Ireland 2011: 63; European Economy Cyprus 2013: 80). Neither was exactly essential for restoring stability in these two countries: indeed, the minimum wage cut in Ireland was reversed when a new government came to power with a clear mandate against it. This was politically damaging: conditionality was seen as inflicting pain rather than trying to cure the patient.

Conditionality certainly managed to upset voters in the countries receiving assistance. The stipulations of budget cuts, tax increases, and the removal of certain protections in a global economic recession were so demanding, causing real hardship, that the quid-pro-quo of unprecedented multilateral support was hardly appreciated. One of the more benign expressions of this voter outrage was the rise of anti-austerity parties like Podemos in Spain, Syriza in Greece, and the Five Star Movement in Italy. When Syriza came to power and was then forced to exercise exactly the austerity they campaigned against, it gave the impression that the EA is no longer a union of formally equal nations (Bellamy and Weale 2015: 259–60, Schimmelfennig 2015: 128). The programs were seen as a brutal diktat, imposed predominantly by Germany making this an even more sensitive issue.

The guarantees given to finance the bond issues by the ESM created political problems in guarantor countries as well. They were grist to the mill of anti-EU parties on the right, such as the French National Front and the Alternative for Germany. These parties amalgamate a quest for sovereignty and national social security with protectionist and xenophobic agendas that question fundamental norms of European integration. When Greek governments proposed referenda, first under Papandreou in 2010 and then under Tsipras in 2015, politicians in guarantor countries were outraged. They had put their jobs on the line to get assistance through parliaments. Referenda in the receiving countries could only compound their difficulties at home, where demands for referenda were immediately raised as well. Cooperative (and right-of-center) governments in Portugal and Spain would have been utterly embarrassed if the Greek government had got away with its demands; the Portuguese and Spanish governments were among the fiercest opponents of accommodating the incoming government in spring 2015 (BBC 2015).

When Prime Minister Tsipras finally held a referendum in summer 2015, it had the predictable outcome of a rejection of the program. The Council ignored the will of the Greek people, in fact setting officially harsher conditions to make up for the losses between the initial agreement and the referendum. This was excruciating to watch for anybody with sympathy for the plight of the Greek people. Yet, it was also hard to see how the majority in the Council could have done anything but ignore the referendum outcome. Representative democracy is constitutive for interstate cooperation. No government could commit credibly to an agreement if it were later open to the vagaries of referenda with their variable participation rates and misinformation campaigns.

The Greek government requested another debt write-down, which it had arguably been promised in 2012.[9] The Council resisted this, but it eased the credit conditions and thus the net present value of Greek debt. This was done by providing long grace periods (on average fifteen years) in which little or no debt service has to be paid, as well as extending the maturities of debt (to an average of forty years) far beyond the maturities that Greece could ever get in the financial markets, and granting a concessionary interest rate (on average 1.2 percent compared to the standard rate of 3.8 percent) (IMF 2016a: 4). Moreover, the Greek government receives all profits from the Eurosystem's holding of Greek bonds (capital gains and interest) that would normally feed into the annual surplus of the ECB (Eurogroup 2012: 2; Darvas and Hüttl 2015). This amounted to an incremental debt write-down equal to an annual transfer of about 3 percent of Greek GDP.[10] But this may still be too little to stop Greece's adverse debt dynamic (IMF 2016a). The Eurogroup of finance ministers thus tried to reconcile irreconcilable demands: to calm down the wrath of domestic opposition, to discipline an impatient Greek government that had challenged the Council so openly, and to respond to the utter despair of a member state's population.

The other program countries exited financial assistance as planned:[11] Ireland in December 2013, Portugal in June 2014, Spain in January 2014, and Cyprus in March 2016. They all remain under post-program supervision until 75 percent of the loans are paid back. All four countries returned to

[9] In November 2012, the Eurogroup (2012) stated that "Member states will consider further measures and assistance ... if necessary, for achieving a further credible and sustainable reduction of Greek debt-to-GDP ratio, when Greece reaches an annual primary surplus, as envisaged in the current MoU, conditional on full implementation of all conditions contained in the programme." The background to this was that the losses from the government debt write-down had to be borne by private bondholders only. About two-thirds of these bonds were held by Greek banks so that the losses wiped out their capital. The cost of their recapitalization came out of the troika program and reduced the effective write-down to only 38 percent (Mabbett and Schelkle 2015: 525).

[10] This figure was mentioned by a senior German official in May 2016.

[11] Information available from the European Commission website: "Financial assistance in EU member states," <http://ec.europa.eu/economy_finance/assistance_eu_ms/index_en.htm>.

government bond markets soon after leaving their programs. But both Spain and Portugal were back in the spotlight of fiscal surveillance by May and July 2016, creating a stand-off between Commission and Council that ended with an exemption from the fine, with the two enforcing bodies switching sides each time (Eder 2016). Sanctions that push a country in (fiscal) trouble into more of the same trouble are unenforceable. It is, in a nutshell, a "dilemma of government responsiveness" (Rodrik and Zeckhauser 1988), a particular manifestation of the commitment problem of collective action.

For the political economy of monetary solidarity, the crucial point is that the Council chose a form of assistance that was generous in terms of the lending volumes but punishing in terms of the strings attached. It seems obvious that this tried to contain the externalities from national bond markets eventually while also sending the signal to member states that this should not be mistaken as a soft stance on future moral hazard. It clearly had adverse political consequences, in distressed countries and in the guarantor countries, even where the programs were concluded as agreed. Management of the EA crisis was thus a very ambiguous statement of European (monetary) solidarity.

6.2 Explaining the Crisis of the Euro Area

In his classic contribution to political economy, Peter Gourevitch (1986) argues that hard times are also the times when our theories of politics and policymaking are put to the test. This fruitful proposition is heeded in the following discussion. The challenge is to provide a coherent interpretation of why the euro area as a whole was so vulnerable to market panic but also to be able to make sense of the diversity of crisis experiences of the five program countries. Moreover, as noted above, the provision of support that was, by historical standards, both extremely high and extremely invasive, requires explanation.

6.2.1 *Revenge of the Optimum Currency Area?*

The mainstream economic explanation for the crisis of the EA generally and of these five countries in particular has recently been formulated by Paul Krugman (2013), using the original version of OCA theory.[12] The explanation runs as follows: joining a currency with other countries may reduce the

[12] Joseph Stiglitz (2016) does not go into the same detail as Krugman (2013) but claims that there was "a consensus among economists" which refers to Mundell (1961) (Stiglitz 2016: 15). Stiglitz is referenced where he supports Krugman; I focus on these two economists because their contributions are recent and influential. Moreover, they are two economists whose work I greatly respect.

transaction costs of trading with each other but this also reduces flexibility when a shock hits one of the members but not others. "It's not just that a currency area is limited to a one-size-fits-all monetary policy; even more important is the loss of a mechanism for adjustment" (Krugman 2013: 440; Stiglitz 2016: 14–15). The lost mechanism is the exchange rate. Krugman takes the example of a housing boom that bursts in some member states. The tradeable sector then suffers from the hangover of the boom time wages and needs a devaluation to achieve a quick adjustment. Iceland was apparently so much luckier than any EA country in this respect, devaluing its wages in "one fell swoop" by 25 percent while Spain had to force down wages in individual wage negotiations.[13] This takes time, as the "daylight saving" argument for exchange rate adjustment emphasizes (Eichengreen and Wyplosz 1993: 60; Section 5.1.1). Furthermore, EA countries also do not have enough labor mobility to prevent unemployment emerging, apparently in contrast to the United States.

This is Mundell's version of OCA theory boldly applied to the EA crisis. It can be examined, first, by asking how much wage adjustment there was, and second whether it had the same consequences in all five countries.[14]

It seems that there was considerable real-wage adjustment by EA countries (Figure 6.1). Ireland is the most extreme case, with a fall in the REER that exceeds Iceland's 25 percent from peak to trough. By contrast, Hungary, a non-EA country which did devalue, showed considerably more volatility, with devaluations apparently only having transitory effects on the REER.

Reductions in REERs occurred in the EA despite depressed demand and extremely low inflation, an economic situation that normally does not bode well for internal devaluation (Shambaugh 2012: 182–4). Real-wage adjustment had to be nominal wage adjustment, which was an extraordinarily painful process. It meant that most of the program countries saw their GDP stagnate relative to the EU-15 (the EU before enlargement of 2004; Figure 6.2). They have hardly got back to the income levels prevailing at the beginning of the currency union, with the exception of Ireland and Spain.

While Krugman is right about the painfulness of the adjustment, it is less clear that flexible exchange rates would have avoided the pain. Compared to Iceland, the program countries except Greece adjusted more quickly in terms of GDP and current account: the Icelandic current account became positive for the first time in mid-2012, almost four years after the krona crashed in late 2008. By 2015, the loss in Icelandic GDP relative to its pre-crisis high in 2007

[13] Krugman (2013) does not mention the capital controls that Iceland maintained for seven years (Milne and Grant 2015).

[14] The question of labor mobility will be taken up in Chapter 8; Krugman (2013: 445) does not consider it a relevant factor in the EA's problems (quoted below).

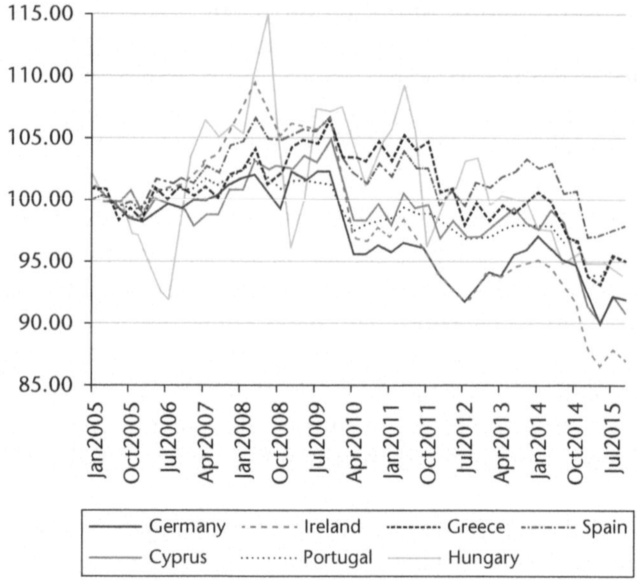

Figure 6.1. Annual real effective exchange rate vis-à-vis forty-two countries
Source: AMECO (price and cost competitiveness), consumer price deflator-based, 2005=100

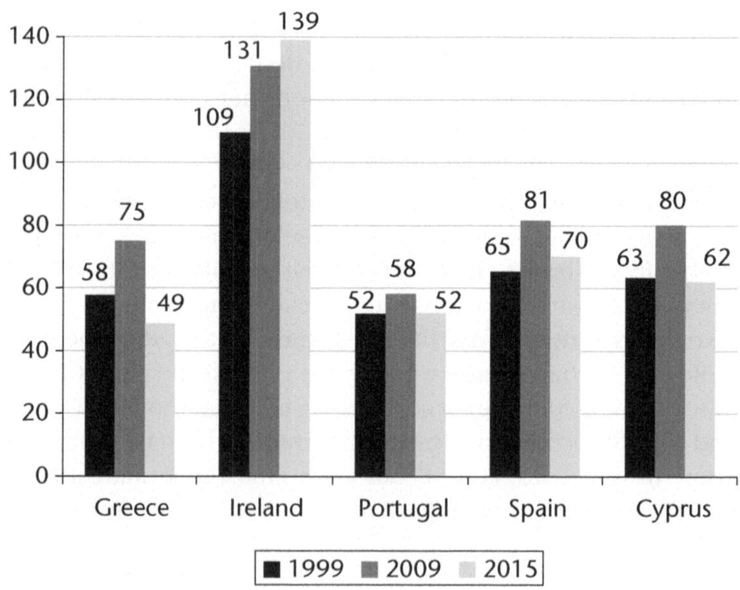

Figure 6.2. GDP at current prices per head of population, relative to EU-15 = 100, 1999–2015
Source: AMECO series HVGDPR

was 28 percent, the fall was steeper only in Greece; Iceland is growing again but so are the other EA countries, except Greece.

The models of Mundell (1961) and McKinnon (1963) perceive the world as made up of "one-product regions," that is each region is so highly specialized that it coincides with a sector, which is why shocks are so specific that each needs their own exchange rate—unless labor market mobility or real-wage flexibility can substitute for it. Since the exchange rate change needed to compensate for the bust of the housing and construction sector in Spain would not be exactly what the tourism industry or car manufacturers need, Spain should have several sectoral or regional exchange rates.

To avoid this *reductio ad absurdum*, Peter Kenen advances a "competing [diversification] principle" (Mundell and Swoboda 1969: 111–13). The ideal adjustment unit of an OCA consists of a bundle of industries that are sufficiently different (Kenen 1969: 49–50). If disturbances are truly random, then a varied production structure provides insurance for the national economy so that a shock to a few sectors can be compensated for by others. Exchange rate change is therefore only needed when there is a general shock. Since the change should be relative to other countries, the shock should be general to the national economy but not shared by others. If other countries have similar production structures, exchange rate adjustment will not be effective. A study by the ECB (2013a: 66–8), based on an index for 250 industries, finds that EA members started out with relatively similar and diversified export structures, and became slightly more similar and more diversified still between 1999 and 2011. This suggests that relative exchange rate adjustment would not serve as an adjustment mechanism.

However, Krugman (2013: 445) fastens onto another aspect of Kenen's contribution to OCA theory: "Kenen has turned out to dominate Mundell: lack of labor mobility has not played a major role in euro's difficulties, at least so far, but lack of fiscal integration has had an enormous impact." If fiscal integration is what matters, an OCA comprises sectors and regions grouped together under a fiscal umbrella. The fiscal unit can reduce adjustment costs: the EA's failure to reduce adjustment costs through appropriate fiscal measures is, for Krugman, its major failing.

But this also means that OCAs are defined by their fiscal arrangements, and for Kenen (1969: 45–8) this had the implication that wider fiscal risk sharing could bring more exchange rate stability. Kenen argued that the stabilizing properties of fiscal federalism—a national market for regionally issued debt securities and discretionary transfers to depressed regions—require fixed exchange rates. A region may have to give up its monetary powers "in order to participate in a major fiscal system" with these benefits (Mundell and Swoboda 1969: 107). The reasons why "fiscal zones should not be larger than monetary zones" are evident from US fiscal and monetary history

(Chapter 4). The central fiscal authority has to nominate a means of payment if it is to avoid collecting taxes in devalued currencies, while sub-national monetary adventurism leads to periodic crises.

More fiscal integration in the EA would have been desirable in the adjustment after 2008 and it is important to understand why fiscal capacity to support adjustment was limited. But OCA theory leads the analysis down the wrong path. In this theory, it must be an asymmetric shock that hit the five countries for which they should have had relief from a central budget, by paying lower taxes and receiving transfers to compensate for their recessions. Krugman (2013: 440) insists: "It is idiosyncratic ('asymmetric') shocks that are the problem: A boom or slump everywhere in a currency area poses no special problems." The reason is that a common monetary policy can respond to a general shock, but not to specific shocks in individual countries. So long as the efficacy of monetary policy is insisted on, the OCA account must interpret the euro crisis as asymmetric rather than general and systemic: "What happened... was the mother of all asymmetric shocks—a shock that was, in a bitter irony, caused by the creation of the euro itself" (Krugman 2013: 444; Stiglitz 2016: 13–14).

There is nothing in OCA theory, given its fixation on external shocks and lack of a financial sector, that would have prepared policymakers for shocks developing as a consequence of monetary integration. Housing booms and busts were decidedly not on the radar screen. It is an understatement to say that "traditional optimum currency area theory paid little attention to banking issues" (Krugman 2013: 445). The theory paid no attention whatsoever to banking and included capital only as a factor of production, not as a stock of wealth. Even endogenous OCA theory, often considered to be its most advanced form,[15] was only about trade in goods and services, without any asset markets. There is no space for the role of a national versus a regional banking system or the negative feedback loop between banks and government balance sheets.

To conclude: it is not clear how listening to those economists who knew all along that the euro area is not an OCA (Krugman 2013: 39) would have helped the protagonists of the common currency or the countries most affected by the crisis. The theory grasps at best the experience of Portugal, facing a longer-term structural shock caused by the entry into global markets of new low labor cost producers. One could even argue that EA crisis management was too impressed by OCA theory, leading to policy mistakes before and in the crisis.

[15] This is because it addressed the Lucas critique that expectations of actors in a model adjust to policy changes, so key parameters may become variables. Trade direction, wage bargains, and price setting are prime candidates for such endogeneity of economic behavior to the drastic change of currency unification.

According to Mundell (1961) and McKinnon (1963), the burden of adjustment in a currency area where labor is relatively immobile must fall on labor costs. OCA theory takes the perspective of the member state and how it can and should adjust, instead of considering how the policies of a group of countries in a currency area can minimize harm to individual members (Mundell and Swoboda 1969: 114). The EU pursued an obsessive agenda of flexibilizing labor markets while the real problems built up in financial markets (Schelkle and Hassel 2013). Once the crisis hit, pro-cyclical budget restraint was advocated in order to force labor markets into adjustment.[16] The "revenge of the Optimum Currency Area" has a double meaning that seems to elude the supporters of the concept: thinking in terms of an "optimum euro area" may have been part of the problem rather than the solution. This is why it is still important to expose the flaws of OCA theory (Schelkle 2013a).

6.2.2 *Incompatible Growth Regimes?*

The comparative capitalism literature addresses questions which the OCA interpretation of events does not grapple with: why did member states with inflexible labor markets try to join a monetary union? And why did they not, after they had joined, become "optimal" by adapting to the requirements of a currency union? The economists' answer to these questions is "politics" (Farhi and Werning 2014: fn 1; Feldstein 2012: 1), usually without much further comment. Comparative capitalism scholars build a bridge between politics and economics. They agree that economic considerations would advise against a currency union between countries with different growth models, but they also explain the institutions and interests that promoted the union as well as the conflicts that have undermined it.

They explain how both the Northern and Southern countries envisaged gains from monetary union. Taking the latter first, the Southern periphery in Europe wanted to enjoy the benefits of low inflation, above all low interest rates and exchange rate stability (Iversen et al. 2016: 10.3–4). This was supported by domestic producer coalitions, especially in non-trade sectors. There was also an economic paradigm shift in favor of monetary stabilization and supply-side reform that elites in most advanced countries came to accept after the tumultuous 1970s (Hall 2014a: 1224). However, the institution of a hard currency does not do away with political-economic forces supporting a

[16] Microeconomic flexibility is a futile and sometimes even counter-productive response to macroeconomic instability. Germany's short time work program that generously subsidized firms hoarding their workforce did just the opposite and successfully stabilized employment (Arpaia et al. 2010: 35).

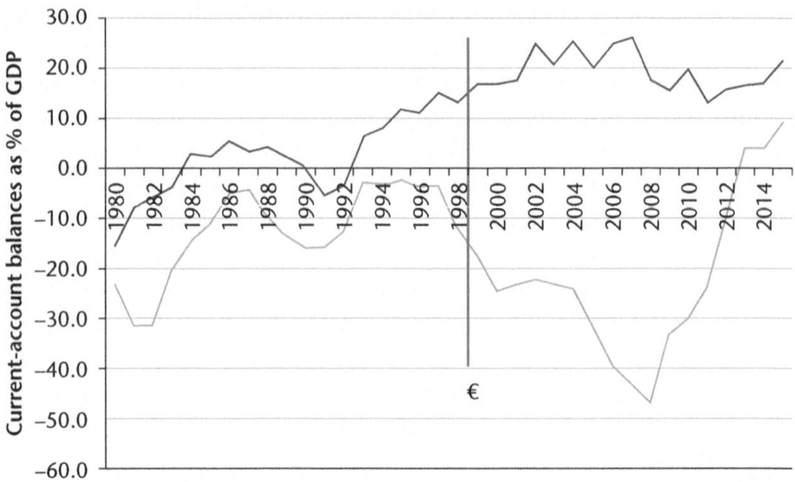

Figure 6.3. Current-account balances of the "South" and the "North," 1980–2015

"Southern" growth model different from that of the North (Hall 2012: 361). In brief, the Northern growth model is said to be "export-led"; the Southern is deemed "domestic demand-led." Unfortunately, the two growth models cannot live together in one monetary union as the South needs periodic devaluations to compensate for its structurally higher inflation or it is doomed to stagnation. The unhappy marriage of the South to the North will continuously run into the current-account constraint and erupt in debt crises.

Figure 6.3, inspired by the intricate analysis of Johnston and Regan (2016: fig. 1), illustrates the point. The "South" comprises Greece, Italy, Portugal, and Spain, plus Ireland; Cyprus is left out for lack of current-account data before 1995. The "North" comprises Austria, Belgium, France,[17] Finland, Germany (West only until 1990), and the Netherlands. Current-account balances are taken as a percentage of GDP at market prices and added up unweighted—otherwise the North is completely dominated by Germany's balance. We can see that until 1998, the current-account balances moved in tandem (were positively correlated); subsequently they moved apart (were negatively correlated). It looks as if, after currency union, the Northern surpluses directly fed on the Southern deficits, with the competitiveness of the North pushing the uncompetitive South into debt (Johnston and Regan 2016: 319; Iversen et al. 2016: 10.5). This seems to illustrate perfectly the internal incompatibility of the export-led and the domestic demand-led models.

[17] Excluding France from the North and including it in the South, as Iversen et al. (2016: 10.2) propose, makes no discernible difference as the French economy had overall a fairly balanced current account.

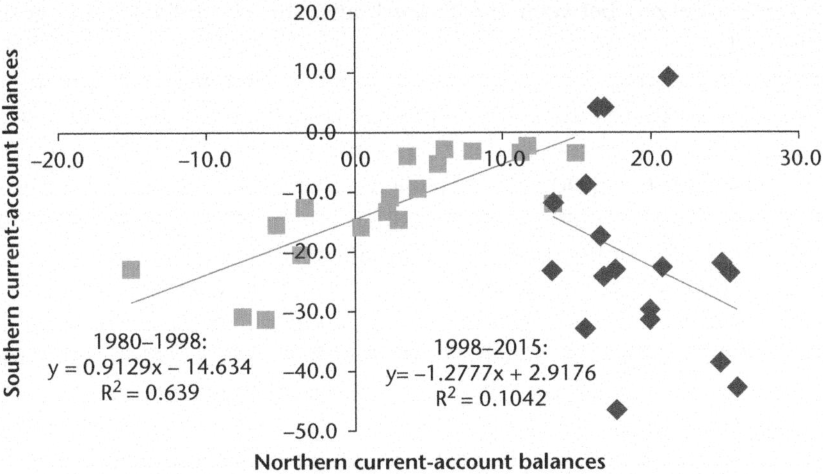

Figure 6.4. Correlation between Southern and Northern balances, 1980–98 versus 1998–2015

Source: AMECO series UBCA, own calculations (unweighted sums of national balances)

Note: Since Johnston and Regan (2016) make a claim about the structural break due to the exchange rate regime, I take 1998 as the year differentiating the two phases, although the positive correlation between Northern and Southern balances appears to break down from around 1992.

The regression equations in Figure 6.4 show that the positive and fairly tight correlation between the balances until 1998 (light quadrants) becomes a steeply negative but also very loose correlation after 1998 (dark diamonds).[18] The aggregate Northern surpluses fluctuate around 20 percent of GDP in the European monetary union while the Southern deficits keep on rising sharply until the crisis in 2008. Johnston and Regan (2016: 319–20) argue that before the fixing of exchange rates in 1999, there was a safety valve for the South in the form of nominal exchange rate devaluation when deficits got too large. At the same time, the ERM provided some spine for inflation-averse national central banks, which to some extent were able to force wage bargains to heed the external constraint. These two mechanisms were abolished with the European monetary union.

If the two mechanisms—an exchange rate safety valve and inflation-averse central banks—had been effective, then it is indeed unclear why any government wanted to get rid of them. But these mechanisms were not effective. There is little evidence that nominal exchange rates moved so as to balance current accounts in the 1980s or 1990s. Nor were national central banks able to pursue exchange rate policies that were right for their domestic conditions:

[18] The coefficient preceding x (for Northern balances) gives the sign and strength of the correlation, the R^2 indicates the tightness of fit which can be between 0 and 1.

they were squeezed between the D-Mark and the US dollar exchange rate (Section 5.1.1).

In the comparative analysis of growth models, the crucial incompatibility between the Northern and Southern models arises from the interplay between wage bargains and central banking (Hall and Franzese 1998; Hancké 2013: 31–4). In the North, export sectors lead a highly coordinated wage-bargaining process across the economy, exercising discipline so as to preserve high-value-added jobs. Tight monetary policy supports this by signaling the need for restraint to powerful export-sector unions in profitable companies; tight fiscal policy ensures that the public-sector unions cooperate as well. No such interaction and discipline works reliably in the Southern political economies: trade unions are relatively strong but often with small membership, competing with each other in the reach and generosity of their bargains to attract more members, while monetary and fiscal policy tend to accommodate these bargains for fear of unemployment and strike action. Only crises or the prospect of extraordinary benefits (like euro membership, which provided a "carrot" for restraint in the 1990s) can suppress excessive wage bargains, and this suppression is necessarily temporary (Hancké and Rhodes 2005; Johnston 2012).

The "competitiveness hypothesis" (Johnston and Regan 2016: 321) that flows from this institutionalist theory of growth models can be looked at more directly using data provided by the ECB (2013) on "intra-euro area trade linkages" before the crisis (Table 6.2). The trade balance is the more relevant indicator for competitiveness, rather than the current account overall which includes cross-border profits and interest payments. The ECB data breaks down intra- and extra-EA exports for trade in goods and services.[19] Among Northern countries, it is noticeable that only Belgium and the Netherlands conform to the hypothesis of Northern growth feeding on Southern deficits in that they have higher surpluses in intra-EA trade than with trading partners beyond the EA.[20] By contrast, Germany had a much higher trade surplus with the rest of the world outside the EA, while Austria and Finland actually had intra-EA deficits. It is also noticeable that not all Northern countries have a net creditor position. In the "South," the countries with the highest deficits, Greece, Portugal, and Spain, have even higher deficits with trading partners outside the EA, while Ireland operated as an export platform for its direct investors and ran large trade surpluses with countries inside and outside the EA (while its current account was in deficit at almost 5 percent of GDP). Almost all had very high external debt, with the exception of Italy.

[19] Unfortunately, this data is not publicly available to extend beyond the time frame provided by the ECB study.

[20] The Dutch intra-EA surplus is overstated, however, due to Rotterdam's role as the EU's biggest harbor (ECB 2013c: 61).

Table 6.2. External trade balance and debt position, 2006–8, in percentage of GDP

	Trade balance*		Net IIP**
	Total	Intra-EA	End of 2008
Austria	−0.2	−5.8	−16.9
Belgium	3.0	5.2	39.8
Finland	2.9	−0.8	−9.7
France	−2.9	−3.2	−12.9
Germany	7.4	2.5	25.0
Netherlands	7.0	19.5	4.2
Greece	−18.1	−8.5	−76.9
Ireland	15.4	11.4	−75.7
Italy	−0.8	−0.5	−24.1
Portugal	−13.6	−10.0	−96.1
Spain	−9.3	−3.9	−79.3

Note: * three-year average 2006–8; ** IIP = International Investment Position
Source: ECB, Monthly Bulletin January 2013: 69

On the basis of this evidence, evaluated when imbalances inside the EA had reached their peak (Figure 6.3), it is doubtful that Northern growth was directly dependent on Southern debt. It makes more sense to turn it round: Southern European countries could finance very high trade deficits, which benefited exporters in the Northern EA but even more those outside the EA (Wyplosz 2013: 5; 19–21). Larger imbalances were an international phenomenon. Pontusson and Baccaro (2015: 21–2, 35) suggest that trade deficits can be caused by wage increases but also by expansions in household credit. A study by the IMF provides some evidence for this link (Chen et al. 2012: 20).

This alerts us to a few problems in the comparative capitalism story which is, at first sight and certainly compared to OCA theory, convincing. There is, first of all, the delineation of countries in a Southern periphery and a Northern core. These homogenous categories do not fit Greece and Ireland (and Cyprus): problems caused by a decline in competitiveness were second order for their crises. Declaring all countries that needed external assistance to be "South" is a post-hoc-ergo-propter-hoc classification. Ireland is not in the South but also not a complete outlier: it shared a crisis pattern with Cyprus and Spain. Similarly, France sits awkwardly in between. Johnston and Regan (2016) include this strong export nation in the North while Iversen et al. (2016) put it in the South because France lacks the wage-bargaining institutions to support a hard currency; Hall's account (2012, 2014a) leaves France out.

Second, this supply-side interpretation of the crisis has some doubtful implications. It must assume a fair amount of myopia and/or recklessness on the part of organized labor in Southern European countries. Carlin (2013) is explicit on this point: her model explains EA imbalances by the irrationality of wage setters in the South and "self-stabilizing" (rational) wage-setting institutions in Germany, compounded by the pro-cyclical effect of a uniform interest rate policy. Furthermore, scholars focus almost exclusively on cost competitiveness as the determinant of external imbalances, while the demand pull from catch-up growth is neglected (Johnston and Regan 2016: 17–20). The focus on wage costs is somewhat anachronistic: competition between advanced economies is largely determined by non-price components, such as branding, quality, and reliability of service (ECB 2003: 68). Hence, even as a supply-side story, the focus on Northern and Southern wage costs is too simple. Chen et al. (2012: 12) find that intra-EA current-account imbalances were driven by (a) the rise of China, displacing Southern European exports in third markets; and (b) the integration of Central and Eastern Europe into the production chain of Germany and other export nations, making the latter more cost-competitive.

Third, if the diagnosis of the comparative capitalism literature is correct, Southern trade unions are largely to blame for the crisis and wage adjustment should be the focus of adjustment programs. The financial system as an explanatory variable is conspicuous by its absence in these explanations. The growth regime literature does not look for national or regime-type differences in financial systems along the lines of Zysman (1983) and Hancké et al. (2007: 21–5), which would have been a natural starting point. This is just as well because the contributions in Hardie and Howarth (2013), Hardie et al. (2013), as well as Grittersová (2014) have put high hurdles in the way of regime-type explanations. They show, on the one hand, that there is a strong trend among cross-border banks to "market-based banking" and, on the other, no evidence for convergence on a crisis-prone, "impatient," liberal financial system in Southern Europe that could explain their calamity.

Comparative capitalist accounts often include the so-called Walters critique of monetary integration, which points out that, with a common nominal interest rate, countries with high inflation will have lower real interest rates, fueling further expansion and inflation (Walters 1988: 503–4). In turn, stagnating economies may have an even harder time to get out of their slump due to relatively high real interest rates. This critique gives monetary policy a big role in the crisis story. But the Walters critique applies to any heterogeneous union: to the UK and the US as well as to the EA (Schelkle 2014b, 2016). It assumes that there are no other policy instruments to rein in inflationary pressures, such as decentralized taxation. The Padoa-Schioppa group also thought that this "endogenous asymmetry" of real interest rates is the most problematic form of heterogeneity that the EA has to contend with (Enderlein et al. 2012: paras 35–6). But they also suggest that a self-financing counter-cyclical fund could easily deal with this source of instability. Other possibilities are counter-cyclical property taxes and macroprudential policies at the national level.

Analyses in the comparative growth model tradition do not extend their arguments consistently to the crisis since 2010. For instance, Hall (2012: 362) argues that it is "a classic debt crisis, fueled by increasing financial speculation and an overweening faith in lightly regulated markets, much like the crisis that exploded in the USA in 2008." Similarly, Iversen et al. (2016: 10.16) assert that "the sovereign debt problems arose because of two institutional deficiencies in the Eurozone... namely, the lack of a banking union and the absence of a credible lender of last resort in government bond markets." In both statements, inadequate institutions that are not central to either growth model are invoked to explain the EA's predicament. The diagnoses are spot on but do not follow from the incompatibility of growth models.

6.2.3 *Incompleteness and Reversal of Risk Sharing?*

The political economy of monetary solidarity does not seek an explanation for the EA crisis in one "root cause" that afflicted all five countries. If one takes diversity seriously, there may be different vulnerabilities that can push economies into crisis. The theory would actually lead one to expect a certain randomness in asymmetric (non-systemic) shocks. From this point of view, an explanation for a *systemic* crisis should be found, first, in hard-to-insure risks and, second, in a setting for risk sharing that cannot prevent collective action failure and may even provide incentives for shirking common responsibility. This failure meant that a self-fulfilling process could run its course, pushing vulnerable economies into devastating crises.

In contrast to OCA theory, the perspective of monetary solidarity highlights the fact that the shock causing the EA crisis was not asymmetric and idiosyncratic, but followed the *common* shock of the financial crisis. Since this shock was largely created by monetary-financial integration between all advanced economies, albeit particularly intensely in the EA, it created problems for banks in all advanced economies. Some banks were prone to insolvency once their dubious assets were properly priced, others were dragged into the abyss because contagion and fire sales of assets led to a crash in asset prices that were actually priced correctly before the crisis.[21] The common shock wiped out loss-absorbing capital of highly leveraged and sound banks alike. Central banks came to the rescue by providing liquidity against collateral and buying assets, to stabilize the prices of these assets and ultimately to prevent a general meltdown that would have destroyed savings of households. Governments took a lot of the financial risks on their books, by becoming shareholders and by acting as guarantors of bank liabilities.

[21] See Brunnermeier et al. (2009: 13–24) for a summary of these propagation and amplification mechanisms.

The commonality of the shock was observable in the real economy as well. Evidence of co-movements in output growth can be found in a research article for the *World Economic Outlook* in October 2013:

> [T]he recent global financial crisis . . . stands head and shoulders above the other events in the sample in terms of inducing strong output comovements. It is literally off the charts, with an impact on output comovements four times larger than that of any other event during the past several decades. (IMF 2013: 86)

The "other events" start with the oil-price shocks of the 1970s and include Black Friday of the mid-1980s, the ERM crisis in the early 1990s, as well as the Asian and Russian crises in the late 1990s. Output growth became highly synchronized, leading to severe recession everywhere and a collapse of international trade.

Commonality of shocks is a problem for insurance. The costs can only be shared with future generations. And governments did this, increasing public debt in a way last seen in the Second World War. They did so in order to bail out domestic banks and their savers, as well as to stabilize the economy with fiscal stimulus packages and automatic stabilizers (Schelkle 2012a). Public debt was also the counterpart to allowing households and firms to deleverage (reduce their indebtedness). For this, they have to achieve a surplus of their earnings over expenditures, for which they need a counterparty that does the opposite. Deleveraging through current-account surpluses (foreign demand and debt) is more attractive, but is counterproductive in a global recession.

The common shock in 2008 and its spreading thereafter highlight the considerable and measurable integration of European financial markets (Coeurdacier and Martin 2009; Waysand et al. 2010: 2; ch. 3.2.3). But increased integration had not been accompanied by the development of a co-extensive supervisory infrastructure and resolution facilities. Financial integration in this situation meant interdependence and heightened exposure to risk, not automatic risk sharing through cross-border asset holdings. As early as June 2010, BIS (2010: 18) indicated in its *Quarterly Review* how much EA banks could lose on their claims against "residents of the euro area countries facing market pressures." At the end of 2009, when the Greek budget data began to unsettle markets and officials, banks in the EA held claims to the tune of around €1,100 billion, that is 62 percent of all foreign bank claims on Greece, Ireland, Portugal, and Spain.[22] This figure related to claims consolidated on an ultimate risk basis; in other words, if those countries defaulted, losses would have to be borne by these EA banks. French and German banks were particularly exposed, holding more than half of the combined exposure

[22] BIS (2010: 18–19), US $ amounts converted at a historical (interbank) exchange rate of 0.7 $/€.

(€345 billion and €325 billion respectively). Exposure went beyond the EA: banks headquartered in the UK were the largest creditors of Ireland (€160 billion) and held large claims on Spain (€98 billion). Last but not least, there was the real threat of a domino effect among vulnerable economies: for instance Spanish banks were the largest creditors of Portugal (€77 billion).

Against this background, it is understandable that governments were reluctant to let Greece or any other sovereign default, for fear of a second Lehman moment. Sandbu (2015: 67–9, 101–4, 116–18) sees this as the greatest mistake in the management of the EA crisis: that no debt default, sovereign and private, was allowed. He sees Denmark as a successful example of a country where banks were allowed to fail; the country got through the crisis relatively unscathed, despite very high household debt.[23] Another example is Hungary where the government effectively wrote off household debt by legislating that households could pay back their mortgages, denominated in foreign exchange, at historical exchange rates. This meant that the claims of the (foreign) banks were written down by about 30 percent and other governments bailed out the foreign-owned banks (Bohle 2014: 935–6; Mabbett and Schelkle 2015: 517–19). But these were essentially national solutions, through self-insurance (Denmark) or burden shifting (Hungary); they could not work for the EA as a whole.

The commonality of the financial instability became less obvious in the months after the major hit arising from the difficulties of Greece, and this became a problem for collective action. Market observers came to perceive some EA members, rightly or wrongly, as more fragile than others. Governments were in the spotlight because, as Paul De Grauwe (2011) wrote in a widely cited paper, the ECB's role as lender of last resort to governments was not assured, by contrast with the backing enjoyed by the British and US Treasuries from their respective central banks. Bond investors started to differentiate between high-risk member states and the rest. Greece was an obvious target because of the adverse trajectory of its public finances. Yet it is not clear that this was the reason why Greek bonds were sold off after late 2009. As argued above, the downgrading of Greek bonds by Standard & Poor's, together with the ECB's announcement that lower standards in collateralized lending would be phased out, was enough to unsettle the markets. This suggests that Greece was simply the weakest link that broke first. The next country in the line of fire was Ireland, in every relevant aspect different from Greece. From summer 2009 onwards, the Irish government had adopted an ambitious orthodox program of budget consolidation that was hoped to yield "expansionary austerity" (Guajardo et al. 2014), only to be attacked in bond markets a year later because the effects were brutally contractionary.

[23] Woll (2014) supports Sandbu's favorable assessment of Danish crisis management which was among the six biggest bank bailout programs she compared.

There was a considerable constructed and self-fulfilling element in this evolution: member states became high risk, or not, depending on market sentiment. For instance, it is not obvious why Belgium with a public debt ratio of 99.5 percent in 2009, up from 87 percent in 2007, was not in the group of countries attacked in bond markets. Two major cross-border banks, Dexia and Fortis, had to be bailed out soon after the Lehman default, in difficult cooperation with French and Dutch authorities (Pisani-Ferry and Sapir 2010: 354–5). Belgium is a divided country, and it had a caretaker government for over 500 days in 2010–11 that was legally constrained in its actions. Belgium's net international investment position was quite concentrated on the countries under pressure: the net claims of its banks on Greece, Ireland, Portugal, and Spain amounted to 50 percent of Belgian GDP at the end of 2008 (Waysand et al. 2010: table 2a).[24] Similarly, Austrian banks and investors could have become victims of contagious currency attacks on non-EA countries in Central and Eastern Europe that were widely feared at the time. Austria's net international investment position included claims against Visegrad countries, Bulgaria and Romania, to the tune of 30 percent of GDP (Waysand et al. 2010: table 2a).

This evidence about individual countries is supported by rigorous cross-national studies. Research has provided evidence that panic and contagion, not fundamentals like high imbalances, explained why certain governments had to pay high-risk premia on their new bond issues. For instance, De Grauwe and Ji (2013) estimated the explanatory power of the current-account balance and the budget balance, both measured as ratios to GDP, for the level of government bond spreads. In no specification does the current-account balance have any significance. The government balance does, but the best specification is non-linear, indicating that expectations of a default, a tail event, play the key role. The authors show that the crisis in 2008 marked a structural break: having underpriced risks on EA government debt before 2008, financial market investors became suddenly oversensitive to these risks. This assessment is based on the observation that non-euro ("stand-alone") countries with similar public debt ratios did not have to pay such risk premia. Only for Greece did De Grauwe and Ji find that fundamentals, specifically government finances, could explain the market reaction; for all others, the market reactions had a self-fulfilling character.

The crucial point for the political economy of monetary solidarity is that there was nothing deterministic in the turn of a common shock into a handful

[24] However, the international investment position is based on location of the immediate lender and borrower, not consolidated on an ultimate risk basis (for instance when the guarantor of a credit is in another country, the claim would be on that other country, not on the countries in distress).

of country crises. It was fundamentally underdetermined whether any particular country would get into deeper troubles and, if so, which one. Greece is the only possible exception but it would, without the previous common shock, have been too small to rock the boat. After the most severe crisis in post-war history, the governments of most member states were vulnerable to bond market attacks. Even France and Germany would have been vulnerable if the EU and the IMF had allowed Greece to default early and markets had taken this as a precedent for further problems, notably in Italy which has the third-largest government bond issue in the world.[25]

Given this widespread exposure to extreme market instability and uncertainty, one might have expected resolute collective action to protect the commons from devastation. Some of this was on display in 2008–9, with the G20 setting an agenda for comprehensive financial reregulation. The EA got relatively well through the first phase of the financial crisis in 2008–9 (Schelkle 2012b) but was less successful in mustering collective action after 2009. How come? The answer has three elements.

First, the Greek calamity looked like the very case of fiscal irresponsibility that fiscal surveillance and the no-bailout clause were meant to prevent. Governments could not simply ignore these institutions; they had insisted that they were necessary for making the commitment to a hard currency credible. If there was some belief in these institutions, decision makers must also have feared that markets would take against the euro if they were lenient with Greece, a serial sovereign defaulter in its modern history (Reinhart 2010: 53). This fear cannot be entirely dismissed as delusion: the fact that the euro was never sold off and remained fairly strong throughout the unfolding crisis vindicates this reading of what markets expected, namely keeping up appearances of rule-based policymaking.

But then followed Ireland and later Spain, neither of which could be portrayed as being addicted to fiscal excess.[26] Here the second element came into play. The panic in bond markets itself obstructed collective action: it lifted the veil of ignorance and divided the risk pool into countries that were a casualty and others that were lucky. Government bond spreads rose for some member states, but not for all. Once the veil lifts, the lucky have an inclination in any insurance scheme to regard their luck as merit and the unlucky as deserving their mishap. The "revelation" of Greece's dismal government statistics—not

[25] In absolute amounts, after the United States and Japan.

[26] One could only argue this under the extended definition of fiscal discipline by Wyplosz (2013: 21–3) who includes financial supervision into fiscal policy: in the absence of monetary financing of sovereigns, governments can only be said to be fiscally disciplined if fiscal resources can cover bank bailouts. It seems to me preferable to see his notion of "fiscal indiscipline" as a problem of an interface between public and private finance rather than as a public-finance problem only—the latter underestimates the amount of uncertainty surrounding bank bailouts.

really news to EU insiders—had already nurtured this inclination. The Irish government's unilateral decision to guarantee all liabilities of Irish banks shortly after the Lehman collapse could be interpreted as self-inflicted harm which was not covered by the insurance contract. The Portuguese and the Spanish governments got somewhat more sympathetic responses as they were honestly struggling to help their households and firms to deleverage. Italy and Greece got technocratic governments, under Mario Monti and Lukas Papademos respectively, that tried hard to appease bond markets.

But just when most policymakers came round to see the self-fulfilling properties of the EA crisis, Cyprus gave new impetus to the conviction that the root cause was a deep divide between a profligate periphery and a prudent core. It is hard not to see self-inflicted harm in the audacious strategy adopted by Cypriot banks, betting on a big gain from a second bailout for Greece (Lütz et al. 2015: 8–9). This chutzpah was only matched by the hubris of the government, which attempted to capitalize on Cyprus' safe-haven status for Russian savers and tax evaders. And so the lucky felt vindicated in treating the unlucky as if it were entirely their fault, albeit some more than others.[27] The acronyms GIPS and GIIPS stand for this pernicious rounding up of the usual suspects.

Beyond these concrete features of the crisis in 2010–12, a third problem for collective action lay in the EA's institutional set-up, which made sovereigns in distress look as if they had failed in their duty to treat budgetary policy as a matter of common concern. Before recent reforms, only the trespassing of fiscal rules could lead to a formal warning by the EU Commission and the Council, while excessive mortgage credit or an unsustainable current-account balance could not. Once the crisis hit, the fiscal accounting rules of Eurostat ensured maximum fiscal transparency, in line with internationally agreed standards, so that the socialization of private debt materialized as liabilities of government.[28] Hence, the crisis in the EA was bound to emerge in government bond markets. When it finally made its highly selective appearance, the apparent "root cause" of sovereign debt provided the pretext for refusing collective responsibility. Given how fiscally stretched all authorities were or felt, there was little incentive for solidaristic gestures, such as introducing a joint debt instrument that would prevent countries being picked off by the bond markets.

[27] Differentiation between program countries came to the fore when German finance minister Schäuble was secretly filmed in February 2012, promising his Portuguese counterpart Gaspar that there was flexibility in the conditions for Portugal once firm decisions on the Greek program had been taken (N-TV 2012). The revelation caused outrage in Germany and Greece.

[28] Mabbett and Schelkle (2016a) go through concrete examples of how the fiscal accounting rules treat bank-rescue packages and the public sector in a recession.

Table 6.3. Cumulative change in public debt over two years before and after program start (in t)

In percentage of GDP	Greece t = 2010/2011	Ireland t = 2010	Portugal t = 2011	Cyprus t = 2012
1 Public debt-to-GDP ratio in t-2	112.9	44.2	83.1	61.3
2 *Change in gross public debt of which:*	*67.9*	*93.8*	*56.4*	*55.2*
2a. Debt-creating flow: *primary deficit*	23.3	39.4	16.8	8.8
2b. Debt dynamic 1: *real interest rate*	26.0	14.9	14.5	11.7
2c. Debt dynamic 2: *real GDP decline*	40.9	3.9	7.7	7.7
2d. Exchange rate depreciation	−0.5	0.0	0.1	0.0
2e. Net privatization proceeds	−1.2	−2.5	−2.8	0.0
2f. Contingent liabilities	8.4	5.8	1.0	0.0
2g. Other (*bank recapitalization*, PSI sweeteners)	43.1	29.3	2.4	14.1
2h. Residual, including *asset change*	−72.0	3.3	16.9	12.9

Note: cumulative figures starting two years before (t-2) and ending two years after (t+2) program started (in t); breakdown for years in the Appendix, including exact sources

Source: IMF (see Appendix); own calculations

Evidence for this explanation of the EA crisis as self-fulfilling can be found first of all in the adverse evolution of public debt that the five vulnerable member states experienced, however different their history was. Table 6.3 summarizes the government debt explosion two years before and two years after the year in which the respective country took recourse to external assistance, for the four countries with full-fledged country programs.[29] Spain had only a financial-sector program without financial IMF involvement. The cumulative figures for Greece cover six years as the country had two programs; the third in 2015 is outside the time horizon. All figures are actual, not forecast.

The first point to note is that Ireland has the most adverse evolution of debt, adding almost 94 percent to its low starting level of 44 percent in 2008 in just five years. The effects of its insolvent banks appear in the primary deficit (covering losses) and contingent liabilities (providing guarantees, etc.), as well as in the specific item of bank recapitalization, which refers to the acquisition of equity. These items make up at least two-thirds of Ireland's debt accumulation. The other big item is the real interest cost of its debt, adding a whopping 15 percent over five years: negative inflation, triggered by cuts in wages and salaries, increases the cost of debt enormously.

Greece is a striking example of self-defeating austerity as negative GDP growth (in row 2c of Table 6.3) added almost 41 percent to the debt ratio. Interest costs also added more to the debt dynamic than the primary budget deficit (rows 2b and 2a, respectively). The country would be showing the most negative development from an already high level if it had not had debt relief

[29] The breakdown by years can be found in the Appendix to this chapter.

in the second bailout program. This is noted in the last row as "asset change" (reducing debt, hence negative). Yet, the gross figure of -78 percent of GDP in 2012 (see Appendix) is misleading. The write-down of government bonds in 2012 was directly responsible for the insolvency of several Greek banks that had to be recapitalized subsequently; this, together with the "sweeteners" for private-sector involvement (PSI),[30] reduced net debt relief by 39 percent, effectively halving it compared with what the IMF deemed necessary (Mabbett and Schelkle 2015: 524–5). But the most striking feature of Greece's debt situation is just how much the dynamic of interest cost and a severe recession fueled debt accumulation (rows 2b and 2c in Table 6.3). These uncontrollable drivers of debt completely outweigh the primary deficit (deficit net of interest payments) for which the government can be held accountable.[31]

The same holds for the other two countries, Portugal and Cyprus: the own dynamic of debt (rows 2b and 2c in Table 6.3) in a slump added at least two-fifths of the total change. In no country could extraordinary measures like privatization proceeds contribute much to debt reduction; a deep recession and the pressure to sell put downward pressure on prices and make a bounty of revenue unlikely. But the programs had projected unrealistically high revenues in order to make the numbers add up (IEO 2016: para 64), presumably in anticipation that the European Council and/or the Board of Governors of the IMF would not pass them otherwise.

Finally, there is an item that is conspicuous for its irrelevance, namely the debt-creating effect of exchange rate depreciation (row 2d in Table 6.3). Stand-alone countries in crisis typically experience a collapse of their exchange rate and, to the extent that the government has foreign currency-denominated debt, this debt will rise due to the devaluation, often quite considerably. Only Greece and Portugal noted some minor effects, depending on whether the euro was strong (reducing non-euro denominated debt) or weak. The effects were minor because even non-EA foreigners held public debt largely denominated in euros. This is an effect of monetary solidarity that was anticipated when governments applied for membership back in the 1990s. The Economic and Financial Committee formed a sub-group to integrate the markets for euro-denominated government bonds (Giovannini Group 2000: para 1.2).

This is easily forgotten because violent exchange rate movements, as shown by Engel (2001) for example, are no longer a problem for those inside the EA. It is also ignored by commentators who highlight the loss of central bank backing suffered by EA member states. For instance, De Grauwe (2011)

[30] The term PSI sweetener is official IMF language. It concerns compensation for private creditors to make them agree to a debt write-down, effectively reducing the net amount of debt relief.

[31] Gourinchas et al. (2016: 18–29) document just how exceptionally deep the Greek crisis was, in historical comparison and in comparison with other country groupings (for instance, strict exchange rate peggers).

emphasizes the value of having a central bank that can act as a lender of last resort to the government. This is the basis of his explanation of why Spain, with better fiscal indicators, is so much more fragile than the UK. This is true if one assumes that, outside the EA, Spain's debt would all have been denominated in domestic currency and the Spanish central bank could simply print the money that sellers of Spanish (government) bonds wanted. It is unlikely that these conditions would have held. Spanish government debt managers might well have been drawn into issuing foreign currency-denominated debt in order to take advantage of lower interest rates, while foreign creditors might well have wanted to get their capital out of Spain. If so, the Spanish government would be equally fragile outside the EA as in it, having to ask for foreign exchange at the IMF or the ECB. This was the case for Hungary and Latvia, although it was the foreign exchange denomination of private rather than public debt which made them fragile (Mabbett and Schelkle 2015).

The upshot of Table 6.3 is that market mechanisms—rising interest rate costs and a depressed economy—make crisis countries look as if they did not tighten their belts but added more debt instead. Officials in the Commission and the IMF, the much maligned technocrats, know that fiscal effort does not readily translate into fiscal outcomes (Larch et al. 2010; Spiegel 2014) although they may have underestimated it. The Independent Evaluation Office of the IMF criticized the Fund for missing the highly adverse effects of austerity on growth and the ensuing debt dynamic (IEO 2016: paras 65–8). The wider public, the media, and other governments may be even less clear about this. Moreover, EU fiscal surveillance does little to dispel the suspicion that rising debt is always a sign of governments not trying hard enough (Mabbett and Schelkle 2016a: 131–6). This played into the hands of those for whom it was more convenient to let these countries fend for themselves. Misperception, systematically created by the institutions of limited cooperation, can thus prevent collective action.

What the five countries have in common is that they were drawn into what are now officially called "bank-sovereign negative feedback loops . . . at the heart of the crisis" (Juncker et al. 2015: 11). The underlying diagnosis is shared by many,[32] even by those who see divergent growth regimes to be the cause for divergence and crisis in the EA (Iversen et al. 2016: 10.17). The fatal nexus can start anywhere. Banking crises were arguably the starting point in three out of the five countries. This resonates with a study of all developed country crises between 1970 and 2010 by Babecký et al. (2012): they find that currency (for the EA read: current-account) crises and sovereign debt crises tend to

[32] The literature on the diabolic or doom loop has exploded since 2010. For influential accounts and/or influential voices see the contributors to the collection by Beck (2012), De Grauwe (2011), and for the US discussion Shambaugh (2012) who added a growth crisis to the loop.

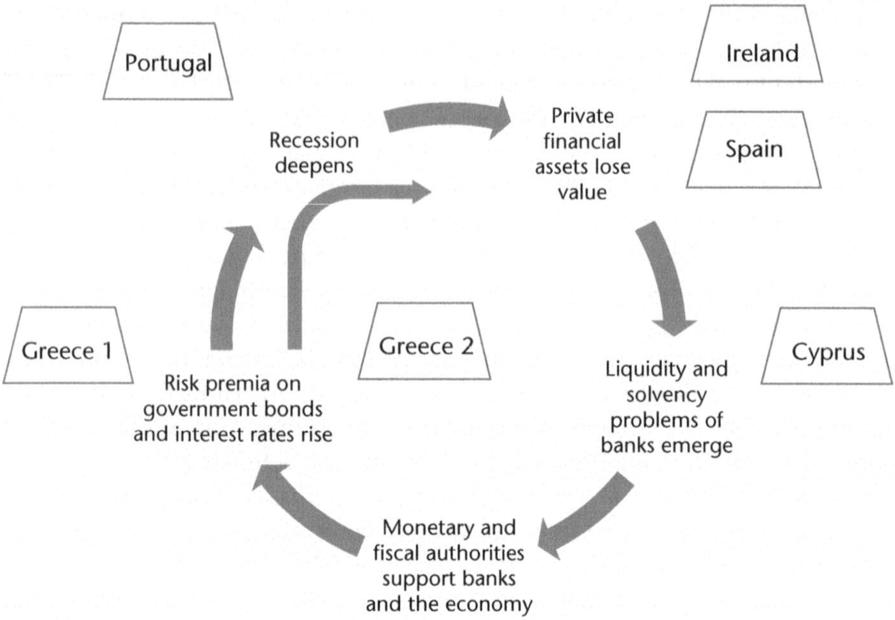

Figure 6.5. Location of program countries in the feedback loop between private and public finances

follow banking crises but not vice versa. Figure 6.5 shows how we can account for the diversity of the countries in terms of the bank-sovereign feedback loop; countries are located where they had their greatest vulnerability at the point when they needed a program (two for Greece).

As Chapter 4 explained for the US, the negative feedback loop can arise whenever a state fiscal authority has to support its banking system and cannot draw on shared fiscal resources or central bank support. Paradoxically, it is exactly this limited risk sharing that forced member states to underwrite truly massive bailout programs. Pre-committed amounts must be large enough to deter speculation that the funds could run out. Otherwise, such speculation has the unfortunate tendency to precipitate a crisis. This is how Charles Kindleberger explained why the IMF could not fully substitute for a central bank that issues the world currency, which was the role of the Federal Reserve Bank under the dollar standard agreed at Bretton Woods (Kindleberger 2000: 216). This was also the insight on which all models of self-fulfilling currency attacks rested, the pre-committed amounts in this context being foreign exchange reserves.[33] The

[33] Krugman (1979) was pioneering in this regard but he never signed up to the second-generation models of purely self-fulfilling attacks (Krugman 1996), unlike Flood and Marion (1996) and Obstfeld (1996).

deliberations about the size of the first emergency funds indicate that decision makers understood the need for large funds that signaled to speculators sufficient "firing power" on the other side. There was soon a discussion about "leveraging" the government-guaranteed funds and two financial instruments were created (EFSF 2013: paras E2, E3). This is particularly relevant when a sovereign re-enters the bond market and needs a back-up in case some market instability occurs and the price of its bonds falls sharply.

Lending programs not only enable a government to finance its activities without entering the bond market; they also act as a firewall for the governments not (yet) in distress. This means that a loan, while made to one country, can be seen as addressing a matter of common concern. This was explicitly emphasized in the European Council conclusions announcing the creation of the ESM. The Council rejected continued reliance on Article 122 (2) TFEU, the provision that was used initially to help countries out of "difficulties beyond the Member State's control" (European Council 2011: para 4). The permanent stability fund, by contrast, is "to be activated if indispensable to safeguard the stability of the euro area as a whole" (Article 136 TFEU). This highlighted how programs could help member states in danger of being next in line, notably Italy and Belgium with their large government bond issues.

The "strict conditionality" attached to every program (European Council 2011: para. 3) underlines that the protection is meant to discourage behavior that makes the need for a program more likely—but it also reveals that the signing governments are aware that their mutual insurance contract can encourage risk taking. Both the size of the programs and the intrusiveness of conditionality extend fiscal risk sharing. Controversial as they have been, the programs are less demanding institutionally than full-fledged fiscal risk sharing, whereby members contribute revenue to a central budget and have current expenditure paid out of it. The counterpart of such budgetary mechanisms is that the member has much less sovereignty over its budget. The troika programs, by contrast, leave the formal sovereignty of a member state intact, for instance by asking it to initiate the negotiations and by putting the eventual Memorandum of Understanding to a parliamentary vote.

This discussion has emphasized how incompleteness of risk sharing is the product of a compromise between recognizing the existence of collective action problems and fearing the possibility that individual countries will exploit collective institutions due to moral hazard. Incompleteness is therefore not necessarily a design flaw that can be "fixed" once it is recognized (De Grauwe 2013). But some manifestations of incompleteness may be more destabilizing than others. It required an existential crisis to prove that the pre-2008 arrangements were untenable. In particular, excluding fiscal difficulties completely from the insurance contract may actually push governments into fiscal difficulties brought about by bond market panic. Chapter 7 analyzes how the contract has been rewritten and shows how monetary solidarity has been extended, albeit reluctantly.

6.3 Monetary Solidarity at Crossroads

The deep dilemma of a heterogeneous union has been repeatedly on display in the EA crisis since 2010: while diversity provides opportunities for risk sharing, it makes it also hard to mobilize the solidarity necessary to realize these opportunities (Imbs and Mauro 2007: 40). And it has become so much harder now. After the veil of ignorance has been lifted, insurance is no longer possible: ex-post compensation and redistribution are required. The policy framework excluded fiscal risk sharing and so a distinct EA crisis was bound to emerge in government bond markets where no safety net was available. Under the strains of crisis, solidarity disintegrated because it was not deeply entrenched in EA institutions, allowing markets to force austerity on vulnerable economies. Crisis management thereby caused risks to be shifted onto the weakest, rather than sharing those risks. The generosity of the programs acted as a firewall for the commons, but was not received with great gratitude in the distressed countries given the level of domestic adjustment requested. From the perspective of the political economy of monetary solidarity, we can see that the firewall for the commons was a by-product of the firewall for the guarantors. Generosity in lending to other sovereigns was based on self-interest.

The commonality of the initial financial crisis could have made governments recognize that they sit in the same boat, increasing the political acceptability of establishing joint liability for bailing out an integrated financial system. International economic diplomacy in the early years of the financial crisis showed some of this insight and a sustained effort of reregulation was its payoff (Pauly 2009; Véron 2014). But the shock was so massive and uncertainty so frightening that member state governments, mindful of their vulnerabilities, regressed towards national ways out. The Irish government's guarantee of all liabilities of Irish banks on September 30, 2008 was the crassest example (Woll 2014: ch.7). The decision was taken without consulting other European partners, led to higher rates for deposits in these Irish banks, and triggered deposit flight from the UK immediately (Acharya and Mora 2013: 30). Subsequently, bond market investors selected the fiscal authorities deemed to be overstretched and promptly they were. But instead of going against this turning of the tables by the financial markets they had just rescued, governments became divided.[34] Domestic audiences turned vehemently against more exposure to risks for taxpayers. The macroeconomic adjustment programs for the worst-hit countries that followed were limited by punishing measures to deter moral hazard (Whelan 2014a: 18). Critics see solidarity becoming ever more limited (Hall 2012: 367–8), with the entire burden of adjustment shifted onto Southern Europe (Matthijs and Blyth 2015: 12).

A closer look, in Chapter 7, shows that new interfaces of risk sharing between monetary and fiscal authorities have been created, and some limitations made less binding. What contributed to the impression of restriction is that every innovation stopped short of accepting joint fiscal liability. The main mode of response was to identify a responsible national fiscal authority and make it shoulder the burden, but this had some destabilizing effects. The major emergency fund for sovereigns and the resolution fund for banks have their fiscal backing from national authorities. A crucial coalition around Germany is not prepared to complete the union by accepting joint fiscal liability, or only in return for such intrusive fiscal surveillance that crucial members like France and Italy backed off. This suggests that the fiscal incompleteness of the EA is deliberate: a hard political constraint. But ways around this constraint have been found, under the exigencies of *Monnet's curse*.

Appendix: Drivers of Debt Accumulation before and after Troika Programs

In Tables 6.1A–6.4A, positive figures increase public debt, negative figures reduce it.

Table 6.1A. Greece, debt sustainability analysis (actual figures)

In percentage of GDP	t − 2	t − 1	t = 2010	t + 1	t + 2	t + 3
Change in gross public debt of which:	5.7	16.8	18.6	22.0	−13.1	17.9
a. Debt-creating flow: *primary deficit*	4.8	10.5	4.9	2.4	1.5	−0.8
b. Debt dynamic 1: *real interest rate*	0.3	2.6	4.5	5.7	5.6	7.3
c. Debt dynamic 2: *real GDP growth*	0.2	3.6	6.7	11.2	12.8	6.4
d. Exchange rate depreciation	0.0	0.0	0.0	0.0	0.0	−0.5
e. Net privatization proceeds	0.0	0.0	0.0	−0.5	−0.1	−0.6
f. Contingent liabilities	0.2	−0.1	0.6	1.3	6.4	0.0
g. Other (*bank recapitalization*, PSI sweeteners)	0.0	0.0	0.0	0.0	39.1	4.0
h. Residual, including *asset change*	0.1	0.3	2.0	1.9	−78.4	2.1

Source: IMF 4th Review (p. 65) and 5th Review (p. 65)

34 Stiglitz (2016: 52–3) suggests that more economic similarity could overcome political divisiveness. But are France and Germany economically more similar or more diverse than Germany and the Netherlands?

Table 6.2A. Ireland, debt sustainability analysis (actual figures)

In percentage of GDP	t −2	t −1	t = 2010	t + 1	t + 2
Change in gross public debt of which:	19.4	20.9	27.3	12.9	13.3
a. Debt-creating flow: *primary deficit*	6.0	9.7	8.1	10.4	5.2
b. Debt dynamic 1: real interest rate	2.0	3.9	3.4	2.5	3.1
c. Debt dynamic 2: *real GDP growth*	0.8	3.5	1.7	−1.9	−0.2
d. Exchange rate depreciation	0.0	0.0	0.0	0.0	0.0
e. Net privatization proceeds[1]	0.0	0.0	0.0	−5.7	3.2
f. Contingent liabilities[2]	0.0	0.0	0.0	5.2	0.6
g. Other (*bank recapitalization*)	0.0	6.8	22.5	0.0	0.0
h. Residual, including *asset change*	10.7	−3.0	−8.4	2.5	1.5

Notes: [1] in 2011 and 2012: drawdown of deposits;
[2] in 2011 and 2012: other including stock-flow adjustments
Source: IMF 7th Review (p. 47) and 12th Review (p. 59)

Table 6.3A. Portugal, debt sustainability analysis (actual figures)

In percentage of GDP	t −2	t −1	t = 2011	t + 1	t + 2
Change in gross public debt of which:	11.5	10.4	13.3	16.4	4.8
a. Debt-creating flow: *primary deficit*	7.3	6.8	−0.1	2.1	0.7
b. Debt dynamic 1: *real interest rate*	2.2	2.2	3.2	4.7	2.2
c. Debt dynamic 2: *real GDP growth*	2.1	−1.1	1.4	3.6	1.7
d. Exchange rate depreciation	0.1	0.1	−0.1	0.0	0.0
e. Net privatization proceeds	0.0	−0.4	−0.3	−1.3	−0.8
f. Contingent liabilities	0.0	0.0	0.5	0.5	
g. Other (*bank recapitalization*)[1]	0.0	0.0	0.6	1.4	0.4
h. Residual, including *asset change*	−0.2	2.9	8.1	5.4	0.7

Note: [1] in 2011 and 2012: drawdown of deposits
Source: IMF 3rd Review (p. 47) and 11th Review (p. 53)

Table 6.4A. Cyprus, debt sustainability analysis (actual figures)

In percentage of GDP	t −2	t −1	t = 2012	t + 1	t + 2
Change in gross public debt of which:	2.8	9.7	14.7	22.7	5.3
a. Debt-creating flow: *primary deficit*	3.0	3.9	3.1	1.6	−2.8
b. Debt dynamic 1: *real interest rate*	1.1	0.7	1.8	3.9	4.2
c. Debt dynamic 2: *real GDP growth*	−0.7	−0.3	1.7	4.6	2.4
d. Exchange rate depreciation	0.0	0.0	0.0	0.0	0.0
e. Net privatization proceeds	0.0	0.0	0.0	0.0	0.0
f. Contingent liabilities	0.0	0.0	0.0	0.0	0.0
g. Other (*bank recapitalization*)	0.0	0.0	0.0	12.6	1.5
h. Residual, including *asset change*	−0.6	5.4	8.1	0.0	0.0

Source: IMF 1st Review (p. 45) and 11th Review (p. 35)

7

Monetary Solidarity by Default and by Design

Maurice Obstfeld, a leading scholar of macroeconomic risk sharing, has offered this perceptive assessment of the EA's monetary and fiscal constitution: "[T]]he purely macroeconomic defenses in the Maastricht treaty proved to be a Maginot line (this time built by Germany) that was inevitably circumvented. By 1940, the nature of ground warfare had changed from what it had been; by 2008, the nature of financial markets had changed" (Obstfeld 2013: 34). Just as the Maginot line was the product of an outdated theory of warfare, so the macro-economic constraints of Maastricht reflected the insights of optimal control theory with its focus on credible commitments to prudent policy rather than the management of financial risks. Defense against financial crises requires fiscal risk sharing, both to prevent negative feedback loops emerging at the national level and to ensure that contagious crises can be prevented by a resolute lender of last resort. It also requires prudential tools that address the systemic externalities that arise from the connectedness of financial firms.

The first section of this chapter returns to the economic literature on risk sharing (Chapter 3) to shed light on what has come of the hopes for stability (low inflation) and catch-up growth (low interest rates) that motivated the adoption of a common currency by a diverse set of member states (Section 5.1.1). Risk sharing is not necessarily confined to consumption smoothing but also entails gainful risk taking, above all through economic specialization and credit-fueled expansion. It is likely that there exists a trade-off between these two goals of risk sharing: more risk taking should lead to higher returns, but at the cost of some stability. This raises the real or perceived issue of moral hazard, that is excessive risk taking, an accusation that has been leveled at governments that needed a bailout program (Economist 2012). Whatever the merit of these accusations in specific cases, the section finds that the stabilizing features of European monetary union prevailed, in line with the institutional emphasis of the Maastricht policy framework.

The second section takes a closer look at the reforms undertaken in response to the crisis. Surveillance of fiscal and macroeconomic imbalances to reduce, rather than share, risks was fortified first. Subsequently, some fiscal capacity building has taken place which has paved the way for the ECB to act as lender of last resort to sovereigns, albeit through the back door. Furthermore, another interface of risk sharing has been developed with the move toward banking union and an expanded prudential mandate for the ECB. This review shows that interfaces of risk sharing have become more articulated and more robust. But the refusal to introduce common fiscal backstops still indicates that major guarantor countries are ready to accept market panic (externalities) as a means of disciplining the governments (and possibly interest groups) in other member states.

The final section of this chapter takes stock by analyzing the overall roadmap for reform that two major reports propose (van Rompuy et al. 2012; Juncker et al. 2015).

7.1 Changing Risk-Return Profiles through Integration

States, their governments, and the electorate do not strive only for stability, but also for expansion of their economic opportunities. Entering a risk pool offers choices: to reduce volatility and insure against permanent shocks or to take advantage of additional protection and incur more gainful risks; obviously a mix of both is also possible. The argument follows the astute observation of Kenneth Arrow (1971: 137), a founder of modern welfare economics: "the mere trading of risks, taken as given, is only part of the story and in many respects the less interesting part. The possibility of shifting risks, of insurance in the broadest sense, permits individuals to engage in risky activities that they would not otherwise undertake." The literature on risk sharing reviewed in Chapter 3 stressed the opportunities of consumption and income smoothing that monetary-financial integration offers, rather than the gains from risk taking under the protection of insurance. This was in the tradition of the theory of OCA with its preoccupation of conventional macroeconomic stabilization. But if risk sharing is economically successful, higher output volatility and even diverging output growth rates could be associated with smoother consumption (Kalemli-Ozcan et al. 2001, 2004). The transmission mechanisms could be levels and volatility of interest and inflation rates. For instance, lower levels of interest rates spur growth for which higher volatility and divergence of inflation rates may be the price. This is a benign interpretation of the Walters (1988) effect that consists of a pro-cyclical movement of real interest rates in diverse monetary union.

A tradeoff between volatility and growth of output should be observed if financial markets reward risk taking. Pioneering work in the area of finance and (endogenous) growth has been done by Obstfeld (1994) and Acemoglu and Zilibotti (1997). They suggest that risk sharing through financial integration can allow investors to take more risks, in the expectation of higher returns that generate higher growth in the aggregate. By contrast, scholars who research trade under uncertainty stress that increased trading of risks through asset markets which accompanies goods trade can reap efficiency gains (Helpman 1988; Saint-Paul 1992). These gains materialize in higher returns on capital, which incentivize more investment and better exploitation of comparative advantage, without necessarily increasing risk. More growth without more volatility would be the aggregate result. The question therefore arises whether there is a tradeoff at all.[1]

Choices that lead to more or less growth and more or less smoothing are not taken by a single decision maker. They are the result of (inter)actions that involve political authorities as well as market actors, who are not uniformly risk averse. Hence, we first have to assess whether the risk-return profiles of countries actually follow any pattern that resembles a tradeoff for risk-averse agents: is lower volatility of output or consumption associated with lower growth, higher volatility with higher growth? Or were there unexploited gains to be had, so that a country with high volatility could sustain growth rates but reduce volatility when entering a hard-currency union?

Figures 7.1 and 7.2 give a simple sketch of the risk-return combinations that members of the Euro area faced before and after joining the currency union. The pre-integration phase is 1971–85, spent "in search of [exchange rate] stability," to paraphrase Meier (1987), after the breakdown of the dollar standard. The integration phase with which it is compared is 1992–2007, when a selection of EU countries set off on the rocky road from Maastricht into the monetary union. The years in between—relatively good years for European economies that saw a revival of ambitions to integrate them more closely—are left out to separate more clearly between a time without the prospect of a monetary union and the time in which the prospect materialized, through politically enforced convergence and anticipation effects.

The return in Figures 7.1 and 7.2 is operationalized as average output growth over each time span while risk is captured by the volatility of annual output growth, measured as the standard deviation. Figure 7.2 gives us a kind of balance sheet of the change, in other words how the risk-return profile of each country moved in terms of gains and losses in volatility and growth.

[1] Obstfeld (1994: 1311) argues the latter, following Arrow's footsteps: risk-taking firms can and must shift some of those additional risks onto banks or investors.

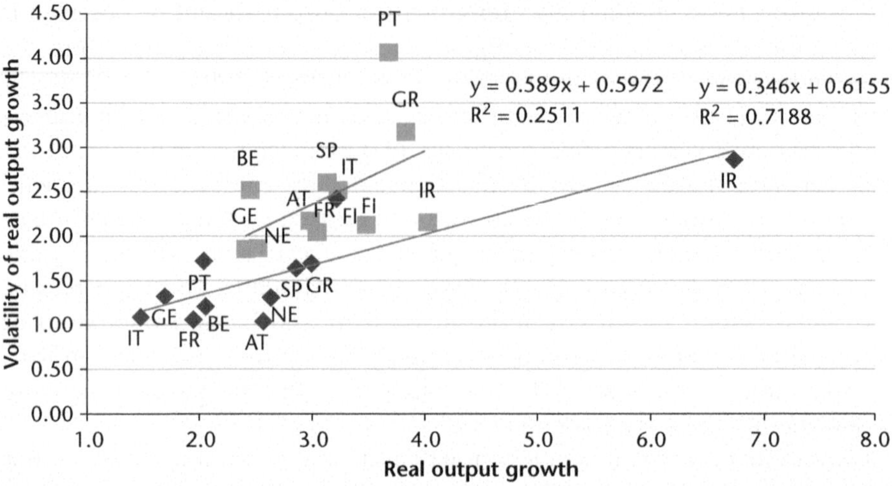

Figure 7.1. EA-11 risk-return profiles of output growth, 1971–85 and 1992–2007

Note: Grey squares depict risk-return combinations for 1971–85, dark diamonds for 1992–2007

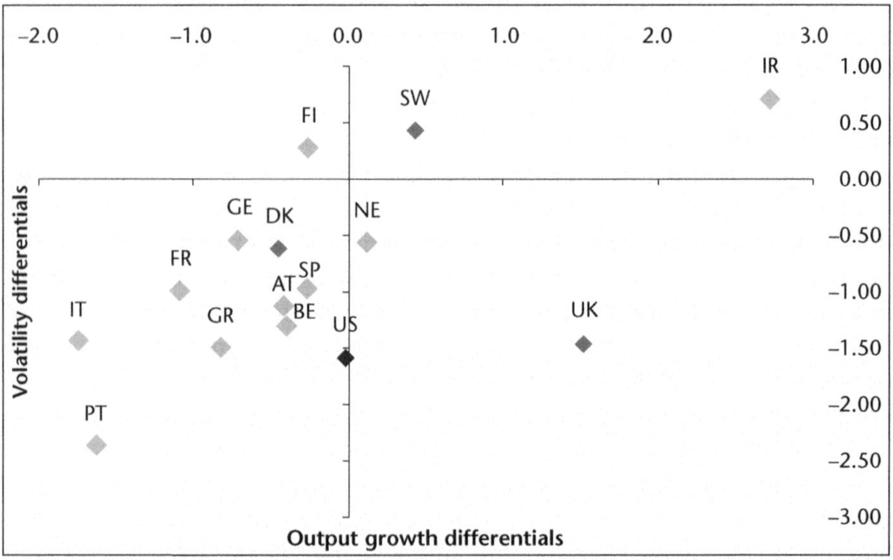

Figure 7.2. Changes in risk-return profiles in output 1992–2007 compared to 1971–85 (in %)

Source: own calculations based on OECD data; dark diamonds depict EA-11 countries, light diamonds non-EA countries in the EU

To this latter "balance sheet" are added four non-Euro countries (Denmark, Sweden, the UK, and the US) for comparison.

The risk-return profiles in Figure 7.1 show a tradeoff for both time spans, in line with the Obstfeld et al. line of reasoning: higher growth is associated with higher volatility. The relationship has a closer fit in 1992–2007 (the R^2 values indicate that the regression explains 72 percent of deviations for 1992–2007 but only 25 percent for 1971–85). The tradeoff is also less steep in the later phase, which implies that a given increase in volatility is accompanied by a higher return, here: a gain in growth. The performance of three countries is responsible for this shift: Greece and Portugal experienced lower volatility, while Ireland had higher growth with similar volatility. Figure 7.2 shows that almost all EA candidates/members ended up in the bottom-left quadrant, gaining stability at the expense of growth. Nine EA member states traded off one good (growth) against another (stability). The hope that more stability could spur growth, at least in the previously more volatile and poorer member state economies like Portugal and Greece, finds no support in Figure 7.2. Only one member state is clearly better off: the Netherlands, along with the non-member UK, enjoyed higher growth performance with more stability. Finland is in "the worst of all possible worlds" quadrant, having less growth and less stability. All three outliers can be explained by exceptionally difficult economic episodes: the Netherlands and the UK had had boom-bust cycles in the previous pre-integration phase, while Finland suffered from the break-up of the Soviet Union in the early 1990s. The US, by contrast, fits best the interpretation that asset trade can reduce risk without loss in growth, supporting the optimistic view that many US economists expressed before the crisis, namely that there are pure benefits to be had from financial liberalization.

Turning from output to consumption, Figures 7.3 and 7.4 show different risk-return profiles. The first observation is that the relationship between risk and return was not a tradeoff in 1971–85: average consumption growth rates between 2 percent and 3 percent could go together with standard deviations (measure of volatility) of less than 2 percent and up to 5 percent; the R^2 is very low. In 1992–2007, countries line up along a tradeoff. The comparison of the two periods in Figure 7.4 shows that Ireland and Spain move into the "Goldilocks" quadrant, with improved consumption growth and lower volatility. Other members gain stability, except Finland, at the cost of growth. The non-members, included again for benchmarking, are either in the best of all possible worlds (Denmark, UK, US) or have a free lunch of more growth with no rise in volatility (Sweden). It is impossible to say whether this is due to a superior national growth performance generally, more opportunities to benefit from economic integration, or, indeed, more effective fiscal policy. All we can tentatively say is that different mechanisms seem to have worked in the EA where the majority "paid" for consumption smoothing with somewhat lower growth.

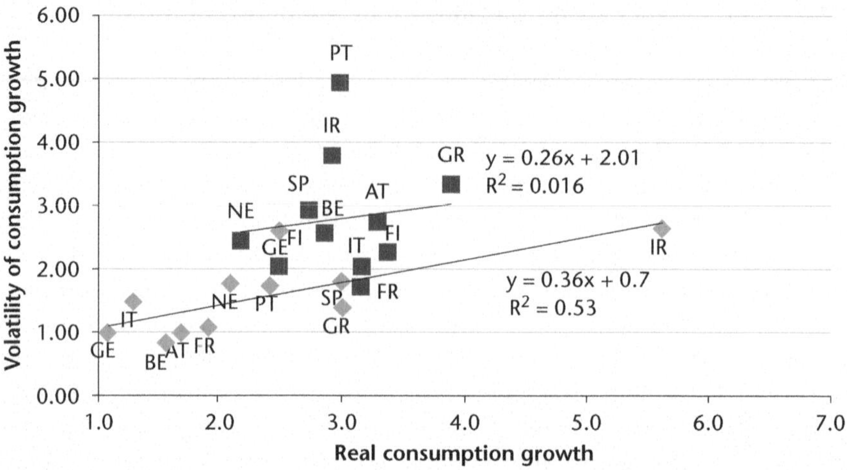

Figure 7.3. EA-11 risk-return profiles of consumption growth, 1971–85 and 1992–2007

Note: Squares depict risk-return combinations for 1971–85, diamonds for 1992–2007

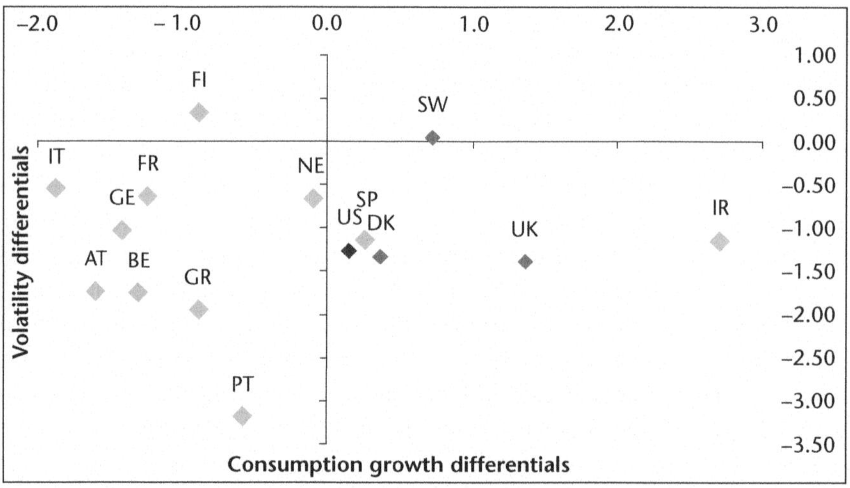

Figure 7.4. Changes in risk-return profiles in consumption 1992–2007 compared to 1971–85 (in %)

Source: own calculations based on OECD data; grey diamonds depict EA-11 countries, dark diamonds non-EA countries in the EU

In about half of EA members, the gain in stability tends to be more pronounced for consumption than for output, which is compatible with what the risk-sharing literature would lead us to expect. The data suggest that Irish firms took higher risks that were rewarded with additional output growth (Figure 7.2), while households enjoyed growth and stability in consumption. Stability in Portugal and Greece came at less cost in consumption than in output. In four countries (Austria, Belgium, France, and Germany), the gain in smoothing was about the same for households (consumption) and firms (output) but consumption growth declined more than output growth. Italian households experienced the same decline in growth as their firms but were not compensated as much by more stability. With the exception of Finland, all cases are compatible with greater risk sharing but the comparison with non-euro countries suggests that financially well-developed economies like Denmark and the UK could achieve this without entering the currency area.

The evidence in Figures 7.1–7.4 suggests, but does not prove, that something has happened as regards risk sharing in the EA member states. It was mostly in one direction, namely towards more stability. Only Ireland can be seen to have a riskier high (output) growth profile with the introduction of the euro, as theory would predict in addition to the existence of a tradeoff (Obstfeld 1994; Acemoglu and Zilibotti 1997). Most others gained stability, in some cases significantly. Even Germany "paid a price" in terms of growth for nominal stabilization as required for membership. But non-EA countries also gained in stability, apparently at hardly any cost to growth. It is tempting to see in this relative performance of EA members and non-members an effect of the Maastricht strategy of contrived convergence. And we may see poetic justice in the fact that the straitjacket was even noticeable for the country that had shaped the policy framework in this restrictive way for others.

7.2 Reforms at the Interfaces of Risk Sharing in Response to Crisis

Despite this evidence for more stability, the common potential for financial instability materialized after 2008. As already mentioned, this was a huge challenge in economic and political terms. Economically, a common financial crisis limited the options for diversification. Public debt was the option used, roping future generations into the risk pool. An IMF study found that the wave of twenty-five systemic and borderline systemic banking crises that affected most advanced economies during 2008–11 had direct fiscal costs of around 5 percent of GDP. This is relatively low compared to previous crises, affecting mostly emerging markets. But the increase in public debt of around 20 percent of GDP was "particularly large" (Amaglobeli et al. 2015: 10) as governments and central banks underpinned their inflated banking systems.[2] The IMF

[2] Amaglobeli et al. (2015) also suggest that the use of counter-cyclical fiscal and monetary policies and larger automatic stabilizers partly explains the pattern, but these factors cannot account for the "stock-flow" discrepancy indicated by the limited role of direct fiscal costs in explaining the increase in public debt.

authors express concern that this pattern of low direct costs and a large rise in public debt will make for longer drawn-out recoveries.

Savers were spared losses alongside the owners of banks. But they had to bear costs in their capacities as current and future taxpayers, while the ensuing recession passed costs on to firms and their employees, especially in the countries in the eye of the storm. Living standards dropped; for some back to where they were at the start of monetary union, as shown in Figure 6.2. Social unrest and mass migration, high government turnover, and the rise of anti-establishment parties across Europe indicate that the status quo was not an option in a union of democratic welfare states.

Reform activism and frantic institution building started as early as late 2008, with the De Larosière report on financial regulatory reform.[3] This section does not try to give an exhaustive account of everything that has been done but Table 7.1 gives an overview. The following sub-sections then hone in on the particularly relevant innovations for the political economy of monetary solidarity: emergency funds and extraordinary monetary policies as nascent interfaces between monetary and fiscal policy, along with banking union and the expanded prudential mandate for the central bank.

Table 7.1 illustrates that no element of the system of risk sharing was left untouched. Dawson (2015) contains an informative discussion of the governance questions raised by these reforms, notably the legal and political accountability of the new institutions. What is of interest here is that the initial reflex was to strengthen containment of risk sharing to nation states, yet this containment strategy could not be sustained.

7.2.1 *Early Interventions to Contain Fiscal Risk Sharing*

Fiscal surveillance to ensure debt sustainability (entry 5 in Table 7.1) was, predictably, one of the first areas on which reform efforts concentrated (Verdun 2015): a "muscular" package of legislation called the Six Pack was shadowed by an almost identical set of measures in the Fiscal Compact, based on bilateral contracts between governments outside the Treaty. This legislative package to toughen and extend sanctions was embedded in a European Semester that linked fiscal surveillance to structural reform oversight and aligned the EU-level process with scrutiny in national parliaments. For all this toughening, no government has been fined, by mid-2016, under either the Six Pack or the Fiscal Compact. Mabbett and Schelkle (2016a) describe this intense activity as "searching under the lamp-post": the EU was institutionally drawn to the brightly lit domain of fiscal policy even though overburdened

[3] See the long list of legislation in Schimmelfennig (2015: 133; table 7.1), which covers the period up to April 2014.

Table 7.1. Evolving channels and interfaces of risk sharing in the EA

	Monetary policy	Fiscal policy	Supervised financial markets
Fiat money	1 ECB with narrow price stability mandate ⇓ Expanded mandate to financial stability and wider set of instruments (macroprudential, Basel III framework)	2 Automatic and discretionary demand stabilization at national level ⇓ Emergency funds (EFSF, EFSM, ESM) for sovereign adjustment programs and debt relief	3 Transmission of monetary policy signals, collateral framework ⇓ European Systemic Risk Board and national macroprudential tools
Public finance	4 Monetary back-up Seignorage shared within ESCB Discount policy to create integrated sovereign bond market ⇓ Lender of last resort for sovereigns in secondary markets (SMP, LTRO, OMT) Monetary stimulus (QE)	5 Debt sustainability No-bailout clause Stability and Growth Pact ⇓ Six Pack and Intergovernmental Fiscal Compact, European Semester Macroeconomic Imbalances Procedure European Stability Mechanism	6 Cost of government debt identical zero risk weighting of government bonds for purposes of regulatory capital calculations ⇓ Collective action clauses in government bonds Single Resolution Mechanism as part of banking union
Private finance	7 Liquidity risk management No explicit lender of last resort role Compensation within European System of Central Banks ⇓ Extraordinary liquidity measures ("qualitative easing," long-term refinancing operations) European Systemic Risk Board, macroprudential mandate	8 Solvency risk management National deposit guarantee schemes with minimum standards set in EU Directive ⇓ Single Resolution Mechanism, planned European Deposit Insurance Scheme Bail-in rule ESM recapitalization instruments	9 Financial stability Harmonized prudential regulation (Financial Services Action Plan) ⇓ Banking union with Single Rulebook and Single Supervisory Mechanism in ECB

Source: own elaboration

public finances were merely a symptom of member states' troubles. The Macroeconomic Imbalances Procedure does little to counter this impression, despite its much wider remit. The creation of the ESM is a much more important change of direction, discussed in Section 7.2.2 on fiscal capacity building.

The reforms to fiscal surveillance fostered the perception that collective action regarding prudent fiscal policy had failed, but they did not facilitate the enforcement of the rules. The Commission looked for ways to give governments leeway to avoid pro-cyclical retrenchment, particularly by emphasizing structural reforms. But lenient assessments of France, particularly in 2014, led the Baltic states, Finland, and Germany to write a critical open letter to the Commission (John and Strupczewski 2014). On the other side, the Italian government under Matteo Renzi became openly defiant (Piccolo 2016), forcing ever more discretionary intervention by the Commission President to give extensions to fiscal trespassers. Jean-Claude Juncker was in turn criticized by the President of the Eurogroup Dijsselbloem (Euractiv 2016). The Commission has not been consistently supportive of the Stability Pact although DG Ecfin, especially Marco Buti and his various co-authors, led the intellectual case for these rules at the start of the European monetary union (Brunila et al. 2001; Buti 2003). But the former Commission President Prodi called the EU's fiscal rules "stupid" for their rigidity (BBC 2002), even before the two social democratic governments in France and Germany openly defied them in 2003. The same two countries played a leading role in launching the more stringent Fiscal Compact under Conservative administrations in 2011. This uneven support by governments from the two most influential countries created enormous political difficulties for the Commission, concerned about its reputation of an independent guardian of the Treaty. Its increasing reluctance to enforce the Pact is hardly surprising, even more so after being sidelined in the creation of the Fiscal Compact.

The Macroeconomic Imbalances Procedure (still entry 5 of Table 7.1) corrects the focus on fiscal excess to some extent. The fourteen headline indicators capture private as well as public debt, house prices as well as wage costs, credit growth, and current-account imbalances. These pertinent indicators of problems do not come with any additional policy instruments for the EU Commission and the Council. Thus it cannot compensate for market responses to countries with twin deficits (of budget and current account), which leave them little room for sequencing adjustment. It also does little to promote symmetric adjustment of surplus countries. The Procedure could actually be said to reinforce the bias against deficit countries as a quick glance at the thresholds for warnings reveals. The most striking example is that a current-account deficit of 4 percent is a threshold while a surplus raises concerns only at 6 percent. Kincaid and Watson (2015: 798) see a deflationary bias in this. They also note the backward-looking nature of the exercise and the tendency to keep on recommending structural reforms that cannot really tackle macroeconomic instability. The macro imbalance procedure, while worthy in its intent, is little more than another reporting requirement for national administrations as long as it is not linked to coordinated macroprudential and fiscal policies.

Reforms to the regulatory treatment of government bonds held by banks (entry 6 in Table 7.1) have been confined to measures that rope the private sector into the risk pool. Under the Basel Accords, government bonds of a certain rating quality can still enjoy zero risk weighting, meaning that banks do not have to hold capital buffers against them. Officials in regulatory bodies have been quite explicit that they think this is a distortion, and some market actors from the banking sector support this view (Goves et al. 2016; Lannoo 2015: 92). But sovereigns themselves have sought to avoid any changes that would make their debt burdens more costly to finance and domestic banking systems more fragile. Only the Dutch and German governments have pushed for a change, officially since April 2016 (Jenkins 2016). A significant measure at this interface of public and private finance was that since 2013 all bond issues by governments in the EA must have a collective action clause. This means that, in the case of sovereign debt restructuring, a minority of private bondholders cannot block the procedure. This ropes private bondholders into the risk pool so they share the insolvency risk. Its workings have yet to be seen: some critics fear that collective action clauses make investors sell such bonds at the slightest rumor of troubles ahead. They may also increase the cost of debt finance, given that they raise the expected probability that private bondholders will have to share the cost of government debt restructuring.[4]

Despite the limitations of the reforms reviewed so far, it must be acknowledged that they brought forth collective action. They were swift, administratively demanding as regards fiscal surveillance, and substantively significant in the case of collective action clauses for government bonds. It would therefore be rather superficial to portray them as evidence for yet more failure to take action, as many observers in the media and in academia did. An interpretation more consistent with the revealed pattern of reforms is that a trade-off between solutions to different collective action problems has been struck in favor of what the guarantor countries wanted. Those supporting and advancing the German position prefer to reduce the risk of market panic (externalities) from perceived fiscal problems; if the risk materializes, however, it is meant to fall largely on distressed countries and their private creditors. This is consistent with deterring moral hazard and extracting a large co-payment if the insurance case arises. The threat of market panic, a classic externality, is used as a stick to enforce fiscal discipline, while the entire official edifice of surveillance has so far not been able to undertake enforcement. The one substantive reform in this context, collective action clauses in sovereign bond issues, means that banks must now share in the risks they incur. The disciplinarian view managed in these early reforms to portray moral

[4] See Bradley and Gulati (2013) for a review of the literature and the empirical evidence.

hazard, of private creditors and public debtors, as the collective action problem that has to be given priority, even though this came at the cost of more financial instability.

There was considerable opposition from national administrations, parliaments, and experts to these early reforms.[5] The reforms shifted the responsibility for a systemic crisis on parties that were too weak to bear them, as subsequent events and reforms confirmed. Naturally, the weaker parties opposed the measures, and they had veto power within the supranational institutions. But this was evaded with the Fiscal Compact, an intergovernmental contract outside the EU Treaty—Bickerton et al. (2015: 704) see this Treaty as a prime example for a "new intergovernmentalism." The German government conditioned its participation in the ESM on the stipulation that those receiving emergency funding had to be signatories of the Compact (Gros and Alcidi 2014). This was accepted at a European Council meeting in January 2012 (ESM 2012: A22), and twenty-five countries signed in March 2012 (the Czech Republic signed in 2014, while the UK and the newcomer Croatia continued to abstain as of 2016).

By shifting to an intergovernmental venue, the obstacles to agreement arising from the supranational conventions of equality and consensus were avoided. The Compact could come into force as soon as twelve member states signed it; it could not be blocked by hold-outs. Such flexibility, here of membership to an agreement, disempowers smaller member states in favor of the influential agenda setters (Martin 2001:138–43). However, the more powerful states did not have it all their own way: for years, the Commission had abstained from writing its report on signatories' transposition of the Fiscal Compact, which meant that the violations of the balanced-budget rule enshrined in it cannot be "automatically" sanctioned as foreseen (Gros and Alcidi 2014).

7.2.2 *Fiscal Capacity Building and Lending of Last Resort to Sovereigns*

EMERGENCY FUNDS

The first significant expansion of fiscal capacity was agreed at a dramatic crisis summit in May 2010, where it was decided to bail out the Greek government (Barber 2010). Such capacity was demanded by then ECB President Trichet in return for embarking on the first bond-buying program, the Securities Market Programme (SMP, entry 4 in Table 7.1). Through the SMP, the ECB bought

[5] The concerns related to the legal uncertainty and political ambiguity, resulting from an intergovernmental treaty that supposedly empowers supranational institutions like the Commission and the European Court of Justice to enforce it (Dehousse 2012). There was also the usual concern that the Compact would force governments to a pro-cyclical policy stance but this would require enforcement that so far has not taken place.

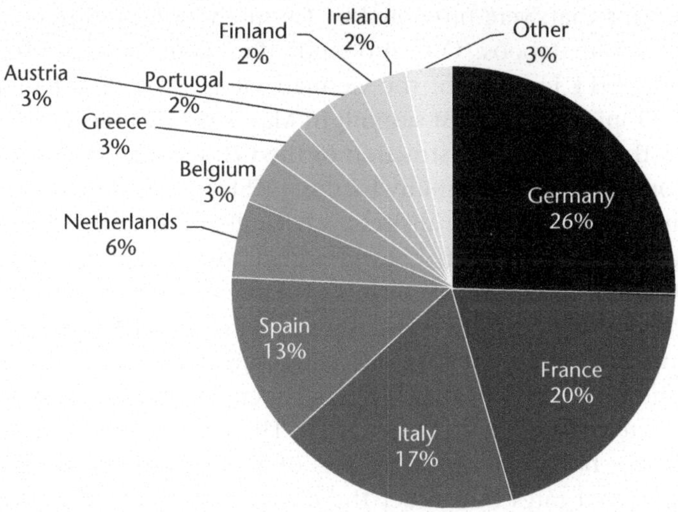

Figure 7.5. Share of EA member states in the paid-up capital of the ECB, as of January 1, 2015

Source: <http://www.ecb.europa.eu/home/html/index.en.html>, "Capital subscription"; (rounded) percentages take the paid-up capital (70 percent of total ECB capital) as basis

government bonds, not least Greek bonds, from banks keen to offload them. The ECB demanded assurance that it could be indemnified if the credit risk from these bonds materialized; since there was no central budget, emergency funds were the next best option from the ECB's point of view (entry 2). Indirect lending to sovereigns, via secondary markets, and emergency funding were thus directly linked. This linkage brought into the open that governments were engaged in risk sharing through the credit risks that the ECB was taking on its books with extraordinary monetary measures since the member states underwrite the ECB's loss-absorbing capital (Schoenmaker 2010; see ch.5). By agreeing to this, risk sharing by default became monetary solidarity.

The key for the extent of solidarity potentially required is each member state's share in the ECB's paid-up capital, which is around 70 percent of the total capital of €10.825 billion; the rest is subscribed by non-euro member states that do not have to pay up. Each country's share is determined by its GDP and its population size, in equal measure. Figure 7.5 shows that France and Germany together would have to bear 46 percent, almost half, of any losses. Despite a similar exposure, French governments were more open to discussions about joint liability while the Merkel administration always ruled out any form of Eurobonds.[6] At the same time, French governments neither

[6] The German opposition parties, notably the Social Democrats in 2012, were in favor of joint liability although subject to acceptance in a referendum (Focus 2012).

blocked reforms that were promoted by Germany nor mobilized support to overcome German taboos. On Eurobonds, President Sarkozy changed his mind in mid-2011 in favor of the German view while President Hollande dropped the topic after his first summit in May 2012 (Reuters 2012).

However, the financial construction of the first emergency fund, the temporary European Financial Stability Facility (EFSF), satisfied neither borrowers nor guarantors. A country in distress was singled out under Article 122(2) TFEU, as a member state with "severe difficulties caused by... exceptional occurrences beyond its control." Loans could be made, but only under non-concessionary terms, in this respect aligned with the IMF terms of facilities that exceed a country's quota. Germany in particular insisted on commercial terms for the first Greek loan while other member states would have been more conciliatory (Bastasin 2012: 185, 187). These terms ended up being a bad compromise for both sides: interest rates of about 5 percent were 2 percent below commercial rates but under the circumstances too high for Greece. This did little to bolster the distressed country's creditworthiness and thus calm down markets.

The guarantor side was not happy with the EFSF either: at Chancellor Merkel's insistence, this was an intergovernmental construct issuing bonds based on identifiable bilateral guarantees (Barber 2010). The Commission had wanted a fund under EU authority, selling a bond with a collective government guarantee. The legal services of the EU backed Chancellor Merkel, insofar as they suggested that the Commission's proposal required a treaty change. A Dutch senior official came up with the idea, in the small hours of an overnight summit, to give the EFSF the legal form of a Special Purpose Vehicle. This meant it lacked its own legal personality. Eurostat then ruled that the guarantees provided should be added to the national debt of the guarantors; the EFSF was treated as holding the claims both against the program country and against the guarantors (ESM 2012: A23). Especially for vulnerable countries like Belgium and Italy, this was most unhelpful. The EFSF could not act as a firewall against contagion if the support provided was treated as a liability of the guarantors for the purposes of fiscal surveillance.

Lessons were learnt from this first botched attempt to create fiscal capacity that was actually increasing risks for all parties involved. With the ESM, a more robust firewall for the commons has been built. The ESM got its own legal (public law) personality based on public law and is able to borrow in bond markets on its own account. The guarantees come in the form of callable capital pledged by the member states, to the tune of €700 billion of which €80 billion has been paid in by member states (according to the usual ECB capital key). Statistically, this is classified as a stake in the ESM, not a liability, as is the case for IMF loans (ESM 2012: A23). This capital backing gives the ESM a lending capacity of €500 billion (ESM 2012: A6); the difference or "overcollateralization" from €700 billion preserves the ESM's triple-A rating, given that not all the member states providing the guarantees themselves have a triple-A rating. Because the ESM is constituted separately to the loans it makes, it is more difficult for guarantors to opt out of a rescue program, as the Slovakian government did from the first Greek rescue program. The ESM also effectively pools the credit ratings of the guarantors, so that financing costs stay low and can be passed on to those receiving assistance. The ESM gives loans, buys bonds from banks, and can buy bonds from the issuing government directly (Article 14–18 of ESM Treaty). This can be done as a precaution, not only after contagion has driven up yields to unsustainable levels. The pricing policy is at the discretion of the ESM Governing Council and, as long as it covers the ESM's own costs, it can be concessionary (Article 20 of ESM Treaty).

However, ESM assistance is still clunky and cannot be mobilized easily—"strict conditionality," laid down in a Memorandum of Understanding, must always be attached. The ESM programs are part of a more general trend observable in IMF programs as well. Bailout programs have become larger with different rounds of financial crises (Barkbu et al. 2011: 15–18). More intrusive and detailed conditionality can also be observed (Griffiths and Todoulos 2014: 12–13) contrary to the IMF's declared intentions. The Fund may not have much choice if an expanding and integrating world economy makes it more likely for country crises to bunch, making guarantor countries in its governing board both nervous and reluctant (Barkbu et al. 2011: 3). But even so, the number of prior actions, benchmarks, and actual conditions for credit disbursement that Greece or Portugal were asked to implement still exceeded the average of IMF programs by a multiple (IEO 2016: para 72).

Last but not least, sovereign debt restructuring as part of these programs became less frequent and less generous, a phenomenon not only but especially in Europe (IEO 2016: paras 61–2). In the case of specific programs, this may have been the outcome of prioritizing the commons rather than the welfare of individual member states. This is how the IMF perceives it when explaining the conflicts over debt restructuring in Greece and bank shareholder bail-in in Ireland:

> The overriding concern of the European authorities was to preserve stability, and especially to preserve the single currency project. In contrast, the IMF's responsibility was also to the individual countries requesting financial assistance . . . In the case of the euro area, debt restructuring was an issue where a conflict could arise between what was good for a country and what was good for the euro area as a whole. (IEO 2016: para 106)

Reluctance to write down debt leaves long legacies of debt, weighing on the recovery of program countries, a point repeatedly and convincingly made by Sandbu (2015).

The ESM also remains a fund of pre-committed size. A program for Italy could easily overstretch €500 billion. Chancellor Merkel categorically rejected a banking license for the ESM that would have made it eligible to draw on ECB funding if necessary. Her view was supported by ECB President Draghi, while the French President Hollande, Italian Prime Minister Monti, and the Austrian central bank governor Nowotny backed a banking license (Reuters 2012; Telegraph 2012). The German position prevailed; the ESM is therefore more a multi lateral fiscal backstop for distressed sovereigns than a common emergency fund.

QUASI-FISCAL MONETARY POLICY

These limitations forced the ECB in turn to provide relief to governments. It had to do this without going against the prohibition on monetary financing. The quid-pro-quo for the first and relatively small bond-buying program, the SMP, was the emergency fund, the EFSF. It did not calm markets, especially after the second bailout program for Greece had forced losses on private bondholders. The crisis escalated further in 2012. There was a visible strain between the ECB and fiscal authorities in the Council. The risk premia in the Italian government bond market, the third largest after the US and Japan, started to rise again. This was preceded by the ousting of the Berlusconi government, to which the ECB openly contributed, which had the intended reassuring effect on the bond market; it was therefore most alarming that risk premia went up again under the technocratic government of Mario Monti.[7]

In this situation, another potential interface between money and public finances emerged in the guise of OMT. In his now famous speech to a bankers' forum in London, ECB President Draghi deviated from the pre-distributed text and assured financial markets that the ECB is ready, "[w]ithin our mandate... to do whatever it takes to preserve the euro," adding: "And believe me, it will be enough" (Draghi 2012). The ECB President had agreed this announcement with a small number of heads of state before consulting the governing board of the ECB.[8] With the announcement of this program, the seemingly unstoppable panic in bond markets miraculously stopped. The two novel features of the OMT were, compared to other bond-buying programs, that (i) the amounts available under OMT are ex ante unlimited and (ii) bonds bought by the ECB under this program will have no seniority compared to privately

[7] In 2011, Trichet and his successor Draghi had jointly signed letters to the Italian and Spanish prime ministers, which outlined the fiscal austerity measures they expected these governments to take in return for buying the country's bonds. The letter to Berlusconi was leaked, to considerable embarrassment of the ECB. When the Italian administration did not honor its side of the bargain, the ECB suspended Italian bond purchases. Alarm in the markets led to Berlusconi's replacement by a technocratic government under Mario Monti (Henning 2016: 182–4).

[8] Based on confidential information given at a Centre for European Reform workshop at Ditchley Park.

held claims in the event of a default (ECB 2012). The OMT assured markets of the ECB's readiness to act as lender of last resort to sovereigns, although confined to sovereigns that already have an ESM program. The OMT was an attempt to make the fiscally limited ESM funding open-ended if necessary, and it therefore represents a massive extension of monetary solidarity with the most distressed countries. This announcement could arguably not have worked its magic without the deafening silence, signifying tacit consent, from Berlin, which trumped resistance by the Bundesbank (Steen 2012).

The political risk that Chancellor Merkel had taken with this tacit agreement to the OMT announcement soon became obvious. The ECB's (2012) press statement on the technicalities of OMT in September 2012 was challenged in the German constitutional court by five different groups of plaintiffs. They came from across the party-political spectrum; one of these challenges, by political moderates, had almost 12,000 signatories. They argued that the OMT program exceeded the mandate of the ECB, which is to ensure price stability, and that it violated the principle of democracy (Case C-62/14: para 6). The aim was to establish that such a program had to be subject to a vote in parliament along with specific authorization by the German government. It took the German constitutional court almost four years to reach a decision, because it referred the case to the European Court of Justice (Case C-62/14 *Gauweiler and others* from June 16, 2015). The referral got ten other member states involved, nine of which (including the Netherlands and Finland) challenged the admissibility of the proceedings.

In the end, the European Court ruling said that the OMT program was legal, subject to certain conditions. These conditions include that the technical implementation must ensure that a member state cannot rely on the ECB buying its bonds, so a certain time span must have elapsed between the first issue of a bond and its buying under OMT. Moreover, the ECB can only buy bonds of countries "which are undergoing a structural adjustment programme and which have access to the bond market again" (Case C-62/14: para. 116)—the intervention is, in other words, confined to reducing excessive spreads and volatility but not replacing the bond market.[9] The European court held, and the German court reiterated, that the ECB can launch an OMT program only to ensure price stability, not to safeguard the stability of the euro area as a whole—this, both courts ruled, is the remit of the ESM (Case C-62/14: para. 64; Bundesverfassungsgericht 2016: para. 194).

[9] As Dolls et al. (2016: 10) put it correctly: "Investors today base their investment calculus at euro area government bond markets on the fact that the ECB is (conditionally) willing to buy crisis country bonds in the secondary market and that this tends to reduce the size of credit risk spreads in this market."

The German court further ruled that the Bundesbank is only allowed to participate in an OMT program if its volume is predetermined by the Governing Council (Bundesverfassungsgericht 2016: paras 199, 206). This is based on a tenuous reading of the European Court's judgment (C-62/14 paras 106, 113, 116) and goes directly against the ECB's announcement that "no ex ante quantitative limits are set on the size of [OMTs]" (ECB 2012). To get around this, the ECB's Governing Council will have to agree on such a large maximum amount that it is sure to exceed the required intervention. Even so, the ruling provides the Bundesbank with huge leverage on such a program, akin to an informal veto player position; an OMT without the Bundesbank's participation is unlikely to calm down markets.

This leaves the ECB with vast lending programs to banks only. These programs can help banks to recapitalize and thus provide relief to fiscal authorities through the monetary back door (Schelkle 2012c). The ECB had tried this arguably before the announcement of the OMT through its LTRO under the incoming President Draghi. This lending, to the tune of €990 billion since December 2011, provided financial institutions with huge credits at a fixed interest rate of 1 percent for up to three years. If they invested the loan in higher yielding assets, not least government bonds, they earned a safe margin out of which they could raise loss-absorbing capital. The responsibility of overburdened governments for recapitalizing their banking systems was therefore partly taken over by the central bank (Schelkle 2012c: 30), the risks marginally underwritten by all EA member states with paid-in capital in the ECB (Schoenmaker 2010). According to Commission estimates for 2008–13, the total amount that governments spent on recapitalization and asset relief to banks in the EA amounted to €484 billion. On top of that, governments provided guarantees and other liquidity measures to banks totaling €932 billion (ECB 2015: 88–9). This amounts to a sum comparable to the €990 billion provided by the ECB under the LTRO. The ECB's own version of what it did was acting as an intermediary that replaced the money market as the ECB (2015: 126) itself recognizes: "non-distressed countries . . . depositing liquidity with the Eurosystem, while distressed countries [were] borrowing liquidity from the Eurosystem." The two accounts are not incompatible, but my emphasis on recapitalization indicates an interface with fiscal policy that, for understandable reasons, the ECB is not keen to highlight. The proud institution had been forced into such a quasi-fiscal policy because it was left alone and firefighting by fiscal authorities in the Council.

These travails illustrate a relevant issue for the theory of interstate cooperation. The ECB's unconventional measure needed political support as it was not strictly covered by the central bank's narrow mandate, as the German constitutional court explains in considerable detail (Bundesverfassungsgericht 2016: paras 188–9). Yet the ECB could not engage in open negotiations with member state governments without conceding from the start that the OMT exceeds the ECB's mandate. Such negotiations would not have been in the interest of anybody who wanted to stamp out panic in the bond market quickly, because the German government's win set was so small that the status quo would have prevailed. This was a two-level game under the exigencies of "emergency politics" (White, J. 2015: 89). Under these conditions, the party that would have been perversely empowered by domestic opposition did not want to exercise its strength: the imperative of preserving the EA overrode the institutional conservatism of the German government. The subsequent challenges in the courts proved that the parties were correct to anticipate that collective action would fail in an open two-level game. Emergency politics proved functionally extremely effective in this case, presumably because it addressed a market audience (Lohmann 2003: 101–2). The OMT calmed markets that trusted the ECB to prevail ultimately, if only to preserve itself as an institution; the later court rulings had not much resonance, even though they constrained OMT.

One of the dilemmas of EA crisis management is that its modus operandi, emergency politics, may be effective in stopping market panic but it is out of sync with democratic processes. We see this not only in the mobilization of opposition in Germany but also in the failure of emergency politics exercised by technocratic governments in Greece and Italy to achieve popular support and electoral legitimation. One of the major benefits of institutionalized risk sharing would be that it would give time and a time horizon to opposition, deliberation, and response in member states (White, J. 2015: 99–100).

7.2.3 *Banking Union and an Expanded ECB Mandate*

Before the crisis, member state authorities were responsible for the prudential supervision of banks, for the resolution of insolvent banks, and for deposit insurance schemes.[10] They conducted these tasks in accordance with EU rules and regulations, but without any shared fiscal resources. Each of these responsibilities may require fiscal intervention. When supervisors order a bank to close, savers may have to be compensated for their losses—in fact, protection of small depositors is typically the main reason for why governments across the party-political spectrum come so readily to the rescue of banks (Brunnermeier et al. 2009: 68). In a systemic crisis, accumulated resolution and deposit insurance funds, typically financed by industry levies, may be too small to deal with the fall-out and governments have to make up the balance, at least in the first instance.

[10] This sub-section covers entries 1, 3, and 7–9 in Table 7.1.

These fiscal obligations meant that the ECB could not be given much of a say in supervision. For the independent central bank to be able to order member states to take fiscally relevant measures would breach the totemic separation of monetary and fiscal policies. An additional constraint for Europeanizing prudential supervision was that financial integration is, legally, a Single Market matter: non-EA members of the EU would not have accepted supervision from the ECB and a special supervisory body would have had to be created. It would in turn have to deal with several central banks: the ECB and the central banks of the non-EA countries.

But keeping supervision, resolution, and deposit insurance as national responsibilities contributed directly to the fragmentation of banking during the crisis as well as to the negative feedback loop between banks and sovereigns (ECB 2015: 88–90). This fragmentation can be seen in the differentiation of interest rates on new loans to non-financial firms in "peripheral countries"[11] compared to non-distressed EA members, as well as shrinking credit to the distressed economies since 2008 (ECB 2015: charts S32 and S34). Banks posted much less cross-border collateral in liquidity operations with the ECB after the crisis, again a tendency driven by distressed countries (ECB 2015: 127). The home bias in banks' holdings of government bonds had fallen before the financial crisis (see Chapter 5), but, by 2015, it had returned to the levels of the early 2000s (ECB 2015: 89). The ECB report gives several reasons for the rising home bias: "moral suasion" to hold their bonds exercised by governments over banks, and "carry trade" (borrowing cheaply from the ECB and investing dearly into high-risk assets), a policy favored by weak banks to build up their profits and recapitalize. In stronger economies, home bias has resulted from attempts to hedge against an exit of peripheral countries. These tendencies all had the effect of concentrating rather than diversifying sovereign risks on banks' balance sheets.

The June 2012 European Council decided to introduce a banking union, amidst dangerously rising risk premia on Italian and Spanish bonds (entry 8 in Table 7.1; Howarth and Quaglia 2013: 113). The EU had upwardly harmonized financial regulation before the crisis, completing the so-called Financial Services Action Plan through a fast-track legislative procedure, known as the Lamfalussy Process. This allowed it to move very fast on a Single Rulebook, already proposed in March 2009 in the De Larosière report. It was the first element of the banking union.[12] Other elements came into force step by step, notably a Single Supervisory Mechanism (SSM) in November 2014 and a Single Resolution Mechanism (SRM) by January 2016. A Bank Recovery and

[11] The ECB (2015: 88) includes in this category the five program countries, Italy, and Slovenia.
[12] See the Commission website on "Banking union" at http://ec.europa.eu/finance/general-policy/banking-union/index_en.htm (accessed December 17, 2015).

Resolution Directive requires bank shareholders to be bailed in first in a bank rescue, a new instrument that was soon to be tested in Italy. Also, the ESM added a Direct Recapitalization Instrument to its arsenal in December 2014, meaning it can acquire loss-absorbing assets in undercapitalized banks without adding to public debt of the banks' home government. All these measures are explicitly geared toward interrupting the negative feedback loop between banks and sovereigns.

A Single Rulebook and the SSM should stop regulatory Balkanization, which increases risk by separating the risk pool. One particularly blatant example arose when national supervisors sought to prevent subsidiaries of foreign banks from repatriating excess liquidity to their parent bank. The German authority Bafin openly admitted this discriminatory practice of "ring fencing liquidity" as late as August 2014; the Commission, spurred by complaints from Italy, had been investigating this for several years but had insufficient legal means to stop it (Arnold 2014).

The assignment of increased supervisory authority to the central bank follows an international trend. The US Fed and the Bank of England, among others, also had their bank supervision mandates expanded after the financial crisis. The rationale underlying this trend is the priority given to internalizing financial externalities, whereas the previous practice that avoided giving central banks much responsibility in supervision prioritized the prevention of moral hazard: specifically the problem that central banks as supervisors have incentives—and the means—to cover up past supervisory failings with fresh money (Goodhart and Schoenmaker 1995). After some wrangling (Howarth and Quaglia 2013: 112–13), the SSM got authority over supervision of all banks in the EA. The ECB directly supervises 120 banking groups that are large in absolute or relative terms (assets above €30 billion or 20 percent of the home country's GDP) or have received assistance from the emergency funds. They represent over 80 percent of EA banks in terms of assets (ECB 2014b).

Putting the ECB at the helm of the SSM created a two-tier Single Market. While open to all EU members, nine non-euro countries stayed out of the SSM, among them Europe's financial center, the UK. The British government did not stop the move, in fact it encouraged it, as it wanted to see the troubled currency union stabilized and accepted "the remorseless logic" towards closer integration, as then finance minister Osborne put it (Giles and Parker 2011). The SSM thus split the risk pool for an integrated financial system in the EU. This does not necessarily create additional problems, as the co-existence of different currencies in the Single Market already limits risk pooling through the ECB. Swap arrangements between central banks can be an alternative way of pooling. They have been used successfully to prevent currency crises in Central and Eastern Europe: a hub-and-spoke system of swap lines ensured that national central banks were not exposed to currency attacks for lack of foreign exchange reserves. Mortgage lending in foreign currencies had the potential to create mayhem at the EA's borders. The ECB established swap lines with the Danish, Hungarian, Polish, and Swedish central banks to cover euro-liquidity shortages which in turn entered into swap agreements with other central banks in Central and Eastern Europe; the ECB in turn could meet its dollar and Swiss franc shortages via swaps from the US Fed and the Swiss National Bank to help Hungary and Poland (Allen and Moessner 2010: 27, 30–1).

The Single Resolution Mechanism is an independent agency linked to the SSM: as soon as the ECB notifies the SRM board that a bank is failing, it decides along uniform lines how to handle the situation. Decision procedures can be quite complex, however, as national authorities have to be consulted and a large bank failure requires the decision to be taken in a plenary rather than in the executive formation. The fund has a volume of €55 billion, from 2024 onwards to be fully paid by the industry itself. It covers at least 1 percent of deposits of the contributing financial institutions. Given this relatively small sum, the main purpose of the SRM can be seen in establishing a clear hierarchy of loss absorption: the bail-in rule puts bank shareholders and creditors (other than insured deposit holders) first in line (ECB 2015: 92). Together with new bank bonus rules, this is likely to ensure that bank managers hold shares and have to bear more losses than they used to. However, the sad case of an Italian pensioner's suicide also revealed that ordinary savers may be caught by the bail-in rule.[13] National authorities are still next in line; if they are overburdened, they can approach the ESM. However, only the Direct Recapitalization Instrument is really a relief as it does not heap more liabilities on the sovereign. Its volume is €60 billion. German, Dutch, and Finnish governments were adamant that the ESM could be used for recapitalization only for future problems, not to resolve the issues currently arising from the financial crisis (Howarth and Quaglia 2013: 112–13).

The final element, a European Deposit Insurance Scheme, was proposed by the Commission in November 2015, eventually to be financed by a levy on the industry. This could stop deposit flight from distressed countries, which has aggravated the liquidity and solvency problems of their banking systems. The proposal met with immediate resistance by German Finance Minister Schäuble, who once again insisted that the scheme should not be used to resolve existing problems. He proposed that risks that are still on banks' books, notably in the form of doubtful government bonds, would have to be removed before the scheme's introduction, for instance through bank

[13] The pensioner had bought savings certificates from his regional bank, for Italians a standard way of saving. But when the bank collapsed, such certificates turned out to be junior bonds that were first in line for loss absorption according to the new EU rules (Münchau 2015).

resolution. He justified this as follows: "Every step we take towards risk-sharing prevents risk reduction. That is why risk reduction has to have priority" (FAZ 2015: 18; own translation). Since the veil of ignorance over who will gain from addressing current problems has been lifted, the deposit guarantee scheme was seen as redistributive towards recipients who have taken on excessive risk. Schäuble's position accepted the principle that there might be stabilizing insurance, but only for future problems, which might be limited with additional regulatory precautions.

Both the resolution mechanism and deposit insurance are institutions of "microprudential" regulation. The idea is to protect the soundness of the financial system with a view to individual banks: the sum of sound parts was meant to deliver a sound whole. But the systemic crisis in advanced countries has led to a macroprudential turn (Hanson et al. 2011). The systemic problem is that credit crunches and asset fire sales can bring down entire economies even if individual banks are fairly sound. The goal of macroprudential measures is "to control the social costs associated with excessive balance sheet shrinkage on the part of multiple financial institutions hit with a common shock" (Hanson et al. 2011: 5). This definition captures the central systemic issue, but it promotes the misleading impression that the financial system was "hit with a . . . shock," whereas the systemic crises before and after 2007–8 were the result of financial integration and innovation itself. An important aspect of the macroprudential turn is therefore to prevent such devastating dynamics from evolving in the first place.

The ECB and national authorities have now been given macroprudential tools in a Capital Requirements Directive (CRD IV) and a Regulation, in line with a framework agreed under Basel III. The main innovation is so-called "mandatory reciprocity" for certain instruments like counter-cyclical capital buffers (ECB 2015: 48): if credit growth is deemed excessive in one member state, other national authorities must impose credit restrictions, in the form of additional capital requirements of up to 2.5 percent, on cross-border banks in their jurisdiction. This is to prevent them from lending into the initiating state's financial markets and thus undermining the restrictive measures. This innovation is a small step by which prudential authority can finally catch up with an integrating financial system.

The Governing Council of the ECB, not the SSM, is the authority for macroprudential policy (ECB 2015: 47). This indicates that macroprudential policy is a way of differentiating the ECB's one-size-fits-all monetary policy regionally, an issue that other central banks, like the Bank of England, also face acutely (Schelkle 2014a). It addresses the Walters (1988) critique of monetary integration: that it brings about a pro-cyclical real interest rate effect; too high in the stagnating regions and too low in the booming regions of a heterogeneous union. The European Systemic Risk Board in the ECB is the coordinating body for this new set of policies at the EU and member state level, necessary because measures may interact in unpredictable ways (entry 3 in Table 7.1). Even outside a monetary union, the one-size-fits-none problem exists in the guise of a global (or rather: US dollar) cycle: countries that are integrated in the world economy have to follow the Fed's interest rate policy more or less closely; otherwise they will be affected by adverse capital flows (Rey 2013).

Macroprudential policies constitute a reversal of the tendency to prioritize financial integration over regulatory control. The instruments of macroprudential policies, such as counter-cyclical buffers and variable loan-to-value-ratios, permit that different rules prevail in different markets (Hanson et al. 2011: 5–16). Insofar as they segment markets and impose rules to prevent evasion and regulatory arbitrage, they are a form of capital control. It is therefore not surprising that the relevant regulation stipulates limits to macroprudential policies, providing that "a measure may only be used if the macro-prudential authority can establish that the measure is necessary, effective and proportionate" (ECB 2015: 48). The macroprudential turn fits into the slow rehabilitation of capital controls at the international level that has occurred ever since the Asian crisis in the late 1990s (IMF 2012; Korinek and Sandri 2015).

Another forceful tool that the extended mandate has given the ECB as a macroprudential regulator is regular stress tests ("comprehensive quality assessments"). Simulating different scenarios and establishing how well banks' capital buffers withstand the imaginary shocks is a way of forcing banks to write down dubious assets and increase their capital. In the exercise that was undertaken as a preparation for the SSM, banks took measures to "strengthen their capital base" amounting to over €200 billion (ECB 2015: 91). The problem is, however, what happens when the stress test finds that capital has to be increased and the bank cannot do this without sovereign support. Only the ESM comes close to providing a pool which governments might draw on to recapitalize their banking systems, and it is heavily hedged around with conditions.

This brings us to the ultimate limitation of the banking union. Reforms have undoubtedly responded to the functional necessities of monetary-financial integration which, as Jones and Underhill (2014) show, are not unique to the EA. Market panic has subsided. Instead of merely monitoring the use of the commons, EA institutions have started to protect it from devastation by financial markets. The banking union is a decisive step towards managing the integration of markets: macroprudential tools can do so by segmenting them temporarily. But the fiscal backstops that have been developed still do not rest on joint liability but on separate national guarantees. The formal obligation for every member to contribute is a form of risk pooling but a relatively weak one, subject to a commitment problem of the guarantors.

7.3 Reforming the Governance of the Commons

How profound or shallow have the reforms of the European monetary union since 2009 been? The sheer number of new policy processes and organizations that has been created in less than seven years is certainly impressive, whatever one's view of their effectiveness. This frantic reform activity defies both journalistic and theoretical accounts that emphasize inertia and a status quo bias. There has been a shift in the underlying paradigm, but the institutional assignment of policy competences has not done away with the fiscal taboo. The clearest example of this is the massive quantitative easing program that the ECB began in 2015, which was still ongoing in late 2016. This program meant to bring inflation up to the 2 percent target, given that the EA suffered from low and even negative inflation, making private and public debt ever more burdensome. The fiscal risks are borne largely by the national central banks in the Eurosystem; only 20 percent are on the ECB's books.[14]

The paradigm change can be inferred from the comprehensive visions of a "genuine" and "complete" European monetary union that the Four and Five Presidents' reports formulated. EU representatives have now firmly adopted the language of risk sharing. In the earlier report, this language still has strong traces of OCA theory, with a focus on asymmetric shocks: "setting up risk-sharing tools, such as a common but limited shock absorption function, can contribute to cushioning the impact of country-specific shocks and help prevent contagion across the euro area and beyond" (van Rompuy et al. 2012: 10). The successor report takes a broader view of risk sharing, while retaining some optimism about the capacity of private markets to spread risk and maintaining the notion that convergence in "competitiveness" is needed for the union to work. It proposes that, in the short term, a banking and capital markets union should provide the mechanisms for private risk sharing when a shock hits any of its members. This would give time for "economic structures [to] converge towards the best standards in Europe" in the medium term, implying unity in minimized diversity. This would eventually prepare the ground for public risk sharing "through a mechanism of fiscal stabilization for the euro area as a whole" (Juncker et al. 2015: 4).

The major attraction of this vision is that it indicates a shift of emphasis from discipline and convergence towards deliberate risk sharing between

[14] The ECB homepage contains the answer to a question on the "Extended Asset Purchase Programme" that reads: "But doesn't the new programme force losses onto national central banks?... It is true that in the new programme some risks are not shared across the Eurosystem but remain with the national central bank. The ECB is committed to the principle of risk-sharing, and that's why 20% of the purchases fall under the regime of full risk-sharing. But the decision also mitigates concerns about potential unintended fiscal consequences." See https://www.ecb.europa.eu/explainers/tell-me-more/html/asset-purchase.en.html (accessed August 14, 2016).

members. But the shift is rather tentative and favors national diversity only within firm bounds; there is still an embrace of best practices or models. We can see in this a manifestation of the political-economic paradox of a diverse union, exacerbated by the battering of trust and goodwill that the crisis and its management have inflicted on all sides. While its leading representatives point to the economic benefits of risk diversification, they try to minimize the political impact of pooling risks across very different states. The problem is that the proposed solution—convergence on best standards—may reduce the benefits to be had from integration. Implicitly, the Five Presidents report' interprets this as a tradeoff or exchange. "Convergence on best standards" allows the EU to pursue a reform agenda that includes everybody. At the same time, it sounds like a concession and assurance to the fortunate member states, always inclined to consider their fortune to be deserved, that the less fortunate will have to "earn" their inclusion into the risk pool. This either reduces the potential benefits of pooling or postpones it forever because convergence does not happen, not least because the "best standards" are moving targets.

The ECB took a different approach to addressing the paradox that diversity increases the potential economic gains but also the political costs of risk sharing. It made the costs of limited risk sharing quite visible; some like Whelan (2014c) would say excessively so. By rationing access to ECB liquidity in ostentatious compliance with its narrow mandate, the Bank repeatedly escalated market panic. It thus put pressure both on the distressed government and the majority in the Council to take some responsibility for crisis management. Escalating market panic made the fortunate members aware that shifting all adjustment pressures onto weaker parties is also costly to themselves. It is difficult to prove this interpretation but it makes sense in light of the sequence of events. In return for the SMP, Trichet forced the heads of state to agree to an emergency fund (Barber 2010). Draghi advanced the role of the ECB as a lender of last resort to sovereigns when extreme circumstances so required but tied OMT interventions to the existence of an ESM program that would give it residual indemnity. The ECB used its capacity for financial stabilization—and the ability to refrain from using this capacity—to raise the costs of political stalemate and discord. The creative exercise of monetary solidarity was thereby made conditional on some political agreement between unequal and divided partners to lend at least partial assistance to each other. The diversity of risks thereby became the lever for political collaboration.

But the ECB's efforts to cajole member states into building institutions for risk sharing are institutionally perilous. The letter by Trichet and Draghi to Prime Minister Berlusconi (see fn 7) highlighted this: it was a step too far even if directed against an utterly disreputable government. The ECB made itself a soft target for criticism for overreaching its powers and lacking transparency in its operations (Schmidt 2015: 31–6). One should not assume that the ECB acted in this way for the greater good of monetary solidarity. Cajoling fiscal authorities was a by-product of the ECB's attempt to get out of a very vulnerable position (Mabbett and Schelkle 2016b). Sole responsibility for crisis management left the ECB exposed to political attacks, from outside and inside the Bank. The Federal Reserve and the Bank of England were engaged in similar maneuvers with their fiscal counterparts, but they enjoyed the support of the executive arm of government, even while the Fed endured incessant attacks in Congress. The late Tommaso Padoa-Schioppa (2004: 180) foresaw that the ECB's separation from any and all governments could leave it isolated, remarking that: "It would be unfortunate if [the ECB's] independence were to be confused with loneliness."

The Five Presidents' report, largely written by teams around ECB President Draghi and Council President Tusk, can be seen as an attempt to set out a plan for monetary-fiscal cooperation, but it received a rather lukewarm reception by heads of state. The reforms since 2009 have extended risk sharing but did not do away with, in particular, the limits on fiscal risk sharing. This keeps the threat of negative feedback loops between banks and sovereign alive and, under extreme stress, tends to concentrate risks on the weakest links. In these extreme situations, the ECB remains lonely—by design, not out of confusion. Seen in this light, the announcement by Mario Draghi (2012) that the ECB will do "whatever it takes to save the euro" is as much a statement of political defeat as of monetary prowess.

Part III

Solidarity in Action

8

Social Solidarity through Labor Market Integration

This chapter is about social solidarity in terms of risk sharing with economic migrants in two monetary unions. There are two reasons for including migration in a study of monetary solidarity. First, there is still a presumption in much commentary on the European monetary union that it needs higher labor mobility in order to function properly. This commentary, in the tradition of the mainstream theory of monetary integration, the theory of OCA, portrays cross-border movement of labor as not categorically different from the movement of labor within borders. This is a distorting simplification and does not speak to the concerns that migration raises in both destination and origin countries. One main point of this chapter is that labor mobility is not an effective and reliable adjustment and insurance mechanism for regions in a monetary union, irrespective of how high or low mobility is.

Second, social solidarity with economic migrants from another member state is a possible risk-sharing mechanism, important for individuals who have fallen on hard times if not of great relevance in the aggregate (Section 8.3.2). This risk sharing in labor markets can be facilitated or hindered by the welfare state. But eminent political economists posit an apparent clash between economic freedoms and social rights; both are seen as citizenship rights that can only go together in a full-fledged political union. Scholars like Maurizio Ferrera (2005, 2009) and Fritz Scharpf (2009) see welfare states and social market economies, respectively, as confined to nationally constituted communities easily upset by economic freedoms. Others, like Caporaso and Tarrow (2009) and Norbert Reich (2008), acknowledge the tension but then analyze judicial ways of mitigating it.

This chapter shows that tensions between the rights of migrants and residents also exist in the United States and do not raise any categorically different issues for Europe's more generous welfare states. But welfare states, far from being an obstacle, are a vehicle of the economic freedom to take up employment in another country, protecting both migrants and resident workers. A consistent conceptualization sees economic freedoms as part of social entitlements. Even so, freedom of movement of persons is an important social insurance mechanism for individuals but a potentially problematic and regressive channel of risk sharing between regions.

8.1 Labor Mobility in a World of Welfare

Labor mobility can be a risk-sharing mechanism inside or beyond a monetary union. It provides an escape route for individuals who cannot find gainful or adequate employment in the country of residence, whether because the economy is in a cyclical downturn or because it is persistently underperforming or is simply poorer and backward. Migration takes place on a great range of terms. The social rights of migrants are among "the critical factors governing the migration process... that differentiate the market for men from the market for shirts" (Piore 1979: 8). These social rights hinge on at least three institutional features: (a) the formal access rights of migrants to another state, (b) the welfare entitlements once migrants are admitted, and (c) the labor market conditions under which migrants can hold onto a job.

In the famous categorization of citizenship rights by T. H. Marshall (1950: 10–11), (a) is a civil right ("the rights necessary for individual freedom"), while (b) and (c) are social rights ("the whole range from the right to a modicum of economic welfare and security to the right to share to the full in the social heritage and to live the life of a civilised being"). Political rights contain the passive and active right to participate in elections ("the right to participate in the exercise of political power, as a member of a body invested with political authority or as an elector of the members of such a body"). His stylized history envisaged a sequence in which social rights beyond the village community were acquired last. EU citizenship and the regulation of free movement of persons and services have a direct bearing on all three determinants but we note from the outset that EU political rights in the Marshallian sense are confined to local and European elections. This raises the political-economic paradox that most of the benefits of migration accrue to destination countries in Western Europe (Atoyan et al. 2016: 5) while the fiercest political resistance to migration also arises within destination countries. In fact, this political resistance to immigration typically extends to European integration since it is EU norms of non-discrimination that tend to constrain domestic practices rather than political representation of immigrants in the democracies where they are resident.

The focus here is on economic migration. Formal employment generally means that the migrant joins, temporarily or permanently, the risk pool that is

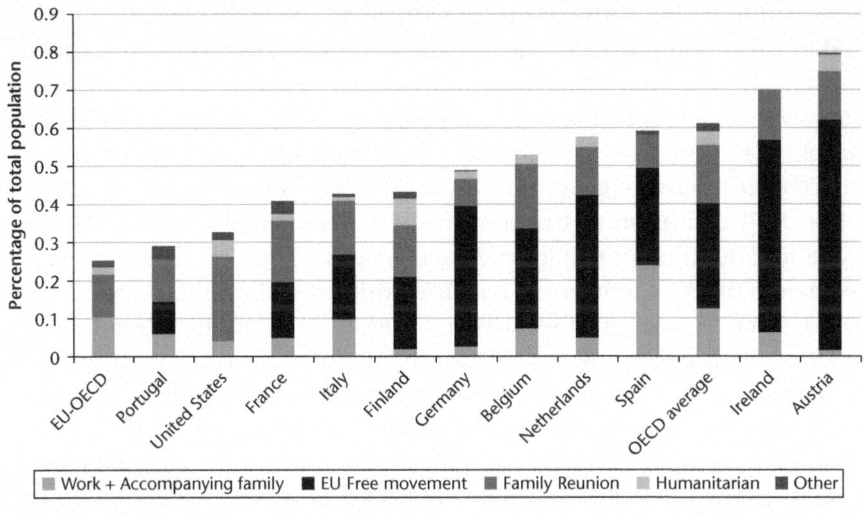

Figure 8.1. Immigration exceeding one year by category of entry or status change, 2012
Source: OECD 2014a

another state's tax-transfer system, but market segmentation and policies limiting the acquisition of social rights may prevent this. Of course, a considerable share of immigration is not driven by economic motives. In the US, the bulk of all immigration is actually related to family reunion (different from "accompanying family of workers"). The importance of family migration is a long-term trend (OECD 2014a: 13). It is somewhat understated in the snapshot for 2012 that Figure 8.1 shows, because this was the first year in which workers from the new member states in Central and Eastern Europe (CEE) could move freely to Austria and Germany. These member states had insisted on the full length of the transitional arrangements that can restrict free movement for seven years after accession.

These figures cover only "permanent" migrants, defined by the OECD as staying in another country for more than a year. In 2012, the OECD (2014a: 13, 24–5) counted a flow of about 4 million permanent new migrants, which compares with 1.9 million temporary migrants who have explicitly timed work permits, such as intracompany transfers or seasonal work. As noted by Piore (1986: 25), many migrants are not "birds of passage" but move with a longer-term perspective or end up staying against their original intention. Recent migrants from CEE have been staying much more permanently than any other group of migrants to Western Europe previously (Atoyan et al. 2016: para. 2).

The article by Mundell (1961) that pioneered OCA theory elevated labor mobility to the prime adjustment mechanism between member states of a monetary union. When member states are differently affected by a macroeconomic shock, the displaced workers in the more severely hit region could move and find work in the less affected region. In this textbook model, there are no important analytical differences between worker movement across sectors, across regions within a country and across state borders—his example was Canada–US migration.[1] Free movement of labor means the absence of restrictive regulation. This perspective is captured in the OECD's (2014a: 147) definition of free movement as "not subject to restrictions on occupation, duration or employer characteristics." The alternative view developed here is that free movement is a differentiated social right to seek employment, residence, and social security in another state, not the absence of any regulation. This perspective follows Piore (1979) in drawing attention to the differences between the market for labor services and the market for shirts.

OCA scholars never dwelt on the political implications of their theory. Regional adjustment through mobility requires real-wage flexibility in the region receiving these displaced workers (McKinnon 1963). Migration is likely to restrain real-wage growth in those segments of the labor market that absorb these workers, mitigated to some extent by the fact that they may also boost demand. Seen as a risk pool for mobile workers, an OCA thus compensates unfortunate workers with access to jobs elsewhere in the monetary union while those fortunate workers elsewhere pay through the dampening effect of migration on their real wages. It is fairly obvious that anti-immigration sentiments may arise in the destination region, although much will depend on the wider context of economic growth and intensity of competition for jobs.

The US is typically cited as the prime empirical example of the labor market flexibility that is required for the smooth functioning of a monetary union.[2] Comparative political economists who study national capitalist institutions and welfare systems grant that the US currency area adjusts through labor mobility and real-wage flexibility. But they maintain that there are other worlds and varieties of mature capitalism that adjust differently while they may deliver as much economic well-being as the US benchmark.[3] They achieve this equivalence with another combination of institutions, above all generous social safety nets, coordinated wage bargains, and long-term credit relationships. Adjustment proceeds not primarily via flexible wages but incremental quantitative as well as qualitative changes in employment, for which both financial stakeholders and the welfare state provide the necessary time.

[1] There are exceptions to the simplistic economists' view of free movement, for instance Boeri (2010).

[2] Barro and Sala-i-Martin (1991) pioneered the comparison, this was taken up by Bayoumi and Eichengreen (1993) and others, recently again by Krugman (2013: 441, 445–6).

[3] See Esping-Andersen (1990) for the classic regime classification of welfare-state regimes, Kitschelt et al. (1999) for a collection of eminent scholars on comparative capitalism, Hall and Soskice (2001) and their collaborators for the most parsimonious liberal versus coordinated classification and Amable (2003) for a comprehensive clustering of diverse capitalisms.

These two approaches, of OCA theory, on the one hand, and comparative capitalism studies, on the other, evaluate migration and especially free movement very differently. For economists, immigration can rejuvenate the workforce and increase the flexibility of labor markets. Parts of the existing workforce may object to this but business interests will support immigration, along with voters who perceive positive fiscal effects and groups who are not in competition with the new arrivals. For comparative political economists, migration can potentially upset an institutional equilibrium, undermining wage bargains and employment standards. This can produce wide adverse effects on the receiving state's labor force, and on the fiscal soundness of its welfare state.

There are also similarities between economic and comparative capitalism diagnoses. Both analyze migration from the perspective of the destination countries. Both see the welfare state as incompatible with openness generally and with the integration of migrants particularly. Against this background, this chapter examines first how free movement is constructed as a distinct social right of migration. Free movement in the EA is compared with free movement *within* the United States to see how the two systems construct this social right. This perspective sides with comparative political economists insofar as it analyzes free movement of workers as movement between different regimes of social rights. Labor market integration is centered on the meta-regulation of social entitlements that in mature welfare states come with a job. The welfare state is the vehicle that can distribute the real or perceived effects on wages and employment conditions of the resident workforce more evenly among taxpayers and thus establish migration as a more equitable insurance arrangement. Furthermore, understanding the efficacy of migration also requires us to consider its effect on the home states. Empirical evidence suggests that the individual insurance provided by migration comes at the cost of the region of origin, although the outcome depends on the socio-economic characteristics of migrants (Huber and Tondl 2012; Atoyan et al. 2016).

The upshot of the comparison that follows is that European welfare states in conjunction with EU regulation are conducive to higher reservation wages and less dualization for those in work than US safety nets; this comes, however, at the cost of higher unemployment among migrants in the EU. This can be seen as a political strategy that reduces conflict in the labor market in destination countries and it arguably also ensures more insurance for regular economic migrants, while the effect on voters is more mixed: migration is seen as a fiscal burden even though this seems to be largely a misperception (Burgoon 2014; Dustmann and Frattini 2014).

The analysis in this chapter casts some doubt on the efficacy of risk sharing through migration in a diverse union. In the origin countries, the loss of predominantly young and better-educated workers has adverse cumulative effects, as predicted by endogenous growth theory and the new economic geography with their emphasis on positive externalities from agglomeration (Atoyan et al. 2016: para. 4). Mass emigration creates skill shortages, reduces potential growth, and removes the political influence of active and educated professionals. In the destination countries, the literature points to the phenomenon of dualization (Bertola 1998; Rueda and Pontusson 2000; Emmenegger and Careja 2012). In these segments or pockets of sectoral labor markets, migrants and resident outsiders are subject to flexible wages and short-term contracts while natives and long-term residents enjoy efficiency wages and decent working conditions. To the extent that a union of mature welfare states reinforces dualization, the insurance that is provided by migration rights is paid for in an inequitable and regressive way (Stiglitz 2016: 134).

None of these considerations deny that labor mobility can help individuals to share the risk of an economic downturn and/or the risk of being left poorer than the rest of the union. But this does not extend to regions or member states of a monetary union. It is striking that US labor mobility has significantly declined while free movement in the EA has increased, in particular during the crisis years of 2008–13 (Beine et al. 2013; Dao et al. 2014; Jauer et al. 2014). But nobody would claim that the EA functioned so much better as a consequence. The evidence suggests that the role of free movement for *interstate* risk sharing—in contrast to individual insurance—is inherently limited and possibly counterproductive.

8.2 The Social Right to Internal Migration in Two Monetary Unions

Free movement of citizens across member states' borders is regulated by the EU and the federal government in the US, respectively. The rules for the EU apply to the EA, as the monetary union is contained within the economic union. The commitment to let citizens of another member state reside on one's territory and give them conditional access to social security[4] is typically seen as part of full-fledged political union, as in a fiscal federation. However social citizenship in the EU is distinct from political citizenship because migrants do not have the right to vote in national elections. This can be compared to the US, where Marshall's sequence holds: political citizenship was established in the nineteenth century (for white males) while social citizenship developed subsequently. It is generally more limited than in the EA.

[4] Social security is used here synonymously with social policy more widely, not confined to old-age security (as in the US) or social insurance only (as in the EU codification).

8.2.1 *Territorial Access and Welfare Entitlements*

The following discussion focuses on ten EA member countries, selected for reasons of data availability. This union of ten states had a combined population size of 309 million in 2012, similar to the US with 314 million. These countries are the founding EA members, namely Austria, Belgium, Finland, France, Germany, Ireland, Italy, the Netherlands, Portugal, and Spain, excluding the city-state Luxembourg. They are one country for purposes of labor mobility, just as normative OCA theory requires, but with different regional welfare systems.

Table 8.1 gives an overview of residency and social security rights attached to migration within the US and EA monetary unions. It provides information on two determinants of risk sharing through migration: (a) the right to reside in another member state and (b) entitlements to social security once resident. It compares the rights of a Spaniard who wants to work in Germany (second column) and those of a migrant from Mississippi who moves to Massachusetts

Table 8.1. Internal migration and immigration as social rights in the EU/EA-10 and the US

	EU/EA-10		US	
	EU nationals (free movement)	Third-country nationals	US citizens (free movement)	Non-US citizens
Formal access rights of migrants to state	*EcActive*: unrestricted, including accompanying family *Ec-Non-Active*: unrestricted for three months	National labor market tests, shortage lists, numerical limits, (PBS for skills and work experience); EU rules for long-term residents, researchers, high skilled, families	Unrestricted	Labor market tests, shortage lists, numerical limits
Welfare entitlements once migrants are admitted	*EcActive*: same as natives; contributory benefits exportable *Ec-Non-Active*: own resources and sickness insurance required for five years of residence, then same as natives	*EcActive*: same as EU nationals for contributory health care and unemployment benefits, contributory and non-contributory pensions; only contributory pensions exportable	Same as state residents; contributory benefits under state administration (unemployment insurance) exportable	Eligible for federally funded means-tested programs after five years, except for previous work history (>ten years) or military service; pension entitlements exportable under bilateral agreements

Note: PBS = Points-based system

Source: Free movement Directive 2004/38; Coordination Regulation 883/2004; EMN 2014; OECD 2014: ch.3; CRS 2014a; US Social Security Administration, "International Programs" at https://www.ssa.gov/international/countrylist3.htm (accessed November 15, 2015)

for work (fourth column). These rights of internal migrants are contrasted with the rights of migrants from outside, say a Turkish citizen moving to Germany for work (third column) and a Mexican to the US (fifth column).

Residency is a starting point for obtaining some social rights of migration. In the EU/EA, free movement entails immediate access to residency in another member state. While this applies to all US citizens for an unlimited duration, for EU nationals the right is conditional on being "economically active": either as a worker or self-employed. The categorization of jobseekers is contested but the Free Movement Directive (2004/38, Article 7(3)) lays down that if EU nationals have worked for over a year in the host state and become involuntarily unemployed, they retain their active status for at least six months. Without previous employment, the status is contestable. After five years' residency, the right to remain becomes permanent.

The Maastricht Treaty established EU citizenship in 1992, historically the first and only case of supranational citizenship that complements national citizenship (Article 20 TFEU). It gives an unconditional right to three months' residence in another member state to all EU nationals. After three months, the right to reside becomes conditional for those labelled economically inactive, typically pensioners and students: they must have sufficient resources to sustain themselves as well as sickness insurance for up to five years. They can be expelled if they fail to fulfil these conditions or seek assistance, although authorities must give due consideration to individual circumstances. A "real link" to the host state can trump this condition.[5]

But even if an EU national is expelled, they can in principle re-enter for another three months. This has led the governments of Austria, Germany, the Netherlands, and the UK to write an open letter to the Council Presidency, asking for the creation of the instrument of a re-entry ban for deported EU citizens (EPRS 2014: 11). While taking pains to stress that they do not question free movement as such, the abuse of this right by non-economic migrants "threaten[s] the acceptance of the European idea of solidarity [in the receiving societies]." The Commissioners who were copied in replied drily that the Free Movement Directive 2004/38 (Article 35) already allows governments to "adopt the necessary measures to refuse, terminate or withdraw any right conferred by this Directive in the case of abuse of rights or fraud, such as marriages of convenience."

Union citizenship thus differentiates economically non-active EU nationals from third-country nationals who would have their visa or work permit terminated if they could not find employment. When it comes to entitlement

[5] Recital 16, Directive 2004/38. This has been established in the landmark case of *Grzelczyk* (C-184/99), a French student residing in Belgium who needed (and had to be granted) social assistance to complete his studies.

to benefits, there is a durational residency requirement for the economically non-active, while workers and the self-employed have immediate and equal access to all benefits upon arrival. For example, if migrants work for low wages, they have a right to any in-work benefit that nationals receive under such circumstances.[6]

In the US, no such residency requirements exist for US citizens although this has been the outcome of protracted legal battles. Residency requirements for receiving social assistance were a favored measure on the part of state and local authorities for deterring poor migrants until the late 1960s, when social activists began to challenge these practices in the Supreme Court as being discriminatory (Schram and Soss 1999: 43). In the most famous case, *Shapiro* v. *Thompson*,[7] the Court ruled forty such durational residency requirements unconstitutional (Schram and Soss 1999: 43) on the grounds that they violated the right to travel. This right to travel was a judicial construction since the word "travel" does not appear in the US Constitution. The judges saw it implied by the Fourteenth Amendment that gives all US citizens "the same privileges and immunities in the several states."[8] A new social right was constructed out of a much older civil right.

But it was not assured. The legality of residency requirements for social assistance came to the fore again with the 1996 welfare reform under the Clinton administration. The Personal Responsibility and Work Opportunity Reconciliation Act authorized "any State receiving a TANF grant to pay the benefit amount of another State's TANF program to residents who have lived in the State for less than 12 months" (*Sáenz*, case summary).[9] Fifteen states introduced new rules subsequent to this authorization, seeking to pay only the lower benefits of the origin state (Allard 1998: 55). In *Sáenz* v. *Roe*,[10] however, the Supreme Court not only struck down California's application of this rule but ruled against the Act's authorization as well: "This Court has consistently held that Congress may not authorize the States to violate the Fourteenth Amendment. Moreover, the protection afforded to a citizen by that Amendment's Citizenship Clause limits the powers of the National Government as well as the States" (*Sáenz* v. *Roe*, case summary). The Californian government advanced a purely fiscal argument for disadvantaging newly arriving citizens. In EU parlance, it maintained that paying the relatively high Californian benefits to newly arriving citizens is a "burden on its

[6] E.g. Case C-22/08 *Vatsouras*, paras 26–32.

[7] *Shapiro* v. *Thompson*, 394 U.S. 618 (1969).

[8] The Amendment itself was regarded dormant because it was included into the Constitution after the abolition of slavery in 1868, as a safeguard against Southern states depriving black Americans of their citizenship rights through so-called Black Codes (Winick 1999: 593).

[9] TANF stands for Temporary Assistance for Needy Families, a means-tested cash benefit that is conditional on the presence of children.

[10] *Sáenz* v. *Roe*, 526 U.S. 489 (1999).

social security system" (Rec.10 and Article 7(1) Directive 2004/38). The Court acknowledged fiscal concerns but rejected a purely contributory rationale for the denial of benefits to new residents. This rationale would permit states to allocate all benefits and services according to past tax contributions which, quoting from *Shapiro* v. *Thompson*, Justice Stevens deemed absurd: it would mean that new residents could be barred from schools and parks or deprived of police and fire protection (Stevens in *Sáenz* v. *Roe*: sect.V).

In the EU regulation of entitlements, the distinction between contributory and non-contributory benefits is a guiding principle for adjudicating on the entitlements of migrating EU nationals. Contributory benefits are "exportable," whereas non-contributory benefits can only be obtained while the migrant is resident in the host state. Regulation 883/2004 on the Coordination of Social Security Systems rules that EU nationals must be allowed to take with them any entitlements they typically acquired through contributions ("social security") if they leave, such as pensions or workers' compensation for accidents.[11] There are rules for the aggregation of benefits (allowing pension entitlements acquired in more than one country to be combined) which had been developed on a bilateral basis before they were then extensively meta-regulated by the EU (Bolderson and Gains 1993: 18). These aggregation rules ensure that a mobile EU national does not lose out because of national requirements that contributions have to be paid for a minimum period of time before benefits can be drawn: contributions paid in one member state count towards the minimum duration in another member state. If a migrant qualifies for benefits in two member states, each government pays pro rata. Double payment for the same period is excluded, however, which means that the more generous state is likely to pay. Non-contributory benefits financed by general taxes are not generally exportable: social and medical assistance and so-called Special Non-Contributory Benefits (SNCB) can be reserved for residents, although not for nationals.[12]

SNCBs are an artificial category of benefits that the EU legislature created to resolve a conflict between some member states and the Court and the Commission.[13] The latter tended to take an expansive view of the contributory nature of benefits, regarding rights acquired during a period of residency as non-wage entitlements that mobile workers should be able to export. Member

[11] The Regulation covers ten "branches of social security" that include health care, old age, employment-related, and family benefits (Regulation 883/2004, Article 3). They do not have to be strictly financed by individual contributions which is one reason for the enormous amount of case law in this area.

[12] Article 3(5) and Article 70(4) of Regulation 883/2004; CJEU judgment of November 11, 2014, C-333/13 *Dano*, para. 63 considers SNCB as "social assistance" in the sense of the Free Movement Directive.

[13] SNCBs must be specifically listed in Annex X of the Coordination Regulation. The haggling over this list between member states and the Commission delayed the implementation of Regulation 883/2004 until May 2010.

state authorities objected that some benefits are meant to ensure social cohesion among residents. SNCBs are typically paid on top of other benefits, such as low public pensions, and are granted to guarantee a certain living standard of elderly or disabled residents, but they are not means tested like social assistance. In *Skalka*[14] the Court accepted the member states' argument that they should be able to restrict certain non-contributory social entitlements to those residing on the territory, even though this tends to favor nationals. Pennings (2012: 330) has an interesting interpretation of the debate and the Court's decision:

> Solidarity was not the reason why social benefits were made accessible to non-nationals; rather, solidarity is referred to in the case law when a particular national scheme is allowed to be defended against foreign nationals, as in the case of special non-contributory benefits, where the Court upheld a residence condition as objectively justified, while referring to the relation between these benefits and the solidarity of the country concerned.

In his view, solidarity is invoked when the Court accepts that free movement and non-discrimination have limits. Pennings (2012) expresses a common understanding of free movement as being opposed to nationally constituted solidarity (Ferrera 2005, 2009).

But it is not entirely correct to say that the Court has never invoked solidarity in order to justify the entitlement of non-nationals to benefits. For instance, in *Grzelczyk* (C-184/99, para. 44) the Court noted that "a certain degree of financial solidarity between nationals of a host Member State and nationals of other Member States" is implied in the stipulation that "beneficiaries of the right of residence must not become an 'unreasonable' burden on the public finances of the host Member State." It can be granted that this is a rather weak and indirect line of reasoning. This implied that free movement is not necessarily the opposite of solidarity but can be its manifestation. Member states are obliged to grant solidarity in the sense of access to domestic support systems but this obligation is bounded by its "reasonableness."[15]

The detailed regulation of the social right of free movement makes it an ex ante mechanism of risk sharing (Section 2.4): the conditions of claiming insurance are specified and rule-based, not left to the discretion of destination countries once the insurance case arises. Claiming insurance here means that an EU national can escape the bad luck of poor employment prospects in his or her home state without becoming a second-class citizen. The comparison with the institutions of access and entitlement for third-country nationals

[14] Case C-160/02, [2004] ECR I-56.

[15] Subsequently, the Free Movement Directive 2004/38 stipulated only that beneficiaries must not become a "burden," which leaves out the adjective "unreasonable" on which the Court's argument relied (Article 7(1)).

(e.g. Turkish migrants to an EU member state) and non-US citizens (e.g. a Mexican immigrant) reveals stark differences. Access is regulated in a discretionary fashion (Table 8.1): labor market tests ask employers to prove that they cannot recruit among residents/nationals; shortage lists regarding desirable occupations and numerical limits on particular nationalities are adjusted in line with the socio-economic and political situation in the destination country, not that of the countries of origin (OECD 2014a: 221–30). In fact, this can lead to tighter rationing exactly when the insurance case arises: as more migrants try to improve on their life chances, a political backlash against a "flood" of foreigners becomes more likely. Point-based systems that some EA-10 countries like Austria have in place give more assurance and transparency to applicants, but they still select the best candidates from the national point of view.

The comparison with the US shows what difference risk sharing through free movement and non-discrimination can make in contrast to risk sharing through citizenship. The US knows no distinction between economically active and inactive citizens as regards the right to reside and receive benefits, at least once the Supreme Court established an extensive constitutional right to travel that includes the entitlement to (non-exportable, non-contributory) social assistance at the destination. The flip side is that US rules draw a sharp distinction between citizens and non-citizens.[16] Immigrant workers are not entitled to needs-based benefits for the first five years and hence there is no risk sharing but only the obligation to sustain oneself through remunerated work. If immigrants are lucky enough to come from an OECD country with which the US has bilateral social security agreements, they will be able to take their pension entitlements with them if they want to retire in their home country. So the majority of legal immigrants, notably from Mexico, can take their pension entitlements with them, provided they were registered to have paid social security payroll taxes for at least ten years.[17] To that extent, old-age poverty is a risk that is shared through the immigration rules laid down in bilateral agreements, similar to the exportability rules in the EU.

[16] The rules for third-country nationals in the EU are less dichotomous: there are different rules for researchers, students, family members, Blue Card holders, and long-term residents. The latter two categories are almost on an equal footing with EU nationals. There are some common EU standards regarding access to social security, family reunion, and intra-EU mobility of third-country nationals but a lot of rules remain subject to member states' discretion (EMN 2013: 34–5, 42–4).

[17] The more problematic issue was an estimated 11–12 million "undocumented" immigrants in the US in 2014. Since 1996, the Internal Revenue Service provided about 21 million immigrants with an individual taxpayer identification number without reporting them to the immigration authorities. Due to their illegal status, they could not get a social security number. It meant that these immigrants paid the social security payroll tax (through their employers) and thus financed an estimated $100 billion of pensions, health care for the elderly, and tax subsidies for other low-income workers, while they could not claim any of these federal benefits themselves (Ohlemacher 2015).

8.2.2 *Dualism in Labor Markets and Risk Sharing*

Labor market conditions can be more or less conducive to economic migrants finding a job, particularly a job matching their qualifications. The large income discrepancies between member states even in the EA-10 but also within the US,[18] and between these monetary unions and the outside world, ensure that there is a highly elastic supply of migrant labor to the richer regions. This elasticity has been reinforced by recent labor market reforms within Europe and the US which made cash benefits to adults of working age conditional on working or at least on training. So-called "activating measures" in the EU, for instance Hartz IV in Germany and the Earned Income Tax Credit (EITC) in the US, are examples of such in-work cash benefits. They have added members of the resident workforce to the labor supply and put them in direct competition with immigrants.

Economists have argued since the late 1980s that, in response to the opening of borders and deindustrialization, an "insider-outsider" structure in the labor market has emerged (Lindbeck and Snower 1986; Bertola 1998). Organized labor, sometimes in collusion with domestic business, supposedly defended the employment conditions of domestic workers, "the insiders," and thus shifted the risks of precarious and low-paid employment onto the reserve army of immigrants and parts of the young and female workforce. Political economists have analyzed in depth why even social democratic parties have allowed such dualism to emerge, for instance by introducing flexible employment contracts for newcomers that do not touch those already established in work (King and Rueda 2008; Palier and Thelen 2010; Emmenegger et al. 2012).

A focus on insiders and outsiders suggests that we will find the answers to what determines risk sharing with migrants in the organization of the supply (worker) side of the labor market. By contrast, the notion of employment dualism developed by Piore (1979, 1986) and Berger and Piore (1980) sees dualism as an inherent feature of capitalist development, rooted in the practices and incentives of employers. Capitalist development tends to generate a supply of menial jobs, through specialization, routinization, and technological progress. At the same time, social norms evolve with rising living standards, meaning that job aspirations and the quest for employment security rise with general income. These social norms become embodied in the political regulation of labor markets and make it increasingly hard to fill the menial jobs. It is then a matter of political choice "whether the dirty, insecure

[18] The coefficient of variation was 27 percent for the (gross) average wages of a single, childless worker in the EA-10 (in 2012) while it was 15 percent for the US states (in 2013). Own calculations from OECD and US census data.

jobs of society are turned over to foreigners, national minorities, or machines" (Berger and Piore 1980: 9–10).

Temporary migrants cater to this demand as do those compelled to take up work by benefit conditionality. Dualism means that those migrants with little education are more likely to be among the working poor (Figure 8.2) which is almost double across OECD countries. The outlier Germany can be explained by higher unemployment (and higher self-employment) among those not born in Germany. Another manifestation of dualism is that the highly educated migrants tend to be overqualified for the jobs they perform. Only in the US do we find no dualism in this regard but a relatively high overqualification rate for both natives and non-natives (Figure 8.3).

The social norms driving political intervention lead to a differentiation of the market for shirts from the market for labor services that produce shirts (Piore 1979: 8). In democracies, this may also reach secondary labor markets and self-employment, as Baldwin's (1990) history of welfare-state development shows in detail. Informal employment also challenges tighter regulated employment in the first labor market through outsourcing and other practices that circumvent regulation. This may then mobilize organized labor and employers interested in a skilled and loyal workforce to lobby the government (Swenson 2002: 17–44). Secondary labor markets may thus become targets of political regulation as well. A decisive intermediate institution is the welfare

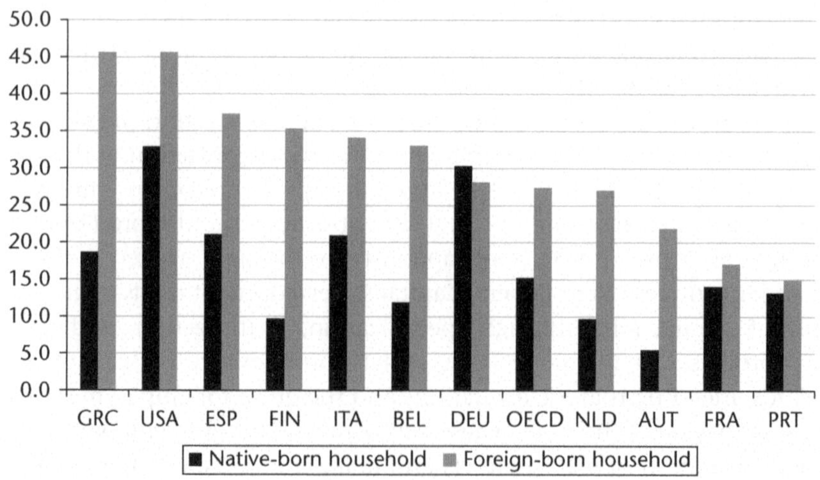

Figure 8.2. In-work poverty risk of households with low-educated household head(s), 2011

Source: OECD 2014

Note: "In-work poverty risk" denotes the share of individuals who live in a household where the equivalized income is below half of the median income of the whole population living in the country. The equivalent scale used is the square root scale.

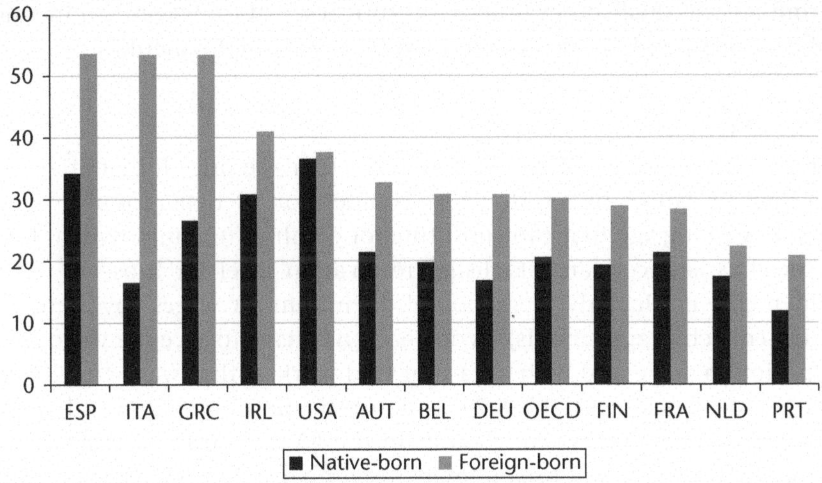

Figure 8.3. Overqualification rates among those with tertiary education in employment, 15–64-year-olds

Source: OECD 2014

Note: Those with tertiary education are considered overqualified if their job is classified as ISCO 4 to 9 (ISCO stands for International Standard Classification of Occupations).

state (Esping-Andersen 1990: 141–7). Welfare-state programs can mitigate dualism, for instance by providing universal benefits such as accessible education and tax-financed health care that insure against poverty traps plus a minimum wage underpinned by social assistance which establishes a reservation wage across the board. Welfare-state programs can also entrench dualism, however, by making more generous social entitlements dependent on formal employment and regular contributions, for instance to health insurance, earnings-related unemployment benefits, and private education. Such welfare states give those without a formal employment history only means-tested social assistance and basic public schooling to fall back on.

The extent of dualism that the welfare state mitigates or generates also depends on whether benefits and standard setting extend to all kinds of employment or are focused on wage-dependent employment only. Self-employment can be an alternative upholding the reservation wage, if it is covered by social programs, or it can be an unregulated sphere of self-exploitation, entrenching dualism. The regulation of qualifications and professional services is an important determinant of the role that self-employment plays.

Against this background, we can see migration as a social right that gives individuals and their families access to economic opportunities underpinned by social security. It is a right, however, that may be only conditionally and partially granted, in which case migration will be closely connected with dualism in the labor market. The following discussion dissects the determinants of dualism, examining in turn reservation wages, competition via the services market, and competition from self-employment.

RESERVATION WAGE LEVELS

An important driver of differentiation is whether the price for labor services has a floor or can be driven down by competition. Benefits for able-bodied adults of working age that can substitute for earnings (unemployment benefits, social assistance) can establish a reservation level for those in regular employment, particularly if supported by minimum wages (by statute or through collective agreements). Workers do not have to accept a wage below the minimum wage and if they cannot find work at that wage they have a safety net to fall back on. Table 8.2 lists statutory minimum wages and the two major cash benefits for working adults in the EA-10 and in US states.[19] The cash benefits selected are unemployment compensation for up to one year and social assistance, both benefits that an internal migrant might want to claim if s/he moves between states in one of these monetary unions. Since actual benefit levels are highly sensitive to family situation and previous earnings, unemployment benefits here are taken for a single person with no children, who was fully employed before losing a job in the state of residence.[20] In the US, a single worker without children would not receive an earnings subsidy from the EITC but would pay federal tax if fully employed at the minimum wage (CBPP 2015). For social assistance, the case shown in Table 8.2 is for a lone parent with two children who is either unemployed or in low-wage full-time employment. For the US, social assistance here means the combined benefit from the Supplementary Nutritional Assistance Program (SNAP), formerly food stamps, and TANF (for which the presence of children is a precondition). Anybody on TANF will be entitled to vouchers under SNAP.

It does not come as a great surprise that the US leaves considerably more room for low wage competition than most EA-10 countries: minimum wage levels are lower and cash benefits for adults tend to be less generous. Even the most generous US states offer only about as much as the least generous EA-10 member states do relative to the average worker in the primary labor market.[21] In most states, the statutory minimum wage for a full-time worker is below the unemployment benefit that previously full-time employed workers would get if they qualified, but above or equal to the social assistance level that lone

[19] See Immervoll (2009) for a detailed assessment of minimum-income benefits.

[20] There is evidence that unmarried individuals are significantly more likely to migrate than those married (Dustmann and Görlach 2015: 27–8).

[21] This observation does not depend on the EA-10 selection that leaves out later members of the EA like Slovakia: as a share of the national average wage, Eastern European countries show as much variety in their benefit levels as their Western neighbors (Immervoll 2009: 12–13).

Table 8.2. Variation in monthly cash benefits for interstate free movement migrants, 2012–14

		US states	EA-10 member states
Statutory minimum wage	As share of average wage in state	27% (federal average) 9–36% (states)[a]	35–51%[a]
	Previously full-employed average worker, single, no children		
Unemployment benefits	Median	$189 (min. benefit) $1754 (max. benefit)	€1272 (gross and net)
	As share of average wage in state	24–58%	30–75% (gross) 51–75% (net)[c]
	Lone parent with two children		
Social	Median	$869[b]	€1506/1626[d]
	As share of average wage in state	14–35%	0–65% (for unemployed)
assistance			30–96% (low-wage employed)

Note:
(a) range of lowest to highest state minimum wage; as of 2013, only six EA-10 members have a statutory minimum wage (Belgium, France, Ireland, Netherlands, Portugal, Spain);
(b) combined benefit of TANF and SNAP before 2008;
(c) net is after income taxes and social security contributions;
(d) the first figure is for an unemployed lone parent with no previous earnings, the second figure is for a lone parent employed at 30 percent of the average wage

Source: Congressional Research Service (CRS 2014b, 2014c); Census for US state benefits and wages; Department of Labor for minimum wages; OECD database on benefits and wages for EA-10

parents with two children would receive.[22] This suggests that unemployment benefits underpin reservation wages in the primary labor market (minimum wages are lower than temporary unemployment benefits), while the minimum wage sets a floor in the secondary labor market (which may be evaded, for instance by self-employment) since it tends to be higher than social assistance.

Eligibility for cash benefits is tightly administered by US states. As regards unemployment benefits, part-time and discontinuous workers often do not meet the requirements of minimum earnings and continuity of employment, even though employers pay earmarked social security taxes for every regular employee. Unemployment must be involuntary, which is a major reason for legal disputes (Baicker et al. 1998: 231). Firms have an incentive to make the worker quit "voluntarily" because of so-called experience rating, which means firms must pay more contributions if they use the insurance more frequently by laying off employees (CRS 2014c: 3). As a consequence of all these restrictions (duration, eligibility criteria, experience rating), the coverage of unemployment

[22] As of 2012–13, the minimum wage in thirty-four US states was higher than social assistance and lower than unemployment benefits, all measured as a share of the average wage in a state. In four states it was lower than unemployment benefits and equal to social assistance for a lone parent with two children. Six states had a minimum wage that was lower than both transfer incomes.

benefits has been eroded: by the 2000s only about a third of all job losers received unemployment benefits, compared to two-thirds in the mid-1970s. The rates are as low as 10 percent for those exiting and re-entering the labor market (Vroman 2009: table 3), while the coverage rate can go up as high as 50 percent in a recession, although benefit levels tend to be reduced in recessions. In the EA-10, only Italy has a lower unemployment benefit recipiency rate (33 percent) than the US (37 percent). Others are above OECD average, topped by Germany and Austria with over 90 per cent.[23] Similarly, means-tested social assistance for lone parents, TANF, is subject to strict limits. Federal law sets maxima for federally funded assistance of five years over a lifetime, and some states have shorter limits (Farrell et al. 2008: ES-1). No EA-10 country has lifetime limits for receiving social assistance.

There is a lot of variation between US states. Unemployment benefits tend to be more diverse between US states than the means-tested TANF and SNAP benefits, which have converged to a very low level. The median benefit leaves a family of three in serious poverty, as the federal poverty level was $1,591 in 2012 (CRS 2014b: table A-5). In the EA-10, it is the other way round: as a share of average wages in a state, unemployment benefits are in a more similar range than social assistance. Some states have no social assistance for some groups (e.g. Italy for young unemployed without previous insurance), while others have assistance levels that are comparable with insurance benefits (e.g. Ireland, for those with children).

The fact that US states have converged on a low level and EA-10 states have widely differing benefit levels for poor households can be seen as supporting evidence by those who fear a race to the bottom in closely integrated welfare states. After all, US states have to pay non-contributory benefits to every resident citizen while in the EA-10, non-national EU citizens are subject to residency requirements if they have never been employed. If they are employed at a low wage, EU nationals are eligible for social assistance, and benefits vary widely. But the pattern of decline in social assistance levels in the US does not support the inference that intra-US migration produces a race to the bottom. Cuts have been most intense in recent years as the political climate generally has become more hostile to "welfare." Reforms giving more discretion to states have encouraged them to shift costs onto the federal government by cutting TANF and promoting the use of federally financed EITC and SNAP (Baicker et al. 1998: 234–5; CRS 2014b: 9–13).

Reservation wage levels are thus lower in the US than in the EA-10: those who cannot find work in the primary labor market are forced to accept work at minimum wages that are very low compared to average wages. The alternative

[23] Figures are for 2007–8 (OECD 2011: fig. 0.9). No data available for Portugal.

of an income from social transfers is low, even compared to federal poverty standards, and very restricted in duration. In the present context, this means that US citizens who are internal migrants enjoy effectively less risk sharing with others in their place of residence than mobile EU nationals. This is not due to citizenship rights but less generous safety nets in the US welfare state.

COMPETITION FROM IMPORTED SERVICES

High reservation wage levels can come under pressure from the import of services, whereby services are provided remotely or by workers temporarily engaged in another ("host") state. In the EU, this is known as posting of workers. For example, a construction contract may be won by an out-of-state provider, which brings in its own cheaper workforce and undercuts the wages of resident construction workers. Thus trade in services can have pronounced effects on labor market regulation.

In the US, the notion of "posting" is not common so rules apply to any worker engaged in "interstate commerce": the federal minimum wage or state minimum wages apply to those workers, whichever is higher.[24] This seems to extend to workers from a state where the minimum wage is set at the federal minimum when s/he provides services in another state with a higher state minimum. Labor standards are otherwise highly federalized but also minimal. For instance, only eight states have statutory paid rest periods and they are also the ones that have minimum meal periods. State labor legislation is much less dense and does not cover issues like holidays and paid sickness or maternity leave.

In the EU, the Posted Workers Directive 96/71/EC regulates the situation where firms from one member state send their employees for a limited amount of time to another in order to provide a service. This Directive was for a long time "one of the most neglected of the modern social policy instruments of the Community" (Davies 2002: 298). Its legal basis is legislation on the freedom of services, yet the preamble of the Directive, and case law referring to it, are explicit about its purpose of protecting both resident and posted workers who are EU nationals in the host country. Hence, the Directive stipulates in Artcle 3(1) that a set of host state rules, such as working time, holiday entitlements, and minimum pay, must apply in the employment of a worker temporarily posted to another EU member state.[25] The applicable minimum wage can be set by the state or by collective agreement (which

[24] This is according to information on the US Department of Labor website at https://www.dol.gov/whd/minimumwage.htm and https://www.dol.gov/whd/state/state.htm (accessed August 15, 2016).

[25] The list enumerates eight terms and conditions of employment, the others concern the supply of workers by temping agencies, health and safety at the workplace, protection of pregnant workers, and non-discrimination principles.

tends to be higher) as long as the latter is universally applicable. Home state or country-of-origin rules on these specified terms and conditions of employment must be applied only if they are more favorable to the worker (Article 3(7)), a clause that was inserted at the insistence of Germany (Barnard 2009: 127).

While the Posted Workers Directive was introduced to protect workers under the freedom of services, it came to be seen as the judicial vehicle for economic freedoms destroying collective bargaining institutions, the pillar of a well-regulated primary labor market (Joerges and Rödl 2008; Höpner 2009; Kilpatrick 2009b). In a series of Court cases, starting with *Laval* C-341/05, the European Court of Justice ruled that national competences such as employment law must be subject to compliance with economic freedoms. It also stipulated that this obligation, originally addressed to governments, applies to disputes between non-state actors such as trade unions and firms. The Court held that certain strike actions by trade unions were a disproportionate infringement of economic freedoms in the internal market. Critical scholars have argued that the judgments restrict the national exercise of rights that the Community has no competence to regulate, putting social rights "on the back foot, having to defend themselves from the economic" (Barnard 2008: 264). An alternative interpretation to this clash of social versus economic is that the EU tries to construct a transnational market for services, different from the market for shirts but also different from that for resident labor (Schelkle 2011).

The Posted Workers Directive was introduced in the aftermath of Southern enlargement to Spain and Portugal in 1986, at the initiative of major destination countries. It went against the trend in international trade negotiations, which was to reduce non-tariff barriers such as host state rules on foreign service providers.[26] All EU members had signed the Rome Convention by 1991,[27] which declared the home state or country of origin principle to be the default option for the employment contracts of workers that provide services in person to another country (Barnard 2009: 123–5). With Eastern enlargement in 2004, the posting of workers became a more noticeable source of competition in services. This was not only because this extension to the East increased the dispersion of income levels in the Union, but also because the freedom of movement of workers was restricted by many existing member states for up to seven years, as was allowed under transitional accession rules "to prevent undue disruption to domestic labor markets." Freedom to provide

[26] The General Agreement on Trade in Services came into effect in 1995, a year before the EU legislation on posted workers. The Agreement stipulates a "national treatment obligation" under Artcle XVII; once a member gives market access to foreign service providers of another member, national treatment really amounts to applying the home state rules so as not to impair the competitive position of the foreign service supplier (Herwig 2008: 18–19).

[27] The "1980 Rome Convention on the law applicable to contractual obligations" has been included in EU law (Official Journal C 027, 26/01/1998 P. 0034–0046).

services was a way around restrictions on free movement of workers. Moreover, throughout the 1990s governments all over Europe announced labor market reforms that made benefit payments increasingly conditional on work and thus lowered the reservation wage of the unemployed. Due to these reforms, the boundaries of the primary labor market became less well defined and competition for jobs in secondary labor markets more intense, even without migration. The Court thus adjudicated the lines in the sand between economic freedoms and social rights of workers in a political environment where destination countries had become more assertive in protecting labor from outside competition while simultaneously challenging safety nets with "activating" reforms at home.

The Posted Workers Directive, and the court cases it triggered,[28] shows that EU regulation, just like a national welfare state, controls the space of secondary labor markets as well as the boundaries of primary labor markets. The Directive rules that temporary workers' service providers must at least be given the nationally defined minimum of employment laws. It determines how much primary labor markets can sustain a clearly defined risk pool where this minimum is exceeded and more generous insurance benefits are reserved to its members, typically due to the strength of industrial relations. In the US, the federal minimum sets a standard that can be exceeded, similar to EU harmonization in goods markets (but not labor markets). This minimum is normally not binding on workers in the primary labor market as minimum wage levels (and other provisions) are quite low.

COMPETITION FROM SELF-EMPLOYMENT

Workers who cannot find a job even in the secondary labor market or try to escape it may be driven into self-employment at an hourly income that is below the minimum wage. With social assistance and perhaps tax credits as the only social safety net,[29] self-employed providers of services may undercut services provided by regular employees. EU regulation now entitles self-employed migrants to the same tax advantages and benefits that self-employed nationals get, such as child benefits. But rules on the (ex-)portability of benefits for workers were extended to self-employed migrants with considerable delay (Baldoni 2003: 8, 13), typically through court rulings that obliged member states to adopt equal treatment. Even so, in most member states, the self-employed are at a disadvantage when it comes to social protection. They either

[28] For helpful analyses by lawyers, see in particular Barnard 2008, 2009; A. Davies 2008; P. Davies 2008; Kilpatrick 2009a, 2009b; and Reich 2008.

[29] There are a few exceptions. For instance, in Germany self-employed individuals can join unemployment insurance voluntarily which they can claim in case they go out of business. In Italy and Spain, unemployed workers can take out their maximum benefits as a lump sum if they start up a business (EEO 2010: 18–21).

pay higher social security contributions for the same benefits, or they receive lower benefits, for instance in terms of maternity leave or pensions, because they can opt out of some parts of the social security system (EEO 2010).

Licensing of professions can establish certain standards and career profiles that make self-employment less prone to self-exploitation and less prone to undercut the conditions under which wage-dependent labor provides the same services. Licenses for hairdressers and barbers, providers of funeral services, and personal trainers in fitness studios can be seen in this light. In the US, about fifty professions are licensed at the state level, typically by private associations. This creates barriers to mobility, albeit often readily surmountable: for example, a hairdresser who qualified in one state must pass an examination if s/he moves to another state (USNEI 2007). The onus is on the migrant to prove that s/he has the necessary aptitude.

In EU parlance, there is no mutual recognition of professional qualifications, even for US citizens. Nor does it exist in the EU. The European Commission has long fought for mutual recognition of qualifications, against the resistance of national professional associations. Mutual recognition means in this context that a qualification obtained in one member state must be accepted in another member state. Secondary legislation, in particular Directive 2005/36/EC on the free movement of professionals, puts down three principles. First, there is qualified mutual recognition of qualifications, meaning that the host state can request an aptitude test or a probation period when national requirements do not fit the "general system" of qualifications (Directive 2005/36 Article 13). Second, there is unqualified mutual recognition of experience in the crafts, commerce, and industry; so a hairdresser who has practiced for three to five years in the home state would be able to do so in another member state without further proof of qualifications (Directive 2005/36 Article 16). And third, there is mutual recognition and partial harmonization with respect to "specific sectors," such as medical professions and architects, for which EU law has laid down minimum requirements for training and curricula. The obstacles to free movement of professionals are, in legal terms, not higher in the EU than in the US: qualifications have to be either accepted or if restricted, national education systems must adapt. The burden of proof that national licensing is in the public interest is on the host states and they are required to adapt national requirements.

The overall comparison with the US provides a differentiated picture of social rights of economic migrants and thus of the scope of this form of risk sharing within the two monetary unions (Table 8.3). The rows compare the two monetary unions while the columns compare conditions for wage labor and self-employment, and summarize the implications for dualization.

At first sight, risk sharing through social rights for migrant workers seems to be surprisingly similar in the two monetary unions. Differences can be seen in

Table 8.3. Summary of rules for risk sharing between internal economic migrants and host states

	Workers	Self-employed persons	Dualism/effect on host state labor market
Euro Area-10 (e.g. EU citizen from Spain to Germany)	Non-discrimination and exportability of contributory benefits; restricted competition from posted workers	Qualified mutual recognition of qualifications; full mutual recognition of experience in vocational skills	Reservation wage levels are comparatively high; standards for self-employment are partly deregulated
United States (e.g. US citizen from Missouri to Massachusetts)	Non-discrimination and exportability of contributory benefits; unrestricted competition from out-of-state service providers	No mutual recognition of qualifications for about fifty professions; licensing requirements for vocational skills at state level	Reservation wage levels are comparatively low; standards for self-employment are state-regulated
Risk sharing between internal migrant and host state	More risk sharing with host state in EA-10: more generous entitlements and some protection from posted workers	More risk sharing with host state in EA-10 due to easier access at acquired qualifications	Dualism more tightly controlled for workers in EA-10, less so for self-employed; the other way round in the US

Source: see references in the text

the following: first, the EA-10 set a higher reservation wage simply because its constituent welfare states are more generous. This may make labor markets in Europe less absorbent, increasing the risk of exclusion through unemployment, however. The net effect on risk sharing is therefore ambiguous and depends on the worker finding regular employment. As regards, second, the ability to compete with resident workers, an internal migrant in the US is only restricted by a fairly uniform minimum wage level but employment practices can vary widely, given that there are few other employment regulations; the Posted Workers Directive covers more minimum standards but minimum pay can vary widely and be much closer to the median wage, especially if set in collective agreements. Finally, the alternative of self-employment is to some extent restricted in both unions; in the US by state licenses for many professions that do not provide massive hurdles and in the EA-10 by harmonized professional standards that the EU Commission has for a long time tried to bring down.

8.3 Interstate Risk Sharing through Free Movement in a Monetary Union

This section asks to what extent the cross-border movements of individuals in search of economic opportunities can help EA member states—in contrast to individuals—to diversify and share risks of its member states. The risks are, on the one hand, temporary downturns in one region but not others, to which temporary migration would be a pertinent response. The financial crisis since 2008 was a massive shock to employment in some member states that allows us to assess how regions adjust through temporary migration. On the other hand, the risk may be inherent in the longer-term growth potential: a low-income region has a high growth potential but the road to realizing it may be bumpy and full of ups and downs, compared to a high-income region with a diminishing growth potential.[30] Migration flows can be attracted by high living standards, as in Northern Europe, or by dynamic growth, as in Spain and Greece before the crisis. The question is whether migration can conceivably help poorer member states to catch up and stabilize demand in richer member states through growing markets, internally and abroad. We might expect temporary migration responses to be limited, because of the sheer cost of moving to another state, which can be an obstacle even in the US (Gruber and Madrian 2002: 22–9).

8.3.1 *Sharing the Risk of Economic Fluctuations?*

The crisis since 2007 (in the US) and 2008 (in Europe) was a systemic and in this sense common shock (Section 6.2.3), yet the secondary effects on labor markets were uneven, not least because welfare states mitigated the ensuing instability differently. So the incidence was idiosyncratic which allows us to observe labor mobility as an adjustment mechanism. Laid-off workers could move elsewhere and find employment; if their families stayed behind migration could stabilize regional income through remittances.

Before the crisis, the path-breaking study by Barro and Sala-i-Martin (1991), confirmed by Asdrubali et al. (1996), had established the ballpark figure for the stabilization effect of migration. It found that, in the US, interstate migration reduced the impact of a state's output shock on household income by 3 percent at most. Recent work on the evolution of internal labor mobility in the US suggests that the contribution has if anything tended to fall (Molloy et al. 2014). Interstate migration has declined since the 1980s, reversing the upward trend earlier in the twentieth century. Various explanations have been put forward, such as the compositional change of the workforce (aging, increasing homeownership) and increased costs of migration.[31] Molloy et al.

[30] A diminishing growth potential is largely deterministic: a constant annual growth rate means exponential growth of the base and this would run into resource constraints. In capitalist economies, resource constraints are signaled by upward price pressures that make investors withdraw as their profits decline.

[31] This was a live issue in the debate about health-care reform under the Obama administration since increasing costs of changing health insurers can create a lock-in effect (Garthwaite et al. 2013).

(2014) and Dao et al. (2014) suggest that lower US mobility could be a signal that labor markets are actually functioning better: there might be better matches between employers and employees to begin with, and employees might be promoted within firms instead of having to change jobs to advance careers. In short, low or declining labor mobility can have many causes and they are not necessarily worrying.

Has the crisis made a difference? A fine-grained OECD study looks at net migration flows between 2005 and 2012, comparing European regions (NUTS-1 and -2 levels)[32] and US states and areas (states and public use microdata areas comparable to NUTS-2). They estimate the level of net flows "produced" by changes in unemployment and income differentials (Jauer et al. 2014: para. 23). The results are remarkable: "the migration response to the crisis has been considerable in Europe, in contrast to the United States where the crisis and subsequent sluggish recovery were not accompanied by greater interregional labour mobility in reaction to labour market shocks" (Jauer et al. 2014: 5). When the researchers split their time series between pre- and post-crisis periods, they find the familiar result that pre-crisis labor mobility in response to region-specific labor market shocks was stronger in the United States than in Europe. With the onset of the crisis, however, Europe showed "a stronger interregional adjustment reaction than the United States" (Jauer et al. 2014: para. 32). The estimates suggest that "up to about a quarter of the asymmetric labour market shock [in Europe] would be absorbed by migration within a year" (Jauer et al. 2014: 5, para. 31). The authors note that this is an upper bound estimate, assuming that all measured population changes in Europe were due to migration for employment purposes. By contrast, Dao et al. (2014: 19–21) do not confirm that the internal migration in the EA is higher than in the US but they do confirm that the former is rising and the latter is declining.

There is a twist, however: this rise in mobility is not due to intra-EA flows but to migration from the new EU member states outside the EA and from third countries (Jauer et al. 2014: para 33). Labor mobility is therefore, strictly speaking, not an adjustment mechanism of the monetary union but a consequence of free movement in the internal market, as the readiness to move is much higher in the new member states in Central and Eastern Europe (Dao et al. 2014: 21; Atoyan et al. 2016: para. 2). By contrast, Beine et al. (2013) argue that there is a statistically significant effect of EA membership on temporary migration: they estimate that over 17 percent of the increase in migration between member states since 1999 was due to the common currency. Yet the

[32] NUTS is the French acronym for the "Nomenclature of territorial units for statistics" and is the EU's own delineation of regions. The main reason is that NUTS-2 regions are the recipients of regional funds. NUTS-1 regions, as of 2013, should have between 3 million and 7 million inhabitants, NUTS-2 between 800,000 and 3 million, NUTS-3 regions between 150,000 and 800,000. Source: http://ec.europa.eu/eurostat/web/nuts/overview (accessed December 29, 2015).

numbers accounted for by this common currency effect, for instance between the Netherlands and Belgium or Germany and Italy, are in the four digits (1,000 and 1,500 migrants per annum, respectively). This seems hardly enough to support the claim that "the inception of the Euro made Europe closer to an Optimum Currency Area" (Beine et al. 2013: 21).

Given that the effect on destination countries is rather small, what is the effect on the countries of origin? Table 8.4 looks at the socio-economic characteristics of recent migrants (Migrants column) and how they compare to their immobile peers in the country of origin. A positive number in the "Diff" column means that the mobile population has a higher share in this characteristic than their compatriots left behind. It cannot be read as a probability though, as the notes to Table 8.4 explain.

The migrants considered are those subject to free movement of persons: they came from and went to EU-27/European Free Trade Area countries or moved within the US, respectively. The comparison with their socio-economic characteristics in the previous year allows us to draw some inferences about the effect on the origin country. The first two pairs of columns show net emigration countries in 2011/12; this marks quite a turnaround since the Southern Europe four (Greece, Italy, Portugal, and Spain) were net immigration countries before the crisis. By comparing employment and unemployment rates in 2011/12 and a year before, we can see that migrants from the new member states and Southern Europe had different characteristics before they migrated: in CEE, they were more likely to be unemployed

Table 8.4. Characteristics of recent free movement migrants compared with natives of the origin region (15–64 years), 2011 and 2012

In %	New member states (CEE)		Southern Europe in EA		Euro area		United States (2011)	
	Migrants	Diff	Migrants	Diff	Migrants	Diff	Migrants	Diff
Employment rate	71	+10	59	+2	60	−4	52	−11
Employment rate one year ago	61	0	51	−6	58	−5	76	+3
Unemployment rate	8	−2	15	0	16	+6	18	+7
Unemployment rate one year ago	13	+2	15	−4	9	−3	12	+1
Share of young (20–34)	70	+38	59	+30	58	+30	50	+20
Share of highly educated	28	+8	41	+20	41	+16	39	+6
Share of highly skilled employed	17	−19	49	+12	50	+8	25	0

Note: The Migrants and Diff figures combined allow us to infer the share of the native population in this characteristic. To take the new member states and their employment rate: if 71 percent of recent migrants from the EU-10 are employed and the difference to their immobile peers is +10 percent, then the employment rate of the residents in the new member states is 61 percent. The difference needs to be transformed before it can be read as a probability: for instance, the unemployment rate of CEE migrants after moving was 8 percent which is 2 percent lower (Diff) than for immobile peers. This means a CEE migrant had a 20 percent better chance (2 relative to 10 percent) of escaping unemployment than those left behind.

Source: OECD from Jauer et al. (2014: table 1)

while the Southern European migrants were less likely to be unemployed.[33] CEE migrants succeeded in becoming employed in their host state; much more so than Southern Europeans. Both groups of migrants improved their (un)employment situation compared to a year before. In both groups of countries, migration drains countries of their younger and better-educated citizens; for the new member states (mainly outside the EA), migration does however offer these groups the prospect of finding employment, and with it perhaps the potential to raise their skills. A more recent IMF study confirms age bias and the brain drain phenomenon for CEE countries (Atoyan et al. 2016: paras 11–14) and adds that remittances are significant for some smaller countries like Latvia.

The last two pairs of columns in Table 8.4 show the pattern of intra-EA and intra-US migration. Interstate migrants in both the EA-17 and the USA do not improve their employment or unemployment situation by migrating, compared to their immobile peers. This may reflect the youth bias among migrants, given that youth unemployment rates are relatively higher and some migration may be related to studying. Brain drain is an issue in the EA as indicated by the overrepresentation of the highly educated and the highly skilled among migrants compared with non-migrants in the EA origin countries. In the US, brain drain played less of a role.

Remittances can compensate home countries for the loss of younger and more educated workers. There is a debate whether remittances rise with the education level of migrants: Schiopu and Siegfried (2006: 20) find this positive association for European migrants while Faini (2007) does not. Remittances tend to be higher if migrants intend to move abroad only temporarily (Dustmann and Görlach 2015: 35–7). The sums involved can be quite substantial but, again, intra-EA amounts are small compared to flows between the EA and its neighboring countries. In the early 2000s, about 85 percent of remittances to Romania were sent by nationals working in the EA, which amounted overall to about 3.6 percent of GDP and exceeded the amount that the country received by way of foreign direct investment (Schiopu and Siegfried 2006: 7).

In summary, recent research suggests that the short-term response of European migrants to the crisis was noticeable and in the expected counter-cyclical direction. But Table 8.4 also shows that even temporary migration is risky. There is no guarantee that newly arriving migrants will find a job despite the likelihood that they will accept sub-standard working and living conditions. Immediate access to social security is therefore an important risk-sharing

33 But Southern Europeans were also less likely to be employed which is less contradictory than it sounds as there is also the category of non-employed (left out for reasons of space), e.g. people who care for children and thus are neither employed nor registered unemployed.

mechanism provided by free movement. It gives individuals a chance to improve their economic situation, although the gain for their home countries is less certain.

The time horizon of migrants makes an important difference for the member states involved. Theory and an emerging body of evidence suggest that temporary migration is more beneficial for origin countries while the behavior of permanent migrants increases the benefits to the destination state (Dustmann and Görlach 2015: 37–42, with further references). Migrants who intend to stay only for a limited time are more likely to underbid prevailing standards of employment and pay. They also invest less in their language and skills acquisition, and save more out of any given income because they send higher remittances, so as to sustain family members back home. This has a negative demand effect on the destination economy (Dustmann and Görlach 2015: 30, 42). Empirically, only a fifth of all migrants to the classically Anglophone immigration countries (Australia, Canada, New Zealand, and the US) leave their destination country within the first ten years while half of all migrants to and in Europe do so (Dustmann and Görlach 2015: 2–3), although research by the IMF suggests that this is not true for migration from the new member states where return migration ("brain gain") is extremely low (Atoyan et al. 2016: para. 15). Migrant employment in some EA countries is weighted towards long stayers: more than 60 percent of employed migrants in 2007 had been there for at least ten years in Austria, Belgium, and Portugal, a share rising to almost 80 percent in France, Germany, and the Netherlands (OECD 2009: table I.2). By contrast, Ireland, Italy, and Spain had predominantly temporary migrants in the sense that more than half of those employed had been in the country for less than a decade.

Rules on the portability of benefits could affect the distribution of gains from migration across sending and receiving states. EU rules for coordinating social security have made pension benefits highly portable. In the US, a national social security system has the same effect. Compared to unregulated or devolved social security, this benefits migrants' state of origin if they choose to return home on retirement. While perhaps a surprising antidote to the Matthew principle in migration patterns ("to those that have shall be given"), facilitation of return migration might reflect resistance to immigration in destination countries, whether temporary or permanent (Burgoon 2014: 367–8).

8.3.2 *Sharing the Risk of Income Divergence?*

Outside the specialist OCA literature, economic migration is studied as a potential vehicle for reducing differences in living standards between countries. In terms of the conceptual framework outlined in Chapter 3, economic migrants are taking risks in order to increase the return from employment. The question for a study of monetary integration is whether this risk-return trade-off can be exploited at the level of regions or member states: does migration advance income convergence between them?

Convergence is what neoclassical growth theory would lead one to expect: factors of production move to where they are scarcest as they will be paid accordingly. Hence, labor moves to resource-abundant or capital-rich regions, bringing down the price of labor services there, raising wages in the state of origin.[34] Yet, this view of equilibrating flows, leading to an equalization of living standards across open economies, contrasts with the experience of agglomeration and urbanization over the twentieth century. The urban population has increased by a factor of more than twelve while world population has grown only fourfold (Ozgen et al. 2010: 537). This suggests that people move to where other people are. Cities are not necessarily capital-rich, as industry tends to move out from city centers, but they provide the market size and the infrastructure that allows for infinite specialization and a niche for every type of service. Positive externalities of agglomeration can trump the negative externalities of congestion: in industries such as fashion and information technology, close personal interaction is likely to be an ingredient of innovation. This gives rise to endogenous growth that is cumulative: growth feeds on growth. Migration can be attracted by growth, and in turn sustains it. But such endogeneity makes it more likely that regional income levels diverge.

So what is the evidence about the role of migration in income convergence in the EA and in the US in normal times, before the 2008 crisis? This simple question does not have a straightforward answer. First of all, reliable data on internal migration are very hard to get. Moreover, studies are less likely to be published if they come to the plausible conclusion that migration has no significant impact on growth in OECD countries because flows, even internally, are simply too small (Balli et al. 2011). Academic publication practices are biased against non-findings, however sound the underlying research. Ozgen et al. (2010) undertake a meta-analysis of sixty-seven estimates, some of them published in mainstream outlets, others in working papers, most of which have been published only since the early 2000s. They cover European countries as well as the US. The short answer to the question of what internal migration does to growth in receiving countries is: of the sixty-seven studies, twenty-seven find a statistically significant positive effect on growth while two studies find a negative effect, significant at the 5 percent level (Ozgen et al.

[34] Barro and Sala-i-Martin (2003) contains an up-to-date discussion of neoclassical growth theory and how it should be empirically assessed. Strictly speaking, convergence results only in the simple textbook model where economies use the same first-best technology and the world is populated by a clone of the representative household, all having the same taste.

2010: fig. 1). The median estimate is 0.18 which means that a 1 percent rise in net internal migration raises growth by about 0.2 percent. Even so, this meta-analysis also tells us that more than half of all studies cannot find a statistically significant effect.

An analysis that covers both internal and cross-border migration, and differentiates the effects on growth in immigration and emigration regions, can be found in Huber and Tondl (2012). They cover NUTS-2 regions from the EU-27 and European Free Trade Area during 2000–7: the period from the introduction of the new currency in twelve EU countries until the year before the crisis broke out in Europe. They find a positive impact of both internal and international net immigration on GDP per capita and on productivity, while there was no significant effect on unemployment. In the first year, the effect is a 0.02 increase in growth and productivity for a 1 percent increase in net immigration which amounts in the long term to a 0.44 percent income growth and 0.20 percent productivity growth. The snag is that this is symmetrical: a 1 percent increase in emigration has a very similar negative effect on GDP per capita and on productivity, in the short and long run. Migration seems to be a zero-sum game. Moreover, immigration regions are typically richer regions and emigration regions poorer, so this would suggest income divergence (Stiglitz 2016: 134). Huber and Tondl (2012: 454) qualify this, since they also find income convergence between NUTS-2 regions during 2000–7, even when controlling for the reverse causation that migrants may be attracted to regions that already grow faster. Migration seems to have slowed down convergence in Europe during 2000–7, but did not trump the higher growth dynamic of poorer regions.

These findings can be illustrated with the smaller sample of the NUTS-2 regions in the EA-10. Figure 8.4 plots the level of GDP per capita at the outset, in 2000, against the growth rate over the following years. GDP here is measured in purchasing power standard euros, taking into account that lower incomes in poorer regions do buy more goods and services (services in particular). Convergence would imply a negative correlation between the two and this is what Figure 8.4 shows.[35]

The effect is weak, however. It is driven by a few high-income regions that experienced weak growth and vice versa. The most extreme case is the capital region around Brussels—with the top regional income but a cumulative decline of 35 percent between 2000 and 2007. The same (high-income levels combined with poor growth) holds for Vienna and a number of Italian regions. In turn, some of the poorest regions in the EA-10 experienced high growth, notably three Spanish and two east German regions.

[35] The low coefficient of -0.0007 is due to the dimensions of the x and y axes (thousands plotted against percentages).

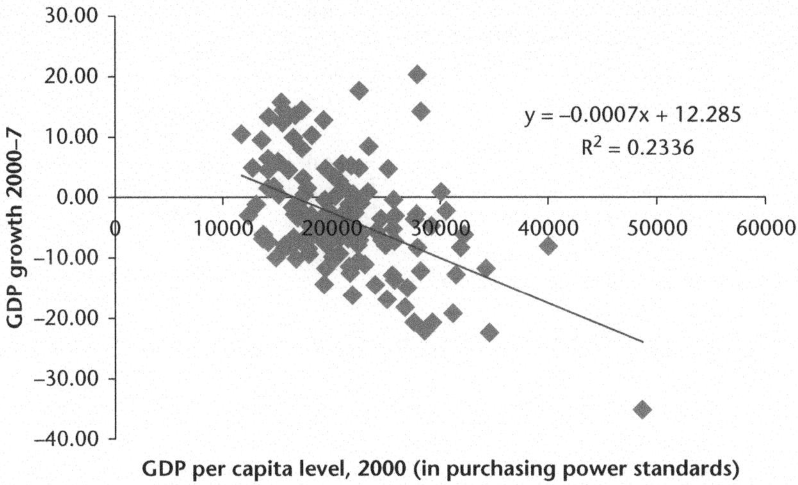

Figure 8.4. Correlation of regional income levels and growth rates, 2000–7

It was mentioned in the introduction that migrants may be attracted by higher income levels or by higher growth rates. In fast-growing regions, migrants can help to alleviate bottlenecks and thus find it easier to get employment, while in rich regions they may get better employment, but they may have to wait (resulting in unemployment) or accept inferior conditions, increasing wage inequality. Unsurprisingly, there was no dominant driver of net migration, income growth, or income levels in the early years of the monetary union. Figure 8.5 shows along the horizontal axes the growth rate and the level, respectively, of GDP in NUTS-2 regions in the EA-10 (again in purchasing power standard euros). The vertical axes show the cumulative net migration, as share of the regional population, that NUTS-2 regions experienced between 2003 and 2007.

We can see that there is no discernible relationship between the indicators on the two axes; the regression line is flat while it should be positive if income growth or income level were significant drivers. It is possible that controlling for other intervening variables or a different choice of determinant would change that. For instance, Beine et al. (2013: 20) find a robust response of bilateral migration flows to the wage ratio between a European destination and a European origin country: a 10 percent increase leads to an 8.5 percent increase in the migration flow. At the regional level, we cannot find a positive relationship between GDP per capita and migration (in the right-hand panel) although GDP per capita and wage levels should be closely correlated. Most EA-10 regions experienced net immigration over these years (115 out of 145) due to inflows from elsewhere in the EU and third countries. Spanish regions experienced the highest immigration; some French and Italian regions also

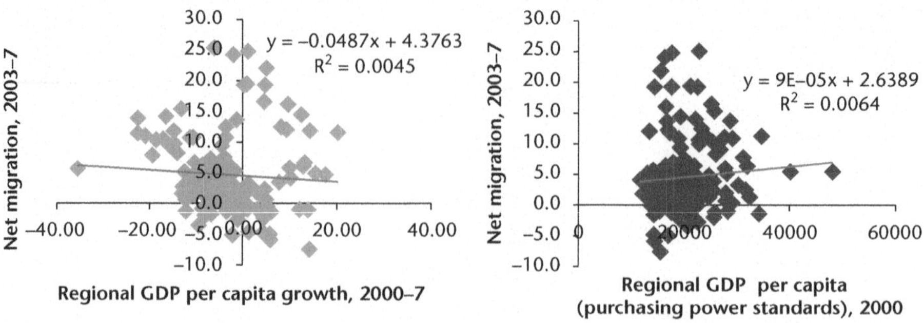

Figure 8.5. Correlation between migration rates and regional income growth and level, 2000–7

Source: Eurostat; the French outer territories of Guadaloupe, Martinique, and Guyane were excluded

experienced double-digit net immigration. The exceptional emigration regions were in peripheral Finland, northern France, eastern Germany, and in southern Italy. Thus France and Italy include both immigration and emigration regions, pointing to considerable intranational movement. In most of the net emigration regions, negative growth and, in national comparison, low income levels combined to push people out. This again confirms that weak convergence, as in the EA-10 between 2000 and 2007, makes income levels and income growth point to different destinations.

As regards the US, Barro and Sala-i-Martin (2003: 492–5) did not find that interregional migration played a role in bringing about convergence in state incomes.[36] This is all the more significant as they looked at flows between 1920 and 1990 when internal labor mobility was higher than after 1990. The few recent studies that look into convergence of US state income and migration come to compatible, if somewhat refined, results. DiCecio and Gascon (2010) use a method that allows them to dig deeper into the pattern of long-term regional convergence. They find that US state incomes actually diverge but that thanks to migration to metropolitan areas, there is income convergence across people. This "convergence across people is driven by the fact that states climbing ranks in the distribution of income are also attracting a larger share of the population" (DiCecio and Gascon 2010: 276). Urbanization and not migration per se drives this process. This finding resonates with the argument of this chapter: free movement is a risk-sharing channel for individuals but not for states or regions. It may actually precipitate a region's decline and divergence within a union.

[36] Nor do Barro and Sala-i-Martin (2003) find an effect of migration on regional income convergence in Japan and five large European countries.

8.4 Free Movement and the Political Economy of Labor Market Integration

This chapter has argued that migration in response to temporary downturns is quantitatively too small for it to be macroeconomically significant, even in the US. In fact, migration responses are not even reliably counter-cyclical as the transaction costs of moving can trump the incentives to move in a recession (OECD 2009: chart I.6). The efficacy of migration as a risk-sharing mechanism for existing income differences is also limited by migrants' self-selection: they are on average much younger and better educated, if not necessarily more skilled, than their fellow citizens in the home state (see Table 8.4, based on Jauer et al. 2014). The benefits of this selection bias accrue mainly to already better-off destination states. This does not share but increases the risk from regional income divergence and associated growth potential.

Such adverse distribution and insurance effects at the state level are not an inherent, deterministic feature. In a union of comparatively well-off member states, the welfare state is not a barrier to risk sharing through mobility but can be its vehicle. Free movement includes migrants in the risk pool of the tax-transfer system in the destination state in that it guarantees, more or less conditionally, equal treatment with long-term residents. If the majority of migrants were unemployed at home, their move would come at little opportunity cost to the tax-transfer system they leave. Yet this is empirically not the case: regular economic migrants are not the most desperate and must have the self-confidence that they have something to offer in order to take the step and uproot themselves (Collier 2013: 38). An alternative benign scenario ensues if, in a converging union, migrants moved primarily to fast-growing rather than rich member states. This could alleviate bottlenecks and thus sustain their catching-up process. But again, there is not much evidence that this was a dominant trend before the crisis (Figure 8.5, left-hand panel). Moreover, high growth also attracts capital flows that may trump any stabilizing effect of migration on prices and competitiveness.

This chapter has also argued that free movement is not an economic freedom opposed to social rights, but is itself a social right. The more rule-based the integration process is, the more it resembles an insurance mechanism, as the rules specify ex ante what the criteria for claiming the insurance of immigration are. This insurance gives individuals the opportunity to escape the bad luck of a temporary downturn or the more permanent state of being born in a poorer region of a union. In principle, social rights for migrants work both ways: they uphold standards to protect migrants but they are also a demand on migrants to justify these standards with the value they add. The latter aspect also protects domestic workers. Minimum wages, underpinned by a right to social assistance, have this character.

The politically tricky issue is, however, that these standards may be so high that they are hard to meet by migrants and some resident workers. This nurtures, rightly or wrongly, the belief that immigration poses a net fiscal burden due to unemployment or poverty. According to Brian Burgoon's intricate study, this belief concerns a majority of voters in twenty-two European countries, surveyed five times between 2002 and 2010, more than issues related to multiculturalism. The consequence is less support for redistribution: "economic nonintegration is more relevant to welfare state politics than is sociocultural nonintegration, and the mechanism by which this is so involves concerns about fiscal costs" (Burgoon 2014: 397). It is as if the political-economic paradox of diversity catches up with the welfare state: while integration can help to reap the benefits of migration, the welfare state is also the first political target if difficulties of integration show up on its balance sheet.

The recent move to the "activating" welfare state may have been, at least partly, a response to this fiscal concern but also made the problem worse. The cut in non-employment benefits, such as unemployment insurance and disability benefits, in favor of in-work subsidies such as tax credits incentivizes workers to accept any job: employment creates the entitlement and the after-tax-transfer income will be the same, regardless of the market wage employers pay. This intensifies competition for low-income jobs; and immigrants may accept harsher employment practices, like overtime and unconventional working hours, than resident workers with families and social norms that militate against these practices. Activation policies make employment of low-wage workers a fiscal burden, to the benefit of private firms. In-work benefits, such as wage subsidies or child benefits for low-income households, do not establish a reservation wage but actually allow low wages to fall further without raising the resistance of workers and organized labor. Policy debates about a "social minimum wage" or the "living wage" in Germany and the UK already reflect this concern that the social security system is exploited by the worst employers (Mabbett 2016: 1241–2, on Germany). Activation policies thus create a new dualism although they shift some of the risk that (resident and immigrant) low-wage workers bear privately to taxpayers.

Either way, dualism separates the risk pool of the welfare state and creates a second pool in which public safety nets are residual. Dualism makes the already doubtful efficacy of migration for interstate risk sharing even more doubtful. It raises the fiscal risks that are entailed in migration across a union with no fiscal risk sharing. They are particularly harmful for the origin countries: cross-border migrants in the EA take the (income) tax base they represent with them which is lost to the emigration country while in the US, it is not lost to the federal tax system (Atoyan et al. 2016: paras 26–30). Similarly, pay-as-you-go pension systems can hardly be sustained in net emigration countries, even if, forty years down the line, they can hope for a rising transfer from pensioners returning from a working life abroad. This is a problem in Southern and Central and Eastern Europe as their demographic dynamic is the same as in Western Europe: aging fast. In the US, the federal social security system does not create problems for Florida which is where many Americans move to when they retire.

The US comparison showed that, while there are differences between the EA and the US, the difference that a political union makes is subtler than most of the literature has it. In either union, access and entitlement comes with the expectation that migrants integrate: there is a strong presumption that migrants get employment. This expectation is particularly transparent in the EU, notably in the differentiated rights of economically active and inactive citizens. In the US, economically inactive migrants have social citizenship, while non-employed EU nationals must first establish a link with the host state by fulfilling a residence requirement. This is routinely assumed to be the case after five years; only then can pensioners and students expect assistance when they fall on hard times (Pennings 2012: 327–9). A foreign immigrant worker attempting to claim any federal benefit in the US faces the same five years requirement. Relative to average wages in a state, the entitlements in the US are often exceedingly low, undercutting even the federal poverty standard. Overall, free movement entitles US citizens to lower benefits and forces them more readily into secondary labor markets than free movement in the EA-10 does. The comparison does not suggest that political union determines the extent of social solidarity; it is the generosity of welfare states that determines it.

Both the EA-10/EU and the US operate regimes of coordinated social security. To an internal economic migrant, the US does not present itself as one welfare state: most programs relevant to adults of working age are co-financed by federal and state governments but administered by the states which give quite different entitlements. To be precise: there is more variation between contributory benefits (unemployment insurance) than between non-contributory benefits (social assistance) in the US while the opposite holds in the EA-10 (see Table 8.2). Contributory benefits are (ex-) portable in both unions, non-contributory benefits are not. The dividing line between these two types of benefits is not easy to draw (Bolderson and Mabbett 1995) which has led to conflicts between state governments and legal activists, often ending up in court. Over time, EU case law developed principles for the exportability of benefits financed through social security contributions that, if in doubt, tend to be favorable to free movement migrants.[37] This repeats the history of the US where equal treatment of internal migrants and residents was also the result of judicial intervention.[38]

Low benefits and less variation in social assistance seem to support the venerable hypothesis that the closer market integration achieved in the US has a dismal effect on social security: free movement of people and capital creates a race to the bottom. Economic freedoms allow marginally employed people to move to the states with the highest benefits, while firms move out of states with the highest taxes and social security contributions, supposedly forcing these "welfare magnets" to slash both (Freeman 1986; Peterson and Rom 1990). The race-to-the-bottom hypothesis has been widely debated and there will always be evidence for both sides of the argument (Bruckner 2000; Schmitt and Obinger 2013).

The persistence of variance in relative benefit levels is counter-evidence to the pessimistic convergence hypothesis (Table 8.2; Schram et al. 1998: 217–19). The decline in benefits arising from the US welfare reforms in the 1990s was not correlated with migration pressures, and the politics of welfare reform point to a host of other explanations (Schwartz 2001). One explanation of particular interest for the comparison with the EU points to the effects of fiscal federalism, with states shifting costs onto the federal government. In the case of social assistance, US states can free ride on federally financed SNAP. State governments can also try to shift workers onto the federally financed EITC. Thus downward convergence in social assistance may have more to do with moral hazard in a fiscal federation than with the alleged incompatibility of welfare states and open economies.

Free movement is a stepping stone in Europe's difficult project of political integration in the form of social security coordination. This is partly a necessity and not just another elite project: if cross-border labor market integration is not supported by welfare-state provisions and left ungoverned, it can easily become politically divisive and socially disruptive (Burgoon 2014; Favell 2009: 186). The shift to activation policies over recent decades is an example of how welfare-state reforms can intensify adverse political effects and regressive distributive effects from immigration. Regulation and contestation around the norms underpinning free movement, non-discrimination, and equal treatment force a heterogeneous union to develop meta-rules with which the various members can live. These norms protect individuals, not institutions. This

[37] As mentioned, if a worker acquired pension rights in two member states simultaneously, s/he must receive the pension from the country with the more generous provision. This aggregation principle was initially introduced to rule out duplication yet tends to be also a mechanism of progressive redistribution, in that richer member states pay higher pensions (Schelkle 2013b). See also Meyer et al. (2013) for a detailed study of pension entitlements of EU internal migrants.

[38] This observation finds support in Dan Kelemen's widely acclaimed work on adversarial legalism in the EU, comparable to the US (Kelemen 2011).

makes them indispensable in a union of liberal democracies but also politically divisive in a monetary union of diverse members. Free movement is a political-legal integration project in its own right, best handled with care and not under the imaginary pressure of an economic imperative (Collier 2013). There is no instrumental necessity for free movement of persons in a monetary union, contrary to what more than half a century of normative economic theory has asserted.

9

Monetary Solidarity in Financial Integration

Since 2008, the idea that financial integration provides channels of interstate risk sharing and thus helps to stabilize economies has been discredited beyond redemption. There are strong theoretical reasons, discussed in Chapter 3, why it is untenable to assume that financial markets as such share and diversify risks. Financial markets allow risks to be taken, sometimes incalculable ones that they are ill-equipped to bear. For financial markets to have a stabilizing effect, they require the permanent provision of collective goods. These include regulation that forces those who take profitable risks to also bear costs on the downside, and safety nets that can draw on fiat money and the pool of future taxpayers (Kindleberger 2000: 216).

This chapter analyses a safety net that is unique to a currency union, namely a unified payments system. This crucial institution distinguishes a currency union from a fixed exchange rate system (Bindseil and König 2011: 4; Garber 2010; Whelan 2014b: 112). It ensures that a euro is accepted as a euro in payment irrespective of whether it is drawn on a bank account in Portugal or the Netherlands, just as a dollar is a dollar throughout the United States even if one district experiences for several years a high inflow of bank deposits from virtually every other district. By zooming in on the payments system between financial firms and central banks of a monetary union, we can demonstrate in a nutshell all the policy tradeoffs that risk sharing in a monetary union faces (Cecchetti et al. 2012: 12–14). Who benefits primarily from the protection? Does a payments system give banks and wealthy individuals too easy an option of capital flight, at the expense of the general taxpayer? Does the insurance provided come at the cost of adjustment to current-account imbalances? Is politically imposed austerity the only way to force a member into adjustment if foreign exchange reserves are no longer a binding constraint?

These questions indicate doubts about the desirability of meeting all demands for cross-border payments and financial transfers, which is what a payments system accomplishes. The chapter argues for the contrary view, that payments systems in the euro area (TARGET) and the US (ISA) are extremely effective stabilizing insurance schemes.[1] They ensured the smooth processing of cross-border payments inside two monetary unions when banks, traders, and savers had lost trust in the financial system. The ex post distributional effects of this insurance are not easy to ascertain. Claims about the effects of TARGET have been the subject of a divisive public debate in Germany, but the following discussion shows that these claims are largely spurious. The comparison with the US enables us to see how a payments system functions within a union where the most devastating political market failures have been institutionally resolved (Section 4.3).

The first section of this chapter outlines the sharp criticism levelled against the payments system of the euro area. Criticism peaked in 2011–12, after Hans-Werner Sinn, a renowned German economist and notorious critic of the euro, was apparently tipped off by former Bundesbank President Schlesinger about the strong increase in claims and liabilities between national central banks. Claims were being accumulated by the Bundesbank in particular. This had been independently noted by Garber (2010) and Whittaker (2011). The insinuation was that the Bundesbank and ultimately German taxpayers were being forced to amass billions of doubtful claims through TARGET2. While this particular charge produced more heat than light, it has to be conceded that those worried about high imbalances in the payments system asked legitimate questions. It turned out that its economic functionality and the legal-financial implications of a participant defaulting were not well understood. But an impressive research effort by a critical mass of scholars produced answers in a relatively short time.

The second section explains why the payments systems in both the EA and in the US began to show huge imbalances after 2007. The fact that the US also registered this phenomenon should have given those who raised the alarm reason to pause, since nobody suggested that the US experienced an internal balance of payments crisis or was about to fall apart. In both monetary unions, extraordinary monetary policy interventions substituted for disrupted interbank markets and the payments systems were the vehicles for this market making of last resort (Buiter 2012; Lubik and Rhodes 2012).

The third section shows how TARGET provided effective insurance against at least three risks: a sudden stop of trade finance, disruption from capital flight, and the eventuality of a euro area break-up. In line with Cecchetti et al. (2012) and Whelan (2014b), the section provides evidence that the various

[1] TARGET stands for Trans-European Automated Real-time Gross settlement Express Transfer System. This characterizes a "settlement system in which processing and settlement [of payments] take place on an order-by-order basis (without netting) in real time (continuously)" (ECB n.d.: 6). TARGET2 stands for the first fully unified system introduced after the EA had already started. ISA stands for the Inter-district Settlement Account in the US which fulfils the same role between Federal Reserve districts in the US.

diagnoses of what was driving the payments imbalances all played a role at some stage; it was not primarily a matter of trade deficits or primarily capital account reversals. For the insurance that TARGET provides, this is also a largely irrelevant question. A functioning payments system of a monetary union is analogous to universal public insurance. It covers all risks (known unknowns) and even uncertainty (unknown unknowns).

The fourth section sums up by addressing two puzzles. First of all, why was there, in the words of an American observer (Wolman 2013: 128), such "uproar" in Europe about an arcane institution? Nothing of the sort has ever been observed in ISA's history, even though the payments system was put to a severe test in the Great Depression (Eichengreen et al. 2014). It is tempting to see the lack of political union and the asymmetric power of Germany as the most plausible explanations. But these explanations leave parts of the puzzle unresolved. From the perspective of the political economy of monetary solidarity, the second puzzle is even bigger. Why was the operation of TARGET not more susceptible to real or perceived collective action problems, real or perceived moral hazard, or commitment problems on the part of Germany? The unified platform of payments in the EA was initially built against some resistance of member state authorities.[2] But apart from a few internal discussions, a glimpse of which outside observers got from a leaked letter by Bundesbank President Weidmann to the ECB, no policymaker questioned the system and certainly none tried to obstruct its working like the Chicago Fed did in 1933. The answers to both puzzles will be sought in the political economy of insurance (Section 2.4).

9.1 The Political Challenge of a Payments System

In a monetary union operated by several member central banks, payments cross internal borders between these members. Payments are initiated by private banks and there is no upper limit on the amounts that can be transacted, which are settled with immediate effect as far as the initiating banks are concerned. The operating central banks may hold the consolidated claims and liabilities against the common central bank or against each other for a certain time (ISA) or indefinitely (TARGET). Typically at the end of the business day, they are netted and either recorded as bilateral claims (ISA) or as claims/liabilities of each against the joint central bank (TARGET). Normally, payments systems work smoothly and consumers and firms do not even notice whether one or two central banks are involved in its operation.

[2] Interviews at the ECB in June 2015. Giavazzi and Wyplosz (2015: 724) recall that observers feared at the time that the ECB would not be able to overcome this resistance against a centralized payments system.

Before the crisis, hardly any student of monetary integration, including myself, paid attention to what seemed to be a mere accounting device. The exception is Peter Garber (1998), a research economist at Deutsche Bank, who suggested that the interbank payments system could fund a speculative attack on weaker currencies during the final stage of forming the euro area when exchange rates were irrevocably fixed but the common currency did not yet circulate. As Garber (2010: fn 1) himself notes, his contribution was part of an alarmist Euroskeptic literature that was produced in abundance throughout the 1990s, by US economists in particular.

The sudden interest in this arcane institution was triggered by anomalous imbalances in the TARGET2 system which Figure 9.1 shows. The top line represents the Bundesbank surplus of bank reserves which has its counterpart in claims against other central banks, while the lowest two lines represent the liabilities of the central banks of Spain and Italy. By mid-2014, the Bank of Italy switched places with the Bank of Spain, bearing the largest liabilities in the TARGET system.[3] At its peak in August 2012, when there was a real prospect of the euro area breaking up, it was understandably worrying that the Bundesbank held claims of more than €750 billion against the TARGET system. Those alarmed argued that the Bundesbank was forced to finance current -account deficits that private capital flows were no longer willing to finance. These deficits were accumulated by "Southern Europe" (relocating Ireland in the process), the "periphery" (including Italy, a founding member of the EU), or the GI(I)PS (Greece, Italy, (Ireland), Portugal, Spain). To see how valid the claims regarding such links are, Figure 9.2 shows the current-account imbalances.

It should be noted, first, that Figure 9.1 depicts the claims and liabilities by national central banks (accumulated stocks), while Figure 9.2 shows the annual imbalances that give rise to claims by net exporting countries and liabilities by net importing countries (flows or change in stocks). Even so, it is evident that there is no close match between the two time series: current accounts tended to diverge after 2003, long before TARGET imbalances emerged in late 2007; and current-account deficits disappeared in all but one member state (France) at exactly the time that TARGET imbalances reached their peak. It is also noticeable that there are two big persistent surplus countries, Germany and the Netherlands, while there is some movement among the large deficit countries: Spain is the biggest net importer until 2009; Italy shows some ups and downs; and France glides from a surplus into the largest deficit without the Banque de France accumulating vast TARGET liabilities.

[3] These data were extracted from national central bank balance sheets and were collected by Steinkamp and Westermann (2014) from the University of Osnabrück.

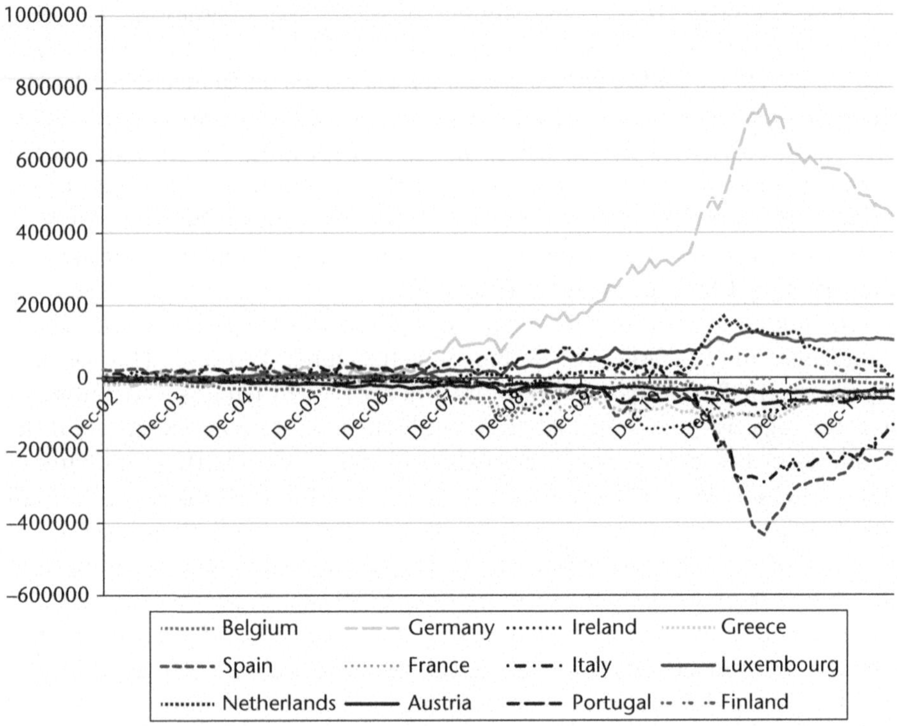

Figure 9.1. TARGET claims and liabilities of the EA-12 member states, 2002–14, in € millions

Source: monthly data from Institute of Empirical Economic Research, Osnabrück University, www.eurocrisismonitor.com

Although a simple explanation was not available, the iconography of exploding TARGET claims and liabilities nonetheless attracted attention. Hans-Werner Sinn raised the alarm with a series of articles in the German media, alongside a co-authored scholarly paper (Sinn and Wollmershäuser 2012). Sinn was a professor of economics and public finance at the University of Munich but not your ordinary academic: an eminently influential figure among German academic economists and known to a wider audience thanks to his popular and populist publications on what went wrong with German unification and what was wrong with the German "bazaar economy" in the early 2000s. At the time of the debate outlined below, he was Director of the CES-Ifo research group. It is instructive to outline the way he launched a media campaign before anybody had the chance to fully understand what was going on, Sinn and those who supported his cause included.

There are direct connections between Sinn's publications on TARGET in 2011–12 and an open letter to the Bundesbank sent by the Bavarian section of the German taxpayers association in February 2012, thirty-one pages long

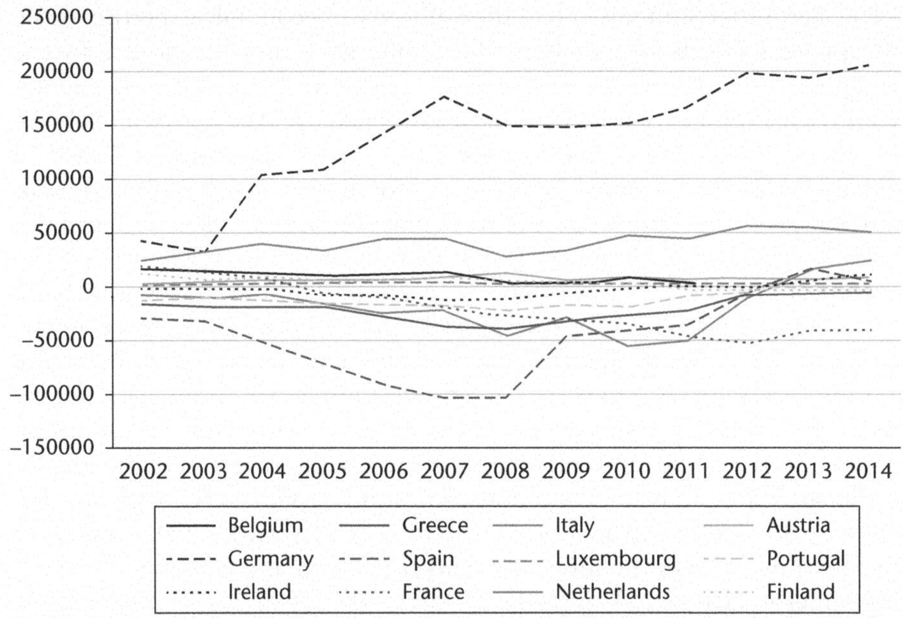

Figure 9.2. Annual current-account balances 2002–13, in € millions
Source: AMECO

with eighty-seven footnotes (Bund der Steuerzahler 2012). This association was a public voice that the two Conservative parties in Germany could not ignore. This open letter followed a rather dry press statement by the Bundesbank in the previous year that triggered more questions than it answered and a more didactic explanation in the March report had to follow (Bundesbank 2011). But to no avail. The open letter was the prelude to a charge of criminal negligence against the Bundesbank management in April 2012, although the criminal court in Frankfurt refused to open procedures. There was some concern in other countries: in the lower house of the Austrian parliament, questions were raised about the size of the Austrian TARGET balances (Jobst et al. 2012: fn 1). Some reverberations of the intense debate were still felt in May 2014 when the TARGET2 balances of the Bundesbank and the alleged liabilities of the German taxpayers made it into the manifesto with which the new Euroskeptic party "Alternative für Deutschland" went into the European Parliament elections. They adopted a proposal originated by Sinn, namely to impose a cap on TARGET imbalances. The new party of Euroskeptics won 7 percent of the popular vote, inflicting massive losses on the Christian Social Union in Bavaria. Its then party leader, the economics professor Bernd Lucke, was well acquainted with Sinn as both were leading lights in a campaign by 200 German economists against the banking union in 2012.

The alarm that Sinn raised had the authority of economic expertise, while his apparent efforts to enlighten the public gave him the license to use metaphors which were as evocative as they were potentially misleading. His introduction to a special issue of *CESifo Forum* on "The European Balance of Payments Crisis" is a case in point. The special issue was published in January 2012 and included eighteen contributions, two by Sinn himself, fourteen by those who support Sinn's concerns, among them former Bundesbank President Schlesinger. The remaining two articles challenged the Sinn position and were written by economists from the Bundesbank (Ulbrich and Lipponer 2012) and the ECB (Bindseil et al. 2012), respectively. Sinn (2012: 3) refers to them as "current representatives of the Bundesbank and the ECB, who wish to convey a sense of normality." So the reader knew from the start that independent experts sided with Sinn, while those opposed were technocrats defending institutional positions. Yet the articles of the latter are more analytical and empirically grounded than the former, and they provide an explanation of why the large TARGET imbalances reflect the abnormal state of the interbank market (Ulbrich and Lipponer 2012: 74; Bindseil et al. 2012: 87).

Sinn's introduction to the special issue was not an editor's introduction but a summary of "the Ifo Institute's views" (Sinn 2012: 3). He insisted that the TARGET system is a way for current-account deficit countries to get whatever they need to continue financing their deficits:

> It is . . . entirely correct to speak of Target credit that the periphery countries were able to draw out of the Eurosystem forcing other euro countries, predominantly Germany, to provide this credit . . . [O]ne could say that the Bundesbank was lending its money printing press to the periphery countries, (Sinn 2012: 5)

The "heuristic" of a printing press evokes the image of a physical flow of money in return for tangible goods and services.

This physical image brings with it two spurious implications (Sinn 2012: 6; Fahrholz and Freytag 2012: 79). First, the outflow of money would lead to the "displacement" of central bank credit to domestic (German) banks. The flood of money to the periphery invokes the image of draining the center when, in fact, no such drastic flows happened (Bindseil et al. 2012: 86–8). Second, the bounty of cheap TARGET credit would prevent adjustment by deficit countries (Sinn 2012: 6):

> Whether good or bad, it is a matter of fact that credit relocation via the ECB System meant that part of the German savings capital was flowing out via the system of central banks, rather than via the interbank markets. This slowed down the adjustment processes in the countries of the periphery, which would otherwise have been enforced by the markets.

Surplus countries like Germany became the passive victims of uncontrolled capital leakage. It is the same physical metaphor that made the price-specie flow mechanism, a stylized textbook explanation of adjustment under the gold standard, so deceptively fathomable. Its operation should lead to equilibrium because countries with a trade deficit lose gold in payment and this lack of means of payment will force their prices and wages down, restoring their competitiveness.[4] But of course, if there is a printing press that replenishes the vanishing gold stock, no such adjustment will take place.

The metaphor of the printing press conveyed to the general reader that trade deficits—creating a demand for money to pay for goods and services—were driving the TARGET imbalances. But Sinn had to grapple with the problem that neither Ireland nor Italy had large and persistent current-account deficits. Sinn (2012: 5) presents the case of Ireland as if it would underline the earlier current-account-competitiveness diagnosis thus:

> In Ireland the situation was even more exceptional and extreme than in the other GIPS countries insofar as outright capital flight took place . . . [T]he breakdown of the interbank market meant that banks from the core countries stopped providing new credit to Ireland and even repatriated their maturing loans, returning the debt titles which backed those loans to the Irish banks.

If his diagnosis for Ireland is correct, it is not simply "even more extreme" but quite different. It is then not consumers in importing countries that are the ultimate beneficiaries of TARGET deficits but holders of assets who are able to reduce their exposure. Principal among these are subsidiaries of core banks, which reduced their periphery assets, cutting lending, and disposing of bonds, while continuing to take deposits (Section 9.3.2).

In Sinn's diagnosis, the surplus countries Germany and the Netherlands are the suffering victims and the GIPS, as he likes to call them, are the benefiting perpetrators. The extent of this victimization is driven home with per capita figures: "Germany's Target claim increased to 463 billion euros in December 2011 or 5.7 thousand euros per capita . . . By November 2011, the Dutch central bank had accumulated a claim of 145 billion euros, which amounted to even 8.7 thousand euros per capita" (Sinn 2012: 4). The figures refer to the recorded claim of national central banks against the ECB, but these are not claims on the taxpayer. There would be a loss if these claims defaulted, and it would indirectly (via central bank profits) accrue to taxpayers, but the magnitude and distribution of these losses bears no relation to the structure of TARGET claims, as will become obvious.

[4] Scholars who study the gold standard can explain that such physical gold flows were the exception rather than the rule as rising interest rates prevented them.

This sorry state of European affairs is contrasted with the US, where market discipline supposedly reins in the deficit districts: "A district that wants to import more goods than it exports must therefore obtain a private loan in other districts, or its central bank must pay its counterparts in other districts with marketable assets" (Sinn 2012: 9).[5] No wonder then that if European deficit countries are given such unrestrained use of a powerful instrument, payments imbalances become the origin of all the calamities that the euro area faces: "[T]he availability of cheap Target credit . . . may very well even have caused the capital flight that it is trying to compensate for" (Sinn 2012: 9). It also interfered with countries' own best interests: "Cheap access to the euro printing press . . . may have kept countries in the eurozone that otherwise would have preferred to exit and devalue to restore their competitiveness" (Sinn 2012: 6). And so the crisis will have to run its course to the bitter end since TARGET prevents the inevitable adjustment:

> Only at the very end, when even the strongest countries have their backs to the wall and have run out of credit, will real internal devaluation in the crisis-stricken euro countries be agreed upon. Only then will the competitiveness of the GIPS countries be restored and the euro area brought into equilibrium. (Sinn 2012: 10)

If there ever was a simple diagnosis of a complex policy problem, we can find it here.

As noted above, these arguments resonated with the German media, organized interests like the Bavarian taxpayers association, a new Euroskeptic party and the wider public. Enraged comments bear witness to this, for instance on blogs by journalists who tried to counter the conspiracy theories and doomsday scenarios that thrived on Sinn's contributions.[6] Finally, on May 31, 2011, Sinn's propositions received worldwide publicity when Martin Wolf (2011) took them up in his widely read blog for the *Financial Times*, "Intolerable choices for the Eurozone." Wolf's blog in turn was endorsed, on June 1, by Paul Krugman (2011), arguing that the TARGET claims and liabilities are evidence for a "slow-motion bank run . . . in the European periphery." Krugman ended on a note that made even Sinn sound hopeful: "If you ask me, the water level has now dropped so far that the fuel rods are exposed. We really are in meltdown territory." Again, the metaphor misleads: the accumulation of

[5] It will become clear that this is a complete misrepresentation of the US system where Federal Reserve districts have no current-account balance and the marketable assets are an expanding portfolio of open-market instruments, generated by similar monetary policy instruments to those that Sinn (2012: 10) vehemently criticizes in the case of the ECB.

[6] See Mark Schieritz on the blog Herdentrieb (http://www.zeit.de/suche/index?q=TARGET2) and Olaf Storbeck on the blog "Economics Intelligence" (http://olafstorbeck.blogstrasse2.de/?cat=15), both in German.

TARGET balances showed a safety valve at work, not a hazardous failure of the main mechanism.

This campaign and its resonance also mobilized an unprecedented effort by scholars and economic journalists to get to the bottom of the TARGET imbalances.[7] The critics emphasized that it was the capital account that unsettled the payments system. This meant that the blame lay not with the deficit countries but with German and other banks that exited the periphery and thus generated a good part of the TARGET surpluses. This analysis also refuted the charge that easy availability of TARGET credit incentivized deficit countries to import more than they export; capital flight instead created a credit crunch. The only point of agreement between the two sides can be summarized by ECB President Draghi's statement that "a decrease in TARGET2 balances is the best sign we have that there has been a gradual return of confidence."[8]

Despite the manipulative rhetoric and outright hysterical overtones, the TARGET debate has proven instructive and the following section draws heavily on the insights that it generated. In my view, the critics of the Sinn position have won the scholarly argument hands down. But this is not necessarily the public perception. Sinn managed to frame the debate in terms that his critics had to accept. Inadvertently, they contributed to the impression that it is Germany that should worry even when arguing that it should not (Dullien and Schieritz 2012). Readers could be forgiven for thinking that the breakdown of the euro area was imminent when leading economists analyzed the consequences. Buiter and Rahbari (2012) proved that Germany would not bear a high cost, while De Grauwe and Ji (2013) proposed ways for Germany to protect itself by discriminating against those choosing it as a safe haven. These assurances were given with an overtly mocking "Calm down, dear!", a sentiment understandably hard to suppress.[9] But it did not exactly help to convince the skeptics. My contribution in the following is to highlight, with the benefit of hindsight, the various insurance roles that TARGET performed and thus turn the arguments of Sinn's critics into a positive case for TARGET imbalances.

[7] The debate can be followed at VoxEU.org (http://www.voxeu.org/taxonomy/term/3064); for the TARGET tag and at the Euro Crisis Monitor (http://www.eurocrisismonitor.com/) which are blogs that give voice to both sides. FT Alphaville also has useful contributions, for instance a thoughtful contribution from Gavyn Davies (2011).

[8] ECB press conference on May 2, 2013, in Bratislava at http://www.ecb.europa.eu/press/pressconf/2013/html/is130502.en.html (accessed December 4, 2014).

[9] For instance, Buiter and Rahbari (2012: 21–2) have some comforting news for those worrying about the worst-case scenario: "With Germany as the only EA member state left, the Bundesbank is the sole owner of the ECB, so it is quite convenient that the institution is located in Frankfurt." And: "If there were a complete disintegration of the euro area ... the Bundesbank, as sole owner of the ECB ought not to have too much trouble collecting on the debt it would be owed by the ECB under Target2."

9.2 Payments Systems of Two Monetary Unions

Both the euro area and the dollar area are "composed of a system of central banks that together administer a single currency" (Wolman 2013: 128). The European currency union started with eleven member states, two years later joined by Greece, which formed the ESCB. National central bank governors are represented in the ECB's Governing Council. These central banks have some limited ability to provide liquidity to banks established in their jurisdiction and are owned, ultimately, by the national governments. The ECB is the sole issuer of central bank money and has its own balance sheet. The Federal Reserve System is made up of twelve district central banks that each represent a number of US states and are owned by private banks that receive a fixed dividend on their shares. The Federal Reserve Board in Washington, DC decides monetary policy through the FOMC on which the governors of the district central banks are represented. Unlike the ECB, the Federal Reserve Board issues central bank money through the New York Fed and has no balance sheet of its own.

Commercial banks established in each member state/district maintain an account with the national/district central bank. A bank is established if it has its headquarters there or is incorporated as a subsidiary, in contrast to merely operating a branch. Payment flows between banks in different member states/districts go through these central bank accounts. Without this highly liquid intermediary, payments would be rather costly as every bank would have to maintain links with every other bank. Payments would also be susceptible to cash flow interruptions, as information about partners and events elsewhere is even less complete than in domestic transactions, leading to cycles of complacency and panic. In the euro area, the payment system TARGET fulfilled these functions from January 1999 by connecting national systems. It was replaced by TARGET2, a single platform, in May 2008. The equivalent in the US is called the Inter-district Settlement Account (ISA), introduced in 1913.

9.2.1 *Payments Systems in Normal Times*

If two currency areas, A and B, decide to form a currency union, it must not make a difference for payments within this newly formed monetary union whether they are (i) operated solely by the joint central bank C, (ii) administered by the two former central banks, or (iii) administered by the central banks in A and B while C is liable for the net balances since it is the one that issues the joint currency (Ulbrich and Lipponer 2012: 74). The first option characterizes the Bank of England in the UK, the second the Federal Reserve System in the US, and the third option was chosen for the ESCB, or Eurosystem. In each case, the payment system is a platform for registered users

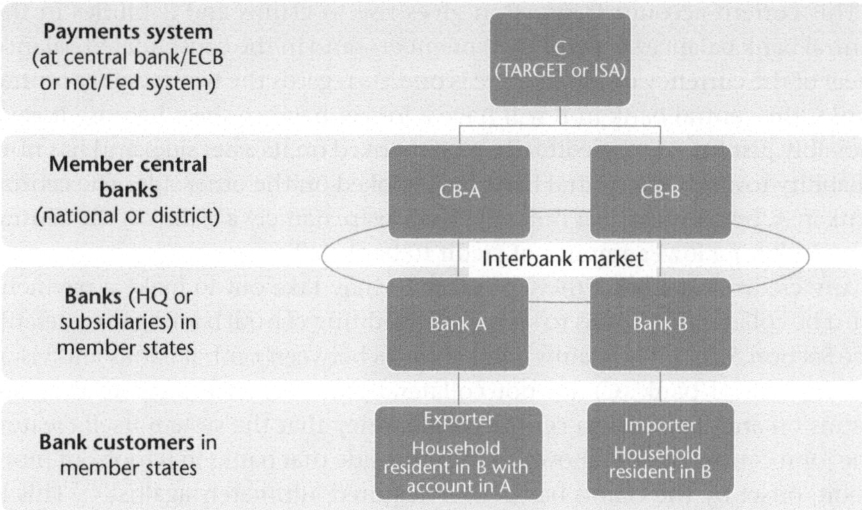

Figure 9.3. Schematic representation of cross-border payments

with access to central bank reserves, typically wholesale and retail commercial banks, to make payments to each other.

There can be many reasons why the authorities ask banks in one member jurisdiction to make their payments to banks in the other area through "their" former central bank. They already have an established infrastructure and member states do not want to lose these jobs; banking supervision may be devolved and the member central banks play some role in it; and the decentralized booking of payments allows regulators to keep track of different liquidity developments in the members' banking systems. A decentralized system certainly creates a lot of employment although the variation is large. In 2009, the euro area had 48,100 central bank staff, or more than 15 per 100,000 inhabitants, of which France had almost 13,000 and Germany over 11,000. The Federal Reserve System had 19,900 staff overall, about 7 per 100,000 citizens (*Economist* 2009).

Since the role of current-account imbalances in contrast to capital flight has been in dispute, the basic exposition distinguishes between them (Bindseil and König 2011: 12–18; Cecchetti et al. 2012: 2–4; Figure 9.3). An example of a current-account transaction is that a wholesale wine importer in B wants to buy produce from a vineyard in A, financed by funds held with her bank in B. The exporting vineyard owner wants to hold all financial wealth with his bank in A. Thus, the bank in B has to make a payment to the bank in A. It does so by instructing the payment system to transfer deposits it holds with the central bank in B (or can get via an overdraft against collateral) to credit the account of the bank in A, which it holds with the central bank there.

This current-account transaction gives rise to claims and liabilities in the central bank balance sheets of each member—and in the consolidated balance sheet of the currency union, if there is one. As regards the two-member central banks, the central bank in B will have a longer balance sheet because it gave (possibly just intraday) credit to bank B (booked on its asset side) and has now a liability towards the central bank in A booked on the other side. The central bank in A, by contrast, just notes an asset swap, namely a claim on the central bank in B for a lower amount of credit to bank A.[10]

Any credit that a bank (here possibly B) may take out to make a payment must be collateralized so as to secure the crediting central bank against default (see Section 5.2.2). The claims and liabilities between central banks and vis-à-vis the central bank (C) are not collateralized. This makes sense: they are claims on and liabilities in central bank money that the system itself creates. The joint central bank C shows on the asset side that banks in B took out more credit, offset by the claims banks in A acquired, ultimately against C. This is how TARGET operates: at the end of each day, the claims that member central banks acquired during a business day are netted and become a claim against the ECB. The ECB is the hub in the "hub-and-spoke structure" of the Eurosystem (Whelan 2014b: 83). In ISA, the hub is constituted by net claims on the pool of interest-bearing securities held by the Federal Reserve System, that is the twelve district banks collectively, since there is no consolidated bank C with its own balance sheet.

In normal times, bank A may now consider that it holds excess reserves with its central bank given the payment it received. Excess reserves carry a low interest rate and bank A may therefore want to lend them at a slightly higher interest rate in the interbank market. In the simplest case, bank B is in a matching position. It may want to replenish its reserves or reduce its borrowing from the central bank, if that borrowing is more expensive than what it has to pay in the interbank market. When the interbank market is functioning, matching occurs: banks in the position of A lend to banks like B. The resulting interbank flow undoes the intrasystem claims and liabilities between the two central banks, including the net claim of bank A on the consolidated bank C. The availability of funds in the interbank market is one of the reasons why before 2007, the intrapayment system claims and liabilities were fairly balanced: liquidity-rich banks financing exporters were happy to lend to liquidity-seeking banks financing importers. The nationality of trading firms and the banks that finance them do not have to be the same. Even a non-euro

[10] This is the supposed "displacement" of central bank credit, namely that central bank A (the Bundesbank) would give less credit to banks in A. No such displacement takes place, this is a mere accounting transaction that happens in normal times.

bank, for instance from the UK, can participate in TARGET via subsidiaries in the euro area.

A capital movement, such as a portfolio investment, generates similar accounting transactions in the payments system. Take the example of wealthy households in B wanting to transfer part of their deposits to banks in A. The reasons can vary: because they often spend their holidays in A, because they want to diversify their bank connections to enjoy full deposit insurance, or because they no longer trust the banks in B. Households would therefore instruct their bank to make a payment to their newly opened account in A. As before, the bank in B requests the central bank in B to take from its reserves or give it credit and transfer the funds to the central bank in A which credits bank A. Deposit holdings and thus liquidity of the banking system in B are reduced, while both have increased for banks in A. As before, the consolidated balance sheet C only shows a change on the asset side to the effect that banks in A need less, and those in B more, central bank liquidity. And again, these traces of a capital transaction would be undone if banks in A lent their excess reserves to banks in B via the interbank market. Bank B may have a liquidity or funding shortage that made it run down its central bank reserves or even take out credit; but in normal times, the interbank market evens out such liquidity shortages and excess holdings promptly.

Thus, the account balances in the payment system do not tell us whether it was current-account transactions or capital movements that originated them. This observational equivalence gave rise to the TARGET debate. Sinn and his supporters saw problems of competitiveness and current-account deficits of Southern European countries as the ultimate drivers of payments imbalances, while his critics insisted that it is more likely that capital flight, not least by German banks, was the villain of the piece. In either case, a thriving interbank market could have prevented the imbalances appearing in TARGET.

9.2.2 *Payments Systems in Extraordinary Times*

The financial crisis in 2007–8 made the interbank market freeze. Banks like A did not want to lend their excess reserves to banks like B anymore, whether within country or cross-border. By holding their excess reserves with the central bank instead, they offloaded the credit risk they perceived in bank B to the central bank. As Section 6.2.3 explained, loss of confidence in periphery banks persisted and deepened when the banking crisis turned into a European sovereign debt crisis in early 2010. As well as weakening banks which held that debt, there were massive capital account transactions, including deposit flight, out of the affected countries. The consolidated central bank balance at the ECB showed that the interbank market was not functioning anymore, so the ECB became the interbank market maker of last resort (Buiter

2012), lending to banks which could not borrow in the interbank market and borrowing from banks which would rather hold excess reserves than lend them to other banks. The consolidated balance sheet of the Eurosystem thus got longer. The banks that were unable to obtain interbank credit could replenish their reserves thanks to the extraordinary monetary interventions that the imminent financial collapse forced the ECB to undertake, including the fixed rate full allotment policy which allowed banks to borrow as much as they wished at an interest rate determined by the ECB. The only limit imposed on the banks was that they had to provide eligible collateral, a constraint that in the euro area is applied uniformly to all banks and for which standards were progressively lowered during the crisis.[11]

Extraordinary monetary policy interventions coincided with widening TARGET balances, as shown in Figure 9.1. If it is correct that this was due to a malfunctioning interbank market, this observation should also apply to the US. The Federal Reserve intervened in unprecedented ways to compensate for a frozen interbank market as well. So how did the ISA balances look at the time? Figure 9.4 shows that they became equally imbalanced and remained so

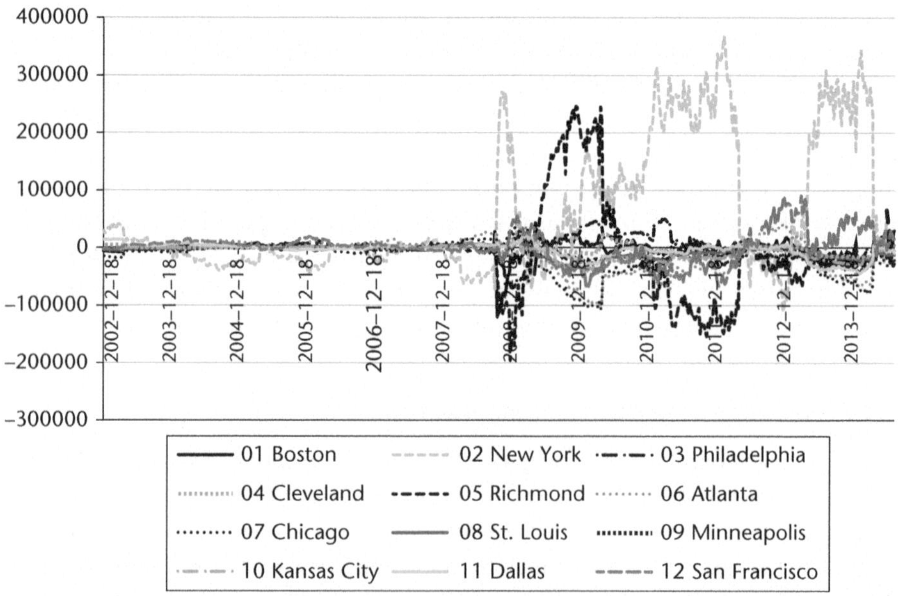

Figure 9.4. ISA claims and liabilities of the twelve US districts, in US$ millions
Source: Weekly data from Federal Reserve Bank of St Louis, http://research.stlouisfed.org/fred2 (accessed November 7, 2014)

[11] See Bindseil and König (2011: 8–12) and Cecchetti et al. (2012: 3–4) for further elaboration of the role that the full allotment policy plays.

even as the US economy recovered. The district of New York was in a similar creditor role to the German Bundesbank, while the districts of San Francisco and Richmond had at times gone into considerable deficit. The figures still look somewhat less frightening as there seem to be reversals from time to time: the district of the Richmond central bank moves from a deficit of $200 billion in mid-2008 to a surplus of almost $250 billion in the first half of 2009. And at its peak in January 2012, New York "only" held claims of less than $370 billion against other district central banks.

Higher volatility and lower overall levels point to a difference between TARGET and ISA that has little to do with their functioning as payments systems, however. TARGET does not settle imbalances between member central banks, in other words claims and liabilities can accumulate for as long as the currency union exists. ISA, by contrast, partially settles balances once a year: district federal reserve banks with claims receive a larger share of interest-bearing assets out of a pool while those with liabilities have to transfer shares and thus end up with a lower share. Federal Reserve publications appropriately speak of rebalancing the portfolio of securities rather than of outright settlement (Lubik and Rhodes: 4; Wolman 2013: 124). If an analogous rebalancing were to take place in TARGET every year, Figure 9.1 would resemble Figure 9.5. For reasons of data availability, the adjustments made for differential developments in currencies and bank reserves in the districts have been left out (Wolman 2013: 126).

The imbalances look much more similar and the maximum claims of Germany are closer to those of the New York Fed ($300 billion/€400 billion). The reverse also holds: "the ongoing increase in the Federal Reserve System's balance sheet, together with the limited tendency for reserve balances to flow from New York to the other Districts, means that without the annual rebalancing, New York...would have a persistently increasing ISA balance" (Wolman 2013: 128). A rough calculation suggests that a figure of $800 billion for the ISA balance of New York would have accumulated between 1999 and 2013, starting at zero in 1999 (Wolman 2013: 138). New York ran ongoing surpluses despite the annual rebalancing: settlement via interest-bearing assets does not mean that the Fed districts with deficits are forced into adjustment.

There was no tendency for the ISA imbalances to recede until mid-2014, because of the expansive monetary policy that the Federal Reserve has operated since 2008 in the wake of a banking crisis. There was no balance of payments crisis among US states that ISA balances prolonged. Bank notes issued by the New York Fed in the course of quantitative easing are subsequently apportioned to the other district central banks, according to a key. This pushes their ISA balance into deficit because the double entry book keeping means that they "buy" securities (Treasury bonds and other assets)

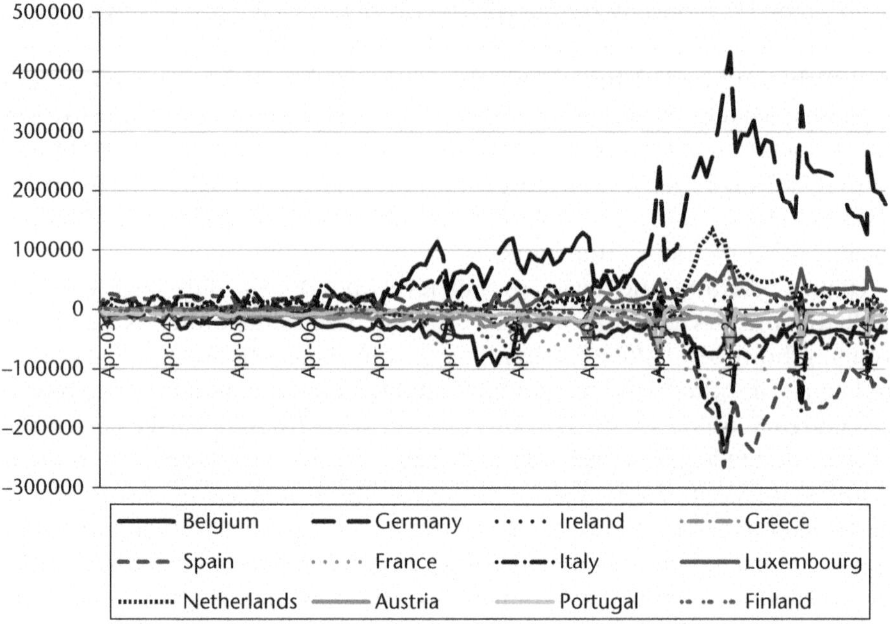

Figure 9.5. TARGET claims and liabilities of the EA-12 member states (ISA method), in € millions

Source: University of Osnabrück, www.eurocrisismonitor.com, own calculations

Note: The TARGET balances here were reset in April of each year, analogous to the domestic securities portfolio in ISA (Wolman 2013: 124–6). The annual average was deducted from the balance in April in the case of net creditor central banks (Germany, Netherlands, etc.) which would receive interest-bearing assets to settle their claim. And vice versa for members that accumulated liabilities over the year (Portugal, Spain, etc.): the annual average was added to their April balance. The balance is drawn towards 0 in April but it would be exactly 0 only if the April balance happened to be equal to the average of the previous year. As a starting point, the balances of all members in the TARGET system were set equal to 0 in April 2003. The starting date was chosen because the estimated monthly data for Ireland are only available since December 2002. The Banque de France shows monthly balances only since July 2007

from the New York Fed with ISA balances (Wolman 2013: 121–2). Conversely, some transactions produce surpluses vis-à-vis the New York Fed. For instance, the New York district can have banks making a lot of payments to other districts. Some monetary policy instruments, such as the Term Auction Facility, were conducted by all twelve central banks. But until 2014, these payment flows in the other direction did not offset the vast amount of money creation that the New York Fed had engaged in since 2008.

There is nothing in the settlement process that would force any district central bank to make these imbalances vanish. Rebalancing was done via a transfer of gold certificates until the mid-1970s, but even this did not force district banks in deficit to impose a local credit contraction. Those with excess gold certificates lent to those with shortfalls, so that the constraint did not become binding (Eichengreen et al. 2014: 12–13).[12] Put differently, the availability of gold certificates has not ever restricted monetary policy or interdistrict payments in the United States (Wolman 2013: 125). In a fairly complicated rebalancing procedure, the gold certificates account served as a mere benchmark for the average reserves-to-notes ratio against which the deviation of the previous year is calculated. This determines how the portfolio of securities held in the System Open Market Account is reallocated. The Federal Reserve System acquires these securities in open-market operations when the money supply expands and reduces its holdings when the money supply contracts. These securities are interest bearing, so those with an ISA deficit over the last twelve months receive less interest income, but these marginal amounts do not induce changes in district policy preferences.

In the Eurosystem, national central banks with net claims also earn interest, at the ECB rate for refinancing operations with banks. These interest earnings and payments feed into the ECB surplus which is distributed according to each member's share in the paid-up capital of the ECB; it does not matter which member earned and which member paid for the amount that governments receive as seignorage (Buiter et al. 2011: 12). Hence, there is no incentive in the TARGET system to run a surplus or a deficit: the ESCB operates a joint profit and loss account (entry 4 in Table 5.1).

Is it possible for a district central bank in the US to experience such enormous capital flight out of its banking system that it would have too few securities to settle its balance with other district Fed banks? For instance, the Richmond District is the seat of the Bank of America, one of the four largest US banks with $1.02 trillion customer deposits as of June 30, 2013.[13] If savers suddenly ran from this bank into banks in other districts, such a situation is conceivable. Would this mean that other central banks of the Federal Reserve System might cease to process payments of banks in Richmond, or start discounting checks to below par value? The short answer is not anymore.

Such bank runs happened between 1917 and 1921 and in 1933 (Koning 2012; Bordo 2014). Mutual accommodation through sharing of gold reserves helped district central banks that ran out of these reserves to settle their balances whenever the need arose, in line with statutory requirements. This

[12] Sinn and Wollmershäuser (2012: 41) see a major design flaw of the euro area in the fact that it imposes no golden fetters on member central banks, in contrast to the US payments system: "According to official statements of the Federal Reserve, the debts are paid with gold certificates and then cancelled. Gold certificates are securities collateralized by gold, issued by the US Treasury, that bear the right to be exchanged for gold on demand." The authors provided no reference to official statements of the Fed that described the present situation.

[13] Wolman (2013: 129) stresses, however, that the Bank of America holds 45 percent of these deposits in branches of other districts, so even a massive deposit flight would affect the Richmond Fed bank only by half of this amount.

happened on average every nine years between 1913 and 1960 (Eichengreen et al. 2014: 13). Only once did a federal district bank, Chicago, refuse to accept checks at par from another district bank, New York (Section 4.2.3). This happened in 1933 at the height of the Great Depression, under pressure from commercial banks in the Chicago District. It caused a major disruption, forcing Roosevelt to declare a bank holiday and capital controls (Eichengreen et al. 2014: 14–16, 20). The Chicago Fed was required to accept checks from New York and honor them at face value. This obligation to maintain the payments system was subsequently formalized in the Federal Reserve Act of 1935. The Federal Reserve System is obliged by law (Sect. 16(14) of the Federal Reserve Act) to clear all checks at par and to maintain the integrity of the payments system. This legislation also eliminated the remaining monetary policymaking powers of the district banks, which had been the basis for the Chicago Fed's defection.[14]

This incident occurred despite there being a political union and a fiscal federation in the US. The Chicago Fed acted in line with the private incentives of its owners while the rest of the country expected the provision of a public good. It was a political market failure of commitment that created a devastating externality for the rest of the Federal Reserve System. Risk sharing was enforced by the Federal Reserve Act which guarantees that "all dollars are treated equally, no matter which private bank or district bank has created them" (Koning 2012). The different treatment of balances in ISA and in TARGET is of little economic significance in a monetary union as a going concern. The focus of both payments systems "is on ensuring the par value of all monetary instruments, not on disciplining individual members," as Koning (2012) puts it in his insightful blog.

9.3 The Beneficiaries of TARGET Insurance

The divergence in ISA balances was fueled by the extraordinary monetary interventions of the Federal Reserve System after 2007–8. The ECB's full allotment policy and long-term refinancing operations did the same for TARGET imbalances. Both responded to a common cause: the breakdown of interbank lending. But since the German Bundesbank does not have the role of the New York Fed in the implementation of monetary policy, it is less clear why the claims would end up so disproportionately with the Bundesbank and De Nederlandsche Bank. Nor are the GIIPS or GIPSIC (including Cyprus) a

[14] "[T]he Federal Reserve Act of 1935 ... gave the Board of Governors in Washington D.C. full control of purchases and sales of securities of regional Reserve Banks via the System account, which significantly facilitated interdistrict accommodation" (Eichengreen et al. 2014: 21).

homogenous group of "peripheral" countries, contrary to what the acronyms suggest (Section 6.1). This statement would even hold if one excluded Ireland, the black swan for all who see a common Southern European malaise of structural current-account deficits at work.

This section argues that the imbalances were the symptoms of TARGET acting as an effective insurance mechanism against at least three risks: first, sudden stops of trade finance; second, the panic of capital flight; and third, exchange rate risks from a break-up of the EA (Cecchetti et al. 2012; Bordo 2014). This implies that TARGET was not a narrowly redistributive transfer mechanism from surplus to deficit countries—nor, in fact, the other way round if one sees capital flight of German banks as the main driver of TARGET imbalances. The system performed insurance services to a variety of pool members afflicted by payments difficulties beyond their control.

It is helpful for the following to briefly recall the basic balance of payments identity (Cecchetti et al. 2012: 4):

Current Account (Ex-Im) + Capital Account (KIm-KEx) ≡ Official Settlement Balance (FEx-FIm).

The identity sign means that a balance of payments is by necessity balanced. So if Sinn (2012) talks of a balance of payments crisis, he means that the current-account deficit (Ex-Im<0) is no longer paid for by a private net capital import (KIm-KEx>0). Thus, the Official Settlement Balance or Financial Account, which normally consists of foreign exchange and gold reserves, becomes negative. The Official Settlement Balance can restrict imports of goods and services if private capital inflows are not forthcoming under a fixed exchange rate system and the central bank cannot borrow foreign exchange in large enough quantities in the market or from other central banks.

For national central banks in the Eurosystem, TARGET balances play the role of foreign exchange reserves (Buiter and Rahbari 2012: 12–13). Current-account deficits can be financed by a capital import from TARGET (FEx-FIm<0) and current-account surpluses can continue because TARGET provides the capital export (FEx-FIm>0) that banks are no longer ready to take onto their books. But even if the current account were balanced, as it was roughly the case for Ireland and Italy, a TARGET deficit may be generated (FEx-FIm<0) by an exodus of capital (KIm-KEx<0) and vice versa for the member state that becomes the safe haven for these capital movements (KIm-KEx>0 leads to FEx-FIm>0). All three balances can be imbalanced of course: before the crisis, Spain had such high net capital imports from German and French banks that they overcompensated even high current-account deficits and the country accumulated small TARGET surpluses and foreign exchange reserves (Chen et al. 2012: 19–20).

9.3.1 *Insurance against Sudden Stops of Trade Finance?*

One interpretation of the TARGET imbalances was that they sustain current-account deficits that can no longer be financed by private capital flows (Tornell and Westermann 2012). It is tempting to make this connection but not self-evident: nobody ever suggested that the ISA imbalances depicted in Figure 9.3 were driven by trade imbalances between Federal Reserve districts. So it would have to be shown that current-account surpluses lead to increases in TARGET balances and vice versa for deficits (Cecchetti et al. 2012: 6–7). Figure 9.6 shows this relationship for the EA-12 in the three years before the crisis (2005–7), and at the height of the North Atlantic financial crisis (2008–10). The cumulative current-account balance over each three-year period is plotted against the corresponding change in the TARGET balance.

We can see that before the crisis (trend line with diamonds) there was virtually no relationship between the volumes needed for trade finance and official payments balances of central banks; instead, private capital and credit financed current-account imbalances. This changed in 2008–10 (trend line with squares) when changes in TARGET claims and liabilities become correlated to the current-account imbalances. Cecchetti et al. (2012: 6) consider this to be evidence in favor of a "(trade) flow interpretation" of TARGET imbalances, at least for this phase of the financial crisis. If so, the correlation implies that up to half of the current-account imbalances of deficit and surplus

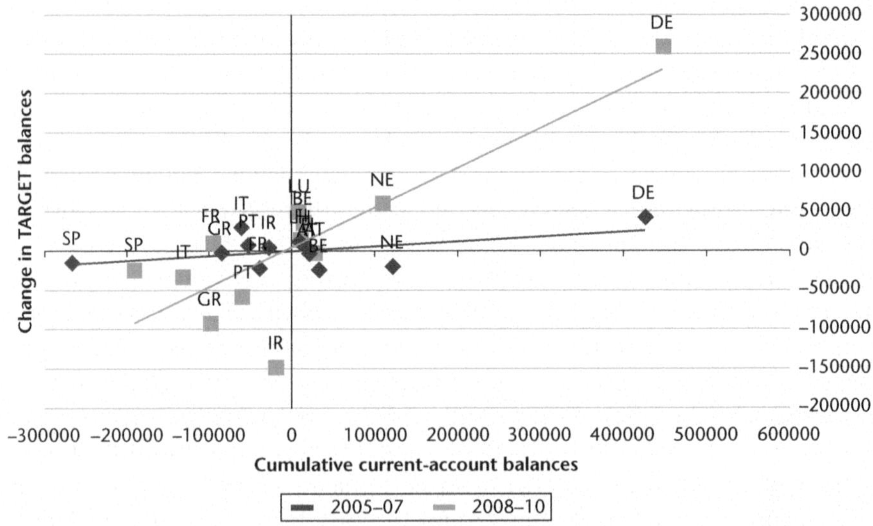

Figure 9.6. Current-account balances and TARGET balances for EA-12, 2005–10, in € millions (annual data)

Source: AMECO, University of Osnabrück (<http://eurocrisismonitor.com>); own calculations

countries could be financed thanks to TARGET (the trendline has a slope of 0.5). Notably, banks financing the importers could obtain credit from the ECB despite being shut out of interbank lending while banks financing the export side could offload the perceived credit risk. This positive relationship still holds if Germany is excluded from the sample.

This change between 2005–7 and 2008–10 is prima facie evidence for TARGET acting as an insurance mechanism against a sudden stop of trade finance. Strictly speaking, this would mean that payments imbalances compensated for the drying up of trade-related capital inflows, rather than for capital outflows (Calvo 1998: 36).[15] Such insurance would be extremely valuable because the international experience of more than 100 sudden stop incidents between 1985 and 2010 suggests that output falls on average by almost 10 percent, possibly more if other measures are used (Hutchison et al. 2010: 2). There is also evidence for developing economies that sudden stops lead to a persistent decline in GDP growth rates, which is largely due to a collapse in investment; smaller firms in the formal sector are the hardest hit, compared to big firms and small informal businesses (Dagher 2010: 5–7). Thus, not only banks but also the non-financial economy, firms, and their employees, might benefit from insurance in the countries afflicted by a sudden stop. This extends of course also to exporting sectors in countries that trade with these countries.

In order to see generally to what extent TARGET may have compensated for a sudden stop, Figure 9.7 depicts the trade balances of Greece, Ireland, Italy, Portugal, and Spain and the change in TARGET balances between 2006 and 2012. The trade balance, recording the export and import of goods and services, is part of the current account. The other two elements are the transfer and the investment balance: the transfer balance records international transfers paid (export) and received (import), the investment balance records interest and profit income received from (for export of capital services) and paid to abroad (for import of capital services).[16]

If TARGET flows compensated only for the sudden collapse in trade finance, they should have the same sign and the same magnitude as the trade balances. This is a plausible interpretation for Greece and Portugal for which both balances closely correspond. However, the other countries do not fit. Spain halved its trade deficit in 2008–9 while the TARGET balances became massively negative from 2010 onwards. Italy has a very minor trade deficit and the TARGET flows developed in a way which is completely unrelated to its need

[15] Gourinchas et al. (2016: 39) define sudden stops as a rise in funding costs but this cannot explain the difference between a sudden stop inside and outside a monetary union.

[16] These two other balances, for transfers and income, were quite important for the smaller of the five countries and explain more of their high deficits than their export performance (Kang and Shambaugh 2013).

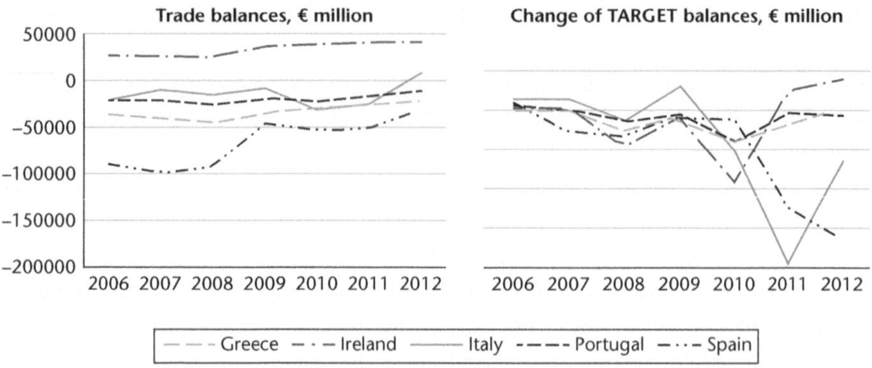

Figure 9.7. Trade balances and change in TARGET balances, 2006–12
Source: OECD, ECB, University of Osnabrück (<http://eurocrisismonitor.com>); own calculations

for trade finance. Ireland had a trade surplus but negative TARGET flows until 2011, clearly a sign that capital account transactions were the major drivers. The deep drop of the Irish TARGET balance in 2008 indicates how much of a credit risk Irish banks had become in the eyes of other financial institutions. The capital exodus was such that the trade surplus could have paid for only half of the capital outflow if Ireland had still had its own currency.

This suggests that the TARGET flows behaved in line with an interpretation that sees them as insurance against sudden stops of trade finance in two out of the five countries (Greece and Portugal). It is arguable though that the smooth behavior of the trade balances in four of the five countries, Spain being the exception, was helped by a functioning payments system (Ilzetzki 2014: 128). In fact, in the context of IMF programs, it has been argued that official financial flows may overly hamper the adjustment of current-account balances. Non-euro EU countries with huge current-account deficits had to cut them by between 25 percent (Bulgaria, Latvia) and 15 percent (Lithuania) of GDP in 2007 to reach balance or even surplus in 2010 (Merler and Pisani-Ferry 2012: 3; Whelan 2014b: 103). Southern European countries with deficits of 15 percent (Greece) and 10 percent (Portugal, Spain) had reduced these to 10 percent (Greece), 7.5 percent (Portugal), and 3 percent (Spain) by 2010. While TARGET is likely to have slowed down adjustment by preventing the sharp credit squeeze that a stop of trade finance otherwise brings, it did not prevent adjustment.

It is a matter for legitimate debate whether buying time for slower adjustment is constructive and valuable or just a delay of the inevitable during which more debt is accumulated (Cecchetti et al. 2012: 12–13; Westermann 2014: 122–3). There is a cost to both. But economists tend to praise "flexibility" and rapid adjustment while neglecting the cost and hardship this entails. Even in purely economic terms, rapid adjustment discourages long-term planning and destroys viable, if import-dependent business and employment along with firms that merely thrived on excessively cheap imports. And when importers have to close down, the claims of exporters and their banks suffer as well. Insurance from TARGET reduced these costs and spillovers.

Spain constitutes a puzzle, however, if the insurance benefit of TARGET is slower adjustment in case a sudden stop strikes. Spain adjusted surprisingly fast as regards its trade balance, and TARGET liabilities accumulated only after trade performance had improved. Ireland also has an odd pattern: its already positive trade balance adjusted steadily upward, yet TARGET balances were volatile and negative. This suggests that something else was driving payments imbalances and something else was forcing these economies to (further) improve their trade performance.

9.3.2 *Insurance but also a Conduit for Capital Flight?*

The majority of those who analyzed the sudden rise in TARGET imbalances concluded that "capital account reversals" were responsible, as Mody and Bornhorst (2012) put it. In this view, the imbalances were not primarily driven by the drying up of trade finance but by savers and financial investors reconsidering where to hold their assets. This then triggered capital outflows that may subsequently have forced countries into current-account (over)adjustment. This could be the key to the puzzles of Spain and Ireland.

If TARGET imbalances are primarily driven by capital flight, the relationship with current-account deficits becomes uncertain. In terms of Figure 9.6, the regression line might become very steep, if capital flight afflicts the deficit countries most (Cecchetti et al. 2012: 7–8). If capital flight is more selective, there may simply be no positive relationship. As Figure 9.8 shows for the three-year period, which includes the first half of 2012, the relationship became negative (line with triangles). It is shown in contrast to the data for 2008–10 reproduced from Figure 9.6.

Despite persistent and even rising current-account surpluses, Germany, the Netherlands, and Luxembourg experienced a reduction in their claims in the latter period (negative TARGET flows). Moreover, the reversal was almost a mirror image of the one for 2008–10. This suggests that capital flight may already have played a role in 2008–10: those who fled into the safe haven of the Bundesbank were unwinding their excess reserves in 2011–13. Moreover, the negative relationship is entirely driven by the Netherlands and Germany—without them, the line of best fit becomes vertical, suggesting no relationship.

What light does this shed on TARGET as an insurance mechanism or risk-sharing channel? Against what risk does TARGET protect if it is a conduit for capital flight? And is this insurance in the public interest of any member state?

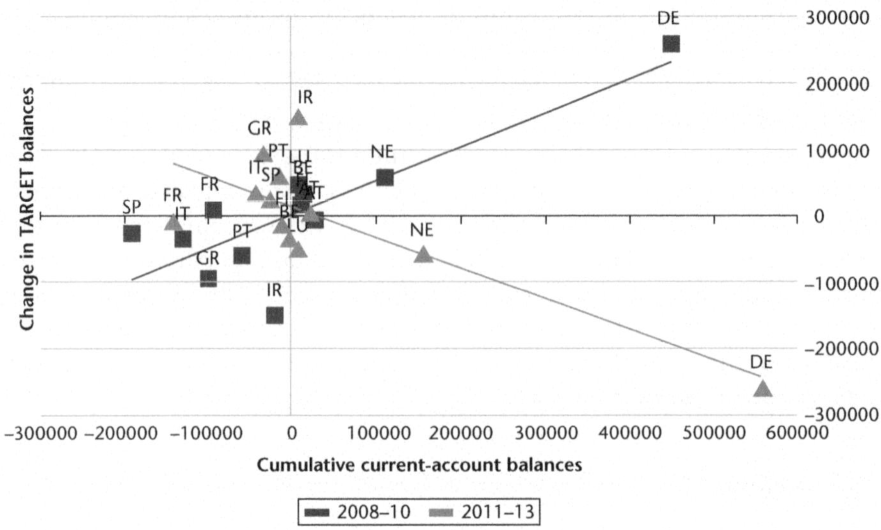

Figure 9.8. Current-account balances and TARGET balances for EA-12, 2008–13, in € millions (annual data)

Source: AMECO, University of Osnabrück (<http://eurocrisismonitor.com>); own calculations

After all, one might see economic value in a payments system that protects trade between the members of a monetary union against the disruption from financial instability. But such value is not obvious if it protects presumably wealthier sections of society and banks whose flight triggered the financial instability in the first place. It might lead to regressive redistribution: the main beneficiaries of the Bundesbank's TARGET claims would be banks in Germany and other rich member states (Cecchetti et al. 2012: 7–8; Hobza and Zeugner 2014a: 12). They withdrew from Southern European countries while German, Dutch, and Finnish export surpluses could still materialize. In line with this argument, Mody and Bornhorst (2012) show that capital-account balances were much more volatile than current-account balances. In particular, Germany's financial flows to the periphery exceeded the latter's financing needs for the bilateral current-account balance before 2007 and fell short of the need for trade finance thereafter, a finding that is more generally elaborated in Chen et al. (2012: 19–22). It would go against the notion of insurance and risk sharing, as understood here, if TARGET were indeed a regressive transfer mechanism, benefiting Germany, possibly Finland, the Netherlands, and Luxembourg while the crisis-stricken member states still experienced the full disruption of capital flight.

If capital flight was occurring, the financial exposure of creditor countries' banks and residents should have declined rapidly. A new database created by Hobza and Zeugner (2014b) from the European Commission allows us to decipher the asset holdings of major creditor countries in Ireland and the Southern European countries between 2010 and 2012. Their database shows privately held stocks and their annual changes as well as the bilateral stock holdings created by official assistance via ESM/EFSF programs and the government bond-buying program of the ECB.

The share that countries receive in stabilization programs is known, while it has to be estimated which (mostly Southern) European Treasury bonds were bought by the ECB under its SMP. Those member states whose bonds were not bought are then considered holders of the SMP bonds according to their share in the capital of the ECB (Hobza and Zeugner 2014a: 7). Similarly, TARGET balances are assigned to bilateral holdings as if the ECB were a mutual fund. Thus, if 21 percent of all TARGET liabilities are owed by Spain, 21 percent of TARGET claims by Germany are assumed to be held vis-à-vis Spain. This is an admissible macroeconomic interpretation of TARGET claims, but it eliminates from the picture the ECB as an entity with its own financial-legal status.[17] But the ECB is such an entity, and this means that, if the debtor countries could not honor the TARGET debt in the case of a break-up of the euro area, Germany would not lose all its TARGET claims but only its share in the paid-up capital of the ECB, which is 27 percent (Buiter and Rahbari 2012: 5).

Asset holdings of two groups of countries—the six countries exposed to bond market attacks and the rest of the euro area—are shown in Figure 9.9. Holdings in a pre-crisis year (2006) are compared with those with the height of the North Atlantic and the EA crisis (2009–12). Figure 9.9 shows that overall asset holdings of the rest of the EA in Cyprus, Greece, Ireland, Italy, Portugal, and Spain do not fall during the financial crisis. A rise of official claims slightly overcompensates for the decline in private debt, from a peak of €2.386 trillion in 2009 to €1.778 trillion in 2012. Equity stays fairly constant, which confirms the expectation in the risk-sharing literature that equity is a (more) reliable source of private insurance than debt. The official interventions through stabilization programs by the EU (with the IMF as the junior partner), the SMP of the ECB, and finally TARGET expand rapidly. There was an astonishing mobilization of official funds within just a few years. Of these official financial stocks, TARGET claims comprise a substantial, albeit falling share, from 100 percent in 2009 to just over 75 percent in 2012, when the remainder is made up of funds from stabilization programs (14 percent) and the SMP (10 percent).

A closer look at the exposure of Germany shows that, by 2012, Germany counts for less than 14 percent of equity in these troubled countries (slightly down from 16 percent in 2006) and for almost 30 percent of private debt

[17] Personal communication with Stefan Zeugner, November 2014.

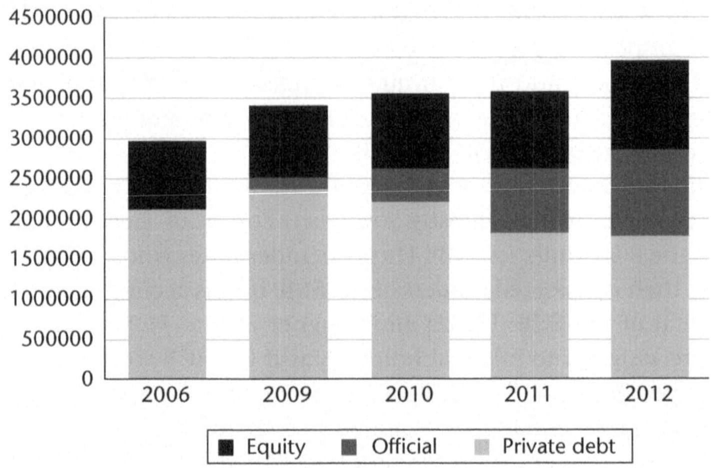

Figure 9.9. Financial assets held by rest of the EA in Ireland and Southern Europe, in € millions

Source: Hobza and Zeugner (2014b); own calculations

(slightly up from its pre-crisis share: 26.9 percent in 2006, 28.4 percent in 2012). The credit claims correspond fairly closely to Germany's economic size in GDP terms while the country is underrepresented in equity terms, indicating that the country acquires its claims through trade, not so much through foreign direct investment. However, Germany held almost 63 percent of all official claims of the rest of the EA in 2012. This is largely due to its high net TARGET claims (almost 70 percent of all TARGET claims) that are attributed to it by the Hobza and Zeugner (2014a) methodology. Together, these figures mean that there was capital flight by German banks but not more than by the rest of the EA banks generally. TARGET was the vehicle for all of them to reduce their exposure.

This finding can be supported by looking at how the exposure of German banks to Greece, Ireland, Italy, Portugal, and Spain relates to the change in German TARGET balances during the North Atlantic financial crisis and then the EA crisis (Figure 9.10).[18] While there was no relationship in 2007–9, the line for 2010–12, with a slope of over 2, suggests that TARGET balances did not merely compensate for the exit of German banks: the TARGET balances changed more than can be explained by German banks reducing their exposure to the distressed countries. There must have been flight into the Bundesbank by banks resident in other countries.

[18] The data for bank exposures are from the quarterly reports of the Bank for International Settlement, aggregated to annual changes in stocks.

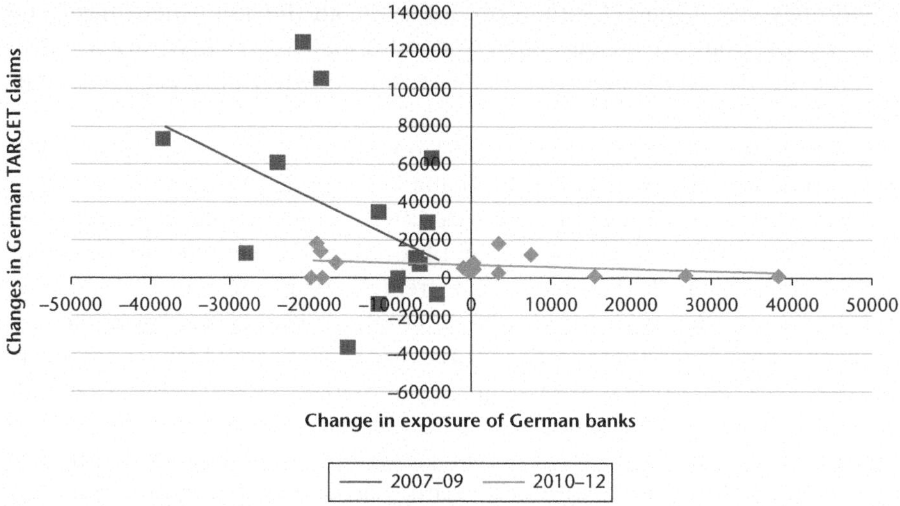

Figure 9.10. Changes in German bank exposure to GIIPS and TARGET claims on GIIPS, in € millions

Source: BIS consolidated banking statistics (ultimate risk basis), University of Osnabrück (<http://www.eurocrisismonitor.com>); own calculations

Note: GIIPS stands for Greece, Ireland, Italy, Portugal, and Spain. Each data point represents a year-country combination, so there are five data points per year and each country has six data points (2007–12)

So TARGET was definitely a conduit for capital flight of banks. There are losers from this: Mabbett and Schelkle (2015) argue that it was not the lack of exchange rate adjustment but the exodus of banks at the height of the Greek crisis that contributed to the country's drop in GDP being so much deeper than in Hungary and Latvia where international banks were kept in. Bastasin (2012: 217–18) claims that an agreement between heads of state at the May 2010 Council to lean on domestic banks and commit them to staying in Greece for three years was broken by French banks; once the Bundesbank revealed the confidential information that French banks were selling their Greek bonds to the ECB under the SMP, other banks felt no longer bound by their promises which were in any case not legally enforceable. Greek banks could substitute borrowing from the central bank for the flight of deposits, but the withdrawal of international banks still meant a credit crunch for Greek business.

This bleak message speaks to the question of whether the insurance of TARGET destroys or at least weakens the signaling function by markets, namely that debt has to be reduced because private investors are no longer willing to hold it. While one might not be too worried about this disempowerment of markets after they failed so badly, there is still the problem that official holders of Greek and other countries' debt are not willing to hold it indefinitely. So, if market signals do not work, all the adjustment has to be imposed by political means, namely conditionality attached to assistance (Section 6.1.2). This would hardly be an encouraging prospect for further European integration.

However, the protection that TARGET provides in the case of capital flight does not immunize economies from market signals. Both the flight from deposits and a withdrawal of claims by international banks made domestic financial institutions lose their sources of funding.[19] Given the breakdown of the interbank market, they faced an extreme version of funding illiquidity, which means that borrowing from alternative sources was prohibitively expensive and drove them to the central bank. They could try to sell assets but they were also up against low liquidity of markets indicated by a sharp fall in prices of assets offered for sale. The fire sale of assets can spread the difficulties of some banks to the financial system as a whole: the decline of asset prices reduces the equity of all banks, even if they are not connected through direct lending and borrowing to each other. This tends to lead to a secondary round of fire sales, amplifying the negative externality on all others (Whelan 2014b: 87). The more the value of assets falls, the higher the probability that banks which had initially only a liquidity problem become insolvent. Negative equity forces any bank to stop trading.

Before it comes to that, banks are likely to reduce new lending to business directly. The knock-on effects of funding illiquidity can include stopping the rolling over and extension of short-term credit lines, notably cancelling the overdraft facilities that non-financial firms need for daily business. Credit access helps them to meet their own payment obligations (wages, inputs) when payments from customers do not coincide. In recessions, such mismatch in payments is likely to become worse as hard-pressed customers, not least from the public sector, tend to postpone payment. The arrears and unmet short-term credit needs of firms are major reasons why recessions can become entrenched and lead to prolonged stagnation. A credit crunch may turn this into a wave of insolvency in the wider economy.[20]

TARGET, and the ECB interventions which it transmitted, could help with funding liquidity and thus rein in the fall in asset prices. To the extent that savers and investors are assured that they can exit at short notice and return without penalty, TARGET helped to retain trust in the currency if not in the

[19] See Brunnermeier et al. (2009: 13–18) for an intricate analysis of this "amplifying dynamic" of asset price falls when banks experience funding and market illiquidity. The alternative view is summarized by Westermann (2014: 118–21) who stresses the policy failure (dynamic inconsistency and risk shifting) that results from maintaining payments despite capital flight.

[20] In Southern Europe, widespread insolvencies were prevented in the first instance by the prevalence of widespread self-employment in family businesses: personal savings compensated for negative equity (Creditreform 2012: 5–7). But these savings run out, of course, if stagnation continues.

banks of some countries. While it was a vehicle for capital flight, the quick unwinding of positions as shown in Figure 9.10 also suggests that this was a reversible process. TARGET thus helped to deal with the crisis on the liabilities side of banks (Brunnermeier et al. 2009: 16) which is crucial. But the payments system could not stop the credit crunch for the wider economy. It is one thing to help banks not to cut overdrafts immediately; it is quite another to extend credit for new business activity in an economy mired in recession. Hence, the protection given by TARGET did not neutralize the effects of capital flight, as the Spanish trade balance (Figure 9.7) illustrates. In fact, one might argue that TARGET cannot give enough protection in that it can do little to prevent the fall-out from capital flight onto credit to non-financial firms.

9.3.3 *Hedging against the Break-Up of the Euro Area?*

Capital flight was not confined to banks inside the EA, but the moves made by financial institutions to reduce their exposure to the five or six beleaguered member states were particularly strong. Cecchetti et al. (2012: 9–12) present circumstantial evidence that non-euro banks, mainly from the UK, instructed their subsidiaries to reduce their asset holdings in Greece, Ireland, Italy, Portugal, and Spain while they maintained their funding (deposit) base in those countries. With these funds, UK banks bought Treasury bonds in the core instead, again using their subsidiaries inside the EA. For example, the Spanish subsidiary of a UK bank bought Bunds, funded by Spanish deposits and possibly credit from the Eurosystem, while the German subsidiary held the payment it received from the Spanish partner institution as excess reserves in the Bundesbank. The authors emphasize that this capital flow reversal via TARGET cannot have been triggered by perceived credit risk since UK banks maintained their stakes in their periphery subsidiaries.

These operations of UK banks amounted to hedging against the break-up of the euro. In the event of break-up, the assets in the core were likely to revalue while the liabilities in the periphery were expected to devalue. Hedging was better conducted through subsidiaries residing in the EA rather than through the headquarters in London: the management presumably feared that in the case of a break-up, banks established inside the EA would be treated more favorably than those from outside (Cecchetti et al. 2012: 10–11; Chen et al. 2012: 20). Figures 9.11 and 9.12 provide evidence, showing how UK banks increased their exposure to the German public sector dramatically, if only temporarily. At the same time, the overall exposure to the five countries under siege dropped, albeit less dramatically (Figure 9.11). With the exception of Ireland, UK banks shunned the periphery public sector in particular, and this tended to be persistent (Figure 9.12).

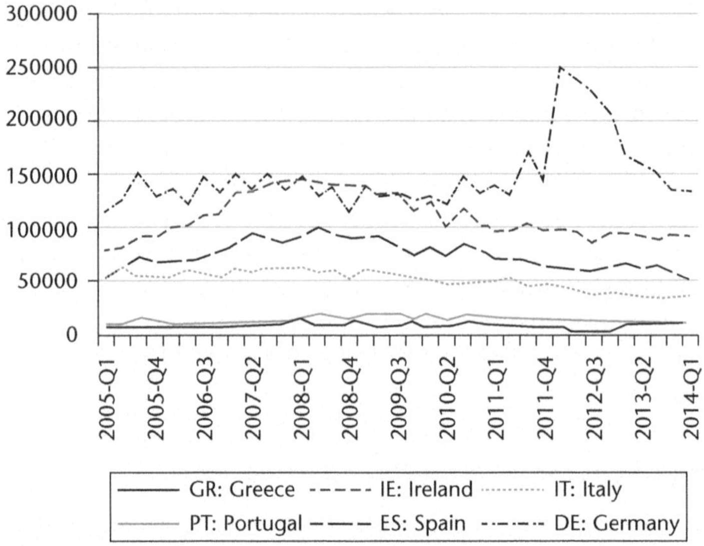

Figure 9.11. Exposure of UK banks on an ultimate risk basis (in € millions)
Source: BIS consolidated banking statistics; own calculations

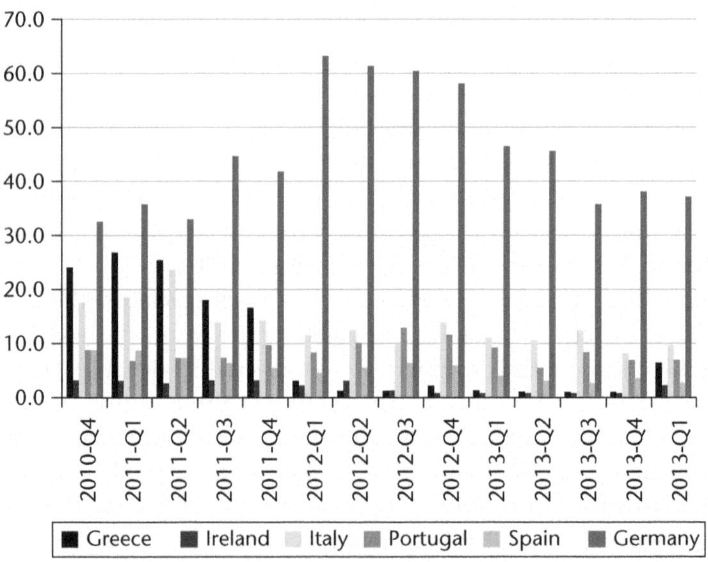

Figure 9.12. Share of UK bank exposure to public sectors (in percentages), 2010-Q4 to 2014-Q1
Source: BIS consolidated banking statistics; own calculations

This situation arose in the six months before ECB President Mario Draghi gave his momentous speech to an investment bankers' forum in London, assuring them that the ECB would do whatever it takes to save the euro (Draghi 2012).[21] At the same time, the TARGET debate reached boiling point in Germany. It is arguable that Draghi's speech, announcing a new monetary instrument full of legal uncertainties, could not have achieved quite the impact it did if there had not been an institution to underpin his claim. TARGET processed the capital flight to hedge against redenomination risk but also prevented it from causing massive disruption. The underlying risk, a break-up of the EA, was beyond any market actors' control; yet collective panic could bring it about. TARGET was an insurance mechanism that helped to sustain the euro despite an existential threat (Bordo 2014).

9.4 TARGET and the Political Economy of Insurance

Contrary to what the heated debate about TARGET imbalances conveyed, the European payments system provided insurance services to a diversity of users. It was neither a progressive nor a regressive transfer mechanism, but spread the risk from a breakdown of interbank lending across the Eurosystem of central banks, just as ISA did in the US. The diversity of users was not simply a matter of core and periphery (Buiter and Rahbari 2012: 48). The cross-border exchange of claims and liabilities benefited current-account surplus and deficit countries, wealth holders and trading companies, domestic savers and foreign investors, euro and non-euro area banks. For some, the value of the insurance consisted in maintaining trade flows and in permitting gradual adjustment to a breakdown of credit. For others, the value of insurance was the ability to secure property rights despite the increasing fragility of the domestic banking system and a non-negligible probability that the currency union could break up.

When the "accident" of a collapse of interbank markets happened and affected so many, TARGET performed the functions that markets no longer performed. In normal times, debt finance is a private form of risk sharing. For example, trade finance allows exporting firms to pass on their claim with the associated credit risk to a bank, rather than have to lend to importers themselves. Yet, as the literature discussed in Chapter 3 explained, risk sharing through debt tends to fail when it is needed most. Equity markets spread the risk among all shareholders but they cannot provide certain services, such as

[21] See Section 7.2.2 for an analysis of the OMT program and the political context of this speech.

short-term trade finance. And sharp movements of share prices can become the transmission mechanism for banking crises.

Systemic market failure is always the result of interdependent risks. A sudden stop of trade finance, capital flight, and the potential break-up of the euro were the interdependent risks that materialized after 2008: when interbank markets froze, trade finance became more difficult immediately and capital flight gradually more opportune. By 2012, the specter of EA dissolution was raised: this in turn gave more reason for capital flight and reluctance to finance trade with certain countries. In the US, the fall in the price of securities had the same effect, confronting investment banks with acute funding illiquidity that made them sell assets, depressing the price of securities and other shares further, rendering markets illiquid (Brunnermeier and Sannikov 2013: 354–9). No private insurance can deal with such interdependent risks since the insurers themselves become victims of the market sentiment that gives rise to the insurance claims against them.

TARGET insures a system, it does not make pay-outs or even grant particular awards. For the political economy of insurance, this is key to understanding the puzzles mentioned in the introduction: why was TARGET not subject to political market failure even when the arcane institution was attacked severely in Germany and apparent exposure extremely high? The US comparison is instructive for answering this question: no such public debate about ISA imbalances occurred in the US. They created no excitement even among Republican members of Congress and Tea Party members who watched every move of the Federal Reserve with utmost suspicion (Broz 2013: 23–8). In his extremely useful report on how ISA works, Wolman (2013: 128) inserted an interesting thought experiment: would the accumulation of balances by the New York Fed create "the same uproar... that it has created in Europe" if these balances were not annually redressed? He gives two reasons for why this is unlikely. First of all, Federal Reserve districts do not correspond to national or even state borders. And second, the accumulation of ISA balances in New York does not reflect a strong economy but its status as a financial center.

It is tempting to read this as the reasoning of a realist political economist: like it or not, the EA is a monetary union of nation states that represent the interests, first and foremost, of domestic constituencies. The union and its nationalist discontents will always come to the fore and trump collective action in a crisis. US history provides some counter-evidence to this nation-state-centric realism, however: the attempt of the Chicago Fed and other district central banks in 1933 to protect their gold reserves by not accepting checks from New York at par shows that quiet cooperation is not guaranteed even if members are part of a larger political union. This happened even though districts were as unrelated to federal state boundaries then as they are now. The institutions of federal monetary policymaking before the 1935

Act provided both incentives and the capacity for non-cooperation (Eichengreen et al. 2014: 18–19).

Furthermore, while the uproar against TARGET occurred in a strong economy of the union, it neither originated nor resonated in the corridors of power in Berlin and Frankfurt. In what might be seen as counter-evidence, a leaked letter by the Bundesbank President to the ECB in February 2012 actually just reiterated Jens Weidmann's well-known request that collateral standards in refinancing operations should be raised (Ruhkamp 2012). His newspaper article on "What's behind TARGET2 balances?" shortly afterwards made in essence the same point (Steen 2012). A rise in collateral standards, if undertaken as requested, would have amounted to a general tightening of liquidity provisions, among them bank credit for TARGET transactions. But it would not have prevented TARGET from processing payments.

It is true that the central banks administering the European payments system map onto member states: the Bundesbank is the German central bank, the Banco de España is the central bank of Spain. Yet, the underlying bank claims and liabilities do not map onto member states: as outlined in the context of Figures 9.10 and 9.11, a Bundesbank claim and a Banco de España liability can reflect transactions between the German and the Spanish subsidiary of a UK bank. In other words, the banks responsible for the build-up of TARGET claims by the Bundesbank were not all German banks. The infrastructure of member central banks administering a payments system is used freely by banks regardless of their national identity. And if losses from the UK bank's TARGET transactions were to materialize, they would be shared by all central banks in the Eurosystem. In this "deterritorialization," TARGET and ISA are actually similar.

Hence, another than the realist explanation seems to be called for. The theory of collective action as introduced in Chapter 2 suggests political market failures, thwarted by the universal insurance character of the insurance provided. TARGET was designed as a cost-effective and robust unified payments platform for cross-border transactions between private parties. It was not designed as insurance of trade finance against capital flight. Yet it turned out to have this universal collective insurance feature and this was quite important for its success: quasi-mandatory, basic in its benefits, covering a broad range of economic sectors against a risk that had not been anticipated and for which coverage was not predefined. It could therefore not only deal with interdependent risks but also uncertainty. However, the social usefulness of an institution as it has evolved to govern the commons is rarely the reason for why it was created in the first place. The by-product theory of collective action tells us that TARGET had to be universal insurance by accident for it to come about: ex ante, universalism is a demanding form of solidarity. It requires considerable trust in other members and/or the robustness of the institution since risk sharing is not conditional on prior contributions and not targeted on the deserving. This should have made it susceptible to all kinds of political market failure: from adverse selection (no prior contributions), moral hazard (no co-payments), commitment (no targeting), and misperception (no targeting on the "deserving").

The political campaign against TARGET in Germany was both an indication of the commitment and the misperception problems that could have led to changes in its set-up, for instance to prevent capital flight. It is likely that such changes would have made capital flight worse, a point to which we come back below. They did not come to pass. Ironically, this political robustness was in all likelihood a consequence of the political attack on TARGET: it provoked a very public defense from a wide variety of sources, not only the central banks themselves but also scholars and journalists, not only in Europe but also in the US. Thus, the payments system became a manifestation of monetary solidarity in the sense of this study: it is now a deliberate institution of risk sharing that has this function officially acknowledged and endorsed.

The political economy of insurance also helps us to explain more specifically why German authorities were unresponsive to the TARGET debate and did not question the rules of the payments system. Sub-groups within risk pools are a threat to insurance if they can (a) identify their interests, for instance as nation states, and if they can (b) act on their interests, for instance because they are a strong economy. While current-account flows give rise to identifiable deficit and surplus members, smooth processing of payments benefits exporters and importers alike. In the case of capital flight, it is even difficult to identify the nationality of those on the run and the banks receiving them, although the receding demand of German banks for Bundesbank credit suggests that they were the main beneficiaries of Germany's safe-haven status. Hence, even though Germany is a strong economy and not a financial center that would necessarily welcome financial inflows, its government and monetary authorities had no interest in disrupting a mechanism that was supporting its strong export economy and providing an exit route for its banks. Even the prospect of losses in the case of major defaults of a banking system on TARGET claims did not give the German authorities much cause for concern, as every member is liable for their pro rata share in the loss (Buiter and Rahbari 2012: 56). In fact, it would be more plausible for other member states to rebel against sharing in the loss, given that they did not benefit from a safe-haven status (and thus low interest rates and abundant credit) as did Germany. But members' interests were aligned as regards the desirability of maintaining a functioning payments system and of preventing a break-up of the EA, in which case TARGET losses would not be the major headache anyhow.

The safe-haven status of some members affected, however, the availability of credit in other countries from which capital fled. This created pressure for adjustment in countries with current-account deficits. A credit squeeze would reduce net imports over time. But this might not be the "right" amount of pressure: the payments system may make capital flight much easier and cheaper than it would be otherwise (Garber 2010: 5; De Grauwe 2011: 3–5), inflicting even more credit squeeze on countries already in dire straits. That capital flight was cheap and easy is undeniable and the flip side of the insurance service provided. The painful credit squeeze should lay to rest the ever present concerns about moral hazard.

It is conceivable that the availability of insurance inside a monetary union reduces the incentives for capital flight. At least this is what the theory of self-fulfilling speculative currency attacks would lead one to expect, a literature that flourished after the 1992–3 ERM crisis (e.g. Flood and Marion 1996; Krugman 1996; Obstfeld 1996). Members of a pegged exchange rate regime still have their own currencies, so the agreed parity can be doubted, however fixed it may seem. If asset holders come to expect a devaluation of the national currency in some distant future, they will try to pre-empt others in order to avoid the loss. Foreign exchange reserves are limited and can be expanded only with the consent of other monetary authorities. Asset owners in a country with its own currency also know that the authorities are left largely on their own in defending it. Hence they may fear the imposition of capital controls as an emergency measure and thus try to get out before they are imposed. If some asset owners get out, along with a sufficient number of like-minded asset holders, they will bring about devaluation even if the parity was sustainable absent an attack.

The incentives—and the ability—to impose capital controls existed even in the EU's Single Market before a banking union came into force since 2014. As outlined in Chapter 7, national authorities imposed hidden capital controls through so-called "liquidity ring fencing." Italian banks complained that the German prudential supervisor Bafin forced subsidiaries of Italian banks in Germany to shore up their balance sheets instead of repatriating excess liquidity to their Italian headquarters (Enrich and Galloni 2012; Arnold 2014). In the absence of collective safety nets, national supervisors tried to protect their domestic banking systems and thus created externalities for others. The example also shows how this lack of coordination during a crisis leads to risks being shifted onto the weakest parts of an incomplete union.

All three features of TARGET that prevent a self-fulfilling attack—no depreciation of the currency as long as the capital flight stays within the EA, no limits on TARGET balances, and freedom of capital movement—reduce the incentives for capital flight that a functioning payments system otherwise facilitates. In theory, it is not clear which effect dominated in the EA crisis and more research is clearly needed. TARGET's ability to act as conduit for as well as a disincentive to capital flight may have made it more robust as an institution because this ambivalence gave all members a stake in it: it made it even less clear ex ante who would benefit most from the elastic liquidity supply through TARGET.

The EA's payments system thus functioned like universal insurance that covers both anticipated and unanticipated risks. Coverage is not based on contributions but on membership. The payments system has created "a community of risk" different from the nation state while the insurance provided does not depend on political union. In other words, TARGET served the "generalized and reciprocal self-interest" (Baldwin 1990: 299) of member states on which monetary solidarity rests.

10

The Experiment of the Euro

This book has proposed a theory of monetary integration that can explain why diverse polities may want to use, and indeed came to use, a common currency. Members of a monetary union can diversify risks to national income that arise both from exogenous shocks and from financial integration. Monetary solidarity between geopolitical entities is, however, rarely the primary and straightforward goal of currency unification. In the US, a common currency was imposed on the defeated Southern parts of the nation and its services adjusted to diverse regional needs in an extended trial and error process (Chapter 4). Crucial elements of monetary solidarity, such as lending of last resort and federal resolution of state banks, were established only as a consequence of the Great Depression. In Europe, monetary integration came about as the side effect of forces within national democracies trying to get more favorable conditions for domestic business and employment; governments supported this in their attempt to transform monetary constraints on domestic policymaking (Chapter 5). The policy framework on which they could agree was based on separate risk-allocation channels, with primarily the monetary channel available for collective risk sharing. Fiscal and financial channels were largely confined to reining in spillovers from domestic problems (Chapter 6). The EA crisis has shaken this framework to the core. The need for risk sharing has been explicitly acknowledged in two high-level reports (van Rompuy et al. 2012; Juncker et al. 2015). Critics emphasize that there is still no fiscal federation, but there has been substantial institution building including some fiscal risk sharing (Chapter 7).

Reaping the benefits of risk diversification requires collective action on a continuous basis to govern the commons. As in all political integration, citizens must tolerate that domestic policy choices may be constrained by considerations of what they do to other members of the monetary union. In a well-functioning union, they can expect reciprocal consideration from other members. In the set-up of the EA, it was anticipated that a common monetary policy would require national adaptation and fiscal demand management have cross-border effects, but the externalities of financial-sector regulation and integration were underestimated. Coordination of these three policy areas—and their interfaces—is essential for the functioning of monetary unions between capitalist democracies, in which financial markets are the gatekeepers to investment and employment. The preceding discussion has provided empirical evidence for this view not only from the crisis of the EA but also the monetary-financial history of the United States.

This evidence shows that, while political market failures can be overcome, there are tradeoffs involved in their solutions and hence ongoing contestation can be expected in the governance of the commons. A recurrent example in both the euro and the dollar area was the tradeoff between addressing externalities, notably the negative feedback loop between failing banks and sovereigns, and avoiding moral hazard, specifically fiscal profligacy or lax credit practices. The more externalities are internalized through risk pooling, the greater the risk of moral hazard, and vice versa. The protracted EA crisis suggests that the monetary-financial union of fiscally sovereign states errs on the side of preventing moral hazard. The long drawn-out process of forming a less crisis-prone US union indicates that coming down more on one or the other side in this tradeoff entails a political process of trial and error that might be shortened, but cannot be replaced, by expert-led policy advice.

The point of departure for this book was the case for diversity. The main argument was that there is little room for risk sharing and monetary solidarity without diversity of members. Yet, one may still wonder whether a monetary union can cope with all kinds of diversity or whether there are limits. The first section addresses this question. In line with the political-economic paradox of diversity, it argues that there are no limits as to how much economic diversity can be accommodated, but political limits do exist. They affect the risk-sharing mechanisms that authorities are able and willing to sustain. The theory of rational interstate cooperation would lead us to expect that the economic gains from diverse ("heterogeneous") membership can be the basis of cooperation, but it will be precarious. Alternatives exist to voluntary cooperation between states, above all hegemony (Snidal 1995: 62–7).

The second section discusses what policy conclusions the risk-sharing approach implies, in comparison with other major proposals. The suggestion that the monetary union needs completion has been eloquently promoted and theoretically well founded by De Grauwe (2013) as well as Jones and Underhill (2014). A different emphasis can be found in a literature on trilemmas of EA governance: it tries to identify sensible policy choices in the face of conflicting goals (Pisani-Ferry 2012; Obstfeld 2013). The discussion here makes essentially two points. First of all, the promotion of monetary solidarity is not the same as the pursuit of economic integration. Indeed, monetary solidarity may be better served by the deliberate and coordinated segmentation of financial and labor markets. Nor does monetary solidarity require fiscal union in the form of a central budget: partial fiscal risk sharing, particularly in the form of insurance and reinsurance against bank failure, can contain the destabilizing potential created by the dependence of financial stability on fiscal resources (the "diabolic loop").

The last section explores two specific issues that European, in contrast to international and comparative, political economy raises. There is first the time-honored problem of the EU's and the EA's democratic deficit. Monetary solidarity as a by-product of currency union is not legitimated by a democratic process. In the context of US monetary-financial history, I have argued that governing the commons is inherently a process of political integration. But this does not mean that political integration necessarily occurs by democratic means: it can occur by accepting the jurisdiction of a transnational court or enhancing the powers of a supranational central bank. Such political integration has to draw on other principles of legitimation than democracy, notably mutual advantage. While this is primarily the basis for the legitimacy of market-type exchanges, we find it in other forms of collective action, notably welfare-state programs and corporatism (Baldwin 1990; Lijphart and Crepaz 1991). It is crucial, if this form of legitimation is relied on, to leave members plenty of leeway for national representation and "reasonable disagreement" (Bellamy and Weale 2015).

The second issue of European political economy concerns the role of expertise in European policymaking. Because there is limited democratic contestation by government and opposition at the EU level, expert policy advice in European political economy often falls on fertile ground. The latest fashion in academic analysis quickly finds its way into the corridors of Brussels; risk sharing is no exception (Juncker et al. 2015). This places a particular demand on the political dimension of academic political economy. It is part of the research effort of expert advisors to recognize how the adoption of their ideas will be affected by the incentives and constraints of policy actors.

10.1 Diversity as Economic Opportunity and Political Challenge

The protagonists of European as well as US monetary integration were fully aware of the diversity that characterized the prospective members of each union: the mottos of "unity in diversity" (EU) and "e pluribus unum" (US) indicate as much. In the US, politically salient diversity was framed around the difference between agricultural-rural states and states dominated by industry and commerce. The underlying economic split of interest was that the regional economies of the South and West depended on elastic seasonal credit while the Northern and Eastern states preferred long-term nominal stability, a split which had particular implications for the choice of currency regime (Frieden 2015a: 50). In Western Europe, salient differences were inflation performance and current-account positions. These created different vulnerabilities to exchange rate instability, especially when the US dollar weakened against the D-Mark (James 2012: 343). This could be framed as an underlying split between political economies dominated by export sectors, which favored low inflation and stable exchange rates, and those dominated by domestically oriented employment, which favored the easy pass-through of rising costs into prices and adjustable exchange rates. This is the split that the comparative capitalisms literature stresses (Hall 2012; Iversen et al. 2016; Johnston 2016). A somewhat less salient split was that between rich and poor members, between those with a tendency to stagnate at a high level, and those hoping to catch up in leaps and bounds. The latter split became ever more important with Southern and Eastern enlargement of the EU and can explain why some new EU member states were so keen to join the EA even during the crisis.

Obviously, diversity makes for different interests in and expectations about the benefits from monetary integration. These differences can be made compatible, but this takes work. Institutional development in the US dollar area eventually reconciled monetary stability and growth-enhancing credit supply, but such reconciliation did not occur until the post-war era, after the specie standard was abolished and new practices of monetary policy, oriented to macroeconomic stabilization, became established. National money and finance became much less divisive. The exchange rate regime of Bretton Woods laid the foundation of the dollar's "exorbitant privilege,"[1] which has survived into the post-Bretton Woods period. In the EA, the compatibility of low inflation and low (market) interest rates was a decisive precondition for a diverse membership to sign up to the experiment of the euro (Section 5.1). Old divisions between hard- and soft-currency areas were thus reformulated and transformed into benefits for both sides. This transformation does not do away with old tensions, although they may become more muted as new divisions and tensions emerge.

The comparative capitalisms literature notes two divisions that are supposedly impossible to reconcile without profoundly altering one regime (Section 6.2.2). First, member states in the North and South allegedly have structurally high or low inflation rates, due to different wage-bargaining regimes that give priority to exposed or sheltered sectors (Carlin 2013; Johnston 2012). Real interest rates then become too low for the inflationary members, fueling asset bubbles, and too high for the stable member

[1] The term was coined by Valéry Giscard d'Estaing in the mid-1960s, when he was French finance minister (Canzoneri et al. 2013: 2n).

economies, leading to stagnation. A second and closely related division is that they supposedly run either current-account surpluses or deficits due to institutions that foster or hinder developing competitive industries. One could add to this other apparent incompatibilities. Member states differ in the role that the financial system plays in supporting growth: patient capital is conducive to steady but relatively low growth, while impatient capital may lead to high average but volatile growth that affords high-risk premia.

These analyses take outcomes like inflation and current-account balances as indicators of institutions that embed certain preferences or tastes. But this ignores the ways that policymakers, especially those under devaluation pressures, used to engineer regime changes through currency unification, and thereby change historic inflation and current-account outcomes. In this they partly succeeded, as the following balance sheet indicates:

- A common monetary policy can achieve a downward convergence of inflation rates, while at the same time former high-inflation countries benefit from low real interest rates for businesses and households. This is exactly what happened, albeit at the cost of financial instability in booming regions and low investment in stagnating regions (Sections 5.1.2 and 7.1).
- Real interest rates fell to historically low levels for all EA members, although more so for the member states that later got into difficulties than the others (Figure 5.1). This manifestation of the Walters effect was an endogenous risk of the hard currency's success. It does not have to lead to boom-bust cycles but can be reined in by macroprudential policies, counter-cyclical property taxation, and long-term measures such as housing policies and urban planning. Large heterogeneous currency areas like the US and the UK have always been subject to regional Walters effects (Section 6.2.2). Low interest rates can spur catch-up growth and afford a longer-term horizon of investments, although at the cost of a higher risk that all ends in a regional bust.
- Permanent current-account surpluses and deficits have the potential to induce crises, but it is important to understand why they occur. Regions in which indigenous producers keep on losing out against import competition will become poor, but they will not become bankrupt unless the imbalances are financed. Capital flows sustained very large imbalances in the EA, leading policymakers to call for new early warning mechanisms, such as the Macroeconomic Imbalances Procedure, in the absence of exchange rate pressures. When capital flows were reversed and interbank markets froze, the common payments system protected member states against a sudden stop of trade finance despite the vast imbalances and the ensuing credit crunch (Chapter 9).

- The US experience shows how the end of a credit boom and collapse of asset prices can be prevented from spilling over into state public finances: lending of last resort to the sovereign and federal resolution capacities for state banks were decisive interventions that were and are still not available in the EA (Chapter 4). The EA has now introduced elements of a banking union that explicitly address the negative feedback loop, although they have not provided full fiscal backing for the ECB or the Single Resolution Mechanism. To keep boom-bust cycles at bay, the EA will have to suppress growth, which given current high debt levels runs the risk of long drawn-out stagnation weighed down by heavy debt service (Sandbu 2015: 106–17). The slow-motion crash of Italy's banking system, noticeable since 2016, is driven by a rising level of non-performing loans, an ominous sign of problems ahead.
- Growth patterns can change and do change despite the institutional forces emphasized (for valid reasons) by the comparative capitalism literature. After World War II, West Germany was a debtor nation (to the tune of 85–90 percent of GDP, all external) and by 1951 it seemed to have fallen back into its "structural" deficit position of the pre-war years (Ritschl 2012: 86–7). It was given a fresh start through a generous debt-relief program and subsequently became a permanent surplus country until German unification led to a domestic investment boom in the 1990s. Ireland has undergone similar fundamental change in its growth pattern, and developed from a poverty-stricken net emigration country to a magnet for people and firms to feed its phenomenal catch-up growth.

These arguments suggest that there is no such thing as a Southern European growth regime that could not be accommodated within the existing EA. Section 6.1 argued in some detail that the five countries which actually needed external assistance were quite different in the run-up to their crises. They obviously had vulnerabilities that financial markets picked up for a reason; but so did countries like Belgium that were spared an attack in bond markets. And vulnerabilities could have quickly developed for supposedly strong economies, like Austria, France, and Germany, the banking systems of which held large claims on Southern and Eastern Europe.

This is not to say that all is well with risk diversification in the EA: market interest rates were arguably too low for former high-inflation countries (Walters effect), destabilizing them in the process, given that no other measures were taken or pro-cyclical public expenditure even fueled the bubble. This had its counterpart in US states like Nevada. Moreover, payments systems like TARGET and ISA cannot prevent capital flight; they actually make flight easier (if also more easily reversible), forcing debtor countries into one-sided adjustment. Again, the EA is not unique in this respect. Of the twenty OECD regions that fared worst between 2000 and 2010, Michigan had the sharpest drop in per capita income and three more US states feature in the list (OECD 2014b: 41).[2]

The upshot is that there is no diversity that cannot, in principle, provide an opportunity for mutually beneficial risk sharing. Imbs and Mauro (2007; see also Callen et al. 2015) tried to find out which groups of countries would benefit most from risk sharing. This would come about by their citizens holding and consuming out of identically structured portfolios of assets. If one member experienced a decline in national output growth, national income would be topped up by the booming economies in the risk pool. It follows that the portfolio should comprise assets from countries with the most asynchronous (negatively correlated) business cycles, as this maximizes the benefits from pooling. The computations for a world sample of over seventy countries, using output growth rates as the measure of volatility, find quite sizeable diversification benefits. The biggest gains result from pooling with countries from other continents and with very different income levels. For instance, a sample of greatly benefiting countries includes Columbia and Costa Rica but also New Zealand and Sweden (Imbs and Mauro 2007: 15, 22–3). The same holds for exchange reserve pooling arrangements between emerging market groups: there are much lower "undiversifiable" exchange rate risks if pools are created across continents rather than regionally. However, these potential members of a risk pool have to consider the enforcement costs necessary to ensure that booming economies really compensate those in a recession (Imbs and Mauro 2007: 7). The authors reckon that the difficulties of enforcement are likely to deter such arrangements across continents and income levels (Imbs and Mauro 2007: 37–9). For instance, it could easily be portrayed as unfair if booming Columbia had to compensate recessionary Sweden. The perceived unfairness of an insurance arrangement is likely to affect enforceability between very unequal parties.

It is thus politically very unlikely that the maximum economic benefits from risk sharing can ever be realized. In this political sense, diversity limits risk sharing and solidarity. The post-crisis distinctions between a periphery and a core, South and North of the EA, GIPISC and the rest, stand for this politically constraining take on diversity. This political-economic paradox that the more beneficial risk diversification would be, the less likely it is to come about, could be detected in the management of the crisis through crisis, or "failing forward" as Jones et al. (2016) put it succinctly. *Monnet's curse* that

[2] The US states adjusted largely through (less) labor utilization, in contrast to (lower) labor productivity. In fact, in Georgia, South Carolina, and Ohio workers were fired faster than firms' revenues declined, raising labor productivity in the process. Interestingly, Spanish regions and the Algarve in Portugal showed the same pattern. French and Italian regions adjusted largely by firms hoarding labor which came at the cost of productivity per worker.

Europe will be forged in crisis materialized in the sense that there was not simply failure to address the crisis. Rather, solutions were achieved: the EA did not break up and a banking union and various other institutions were created. But these reforms reflected the concerns and domestic constraints of those providing guarantees: renewed commitments to fiscal restraint were introduced and strong precautions against moral hazard were taken by imposing high political costs on borrowers under conditional lending programs. Furthermore, the threat of financial market "discipline" has been maintained, insofar as all reforms stopped short of putting two effective circuit breakers for negative bank-sovereign feedback loops in place: joint fiscal backing for the ECB and for the Single Resolution Mechanism. Not all of these limits on risk sharing were imposed by governments. In the case of the OMT, analyzed in Section 7.2.2, popular resistance materialized in the involvement of Germany's constitutional court. Its decision put the Bundesbank in a very strong position to determine the specifics of the program.

The outcome of crisis management was a limited form of monetary solidarity. One alternative is that a hegemonic power takes on the task of stabilization and contributes disproportionately to it. The German government was reluctant to fill this role (Bulmer and Paterson 2013), constrained as it was by weak international legitimacy and domestic opposition. The Merkel government insisted that every contingent commitment of fiscal resources, such as sovereign bailouts and bank resolution, was based on institutionalized burden sharing according to the key provided by the share in the ECB's paid-up capital (Section 7.2). For their part, other governments resisted Germany's substantial influence, suggesting that hegemony is also affected by the political-economic paradox of diversity: economic strength cannot overcome resistance to alien power. Germany's reluctance to take on a disproportionate burden, and the reluctance of other members to accept German hegemony, ensured that monetary solidarity was the only way forward.

But political market failures can still undermine the environment in which risk sharing is mutually beneficial. There is the inclination of the fortunate to renege on their commitments as well as the tendency to see the others as the authors of their misfortunes. There is always some risk taking that may have been incentivized by the availability of a safety net and can be portrayed as moral hazard if things go wrong.[3] Moreover, the characteristics of another member's political economy that are different tend to be perceived as responsible for any

[3] Westermann (2014: 121) specifies the tragedy in the context of TARGET as follows: "Let us consider the national central bank's (or national regulators) decision problem when assessing whether a private bank is solvent or not: it will compare the marginal benefit of not having to bear the resolution cost for taxpayers, with the average cost, which might occur in terms of inflation, or write-downs on losses at the later stage. The former (inflation) would spread across Europe in an integrated economy, and the latter (losses) will be shared with the ECB's capital key."

calamity that befalls them. Support is then made conditional on these characteristics being transformed: all have to converge on some "best practice" (Juncker et al. 2015: 4; van Rompuy et al. 2012: 9).

The tendency to regulate other members in one's own (idealized) image is a symptom of political market failures. Indicators of this tendency included structural conditionality in bailout programs, which had little to do with the underlying causes of the country's financial difficulties (Section 6.1.2), and the tightening up of fiscal surveillance (Section 7.2.1). It created the impression that a German consensus was taking hold of the EA (Bronk and Jacoby 2013: 20–9; Blyth 2013). These political processes may mean that diversity in a heterogeneous union diminishes over time.

The risk-sharing perspective on international cooperation suggests that it is imperative for the pool to maintain the diversity it has. Existing arrangements must nurture diversity for its own sake but also in order to keep up the rationale for collective action. Bronk and Jacoby (2013) endorse mutual recognition and the open method of coordination on these grounds. Franzese and Mosher (2002) argue that trade and capital flows reinforce domestic institutional equilibria counteracting convergence. If so, institutional inertia and economic rationale are aligned. But political market failures work against these diversity-preserving forces.

It will be crucial to dispel the impression of one-sided transfers, in other words that only "the South" would gain from the risk-sharing arrangement or that "the North" has written all the rules in its favor. This was the lesson that can be taken from the example of TARGET: its insurance benefits were hard to pin down and so widespread that very diverse members had a stake in it. A migration regime can be set up such that it strikes a balance between more and less well-off member states. In migration, rules need to compromise between the imperative to rejuvenate the workforce and receive impulses for social innovation, on the one hand, and the desire to give additional opportunities to young people who cannot find adequate training and employment at home on the other. Similarly, banking regulation can find a compromise that gives (less than full) protection to creditors and debtors.

10.2 Policy Implications

The political economy of solidarity has two policy implications that differ significantly from other approaches. First, diversity has to be fostered rather than eliminated. Second, solidarity does not necessarily require "ever closer union," meaning ever more integration and centralized policy capacity. On the contrary, it can mean foregoing more integration so as not to jeopardize the risk sharing achieved. This can be illustrated with the arguments about financial integration and migration developed earlier in the book. The discussion in previous chapters has also raised doubts about whether more integration in the guise of a full fiscal union with a common budget would necessarily improve monetary solidarity.

These policy implications can be contrasted with others in the literature. They fall into two categories. One seeks to complete the incomplete policy architecture of the EA. Jones and Underhill (2014: 11) develop a theory that sees financial integration as the ultimate goal of currency unification and identify six crucial institutions of "Optimal Financial Areas."[4] They support their theory with historical case studies of Canada, the UK, and the US to show how (a functional equivalent of) the six institutions emerged. While none of them is perfect, Canada comes close (Jones and Underhill 2014: 27–8, 32, 36–7). Similarly, De Grauwe (2013) analyzes the "design failures" of the EA. He considers two in particular: national economies still experience boom-bust cycles that were not "disciplined into a union-wide dynamic" and probably even exacerbated by the one-size-has-to-fit-all monetary policy (De Grauwe 2013: 6–7). At the same time, currency unification has taken away national lenders of last resort which can lead to self-fulfilling liquidity and solvency crises. Completion requires a phasing in of banking and fiscal union, with the important intermediary steps of the ECB acting as sovereign lender of last resort and the adoption of mechanisms to force member states to symmetric macroeconomic adjustment. This "completion" approach to monetary-financial integration rests on the idea of finalité, a normative benchmark of a functioning union. The value of such studies is that they reveal how policy choices are guided by an overall goal. However, even if everybody did share the goal of ever closer union, this means very different things to different decision makers.

An alternative to completion is to optimize a tradeoff by choosing consistent combinations out of a trilemma. This is how two widely cited studies, one by Pisani-Ferry (2012) and the other by Obstfeld (2013), proceeded. The "new impossible trinity"[5] that Jean Pisani-Ferry (2012: 8–9) considered consists of the two norms of EA governance that there must not be monetary financing of public spending nor joint liability for public debt, alongside the fact of the political, legal, and economic interdependence of national banks and national public finances. It is consistent with the stability of the system to give up one

[4] The notion of Optimal Financial Areas is a deliberate attempt by the authors to propose an alternative to OCA theory. But the term does not do justice to the profound analysis of Jones and Underhill (2014) in that it is based on studies of existing, non-optimal currency unions, not deduced from some outdated economic model.

[5] It builds on the old impossible trinity stipulated by Robert Mundell suggesting that it is impossible to have simultaneously perfect capital mobility, stable exchange rates, and monetary policy autonomy (Pisani-Ferry 2012: 8).

of these elements of the trinity. Financial stability could be secured by breaking the link between national banking and national budgets and supervision. Sovereign debt crises could be prevented if the ECB's mandate was extended to allow lending of last resort to sovereigns, giving up on the norm of no monetary financing, or if a fiscal union was created by giving up the no-joint-liability norm. Pisani-Ferry believed, in January 2012, that fiscal union was politically the most likely option; we have seen, however, that incomplete versions of the other two have been partially realized instead, with the banking union agreed in June 2012 and the announcement of the OMT program a few weeks later (Sections 7.2.2 and 7.2.3).

Obstfeld's financial-fiscal trilemma takes off from the observation that "in today's global financial environment, financial integration and stand-alone national fiscal policy are not compatible with financial stability" (Obstfeld 2013: 24). Obstfeld endorses a mixture of banking and fiscal union, namely centralized banking supervision and joint fiscal liability for bank bailouts as a last-resort safety net when privately funded resolution mechanisms and deposit insurance are overwhelmed (Obstfeld 2013: 37–41; Shambaugh 2012: 205–6). This analysis, like that of Pisani-Ferry, is helpful in focusing on the hard policy choices facing decision makers and highlighting considerations of political economy. But while trilemmas are of great didactic value, they tend to become fuzzy and of little explanatory value when partial solutions become inconsistently implemented as time moves on.

The approach taken in this book was to set out the logically complete system of interfaces and channels of risk sharing that characterize any mature currency union (Tables 4.1, 5.1, 7.1). It is in this respect similar to the completion approach, especially of the more institutionalist variant of Jones and Underhill (2014).[6] But the emphasis of the analysis is on the entries that are left void and the risks that remain uninsured (Table 3.1). These *flaws by design* can be deliberate, in other words *flaws by design*, as the fear of moral hazard can justify less than complete insurance or the externality of market panic can be used to reinforce fragile commitments to fiscal rules. Hence, the approach concedes tradeoffs analogous to the "impossible trinity" framework. This systemic perspective generates no expectation of a small finite number of consistent policy choices, since the variety of political market failures and their inherent tradeoffs leave more possibilities open. Even so, this approach reveals risk-sharing priorities inherent in a policy framework, explains them in terms of political market failures or compromises, and assesses their costs in terms of missed risk-sharing opportunities.

[6] A variant of the systemic approach is Dolls et al. (2016), focusing on fiscal risk sharing. They start with a complete view of what a fiscal union can entail, along the lines of Fuest and Peichl (2012).

10.2.1 *Solidarity and Integration*

The "completion" and "impossible trinity" perspectives converge on one point: that any policy solution consists of more integration. The completion approach would "fix" the design failures of the EA with the adoption of more common policies and institutions (De Grauwe 2013). Those focusing on impossible trinities recommend choices that are more consistent with integration, which is taken as a fact. The thrust of Ostrom's work on governing the commons is, by contrast, to explore how collective solutions might be found without ceding power to a central authority. These solutions rely on parties' recognition of their interdependence, which brings both the prospect of gains from cooperation and the potential for conflict. Defining boundaries is an essential part of creating a sustainable commons, "as much a result as a cause of successful cooperation" (Snidal 1995: 51). Outcomes do not necessarily maximize gains from cooperation; rather, they find arrangements which are sustainable in terms of managing conflict. The incompatible growth literature points in a similar direction but suggests boundaries along country-regime lines (Section 6.2.2) while my approach suggests boundaries with regard to certain policy functions.

The creation and limitation of insurance pools reflects this balancing of cooperation and conflict. Risk sharing provides a reason to participate, but conflicts readily arise over perceived moral hazard. Insurance is such a "political success," as the great sociologist and historian of insurance, François Ewald, put it, because "[i]nsurance provides for a form of association which combines a maximum of socialization with a maximum of individualization. It allows people to enjoy the advantages of association while still leaving them the freedom to exist as individuals" (Ewald 1991: 204). Participation is sustained through "generalized and reciprocal self-interest," not ethical beliefs or community solidarity (Baldwin 1990: 299). By understanding cooperation between states in this way, it is evident that limits on integration can be necessary to maintain the common pool resource of a single currency and the insurance that comes with it.

The endogenous nature of risks that may arise in financial integration implies that integration can become itself the source of risks, so more is not always better. The adoption and extension of macroprudential policies exemplify this point. As outlined in Section 7.2.3, these measures try to prevent a common shock from turning into a systemic crisis (Hanson et al. 2011: 5). The turn to a macroprudential perspective follows from the insight that financial markets tend to cumulate risks due to their connectedness. Without appropriate safety nets and circuit breakers, financial integration is therefore not necessarily a channel of risk sharing but of shock propagation (Brunnermeier et al. 2009). Macroprudential instruments try to segment financial markets, by setting stricter conditions on banks as regards capital or liquidity if a regional market is overheating. Research done at the ECB suggests that macroprudential tools can be used to tackle the EA's imbalances by enabling monetary conditions to be differentiated along regional lines (Brzoza-Brzezina et al. 2013: 5). Monetary solidarity in this context means that authorities support each other's regulatory endeavors, imposing constraints such as capital surcharges on banks under their supervision if they might otherwise extend credit to the overheating market in question. The Basel III framework, transposed into EU legislation, requires exactly such collective action. It stipulates policy coordination to prevent contagion through market integration.

Economic migration, regarded by the mainstream theory of monetary integration as an adjustment mechanism replacing the exchange rate, is another example in which sustainable risk sharing does not call for ever closer market and policy integration. Full integration of labor markets, in the sense of seamless migration, cannot be the maxim of social solidarity. If we take regions rather than individuals as the unit of analysis, we see an inherent regressive bias in migration that only the politically most unlikely redistribution scheme could neutralize. The benefits of migration accrue predominantly to destination countries, after all they are destinations because they offer more gainful opportunities. Origin countries lose, on average, younger and better-educated members of the workforce, for whom they provided child care and schooling and may later have to provide some benefits for their retirement. In other words, migrants tend to spend the economically unproductive and fiscally expensive phases of life in their home countries and thus disadvantage their home country further. All this can be ameliorated, but research suggests that the net costs for origin countries are the mirror image of the net benefits for destination countries (Huber and Trondl 2012; Section 7.3). EU rules on exportability of benefits and non-discrimination of migrants and their families try to redress some of the inherently regressive tendencies of migration, but this is controversial and has to tread carefully or risk a backlash.

Most discussion of the effects of EU migration has focused on the destination countries:[7] particularly on the question of whether migration undermines their welfare states and promotes a "race to the bottom." The "integrationist" solution would be to establish a common social security system, operating through a central budget. In my view, this is no solution at all, as it is politically unsustainable. It would at best be feasible at a low common denominator. Furthermore, the existing EU rules which coordinate, but do not harmonize, the social security systems of member states are

[7] This is changing now, as the study of the IMF (Atoyan et al. 2016) indicates.

workable in contrast to what many critics say.[8] The guiding principle is non-discrimination to ensure that acquired entitlements can be exported and individuals with a real link to their place of residence get benefits irrespective of their nationality. This cannot protect resident low-income workers entirely from competition; but welfare states can contain competition between migrants and low-income residents by setting minimum conditions and by underpinning them with redistributive measures. Coordination in favor of individual entitlements rather than systems harmonization strikes a balance between at least three norms: social solidarity with EU citizens, the imperative of safeguarding the viability of welfare states at each level of development, and the obligation to adapt domestic institutions to support and facilitate integration.

The US comparison on migration and financial stability (Chapters 8 and 9) should caution both against deterministic pessimism that a heterogeneous union can never work and against the optimism of integration as complete risk sharing. Even if the latter could be attained, more complete integration could backfire. The theory of collective action, in markets and policymaking, suggests that more complete risk sharing encourages more risk taking. Some of it will be moral hazard that shifts downside risks on others, some of it will be perceived as moral hazard once the downside risk materializes even though the risk takers acted in good faith. Rightly or wrongly, any realization of downside risks can be perceived as willful free riding on other members, undermining trust in risk-sharing arrangements. The more comprehensive these arrangements are, the more likely this is to happen. More complete risk sharing, prioritizing the internalization of externalities through closer integration, can thus undermine solidarity.

10.2.2 *Fiscal Risk Sharing through Reinsurance*

The limits of fiscal risk sharing in the EA have been noted in Chapters 5–7. Many commentators see that the only way forward for the EA is a fiscal union.[9] This can mean a number of things, as Fuest and Peichl (2012) note in their useful survey: (1) fiscal surveillance; (2) a crisis-resolution mechanism; (3) a joint guarantee for government debt; (4) redistributive transfers between unequal regions; and (5) a centralized budget at the EU level. The EA

[8] See, for instance, Chalmers et al. (2016b: 15) where the authors criticize, in the same paragraph, that the EU tries to replace national citizenship by giving migrants equal access to entitlements but that its way of dealing with the inherent tension also makes migrants "second-class denizens" exposed to racism and marginalization.

[9] See Bargain et al. (2013: 378–83) for a literature review; the authors argue against a full-fledged federal budget (see also Dolls et al. 2016). De Grauwe (2011, 2013) and all authors mentioned above (Jones and Underhill 2014; Pisani-Ferry 2012; Obstfeld 2013) endorse at least a common debt instrument ("Eurobond").

framework that was in place by mid-2016 retained the original emphasis on (1) fiscal surveillance and had (4) minimal transfers in the form of regional funds. In the course of the crisis, (2) was added, in the guise of the ESM. We have seen that this left the ECB in the role of substituting for (3) and (5) over several years. Its bond-buying programs first compensated for the limitations of the ESM, and provided lending of last resort to governments through the back door. Since early 2015, quantitative easing has continued this process but also substitutes for a coordinated fiscal stimulus (5), in the face of negative inflation rates. These monetary innovations highlight that automatic stabilizers at the member state level have been switched off with the focus on fiscal consolidation.

The functional theory of fiscal federalism supports central financing for macroeconomic stabilization and redistribution. However, fiscal federalism has ambiguous effects on stabilization, as was noted for the US in Chapters 4 and 8. States shift the cost of bank rescues, macroeconomic stabilization, and social security to the federal level. This is fine as long as the political support for federal risk sharing is there, but, even in a long-lasting political union like the US, this should not be taken for granted. The functional logic leaves very little for lower levels of government to do (Oates 2005: 352) and ignores their agency, whereby they protect their budgetary commons at the cost of central government and free ride on the stabilization effort of others. These considerations about the political strains of centralization and the potential for dysfunctional interaction between levels of government suggest that alternatives to the functional theory should be considered. The following discussion considers ways in which the federal or supranational level can act as "reinsurer," complementing rather than substituting for stabilization by member states.

FISCAL STABILIZATION

The risk-sharing literature, reviewed in Chapter 3, attracted attention with its finding that compared to credit and capital markets the central budget in the US stabilizes only a small fraction of an output shock (Figure 3.2). In the original Asdrubali et al. (1996: 1092) study, the budget accounted for 13 percent of smoothing an idiosyncratic output shock to a US state, credit markets for 23 percent, and capital markets for a whopping 39 percent. This low contribution would be even lower if Asdrubali et al. (1996) had taken into account that fiscal policies in the states tend to counteract the stabilization effort at the federal level (Follette et al. 2008; Svec and Kondo 2012).

This free riding on the stabilization effort of the federal budget is a moral hazard problem of collective stabilization in federations (Section 4.3.4). Rodden and Wibbels (2010) show that this is a general pattern with a study of seven federations. They found that regional or state governments tend to run procyclical expenditure policies, neutralizing some of the counter-cyclical effects of the federal budget. Balanced budget rules are one driver of this pro-cyclicality: lower-level governments tend to cut expenditure when tax revenue falls in an economic downturn. Grants from central government also tend to be pro-cyclical (Rodden and Wibbels 2010: 42), in other words grants are generous when the economy does well and tax revenue is high, and vice versa in a recession. The two effects together make stabilization in federations less responsive than in a unitary state. While there may be high capacity to implement a counter-cyclical policy at the federal level, this is undermined by the incentives for pro-cyclicality at the lower levels.

This also applies to the stabilization of individuals' incomes that welfare-state programs try to achieve: cash benefits in states tend to be extremely low compared to Europe but also the federal poverty standard (Section 8.2.1). Federal programs like SNAP and TANF take up the slack. Some states have raised the minimum wage above the federal level, making employers share in the cost of working poverty relief rather than the federal government with its EITC. Unemployment insurance which is fully administered but only partly financed by the states is paid only to a fraction of the unemployed. This contributes to the relatively low automatic stabilizers to be activated when there is a shock to employment in the US (Section 4.3.4). The study by Dolls et al. (2010: 31–2) found that states do not even contribute their small share of 4 percent to a 32 percent stabilization of income when unemployment hits a region. By contrast, the member states in the EU stabilize incomes on average by 48.5 percent when an unemployment shock hits the economy. It is remarkable that without a central budget, fiscal policy is a more effective stabilizer in the EA than in the US.

Completing the monetary union by a fiscal union is therefore unlikely to increase the stabilizing capacity of the EA linearly with the centralization of budgetary policy. The political incentives of lower levels of government have to be taken into account. Any conceivable fiscal federation of the EA would probably feature a close expenditure-tax link in a decentralized setting. This would bode well for the goals of low budget deficits and low inflation but badly for stabilization (Rodden and Wibbels 2002). Simulations of a fiscal union come to similar discouraging results (Bargain et al. 2013). There are stabilization gains to be had from replacing one third of national taxes and transfers of EA member states by a central budget, but the redistributive effects would be quite large. Moreover, a fiscal equalization scheme might not only be too redistributive to be politically sustainable; it could also weaken the stabilizing capacity of the EA, because large-scale redistribution is liable to have negative incentive effects on economic activity, lowering the tax capacity of the system and hence its ability to implement counter-cyclical stabilization.

All these findings commend stabilization schemes that complement national measures, rather than a wholesale fiscal federation. A proposal for such a Community stabilization mechanism was developed in the early 1990s, but rejected by the Council (Italianer and Vanheukelen 1993). The central idea has recently been revived by Dullien (2014) in the form of a supplementary unemployment scheme. Dolls et al. (2016) combine an income-stabilization mechanism with the proposal for sovereign insolvency that a team of IMF and Bruegel authors recently ventured, which is discussed further below (Gianviti et al. 2010). Interestingly, they argue that an EU-wide insurance scheme for short-term unemployment and insurance for sovereigns in the case of overindebtedness would steer successfully between two political market failures: moral hazard on the one hand and internalizing the externalities of market panic on the other (Section 7.2.1). An automatic stabilizer on top of effective national unemployment schemes would allow a country to get over a temporary shock. It would not be forced to switch off automatic stabilizers with pro-cyclical measures, while the deterioration of budget balances would be kept at bay.

This contribution of Dolls et al. (2016) is important because it supports the case that there is an alternative to a sizeable central budget at the EU level to smooth income fluctuations of member states. Southern European countries should be encouraged to increase the responsiveness of their tax systems and unemployment benefits, for instance through more progressive tax schedules and better coverage of unemployment insurance. Adjustment programs under the surveillance of the troika could help to bring this about and this rationale for requested institutional reforms should be explicit, so as to make them contestable and open to proposals that achieve the same goal of increased stabilizing capacity. For instance, the first bailout program for Greece contained prescriptions for a more progressive income tax structure on grounds of equity (European Economy Greece 2010: para. 24). This justification is problematic and seems opportunistic: pursuing redistributive goals through member states' tax systems is not an EU competence. However, it is "a matter of common concern" that some member states raise the effectiveness of automatic stabilizers; a more progressive income tax schedule can be a way to achieve this.

The example also illustrates that such complementarity does not do away with the need for political integration, as Münchau (2016) points out. Creating a supranational unemployment reinsurance scheme would call for a high level of cooperation: this is political integration of a kind, regardless of the particular institutions through which it is developed and implemented.

FISCAL BACKSTOPS

As important as more counter-cyclical fiscal capacity is in the EA, this was a second-order problem in the aftermath of the financial crisis. The first-order problems arose from unsustainable stocks of debt that turned into a downward spiral of private and public insolvency. These first-order problems also emerged repeatedly in US history (Chapters 4 and 6). What put an end to this history of financial instability in the US were advances in central banking and the introduction of federal fiscal backstops as part of the New Deal.[10] The fiscal backstops rest on the availability of a national debt instrument, US Treasury bonds, that in turn backs up federal fiscal capacity.

Fiscal backstops in the EA context would mean joint liability of member states for their debts, supplementing their national liability. The idea of a Eurobond is to have "joint and several liability," while there is only several (national) liability today. The joint liability would act as a reinsurance mechanism when the national liability is insufficient to honor the claims. This is analogous to the reinsurance that private insurers take out to guard against the tail risk of a catastrophic concentration of adverse events.

The foremost commitment problem of sovereigns is that the present value of net taxes may be too small to guarantee the liabilities of a collapsing financial system, destroying the security of saving households and disrupting the payments system. Iceland and Ireland were the most glaring examples of this in the financial crisis of 2008. But Luxembourg, Switzerland, and the UK could also have this problem (Buiter 2008: 278–81). Other sovereigns have the commitment problem that the legacy of public debt is so burdensome that a small change in parameters, for instance a rise in interest rates or stagnating growth, raises doubts about the country's solvency. If holders of bonds—or the credit agencies rating them—do not believe bonds will be paid back as promised and move out, their skeptical beliefs become self-fulfilling. This is a commitment problem for any new administration in Belgium or Italy due to their high public debt, even if an incoming government has the best intentions of stabilizing public finances. The problem is heightened in the EA because governments have no longer a central bank that could provide liquidity directly (De Grauwe 2011: 2–5).

A common debt instrument is a risk-pooling device, exploiting the fact that not all member states will experience a shock or a bond-market attack at the same time. In fact, if some member states have a safe-haven status and others have a traditionally precarious status in financial markets, then their risks are negatively correlated and pooling can bring down the aggregate risk of the pool.

Ideas for a Eurobond, analogous to federal debt in the US, have been floated for a while.[11] It is arguable that the ESM is one limited version, insofar as it

[10] The S&L crisis of the 1980s was due to the unwinding of the early post-war regime of financial repression; it ended only when federal fiscal backstops were applied in the guise of the FDIC (Section 4.2.5).

[11] See Schelkle (2012c: 31–2) for a comparison of main proposals.

allows the Commission to borrow up to €60 billion in capital markets and lend it on to countries. The ESM is securitized by the EU budget which ropes non-euro countries into the risk pool and hence cannot be easily increased. De Grauwe and Moesen (2009) propose that EA members should have guaranteed access to a common financing instrument but at national interest rates. The red and blue bond proposal by Delpa and von Weizsäcker (2010), as well as that of the German Council of Economic Advisors (Sachverständigenrat 2012), would primarily try to use Eurobonds in order to reduce the legacy of debt, in other words it pools the risk of insolvency rather than that of liquidity. Finally, so-called ESBies, European Safe Bonds, have been proposed. They would use structured financing techniques to create a private-sector equivalent to a Eurobond (Brunnermeier et al. 2011). This demonstrates that Eurobonds do not have to come about as part of quasi-federal public-debt management.

Joint liability instruments can also be more targeted, acting as specific circuit breakers of a negative feedback loop. Such a specific backstop is exactly what the FDIC in the US provides for state banks, financed out of fees from its member banks and invested in US Treasury bonds. An alternative to a targeted Eurobond for bank resolution is to give the ESM a banking license that would give it access to the ECB in well-defined circumstances such as a systemic banking crisis in a member state. In other words, the question before heads of state will be whether extreme emergencies require joint fiscal liabilities or the fiscalization of central banking; and it might be wise to have both instruments available instead of relying on only one.

Each extension of public safety nets raises the issue of moral hazard, not only among the unequal members of the risk pool but also elsewhere in the financial system. Commercial incentives inherently lead to bets on the availability of insurance. This has led some experts to advocate an insolvency procedure for sovereigns that would force the private sector to bear some losses and thereby reduce the moral hazard that arises from provision for joint bailouts. Gianviti et al. (2010) propose a "viable insolvency procedure for sovereigns" that would give a country up to three years under an ESM program to get back on a sustainable trajectory or write down debt, as an ultimate threat to careless private lenders to governments. Debt restructuring is needed to make it credible that a bailout will not be forthcoming, as disorderly default would lead to a banking crisis. The proposal faces the political difficulty that losses will be inflicted on lending countries' banking systems when another EA member state defaults. Reining in moral hazard comes at the cost of externalities.

Another way to address negative feedback loops is to prevent real or perceived collusion between national policymakers and national bankers by changing the rules for risk weighting of bond holdings on banks' balance sheets (Dolls et al. 2016: 8–9, 22). Holding sovereign bonds of the country in which a bank has its headquarters or is registered as a subsidiary should have a higher positive risk weight than for that of other member states, meaning a bank has to set aside more loss-absorbing capital. This would give banks incentives to diversify their bond holdings and make them less susceptible to pressures from officials to invest in domestic bonds. This reduction of the home bias through diversification would greatly reduce the basis for a negative feedback loop. A requirement to diversify is likely to increase the cost of the government debt of weaker states at first and thus needs to be phased in, but since it will reduce the risk of feedback loops, this should only be a transitory phase.

These policy implications for fiscal risk sharing address the fact that the European monetary union consists of political economies that are diverse in economic and political terms. Targeted reinsurance is more pertinent for such a union than generalized joint liability. Regulatory ways of making private finance diversify rather than concentrate sovereign risks would help its members with a problem that they find hard to avoid on their own. All this is to say that policies must help member states to sustain but also to benefit from their diversity.

10.3 European Political Economy

The European economic and monetary union is politically integrated, albeit differently from nation states (Section 5.3). The amount of harmonized legislation, fiscal surveillance, and policy coordination that member state administrations engage in surpasses some federations. But it is a union of democracies and not a democratic union. This is of course the constitutional reason why risk sharing in a fiscal federation is taboo. But just as there can be other ways to do fiscal risk sharing, so there can be other ways to achieve political integration, in the sense of developing capacity to resolve collective action problems. The legitimacy of monetary solidarity does not rest on majoritarian decision-making processes, yet it has to work through the cooperation of governments that can only function within the constraints of those processes.

One feature of the processes that do prevail is that expert policy advice has an influential political role; this is the counterpart of the inherently weak democratic underpinning of the EA/EU. This imposes a duty of reflexivity upon academic researchers and experts: if an idea is enthusiastically taken up by policymakers, the researcher should pause to reflect on what selective incentives have been triggered to make the authorities so receptive. Reflection on the current embrace of the concept of "risk sharing" by the European

Commission suggests that the risks posed by financial integration are deliberately downplayed. Those drawing on OCA theory to advocate "an ever closer union" should also reflect on the likelihood that member states will impose limits on risk sharing that undermine the putative benefits of integration.

10.3.1 *Political Legitimation of Monetary Solidarity*

Monetary solidarity between democracies is a peculiar form of political integration. Some of the most obvious expressions of monetary solidarity analyzed in previous chapters can illustrate this: the large membership with which the European monetary union started, pooling former hard-currency and soft-currency areas; the formerly egalitarian set-up of the ECB, giving each governor a vote that is disproportionate to national size;[12] the equal treatment of all member state bonds in collateralized lending by the central bank; extraordinary monetary policies during the crisis that provided lending of last resort to national banking systems and indirectly to sovereigns; the maintenance of a cross-border payments system when banks did not want to acquire any claims against each other while they and their clients depended on the processing of payments; the unprecedented size of the stabilization programs under the watch of the Commission, the IMF, and the ECB, guaranteed by member states that were themselves in dire straits. Only the first (euro membership) and the last (troika programs) qualify as political phenomena that easily capture the public imagination. But a weak potential for politicization does not make these developments apolitical. Moreover, the heated argument in Germany about the risks involved in TARGET imbalances illustrated how quickly this can change (Section 9.1).

These instances of monetary solidarity have in common that they did not rest on majoritarian decision making. To be sure, decisions were taken by elected representatives of government. But they usually concerned institutions, for instance in determining the rules on how an applicant country can qualify for EA membership, and the decisions of parliaments or referenda deciding on EA membership were secondary to this qualification.[13] A similar logic applied to the ECB. Elected governments decided on the nature of its independence which then allowed the ECB to adopt policies it saw as being in line with fulfilling its legislated mandate. Once the institution was set in place by majoritarian procedures, it was to a considerable degree isolated against

[12] The rotation system in place since the accession of Lithuania in January 2015 means that ECB governors have periodically no voting right. Governors from smaller member states must abstain more often than those from larger member states.

[13] Troika programs are an exception in that each has to be signed off by the German Bundestag, an obligation that the German Constitutional Court stipulated as a democratic requirement.

shifting majorities in member states. The same holds for TARGET or the Commission's role in fiscal surveillance and stabilization programs for distressed member states.

This isolation is deliberate. For reasons of commitment when the veil of ignorance has been lifted, an insurance arrangement must be immune to opportunism by the fortunate. An ECB must be free to support the less fortunate in order to preserve the integrity of financial markets in the monetary union as a whole, even if it is thus redistributing from the fortunate to the unfortunate. This upholding of insurance arrangements has parallels in the insurance arrangement that is the welfare state. The norm of equality often promotes an extension of social policy programs to beneficiaries that were not the target group when the program was legislated. Democratic control is exercised over the broad principles of entitlement in a welfare-state program, not over who exactly benefits. Obviously, if a majority of voters no longer endorses the principles used to target a program, then it is up to their political representatives to propose changes.

Anybody who deplores a democratic deficit of the EA (and by extension the EU) has to come to terms with the fact that it was parliaments, and in some cases electorates directly, that voted with sizeable majorities to become part of a system that was transparent about this democratic deficit. Even if electorates had not fully understood the mandate of the ECB, no Irish, Italian, or German voter could be under any illusion that the common central bank would make monetary policy for Ireland, Italy, or Germany alone. Furthermore, it could not be expected that the ECB would respond to the domestic concerns of shifting national majorities; membership entails that policies will be conducted with regard to others. This is the essence of EU/EA membership, reflecting the inherent tension in being "governing together but not as one" (Nicolaïdes 2013: 4).

Monetary solidarity is also not merely compliance with international treaties, such as the Refugee Convention or World Trade Organization trade agreements. Rather than committing to certain national policies, it rests on delegating monetary (and since 2014 financial supervisory) policy authority to supranational bodies. Majone (2001) argued that the delegation of policy powers to the ECB is more pertinently described as a fiduciary relationship than as a principal–agent relationship. The description of the ECB as a trustee rather than an agent is pertinent if the delegating governments do not necessarily want the central bank to have the same preferences as they have and if the policy area is beset with considerable uncertainty so that the contract cannot be fully specified ex ante. Such trustees are an answer to the commitment dilemma that is inherent in democracy: elected governments rule only for a limited time while international agreements are meant to last (Majone 2001: 106–7).

The conundrum for legitimacy is precisely formulated by Richard Bellamy and Albert Weale (2015: 264): how is it "legally and constitutionally possible" for a member state "to enter into and honour international agreements that are in its interests and in the interests of other states who are party to the agreement, whilst at the same time retaining the principle of the democratic self-determination of [its] people"? The contracting governments wanted the ECB to have preferences that would depart from those of predecessor central banks (of others and their own) that created exchange rate instability and/or forced them to raise interest rates at inconvenient times (Section 5.1). The Bundesbank was the *bête noir* for governments of soft-currency areas; the Banca d'Italia or the Banque de France played similar roles for authorities of hard-currency areas. By applying for the European monetary union, they accepted that the future central bank would conduct monetary policy not with a view to any one of them, although it was of course expected to be more stability-oriented. This was not a worry as long as the ECB managed to give both sides what they wanted: both lower interest rates and stable low inflation.

The idea was that these politically desired policy outputs legitimized the ECB, in line with the useful distinction between input and output legitimacy developed by Scharpf (1999). It was rarely noted at the time—since the Treaty mentions price stability only—that the delegation of policy authority suited at least two goals: inflation, which the ECB was meant to control, and low-risk premia, which the ECB would thus achieve. With hindsight, it seems obvious that serving different economic aspirations is enormously important for the diverse political community that underpins monetary union. Otherwise, the commitment of the various states is not credible (Bellamy and Weale 2015: 263): if the collective agreement at the EA level runs counter to democratic majorities or important constituencies in the member states, administrations cannot rationally trust each other to honor the agreement.

This follows from "the normative logic of two-level games" (Bellamy and Weale 2015: 259) which is an important variation on the positive logic of two-level games. The domestic level is a constraint on the supranational level in the sense that the latter cannot legitimately ask for compliance and consideration of other member states' concerns if the international agreement subjects national democracies to outdated or narrowly based commitments. Fiscal surveillance suffered from a violation of this normative logic and the international agreement was repeatedly disregarded, including a social democratic administration in Germany. The problem is that those in support of strict fiscal surveillance take this as an indicator that the defying states cannot or will not honor any commitments.

For the normative logic to be respected and followed, each member state must acknowledge that other governments act as representatives of their state, and they should expect reciprocal acknowledgment. This is the principle of demoicracy rather than a European democracy (Cheneval and Schimmelfennig 2013: 334; Nicolaïdes 2013: 1–2). There must be domestic ways in which the political authority at the international level can be "openly and consequentially disputed" (White, J. 2015: 88), for it to back off, change tack, or base its decisions on a more inclusive rationale.[14] Financial stability has become the case in point since 2010. There are proposals, like those of Dolls et al. (2016) discussed above, that show ways in which the EA institutions could respond to this evolution without losing its constitutional identity as a union of democracies that formed a hard-currency area.

At the moment, the democratic concerns are taken up by constitutional courts, prominently in Germany but also quite effectively in Portugal (Bellamy and Weale 2015: 258). The Portuguese court declared certain agreements in memoranda of understanding unconstitutional (Lütz et al. 2015), the German court ruled that only a pre-committed amount for bond buying under the OMT program is compatible with the democratic prerogative over fiscal resources. Bellamy and Weale (2015: 264) see the "doctrine of delegation" that the German court developed as a possible solution to the conundrum of legitimacy: "So long as the international agreement could be said to rest on the delegated authority of the member state and the Bundestag retained the power of revoking Germany's participation in the international agreement, then the principle of democratic self-determination was respected."

However, the final OMT judgment of the German court, not known to Bellamy and Weale (2015), also indicates the limits of this judicial way out (Section 7.2.2). The court did not simply obligate the national parliament to review a major innovation in monetary policy. It also sought a specific reason why this is necessary for the OMT, which it found in the potential liabilities of German taxpayers. Like all courts, it tried to maintain continuity by constructing an analogy with cases which have gone before, and the analogy it found was fiscal. This analogy is contested among economists but reflected the Bundesbank's view (Steen 2012).[15] The problem with national judicial governance of the two-level game is that, by its very nature, it cannot provide a way out of the "practical contradiction at the heart of EMU" (Bellamy and Weale 2015: 265): that governments were asked at the time to agree to fiscal

[14] The infamous incident in which the German finance minister promised his Portuguese counterpart that adjustments can be made once the Greek program will have been agreed is one example for adjustments to domestic opposition in an otherwise cooperative member state (Chapter 6, fn 24).

[15] On the grounds of open-ended commitment, full allotment repos, another extraordinary monetary policy measure, should have been subject to approval by national parliaments as well because collateral under this open-ended lending program can also default.

rules and a narrow mandate of the central bank as if these would cover all future contingencies in member states and the union, with no further democratic legitimation required. National courts are ill-equipped to deal with the "predictable unpredictability of monetary union" (Bellamy and Weale 2015: 265) and have an institutionally rational conservative bias. Only elected, representative governments can deal with the open-ended nature of a diverse monetary union. This maxim is, by mid-2016, respected in the breach rather than in the observance of fiscal rules, while a lonely central bank struggles to provide policy innovations to develop its mandate.

10.3.2 *Reflexive Policy Advice*

This brings us finally to the role of those researching the experiment that is the EU generally and the euro especially. Research in European political economy acts to some extent as a substitute for limited political contestation over policies at the EU level. A striking example was the article "The advantage of tying one's hands: EMS discipline and central bank credibility" by Francesco Giavazzi and Marco Pagano (1988) that clearly supported the limited risk sharing enshrined in EA institutions.[16] The article provided a justification for the irrevocable fixing of the exchange rate on the grounds that it was a rational strategy to discipline wage bargainers and escape cycles of inflation and devaluation.

This was research at its most influential, particularly in Italy where policymakers had not found other solutions to the inflation-devaluation cycle. It could be read as turning the theory of OCA on its head. A non-optimal candidate, with too high inflation, can be made optimal through monetary integration, by taking away the instrument that allowed it to accommodate its excessive inflation. All that was required was to apply the then fashionable methodological assumption of rational expectations to the mainstream view of monetary integration.

Such research falls on fertile ground in a "democratic" union that is forever in search of new policy ideas, but lacks contestation between government and opposition spurred on by the prospect of an election. Hence, the competition for policy ideas—and support for policies from outside EU institutions—must partly substitute for the political contestation associated with democratic processes. If targeted in this way, research in European political economy becomes a form of politics in the sense of Jon Elster (1986: 128):

[16] In 2005, Francesco Giavazzi was asked to look back at this article in light of what we knew then about the EA. My contribution (Schelkle 2006) was prompted by the fact that in a series of such exercises, he was the only contributor who did not honor his commitment to write up his seminar presentation.

> It is the concern with substantive decisions [ultimately on economic matters] that lends the urgency to political debates. The ever-present constraint of time creates a need for focus and concentration that cannot be assimilated to the leisurely style of philosophical argument in which it may be better to travel hopefully than to arrive. Yet within these constraints arguments form the core of the political process. If thus defined as public in nature, and instrumental in purpose, politics assumes what I believe to be its proper place in society.

Participating in debates about policies is in this place a valid and important political activity of scholars.

Yet, it is the realm of politics and not of applied research. After all, advising European institutions leads, if successful, to the paradoxical situation that research comes to chase a moving target of which it is itself a driving force. This is rarely compatible with unbiased research; rather, it is a sign of successful political engagement. The contribution of many scholars to the TARGET debate can be seen as a striking example of such a successful engagement, and it had academic as well as political payoffs (Section 9.1). What made this debate constructive was exactly the seriousness with which (most) participants tried to understand what was going on rather than finding forever fault with the imperfect world around them and giving in to the urge to recommend reforms to the TARGET system.

This political use of research gives the EA a "constructivist" touch. Wide-ranging policy changes are driven through with the backing of theories and models that may have their empirical evidence from rather different contexts and may have been based on assumptions that seem problematic with the benefit of hindsight. Economic research lends itself more easily to such instrumental use than political science or sociological research on Europe. This would not necessarily be a problem if the latter were still part of the debate on economists' policy ideas. But too often they are not. The great scholar of central banking, Charles Goodhart (1989: 482), noted with respect to the debate on economic governance in the EU early on a "lack of interdisciplinary inputs" and the "narrow professionalism" of economists dominating the debate. Such scholarship becomes part of a technocratic infrastructure, narrowing down the perspective on European integration rather than widening and enriching it for the benefit of a diverse union. Fortunately, this is no longer the case and political scientists as well as political economists have left their marks on the interpretation of the EA crisis.[17] Their advice is now sometimes invited by the ECB, the IMF, and the Director General for Economic and Financial Affairs, although it is marginal compared to economists.

[17] To name just a few edited volumes: Genschel and Jachtenfuchs (2014); Cramme and Hobolt (2015); Matthijs and Blyth (2015); Caporaso and Rhodes (2016); and Chalmers et al. (2016a); These have been compounded by an impressive number of special issues of political economy journals.

The by-product theory of collective action also applies to this political use of research: policy ideas are taken up by the Commission or uploaded by member states when they have selective incentives to draw on it. This insight suggests a reflexive attitude to policy advice: whenever a policy idea falls on fertile ground, one might ask whose selective incentives made the policy authorities so receptive. This may be grounds for reconsidering whether the advice is robust to furthering an agenda different from what the research had in mind.

The concept of risk sharing is a case in point. As indicated earlier, it already figures prominently in the high-level report on how to "complete" EMU (Juncker et al. 2015), drawing heavily on the literature reviewed in Chapter 3. This review indicated that the literature saw financial markets as reliable channels for allocating risk efficiently and located the only source of instability in exogenous output shocks. These assumptions are indefensible in 2015, in the aftermath of the financial crisis. But the Juncker et al. report follows this literature closely because it suits the agenda of building a banking and capital markets union quickly and allows a neat distinction to be drawn between private and public risk sharing (Kalemli-Ozcan et al. 2013). Member states that do not wish to discuss specific interfaces of fiscal risk sharing can live with this use of the research, since the sequencing postpones the debate about public (read: fiscal) risk sharing for a while.[18] This closing off of a debate supports, however, a policy of moving first towards a capital market union without the necessary safety nets in place. If, for instance, a large cross-border insurer fails in a stock-market crash and policy holders in different countries lose their old-age security, the same issues arise as in the default of a cross-border bank. The low-interest environment poses risks to financial conglomerates like Deutsche Bank and Allianz that are largely unknown in their ramifications (IMF 2016b: 29–32).

It is a serious allegation but sometimes one cannot help but see in this a political strategy that instrumentalizes Monnet's dictum about crisis as a force for European integration: that the next crisis will force the hands of governments and lead to another quantum leap in European monetary integration. The historical evidence in Chapters 4 and 6 indicated, however, that crisis politics is ruled by the selective incentives of short-termist "sauve qui peut," a rush to the exit that blocks the exit for everybody. Understandably, the overriding impulse is to evade the uncertain fall-out from catastrophe by shifting the costs onto others even if they are conceivably too weak to bear them. Monnet's statement is a prediction to fear, not a recipe to follow.

[18] In fact, between the Four Presidents' report in 2012 and the Five Presidents' report in 2015, the shock-absorption function for a monetary union highlighted in the former report (van Rompuy et al. 2012: 12) was edited out because of objections from the usual Northern contingent.

Experts who insist, with the best intentions, that ever closer union is needed may undermine the monetary union by imposing on it political demands that it cannot meet. This leads to political integration by latent conflict rather than by open contestation for a compromise among representative governments. Lingering conflicts create lasting alienation between member states: it will take years to forget the bad blood that troika programs created on all sides. Institutional complexity is invariably the result post-crisis when EU bodies scramble to find ways around ill-conceived ad hoc constructs, such as the Fiscal Compact or the first emergency fund. Ever closer union, even if it were desirable, is not necessarily viable.

The approach adopted in this book shifts attention from institutional design to institutional evolution. International collective goods are rarely the outcome of primary intentions (Broz 1998), they evolve in context-specific practices of "governing the commons" (Ostrom 1990). The inherently constructivist tendency of EU institution building needs to be complemented by a hermeneutic contribution to policy debates. By this I mean furthering our understanding of how policy ideas enshrined in existing institutions change with the interests in using these institutions. Independent central banking means something very different in 2010 from what it meant in 2000; I have argued that it has dispersed more risks effectively than previously envisaged. The insistence on fiscal sovereignty has also changed its impetus; it has been revealed as the last Maginot line (Obstfeld 2013) that upholds financial panic as an arbitrary disciplining threat while it was hoped to be a freedom gained when a single currency reins in foreign exchange markets. The hermeneutic thrust of research is an antidote to both the emphasis on recommending new policy ideas for ever more integration and the critique that the design of the union is incomplete. Completion implies uniform principles and one functional logic. Such stringency can be intellectually stimulating for scholars although even academic debates usually benefit from a diversity of views, approaches, and empirical strategies. When research enters the realm of political engagement, however, it is worth reminding ourselves that a union of democracies using a single currency might thrive on diversity for political as well as economic reasons.

Bibliography

Abdelal, R. (2007). *Capital rules. The construction of global finance*. Cambridge, MA: Harvard University Press.

Acemoglu, D. and Zilibotti, F. (1997). Was Prometheus bound by chance? Risk, diversification, and growth. *Journal of Political Economy, 105*(4), 709–51.

Acharya, V. and Mora, N. (2013). A crisis of banks as liquidity providers. *Working Paper 070913*. New York: Stern School of Business.

Acharya, V., Philippon, T., Richardson, M., and Roubini, N. (2009). The financial crisis of 2007–2009: Causes and remedies. *Financial Markets, Institutions and Instruments, 18*(2), 89–137.

Akerlof, G. (1970). The market for lemons: Qualitative uncertainty and the market mechanism. *Quarterly Journal of Economics, 84*(3), 488–500.

Alber, J. and Gilbert, N. (2010). *United in diversity? Comparing social models in Europe and America*. Oxford: Oxford University Press.

Alberola, E., Trucharte, C., and Vega, J. L. (2011). *Central banks and macroprudential policy. Some reflections from the Spanish experience*. Documentos Occasionales No. 1105. Madrid: Banco de España.

Allard, S. W. (1998). Revisiting Shapiro: Welfare magnets and state residency requirements in the 1990s. *Publius, 28*(3), 45–65.

Allen, W. A. and Moessner, R. (2010). Central bank co-operation and international liquidity in the financial crisis of 2008–9. *BIS Working Papers, No. 310*, May. Basel: Bank for International Settlements.

Amable, B. (2003). *The diversity of modern capitalism*. Oxford: Oxford University Press.

Amable, B. (2010). Morals and politics in the ideology of neo-liberalism. *Socioeconomic Review, 9*, 3–30.

Amaglobeli, D., End, N., Jarmuzek, M., and Palomba, G. (2015). From systemic banking crises to fiscal costs: Risk factors. *IMF Working Paper, 15/166*. Washington, DC: IMF.

AMECO (2005). *AMECO list of variables*. Brussels: European Commission.

Arnold, M. (2014). ING chief hits out at German financial regulator BaFin. *Financial Times online*, August 6.

Arpaia, A. and Pichelmann, K. (2007). Nominal and real wage flexibility in EMU. *European Economy Economic Papers, 281* (June). Brussels: European Commission.

Arpaia, A., Curci, N., Meyermans, E., Peschner, J., and Pierini, F. (2010). Short time working arrangements as response to cyclical fluctuations. *Occasional Papers, 64* (June). Brussels: European Commission.

Arreaza, A., Sørensen, B., and Yosha, O. (1998). Consumption smoothing through fiscal policy in OECD and EU countries. *NBER Working Papers, 6372*. Cambridge, MA: National Bureau of Economic Research.

Arrow, K. J. (1963). Uncertainty and the welfare economics of medical care. *American Economic Review, 53*(2), 941–73.

Arrow, K. J. (1971). *Essays in the theory of risk-bearing*. Chicago: Markham.

Artis, M. and Hoffmann, M. (2008). Financial globalization, international business cycles and consumption risk sharing. *Scandinavian Journal of Economics, 110*(3), 447–71.

Asatryan, Z., Feld, L. P., and Geys, B. (2015). Partial fiscal decentralization and sub-national government fiscal discipline: Empirical evidence from OECD countries. *CESifo Working Paper, No. 5279*, March. Munich: CESifo.

Asdrubali, P., Sørensen, B. E., and Yosha, O. (1996). Channels of interstate risk sharing: United States 1963–90. *Quarterly Journal of Economics, 111*(4), 1081–110.

Atkeson, A. and Bayoumi, T. (1993). Do private capital markets insure regional risk? Evidence from the United States and Europe. *Open Economies Review*, IV, 303–24.

Atkinson, A. B. (1999). *The economic consequences of rolling back the welfare state*. Cambridge, MA: MIT Press.

Atkinson, A. B. (2015). *Inequality: What can be done?* Cambridge, MA: Harvard University Press.

Atoyan, R., Christiansen, L., Dizioli, A., Ebeke, C., Ilahi, N., Ilyina, A., Mehrez, G., Qu, H., Raei, F., Rhee, A., and Zakharova, D. (2016). Emigration and its economic impact on Eastern Europe. *IMF Staff Discussion Note, SDN/16/07* (July). Washington, DC: IMF.

Auerbach, A. J. and Gorodnichenko, Y. (2011). Fiscal multipliers in recession and expansion. *NBER Working Paper, 17447*. Cambridge, MA: NBER.

Axelrod, R. M. (1984). *The evolution of cooperation*. New York: Basic Books.

Babecký, J., Havránek, T., Matějů, J., Rusnák, M., Šmídková, K., and Vašíček, B. (2012). Banking, debt, and currency crises. Early warning indicators for developed countries. *ECB Working Paper, No. 1485*. Frankfurt: ECB.

Backus, D. K., Kehoe, P. J., and Kydland, F. E. (1992). International real business cycles. *Journal of Political Economy, 100*(4), 745–75.

Bagehot, W. (1882). *Lombard Street: A description of the money market* (8th ed.). London: Kegan, Paul, Trench.

Baicker, K., Goldin, C., and Katz, L. F. (1998). A distinctive system: Origins and impact of U.S. unemployment. In M. D. Bordo, C. Goldin, and E. N. White (Eds), *The defining moment: The Great Depression and the American economy in the twentieth century* (pp. 227–64). Chicago, IL: University of Chicago Press.

Baker, T. and Moss, D. A. (2009). Government as risk manager. In D. A. Moss and J. Cisternino (Eds), *New Perspectives on Regulation* (pp. 87–109). Cambridge, MA: Tobin Project.

Baldoni, E. (2003). The free movement of persons in the European Union: A legal-historical overview. *PIONEUR Working Paper No. 2*, PIONEUR network.

Baldwin, P. (1990). *The politics of social solidarity*. Cambridge: Cambridge University Press.

Balli, F., Balli, H. O., and Louis, R. J. (2011). Decomposing the income insurance channel across OECD and emerging markets. *International Review of Finance, 11*(4), 515–35.

Balli, F., Kalemli-Ozcan, S., and Sørensen, B. E. (2012). Risk sharing through capital gains. *Canadian Journal of Economics, 45*(2, May), 472–92.

Barber, T. (2010). Dinner on the edge of the abyss. *Financial Times*, October 11, 7.

Barberis, N. C. (2013). Thirty years of Prospect Theory in economics: A review and assessment. *Journal of Economic Perspectives, 27*(1), 173–95.

Bargain, O., Dolls, M., Fuest, C., Neumann, D., Peichl, A., Pestel, N., and Siegloch, S. (2013). Fiscal union in Europe? Redistributive and stabilizing effects of a European tax-benefit system and fiscal equalization mechanism. *Economic Policy, 28*(75), 375–422.

Barkbu, B., Eichengreen, B., and Mody, A. (2011). Financial crises and the multilateral response: What the historical record shows. *NBER Working Paper, No. 17361*. Cambridge, MA: NBER.

Barkbu, B., Eichengreen, B., and Mody, A. (2012). Financial crises and the multilateral response: What the historical record shows. *Journal of International Economics, 88*(2), 422–35.

Barnard, C. (2008). Social dumping or dumping socialism? *Cambridge Law Journal, 67*(2), 262–4.

Barnard, C. (2009). The UK and posted workers: The effect of commission v Luxembourg on the territorial application of British labour law. *Industrial Law Journal, 38*(1), 122–32.

Barr, N. (1992). Economic theory and the welfare state: A survey and interpretation. *Journal of Economic Literature, 30*(2), 741–803.

Barr, N. (2012). *Economics of the welfare state* (5th ed.). Oxford: Oxford University Press.

Barro, R. and Sala-i-Martin, X. (1991). Convergence across states and regions. *Brookings Papers on Economic Activity*, 107–58.

Barro, R. and Sala-i-Martin, X. (2003). *Economic growth* (2nd ed.). Cambridge, MA: MIT Press.

Barta, Z. and Schelkle, W. (2015). At cross-purposes: Commercial versus technocratic governance of sovereign debt in the EU. *Journal of European Integration, 37*(7), 833–46.

Bastasin, C. (2012). *Saving Europe. How national politics nearly destroyed the euro.* Washington, DC: Brookings Institution.

Baxter, M. (2012). International risk-sharing in the short run and in the long run. *Canadian Journal of Economics, 45*(2, May), 376–93.

Bayoumi, T. and Eichengreen, B. (1993). Shocking aspects of European monetary integration. In F. Torres and F. Giavazzi (Eds), *Adjustment and growth in the European Monetary Union*. Cambridge: Cambridge University Press, 193–240.

Bayoumi, T. and Masson, P. R. (1996). What can the fiscal systems in the United States and Cannada tell us about EMU? In P. J. J. Welfens (Ed.), *European Monetary Integration: EMS Developments and International Post-Maastricht Perspectives* (3rd ed.). Berlin: Springer-Verlag, 307–31.

BBC (2002). Budget rules are still "stupid," Prodi says. *BBC News*, October 21, <http://www.news.bbc.co.uk/1/hi/business/2345653.stm> (accessed July 2, 2016).

BBC (2015). Greece bailout: EU "mediating" Greek row with Spain and Portugal. *BBC News*, March 2, <http://www.bbc.com/news/world-europe-31696596> (accessed August 13, 2016).

Beck, T. (Ed.) (2012). *Banking union for Europe. Risks and challenges*. London: CEPR.

Becker, S. O. and Hoffmann, M. (2006). Intra- and international risk-sharing in the short run and the long run. *European Economic Review, 50*, 777–806.

Beetsma, R. (2001). Does EMU need a stability pact? In A. Brunila, M. Buti, and D. Franco (Eds), *The Stability and Growth Pact. The architecture of fiscal policy in EMU*. Houndmills: Palgrave Macmillan.

Beine, M., Bourgeon, P., and Bricongn, J.-C. (2013). Aggregate fluctuations and international migration. *Working Paper No. 437*. Munich: CESifo.

Beine, M., Burgoon, B. B., Crock, M., Gest, J., Hiscox, M., McGovern, P., and Thielemann, E. (2014). Measuring immigration policies: Preliminary evidence from IMPALA. *Working Paper, No. 5109*. Munich: CESifo.

Belke, A. and Gros, D. (2009). On the benefits of fiscal policy coordination in a currency union: A note. *Empirica, 36*(1), 45–9.

Bellamy, R. and Weale, A. (2015). Political legitimacy and European monetary union: Contracts, constitutionalism and the normative logic of two-level games. *Journal of European Public Policy, 22*(2), 257–74.

Bénassy-Quéré, A. and Turkisch, E. (2009). The ECB governing council in an enlarged Euro Area. *Journal of Common Market Studies, 47*(1), 25–53.

Berger, S. and Piore, M. J. (1980). *Dualism and discontinuity in industrial societies*. Cambridge: Cambridge University Press.

Bermeo, N. (2010). Beyond the tragedy of the commons: A discussion of governing the commons: The evolution of institutions for collective action. *Perspectives on Politics, 8*(2), 570–2.

Bertola, G. (1998). Microeconomic perspectives on aggregate labor markets. *EUI Working Paper ECO No. 98/23*. Florence: EUI.

Bickerton, C. J., Hodson, D., and Puetter, U. (2015). The new intergovernmentalism: European integration in the post-Maastricht era. *Journal of Common Market Studies, 53*(4), 703–22.

Bindseil, U. and König, P. (2011). The economics of TARGET2 balances. *SFB 649 Discussion Paper, 2011–35*.

Bindseil, U., Cour-Thimann, P., and König, P. (2012). Target2 and cross-border interbank payments during the financial crisis. *CESifo Forum, 13*, 83–92.

Bini-Smaghi, L. (2011). Risk management in central banking. Speech, International Risk Management Conference, Free University of Amsterdam, June 15. <https://www.ecb.europa.eu/press/key/date/2011/html/sp110615.en.html> (accessed November 4, 2015).

BIS (2010). *Quarterly review*, June. Basel: Bank for International Settlements.

Blanchard, O. (1990). Suggestions for a new set of fiscal indicators. *OECD Department of Economics and Statistics Working Paper No. 79*. Paris: OECD.

Blanchard, O. E. and Leigh, D. (2013). Growth forecast errors and fiscal multipliers. *IMF Working Paper, No. 1301*. Washington, DC: IMF.

Blyth, M. (2013). The austerity delusion: Why a bad idea won over the West. *Foreign Affairs, 92*(3), 41–56.

Board (2005). *The Federal Reserve System. Purposes and functions* (9th ed.). Washington, DC: Board of Governors of the Federal Reserve System.

Boeri, T. (2010). Immigration to the land of redistribution. *Economica, 77*(308), 651–68.

Bohle, D. (2014). Post-socialist housing meets transnational finance: Foreign banks, mortgage lending, and the privatization of welfare in Hungary and Estonia. *Review of International Political Economy, 21*(4), 913–48.

Bohle, D. and Greskovits, B. (2012). *Capitalist diversity on Europe's periphery*. Ithaca, NY: Cornell University Press.

Bolderson, H. and F. Gains (1993). *Crossing national frontiers: An examination of the arrangements for exporting social security benefits in twelve OECD countries*. DSS Research Report. National Archives.

Bolderson, H. and Mabbett, D. (1995). Mongrels or thoroughbreds: A cross-national look at social security systems. *European Journal of Political Research, 28*, 119–39.

Bordo, M. (2014). TARGET balances, Bretton Woods, and the Great Depression. *VoxEU blog*, March 21, http://www.voxeu.org/article/historical-lessons-target-imbalances (accessed June 8, 2015).

Bordo, M. and Wheelock, D. C. (2011). The promise and performance of the Federal Reserve as lender of last resort 1914–1933. *NBER Working Paper, No. 16763*. Cambridge, MA: NBER.

Bordo, M., Eichengreen, B., Klingebiel, D., and Martinez-Peria, M. S. (2001). Is the crisis problem growing more severe? *Economic Policy, 16*(32), 52–82.

Borio, C. and Zhu, H. (2012). Capital regulation, risk-taking and monetary policy: A missing link in the transmission mechanism? *Journal of Financial Stability, 8*(4), 236–51.

Boughton, J. M. (2012). *Tearing down walls. The International Monetary Fund 1990–1999*. Washington, DC: IMF.

Bradley, M. and Gulati, M. (2013). Collective action clauses for the Eurozone. *Review of Finance, 18*(6), 2045–102.

Branson, W. (1993). Comments and discussion. In B. Eichengreen, C. Wyplosz, W. H. Branson, and R. Dornbusch (Eds), *The unstable EMS. Brookings Papers on Economic Activity*, 1, 125–9.

Bronk, R. and Jacoby, W. (2013). Avoiding monocultures in the European Union: The case for the mutual recognition of difference in conditions of uncertainty. *LEQS Paper No. 67/2013*. London: London School of Economics and Political Science.

Broz, J. L. (1997). *The international origins of the Federal Reserve System*. Ithaca, NY: Cornell University Press.

Broz, J. L. (1998). The origins of central banking: Solutions to the free-rider problem. *International Organization, 52*(2), 231–68.

Broz, J. L. (2013). *The federal reserve as global lender of last resort, 2007–2010*. Paper presented at the International Political Economy Society, University of Virginia.

Bruckner, J. K. (2000). Welfare reform and the race to the bottom: Theory and evidence. *Southern Economic Journal, 66*(3), 505–25.

Brunila, A., Buti, M., and Franco, D. (Eds). (2001). *The Stability and Growth Pact. The architecture of fiscal policy in EMU*. Houndmills: Palgrave Macmillan.

Brunnermeier, M. K. and Sannikov, Y. (2013). Redistributive monetary policy. Federal Reserve Bank of Kansas City Economic Conference Proceedings. *Jackson Hole Symposium 2012*, 331–84.

Brunnermeier, M. K., Crockett, A., Goodhart, C., Persaud, A. D., and Shin, H. S. (2009). *The fundamental principles of financial regulation*. Geneva and London: International Center for Monetary and Banking Studies and Centre for Economic Policy Research.

Brunnermeier, M. K., Garicano, L., Lane, P. R., Pagano, M., Reis, R., Santos, T., and Vayanos, D. (2011). European Safe Bonds (ESBies). *Euronomics Group Working Paper*, <http://www.columbia.edu/~rr2572/papers/11-ESBies.pdf>.

Brzoza-Brzezina, M., Kolasa, M., and Makarski, K. (2013). Macroprudential policy instruments and economic imbalances in the euro area. *ECB Working Paper Series, No. 1589* (September). Frankfurt: ECB.

Buchanan, J. M. (1965). An economic theory of clubs. *Economica, 32*(125), 1–14.

Buiter, W. (2004). To purgatory and beyond: When and how should the accession countries from Central and Eastern Europe become full members of the EMU? *CEPR Discussion Paper, No. 4342*. London: Center for Economic Policy Research.

Buiter, W. (2007). The central bank as market maker of last resort. Willem Buiter's *Maverecon* blog, August 12, <http://www.blogs.ft.com/maverecon/2007/08/the-central-banhtml/#axzz3ceSZllEE> (accessed June 10, 2015).

Buiter, W. (2008a). Quantitative easing and qualitative easing: A terminological and taxonomic proposal. Willem Buiter's *Maverecon* blog, January 9, <http://www.blogs.ft.com/maverecon/2008/12/quantitative-easing-and-qualitative-easing-a-terminological-and-taxonomic-proposal/#axzz3KT8DzOs4> (accessed June 8, 2015).

Buiter, W. (2008b). Debate: Why the UK should join the Eurozone. *International Finance, 11*(3), 269–82.

Buiter, W. (2012). The role of central banks in financial stability: How has it changed? *CEPR Discussion Paper, No. 8780*. London: CEPR.

Buiter, W. H. and Rahbari, E. (2012). Target2 redux: The simple accountancy and slightly more complex economics of Bundesbank loss exposure through the Eurosystem. *CEPR Discussion Paper 9211*. London: CEPR.

Buiter, W. and Sibert, A. (2005). How the Eurosystem's treatment of collateral in its open market operations weakens fiscal discipline in the Eurozone (and what to do about it). *CEPR Discussion Paper, 5626*. London: Centre for Economic Policy Research.

Buiter, W. H., Rahbari, E., and Michels, J. (2011). The implications of intra-euro area imbalances in credit flows. *CEPR Policy Insight, 57*, August.

Buiter, W., Rahbari, E., Giani, G., and Michels, J. (2013). Cyprus is systemically important—it changed the rules of the game. *Citi Research Economics*, April 10.

Bulmer, S. and Paterson, W. E. (2013). Germany as the EU's reluctant hegemon? Of economic strength and political constraints. *Journal of European Public Policy, 20*(10), 1387–405.

Bund der Steuerzahler (2012). Strafanzeige in Sache Target2. <http://www.querschuesse.de/strafanzeige-in-sache-target2/> (accessed November 26, 2014).

Bundesbank (2011). The dynamics of the Bundesbank's TARGET2 balance. In Deutsche Bundesbank (Ed.), *Monthly Report March*, 34–5.

Bundesverfassungsgericht (2016). BVerfG, Urteil des Zweiten Senats—2 BvR 2728/13—Rn. (1–220), June 21, <http://www.bverfg.de/e/rs20160621_2bvr272813.html> (accessed August 1, 2016).

Burgoon, B. (2014). Immigration, integration and support for redistribution in Europe. *World Politics* 66(3), 365–405.

Buti, M. (Ed.) (2003). *Monetary and fiscal policies in EMU: Interactions and coordination*. Cambridge: Cambridge University Press.

Buti, M., Eijffinger, S. C. W., and Franco, D. (2003). Revisiting the Stability and Growth Pact: Grand design or internal adjustment? *CEPR Discussion Paper, No. 3692*. London: Centre for Economic Policy Research.

Callen, M., Imbs, J., and Mauro, P. (2015). Pooling risk among countries. *Journal of International Economics, 96*(1), 88–99.

Calvo, G. A. (1998). Capital flows and capital-market crises: The simple economics of sudden stops. *Journal of Applied Economics, 1*(1), 35–54.

Canzoneri, M., Cumby, R., Diba, B., and López-Salido, D. (2013). Key currency status: An exorbitant privilege and an extraordinary risk. *Working Paper*. Washington, DC: Georgetown University.

Capie, F., Goodheart, C., Schnadt, N., Greenspan, A., Trichet, J.-C., and Mieno, Y. (1994). The development of central banking. In *The Future of Central Banking: The Tercentenary Symposium of the Bank of England* (pp. 1–261). Cambridge: Cambridge University Press.

Caporaso J. A. and Rhodes, M. (Eds) (2016). *The political and economic dynamics of the Eurozone*. Oxford: Oxford University Press.

Caporaso, J. A. and Tarrow, S. (2009). Polanyi in Brussels: Supranational institutions and the transnational embedding of markets. *International Organization, 63*(04), 593–620.

Carlin, W. (2013). Real exchange rate adjustment, wage-setting institutions, and fiscal stabilization policy: Lessons of the Eurozone's first decade. *CESifo Economic Studies, 59*(3), 489–519.

Carney, M. (2015). Fortune favours the bold. Lecture to honour the memory of The Honourable James Michael Flaherty, P. C., Iveagh House, Dublin. Speech. January 28.

CBPP (2015). Policy basics: Earned income tax credit. Washington, DC: Center on Budget and Policy Priorities, <http://www.cbpp.org/cms/?fa=viewandid=2505>.

CEC (1990). One market, one money. An evaluation of the potential benefits and costs of forming an economic and monetary union. *European Economy, 44*, October. Brussels: Commission of the European Communities.

Cecchetti, S. G., McCauley, R. N., and McGuire, P. M. (2012). Interpreting TARGET2 balances. *BIS Working Papers No. 39,3*. Basel: Bank for International Settlement.

Cesa-Bianchi, A., Imbs, J., and Saleheen, J. (2016). Finance and synchronization. *CFM Discussion Paper, 2016-22*. London: London School of Economics, Centre for Macroeconomics.

Chalmers, D., Jachtenfuchs, M., and Joerges, C. (Eds). (2016a). *The end of the Eurocrats' dream. Adjusting to European diversity*. Cambridge: Cambridge University Press.

Chalmers, D., Jachtenfuchs, M., and Joerges, C. (2016b). The retransformation of Europe. In D. Chalmers, M. Jachtenfuchs, and C. Joerges (Eds), *The end of the Eurocrats' dream. Adjusting to European diversity* (pp. 1–28). Cambridge: Cambridge University Press.

Chen, R., Milesi-Ferretti, G. M., and Tressel, T. (2012). External imbalances in the euro area. *IMF Working Paper, WP/12/236*. Washington, DC: IMF; also published as Chen, R., Milesi-Ferretti, G. M., and Tressel, T. (2013). External imbalances in the Eurozone. *Economic Policy, 28*(73), 101–42.

Cheneval, F. and Schimmelfennig, F. (2013). The case for demoicracy in the European Union. *Journal of Common Market Studies, 51*(2), 334–50.

Cheun, S., von Köppen-Mertes, I., and Weller, B. (2009). The collateral frameworks of the Eurosystem, the Federal Reserve System and the Bank of England and the financial market turmoil. *ECB Occasional Paper Series, No. 107*. Frankfurt: ECB.

Chislett, W. (2014). Spain's banking crisis: A light in the tunnel. *ARI 11/2014*, February. Madrid: Real Instituto Elcano.

Christev, A. and Melitz, J. (2011). EMU, EU, market integration and consumption smoothing. *CEPII WP No 2011-21*.

Chwieroth, J. and Walter, A. (2013). From low to great expectations: Banking crises and partisan survival over the long run. *Working Paper*, <http://www.ssrn.com/abstract=2258980>.

Coase, R. H. (1960). The problem of social cost. *Journal of Law and Economics, 3*, October, 1–44.

Coeurdacier, N. and Martin, P. (2009). The geography of asset trade and the euro: Insiders and outsiders. *Journal of Japanese and International Economies, 23*(2), 90–113.

Collier, P. (2013). *Exodus: How migration is changing our world*. Oxford: Oxford University Press.

Collignon, S. and Schwarzer, D. (2002). *Private sector involvement in the Euro: The power of ideas*. London: Routledge.

Committee (1989). *Report on economic and monetary union in the European Community (Delors report)*. Brussels: Committee for the Study of Economic and Monetary Union.

Corsetti, G., Meier, A., and Müller, G. J. (2012). What determines government spending multipliers? *Economic Policy*, October, 521–65.

Cour-Thimann, P. and Winkler, B. (2013). The ECB's non-standard monetary policy measures the role of institutional factors and financial structure. *ECB Working Paper Series, No. 1528*, April. Frankfurt: ECB.

Cour-Thimann, P. and Winkler, B. (2016). Central banks as balance sheets of last resort: ECB's monetary policy in a flow-of-funds perspective. In D. Cobham (Ed.), *Monetary analysis at central banks* (pp. 53–92). Basingstoke: Palgrave Macmillan.

Cramme, O. and Hobolt, S. B. (Eds) (2015). *Democratic politics in a European Union under stress*. Oxford: Oxford University Press.

Creditreform (2012). *Insolvencies in Europe 2011/12. A survey by the Creditreform economic research unit*, <http://www.creditreform.com/uploads/media/Insolvencies_in_Europe_2011-12_04.pdf> (accessed November 9, 2016).

CRS (2014a). Noncitizen eligibility for federal public assistance: Policy overview and trends. *CRS Report for Congress, RL33809* (Ruth Ellen Wasem). Washington, DC: Congressional Research Service.

CRS (2014b). Temporary Assistance for Needy Families (TANF): Eligibility and benefit amounts in state TANF cash assistance programs. *CRS Report for Congress, R43634* (Gene Falk). Washington, DC: Congressional Research Service.

CRS (2014c). Unemployment insurance: Program and benefits. *CRS Report for Congress, RL 33362* (Julie Whittaker, Kateline Isaacs). Washington, DC: Congressional Research Service.

CRS (2014d). Unemployment insurance: Consequences of changes in state unemployment compensation laws. *CRS Report for Congress, R41859* (Kateline Isaacs). Washington, DC: Congressional Research Service.

Curry, T. and Shibut, L. (2000). The cost of the savings and loan crisis: Truth and consequences. *FDIC Banking Review*, 26–35.

Dagher, J. C. (2010). Sudden stops, output drops, and credit collapses. *IMF Working Paper 10/176*. Washington, DC: IMF.

Dao, M., Furceri, D., and Loungani, P. (2014). Regional labor market adjustments in the United States and Europe. *Working Paper 14/26*. Washington, DC: IMF.

Darvas, Z. and Hüttl, P. (2015). How to reduce the Greek debt burden? *Bruegel blog*, January 9, <http://www.bruegel.org/2015/01/how-to-reduce-the-greek-debt-burden/> (accessed June 23, 2016).

Davies, A. (2008). One step forwards, two steps back? The Viking and Laval cases in the ECJ. *Industrial Law Journal, 37*(2), 126–48.

Davies, G. (2011). The ECB and Target2 imbalances. *Financial Times blog*, June 10. http://www.blogs.ft.com/gavyndavies/2011/06/10/the-ecbs-sinnful-behaviour/ (accessed November 9, 2016).

Davies, P. (2002). The posted workers directive and the EC Treaty. *Industrial Law Journal, 31*(3), 298–306.

Davies, P. (2008). Case C-346/06, *Rüffert* v *Land Niedersachsen* [2008] IRLR 467 (ECJ). *Industrial Law Journal, 37*(3), 293–5.

Dawson, M. (2015). The legal and political accountability structure of "post-crisis" EU economic governance. *Journal of Common Market Studies, 53*(5), 976–93.

De Grauwe, P. (2006). What have we learnt about monetary integration since the Maastricht Treaty? *Journal of Common Market Studies, 44*(4), 711–30.

De Grauwe, P. (2011). The governance of a fragile Eurozone. *CEPS Working Document 346*. Brussels: CEPS.

De Grauwe, P. (2013). Design failures in the Eurozone: Can they be fixed? *LEQS Paper No. 57/2013*. London: London School of Economics, European Institute.

De Grauwe, P. (2015). *Economics of monetary integration* (10th ed.). Oxford: Oxford University Press.

De Grauwe, P. and Ji, Y. (2013). Self-fulfilling crises in the Eurozone: An empirical test. *Journal of International Money and Finance, 34*, April, 15–36.

De Grauwe, P. and Moesen, W. (2009). Gains for all: A proposal for a common euro bond. *Intereconomics*, May/June, 132–5.

Degiannakis, S., Duffy, D., and Filis, G. (2014). Business cycle synchronization in EU: A time-varying approach. *Scottish Journal of Political Economy, 61*(4), 348–70.

Dehousse, R. (2012). The "fiscal compact": Legal uncertainty and political ambiguity. *Notre Europe Policy Brief, 33*, February, <http://www.ftp.infoeuropa.eurocid.pt/database/000048001-000049000/000048296.pdf> (accessed July 3, 2016).

Del Negro, M. (2002). Asymmetric shocks among U.S. states. *Journal of International Economics, 56*, 273–97.

Delpla, J. and von Weizsäcker, J. (2010). The Bluebond proposal. *Bruegel Policy Brief, 2010/03.*

Denk, O. (2015). Financial sector pay and labour income inequality: Evidence from Europe. *OECD Economics Department Working Papers, No. 1225.*

Deutsche Bundesbank (1991). Geschäftsberichtder Deutschen Bundesbank für das Jahr 1991. Frankfurt: Deutsche Bundesbank.

Deutsche Rentenversicherung (2014). *Rentenversicherung in Zeitreihen.* DRV Schriften Bd.22. Würzburg: DRV.

Diamond, D. W. and Dybvig, P. H. (1983). Bank runs, deposit insurance, and liquidity. *Journal of Political Economy, 91,* 401–19.

DiCecio, R. and Gascon, C. (2010). Income convergence in the United States: A tale of migration and urbanization. *Annals of Regional Science, 45*(2), 365–77.

Dinger, V., Steinkamp, S., and Westermann, F. (2014). The tragedy of the commons and inflation bias in the euro area. *Open Economies Review, 25*(1), 71–91.

Directorate-General (1990). One market, one money. *European Economy, 44,* October. Brussels: Directorate-General of Economic and Financial Affairs.

DNB (2012). Target 2 balances: Indicator of the intensity of the European debt crisis. De Nederlandsche Bank, April 12, <http://www.dnb.nl/en/news/news-and-archive/dnbulletin-2012/dnb271217.jsp> (accessed November 22, 2014).

Dolls, M., Fuest, C., and Peichl, A. (2009). Automatic stabilisers and the economic crisis: EU vs US. *IZA Discussion paper, No. 4310.* Bonn: IZA.

Dolls, M., Fuest, C., and Peichl, A. (2010). Automatic stabilizers and economic crisis: *US* vs. *Europe. NBER Working Paper, No. 16275* (August). Cambridge, MA: NBER.

Dolls, M., Fuest, C., Heinemann, F., and Peichl, A. (2016). Reconciling insurance with market discipline: A blueprint for a European fiscal union. *CESifo Working Paper, No. 5767* (August), Munich: CESifo.

Domanski, D., Gambacorta, L., and Picillo, C. (2015). Central clearing: Trends and current issues. *BIS Quarterly Review, Q4,* December, 59–76.

Dornbusch, R. (1993). Comments and discussion. In B. Eichengreen, C. Wyplosz, W. H. Branson, and R. Dornbusch (Eds), The unstable EMS. *Brookings Papers on Economic Activity, 1,* 130–6.

Draghi, M. (2012). Speech by Mario Draghi, President of the European Central Bank at the Global Investment Conference in London July 26, <http://www.ecb.europa.eu/press/key/date/2012/html/sp120726.en.html> (accessed November 25, 2014).

Drezner, D. W. (2013). The tragedy of the global institutional common. In M. Finnemore and J. Goldstein (Eds), *Back to basics: State power in a contemporary world* (pp. 280–310). New York: Oxford University Press.

Dubois, E. (2016). Political business cycles 40 years after Nordhaus. *Public Choice, 166*(1), 235–59.

Dullien, S. (2014). A European unemployment benefit scheme. How to provide for more stability in the Euro zone. Gütersloh: Verlag Bertelsmann Stiftung.

Dullien, S. and Guérot, U. (2012). The long shadow of ordoliberalism. *ECFR Commentary,* July 27.

Dullien, S. and Schieritz, M. (2012). German savers should applaud the growing TARGET balances. *VOX CEPR's Policy Portal* (7 May). http://www.voxeu.org/

article/german-savers-should-applaud-growing-target-balances (accessed November 9, 2016).

Dullien, S. and Schwarzer. D. (2007). Integrating the macro-economic dimension into the EU budget: Reasons, instruments and the question of democratic legitimacy. *EU-CONSENT Budget Working Paper, No. 4.*

Dustmann, C. and Frattini, T. (2014). The fiscal effects of immigration to the UK. *Economic Journal Online.*

Dustmann, C. and Görlach, J. S. (2015). The economics of temporary migrations. *Journal of Economic Literature*, published as: SOEP papers on Multidisciplinary Panel Data Research 729–2015. Berlin: DIW.

Dynan, K. (2010). The income roller coaster: Rising income volatility and its implications. *Pathways*, Spring, 3–6.

Dyson, K. and Featherstone, K. (1999). *The road to Maastricht: Negotiating economic and monetary union.* Oxford: Oxford University Press.

ECB (1999). *Annual report.* Frankfurt: ECB.

ECB (2003). *Monthly bulletin*, August. Frankfurt: ECB.

ECB (2011). TARGET2 balances of national central banks in the euro area. *Monthly bulletin*, October. Frankfurt: European Central Bank, 35–40.

ECB (2012). Press release: Technical features of outright monetary transactions. Frankfurt: European Central Bank.

ECB (2013a). *Collateral eligibility requirements: A comparative study across specific frameworks.* Frankfurt: ECB.

ECB (2013b). ELA procedures. October 17. Frankfurt: ECB.

ECB (2013c). *Monthly bulletin* 1/2013. Frankfurt: ECB.

ECB (2014a). *Collateral eligibility and availability*. July. Frankfurt: ECB.

ECB (2014b). ECB assumes responsibility for euro area banking supervision. November 4. Frankfurt: ECB.

ECB (2015a). Rotation of voting rights in the Governing Council, <https://www.ecb.europa.eu/explainers/tell-me-more/html/voting-rotation.en.html> (accessed January 12, 2016).

ECB (2015b). Financial integration in Europe. *Annual Report*, April. Frankfurt: European Central Bank.

ECB (2016). What is the expanded asset purchase programme? Updated March 31, <https://www.ecb.europa.eu/explainers/tell-me-more/html/asset-purchase.en.html> (accessed July 13, 2016).

ECB (n.d.). TARGET2 glossary. Frankfurt: ECB, <http://www.ecb.europa.eu/paym/t2/shared/pdf/target2_glossary.pdf>.

Economist (2009). In the bank. Which central bank has the most employees? December 4, <http://www.economist.com/node/15048548> (accessed August 17, 2016).

Economist (2012). Hazards, moral and otherwise. *Free Exchange blog*, April 10, <http://www.economist.com/blogs/freeexchange/2012/04/euro-crisis-2> (accessed August 13, 2016).

Eder, F. (2016). Wolfgang Schäuble bails out Spain, Portugal. *POLITICO blog*, July 27, <http://www.politico.eu/article/wolfgang-schauble-bails-out-spain-portugal-sanctions-juncker-german-finance-minister/> (accessed August 10, 2016).

EEO (2010). *Self-employment in Europe*. European Employment Observatory Review. Birmingham: EEO network services.

EFSF (2013). FAQ: European financial stability facility, <http://www.efsf.europa.eu/attachments/faq_en.pdf> (accessed January 19, 2016).

Eichengreen, B. (1987). Hegemonic stability theories of the international monetary system. *NBER Working Paper, No. 2193*. Cambridge, MA: NBER.

Eichengreen, B. (2008). Sui generis EMU. *NBER Working Paper, 13740*, January. Cambridge, MA: National Bureau of Economic Research.

Eichengreen, B. and Frieden, J. A. (2001). *The political economy of European monetary unification* (2nd ed.). Boulder, CO: Westview Press.

Eichengreen, B. and Wyplosz, C. (1993). The unstable EMS. In B. J. Eichengreen, C. Wyplosz, W. H. Branson, and R. Dornbusch (Eds), The unstable EMS. *Brookings Papers on Economic Activity, 1*, 51–124.

Eichengreen, B., Mehl, A., Chitu, L., and Richardson, G. (2014). Mutual assistance between Federal Reserve Banks, 1913–1960 as prolegomena to the TARGET2 debate. *NBER Working Paper 20267*. Cambridge, MA: NBER.

Ellsberg, D. (1961). Risk, ambiguity, and the savage axioms. *Quarterly Journal of Economics, 75*(4), 643–69.

Ellul, A., Pagano, M., and Schivardi, F. (2015). Employment and wage insurance within firms: Worldwide evidence. *CEPR Discussion Paper, No. DP10711*.

Elster, J. (1979). *Ulysses and the sirens*. Cambridge: Cambridge University Press.

Elster, J. (1986). The market and the forum: Three varieties of political theory. In J. Elster and A. Hylland (Eds), *Foundations of social choice theory* (chapter 6). Cambridge: Cambridge University Press.

Emmenegger, P. and Careja, R. (2012). From dilemma to dualization: Social and migration policies in the "reluctant countries of immigration." In P. Emmenegger, S. Häusermann, B. Palier, and M. Seeleib-Kaiser, M. (Eds), *The age of dualization: The changing face of inequality in deindustrializing societies* (pp. 124–48). Oxford: Oxford University Press.

Emmenegger, P., Häusermann, S., Palier, B., and Seeleib-Kaiser, M. (Eds) (2012). *The age of dualization: The changing face of inequality in deindustrializing societies*. Oxford: Oxford University Press.

EMN (2013). Intra-EU mobility of third-country nationals. *European Migration Network Study 2013*. Brussels: European Commission.

EMN (2014). Migrant access to social security and healthcare: Policies and practice. *European Migration Network Study 2014*. Brussels: European Commission.

Enderlein, H., Bofinger, P., Boone, L., De Grauwe, P., Piris, J.-C., Pisani-Ferry, J., João Rodrigues, M., Sapir, A., and Vitorino, A. (2012). Completing the Euro. A road map towards fiscal union in Europe. A report of the Tommaso Padoa-Schioppa Group. Berlin: Notre Europe-Jacques Delors Institute.

Engel, C. (2001). A retrial of the case against the EMU: Local-currency pricing and the choice of exchange-rate regime. In B. Eichengreen and J. A. Frieden (Eds), *The political economy of European monetary integration* (2nd ed., pp. 77–110). Bolder, CO: Westview Press.

English, W. B. (1996). Understanding the costs of sovereign default: American state debts in the 1840s. *American Economic Review*, *86*(1), 259–75.

Enrich, D. and Galloni, A. (2012). Turmoil frays ties across continent. *Wall Street Journal Online*, May 31, <http://www.wsj.com/articles/SB10001424052702304065704577426560281463958> (accessed December 16, 2014).

EPRS (2014). Freedom of movement and residence of EU citizens. Access to social benefits (E.-M. Poptcheva). Brussels: European Parliament.

Epstein, R. A. (2014). When do foreign banks "cut and run"? Evidence from west European bailouts and east European markets. *Review of International Political Economy*, *21*(4), 847–77.

ESM (2012). Frequently asked questions on the European Stability Mechanism (ESM). *European Stability Mechanism*, October 8, <http://www.esm.europa.eu/pdf/FAQ%20ESM%2008102012.pdf> (accessed July 3, 2016).

Esping-Andersen, G. (1990). *The three worlds of welfare capitalism*. Cambridge: Polity Press.

Euractiv (2016). Dijsselbloem berates Juncker for failing to apply EU pacts. June 3, <http://www.euractiv.com/section/euro-finance/news/dijsselbloem-raps-juncker-for-failing-to-apply-eu-pacts/> (accessed July 1, 2016).

Eurogroup (2012). Eurogroup statement on Greece. November 27, <http://www.consilium.europa.eu/uedocs/cms_data/docs/pressdata/en/ecofin/133857.pdf> (accessed June 23, 2016).

European Commission (2010). Report on Greek government deficit and debt statistics. *COM(2010) 1 final*, January. Brussels: European Commission.

European Commission (2016). Stability and Growth Pact: Update on the fiscal situation of Spain and Portugal. *Press Release*, July 7. Brussels: European Commission.

European Council (2011). *European Council 16–17 December 2010, conclusions*. General Secretariat of the Council, <http://www.consilium.europa.eu/uedocs/cms_data/docs/pressdata/en/ec/118578.pdf>.

European Economy (1993). Stable money—sound finances: Community public finance in the perspective of EMU. *European Economy report, No. 53*. Brussels: Commission of the European Communities.

European Economy Cyprus (2013). The economic adjustment programme for Cyprus. *Occasional Papers, 149*, May. Brussels: European Commission.

European Economy Greece (2010). The economic adjustment programme for Greece. *Occasional Papers, 61*, May. Brussels: European Commission.

European Economy Ireland (2011). The economic adjustment programme for Ireland. *Occasional Papers, 76*, February. Brussels: European Commission.

European Economy Portugal (2011). The economic adjustment programme for Portugal. *Occasional Papers, 79*, June. Brussels: European Commission.

European Economy Spain (2012). The financial sector adjustment programme for Spain. *Occasional Papers, 118*, October. Brussels: European Commission.

Eurostat (2004). *Report by Eurostat on the revision of the Greek government deficit and debt figures*. November 22. Luxembourg: European Commission.

Eurostat (2010). *Report on Greek government deficit and debt statistics*. COM(2010) 1 final. January. Brussels: European Commission.

Eurostat (2013). Statistical classification of the European Stability Mechanism. *Decision of Eurostat on deficit and debt*, Ref. Ares(2013)117666—30/01/2013, <http://www.ec.europa.eu/eurostat/documents/1015035/2041337/Eurostat-Decision-on-ESM.pdf/6e87bbe1-f081-43a4-8543-cc62f32eefc1> (accessed March 29, 2016).

Eurostat (2014). Supplementary table for the financial crisis. Background note, October. Luxembourg: European Commission.

Ewald, F. (1991). Insurance and risk. In G. Burchell, C. Gordon, and P. Miller (Eds), *The Foucault effect. Studies in governmentality* (pp. 197–210). Chicago, IL: University of Chicago Press.

Facchini, G. and Mayda, A. M. (2009). The political economy of immigration policy. *Human Development Research Paper 2009/3*, UNDP.

Fahrholz, C. and Freytag, A. (2012). A way to solve the European balance of payments crisis? Take a chance on market solutions! *CESifo Forum*, *13*(January), 77–82.

Faini, R. (2007). Remittances and the brain drain: Do more skilled migrants remit more? *World Bank Economic Review*, *21*(2), 177–91.

Farhi, E. and Tirole, J. (2014). Deadly embrace: Sovereign and financial balance sheets doom loops. *Working Paper*, April.

Farhi, E. and Werning, I. (2014). Fiscal unions. *Working Paper*, July. Cambridge, MA: Harvard and MIT Press.

Farrell, M., Rich, S., Turner, L., Seith, D., and Bloom, D. (2008). *Welfare time limits. An update on state policies, implementation, and effects on families*. Washington, DC: Lewin Group and MDRC for the Office of Planning, Research, and Evaluation, Administration for Children and Families, US Department of Health and Human Services.

Favell, A. (2009). Immigration, migration, and free movement in the making of Europe. In J. T. Checkel and P. J. Katzenstein (Eds), *European identities*. Cambridge: Cambridge University Press, 167–92.

FAZ (2015). Schäuble nennt Bedingungen für europäische Einlagenversicherung. *Frankfurter Allgemeine Zeitung*, *286*, December 9, 18.

FDIC (1998). A brief history of deposit insurance in the United States. September. Washington, DC: Federal Deposit Insurance Corporation.

FDIC (2014). Who is the FDIC? <https://www.fdic.gov/about/learn/symbol/WhoistheFDIC.pdf> (accessed January 21, 2016).

Feldstein, M. (2012). The failure of the euro. The little currency that couldn't. *Foreign Affairs*, January/February, online version.

Ferguson, E. J. (1962). Public finance and the origins of Southern sectionalism. *Journal of Southern History*, *28*(4), 450–61.

Ferguson, W. (2013). *Collective action and exchange. A game-theoretic approach to contemporary political economy*. Stanford, CA: Stanford University Press.

Ferrera, M. (2005). *The boundaries of welfare: European integration and the new spatial politics of social protection*. Oxford: Oxford University Press.

Ferrera, M. (2009). The JCMS annual lecture: National welfare states and European integration: In search of a "virtuous nesting." *Journal of Common Market Studies*, *47*(2), 219–33.

Fitoussi, J.-P., Atkinson, A. B., Blanchard, O. E., Flemming, J. S., Malinvaud, E., Phelps, E. S., and Solow, R. M. (1993). *Competitive disinflation. The mark and budgetary politics in Europe*. Oxford: Oxford University Press.

Flood, R. P. and Marion, N. P. (1996). Speculative attacks: Fundamentals and self-Fulfilling prophecies. *NBER Working Paper, No. 5789*, October. Cambridge, MA: NBER.

Flood, R. P., Marion, N. P., and Matsumoto, A. (2012). International risk sharing during the globalization era. *Canadian Journal of Economics, 45*(2), 394–416.

Focus (2012). Bevölkerung soll über Euro-Bonds abstimmen. SPD-Chef Gabriel für gemeinsame Schuldenhaftung. *Focus Online*, August 8, <http://www.focus.de/finanzen/news/staatsverschuldung/bevoelkerung-soll-ueber-euro-bonds-abstimmen-spd-chef-gabriel-fuer-gemeinschaftliche-schuldenhaftung_aid_794076.html> (accessed July 3, 2016).

Follesdal, A. and Hix, S. (2006). Why there is a democratic deficit in the EU: Response to Majone and Moravcsik. *Journal of Common Market Studies, 44*(3), 533–62.

Follette, G., Kusko, A., and Lutz, B. (2008). State and local finances and the macroeconomy: The high-employment budget and fiscal impetus. *Finance and Economics Discussion Series (FEDS)*. Washington, DC: Board of Governors of the Federal Reserve System.

Frankel, J. A. (1996). Recent exchange-rate experience and proposals for reform. *American Economic Review, 86*(2), 153–8.

Frankel, J. A. and Rose, A. (1998). The endogeneity of the optimum currency area criteria. *Economic Journal, 108*, 1009–25.

Franzese, R. J. (2002). Electoral and partisan cycles in economic policies and outcomes. *Annual Review of Political Science, 5*, June, 369–421.

Franzese, R. J. and Mosher, J. M. (2002). Comparative institutional and policy advantage: The scope for divergence within European economic integration. *European Union Politics, 3*(2), 177–203.

Freeman, G. P. (1986). Migration and the political economy of the welfare state. *Annals of the American Academy of Political and Social Science, 485*(May), 51–63.

Frenkel, J. A. and Mussa, M. L. (1984). Asset markets, exchange rates and the balance of payments. *NBER Working Paper, No. 1287*. Cambridge, MA: NBER.

Frieden, J. A. (2002). Real sources of European currency policy: Sectoral interests and European monetary integration. *International Organization, 56*(4), 831–60.

Frieden, J. A. (2015a). *Currency politics: The political economy of exchange rate policy*. Princeton, NJ: Princeton University Press.

Frieden, J. A. (2015b). Early American monetary and financial history: Lessons for the euro. March, unpublished typescript of presentation to Absolute Strategy Research, London.

Frieden, J. A. (2016). The governance of international finance. *Annual Review of Political Science, 19* (pre-publication online), *3*, 1–3.16.

Friedman, M. and Schwartz, A. J. (1963). *A monetary history of the United States 1867–1960*. Princeton, NJ: Princeton University Press.

Fritz, B. and Metzger, M. (Eds) (2006). *New issues in regional monetary coordination. Understanding north-south and south-south arrangements*. Basingstoke: Palgrave Macmillan.

Fuest, C. and Peichl, A. (2012). European fiscal union: What is it? Does it work? And are there really "no alternatives"? *CESifo Forum, 13*(1), 3–9.

Galati, G. and Moessner, R. (2011). Macroprudential policy—a literature review. *BIS Working Papers, 337,* February. Basel: Bank for International Settlement.

GAO. (1990). Failed thrifts: FDIC oversight of 1988 deals needs improvement. *GGD/90/93,* Washington, DC: US General Accounting Office.

Garber, P. (1998). Notes on the role of TARGET in a stage III crisis. *NBER Working Paper.* Cambridge, MA: National Bureau of Economic Research.

Garber, P. (2010). The mechanics of intra euro area capital flight. *Special Report.* Deutsche Bank Securities.

Garthwaite, C., Gross, T., and Notowidigdo, M. J. (2013). Public health insurance, labor supply, and employment lock. *NBER Working Paper,* No. 19220. Cambridge, MA: NBER.

Gaspar, V. (2015). The making of a continental financial system: Lessons for Europe from early American history. *Journal of European Integration, 37*(7), 847–59.

Genschel, P. and Jachtenfuchs, M. (Eds) (2014). *Beyond the regulatory polity? The European integration of core state powers.* Oxford: Oxford University Press.

Gerlach, S. and Hoffmann, M. (2008). The impact of the euro on international stability and volatility. *Economic Papers 309.* European Commission.

Giannini, C. (2011). *The age of central banks.* Cheltenham: Edward Elgar.

Giannone, D., Lenza, M., and Reichlin, L. (2009). Business cycles in the euro area. *Working Paper No. 1010.* Frankfurt: ECB.

Gianviti, F., Krueger, A. O., Pisani-Ferry, J., Sapir, A., and von Hagen, J. (2010). *A European mechanism for sovereign debt crisis resolution: A proposal.* Brussels: Bruegel.

Giavazzi, F. and Giovannini, A. (1987). Models of the EMS: Is Europe a greater deutschmark area? In R. C. Bryant and R. Portes (Eds), *Global Macroeconomics.* London: Macmillan.

Giavazzi, F. and Pagano, M. (1988). The advantage of tying one's hands: EMS discipline and Central Bank credibility. *European Economic Review, 32*(5), 1055–75.

Giavazzi, F. and Wyplosz, C. (2015). EMU: Old flaws revisited. *Journal of European Integration, 37*(7), 723–37.

Giles, C. and Parker, G. (2011). Osborne urges Eurozone to "get a grip." *Financial Times Online,* July 20.

Giovannini Group (2000). Co-ordinated public debt issuance in the euro area. *Report of the Giovannini Group,* November 8. Brussels: Economic and Financial Committee.

Goldstein, J. L. and Steinberg, R. H. (2010). Introduction. In J. L. Goldstein and R. H. Steinberg (Eds), *International institutions* (Vol. I). London: Sage.

Goodhart, C. A. E. (1989). *Money, information and uncertainty* (2nd ed.). London: Macmillan.

Goodhart, C. A. E. (1998). The two concepts of money: Implications for the analysis of optimal currency areas. *European Journal of Political Economy, 14,* 407–32.

Goodhart, C. A. E. (2011). Europe: After the crisis. *VOX CEPR's Policy Portal,* November 25.

Goodhart, C. A. E. and Schoenmaker, D. (1995). Should the functions of monetary policy and banking supervision be separated? *Oxford Economic Papers, 47,* 539–60.

Goodhart, C. A. E. and Smith, S. (1993). Stabilization. *European Economy, 5*, 417–55.

Goodhart, C. A. E., Tsomocos, D. P., and Sunirand, P. (2004). *A model to analyse financial fragility: Applications*. London: London School of Economics and Political Science, Financial Markets Group.

Goodhart, D. (2004). Too diverse? Is Britain becoming too diverse to sustain the mutual obligations behind a good society and the welfare state? *Prospect*, February.

Gottschalk, P. and Moffitt, R. (2009). The rising instability of U.S. earnings. *Journal of Economic Perspectives, 23*(4), 3–24.

Gourevitch, P. A. (1986). *Politics in hard times: Comparative responses to international economic crises*. Ithaca, NY: Cornell University Press.

Gourinchas, P.-O., Philippon, T., and Vayanos, D. (2016). The analytics of the Greek crisis. *GreeSE Paper*, No 100 (July). London: Hellenic Observatory, LSE.

Goves, P., Spies, M., and Tentori, A. (2016). Regulatory treatment of sovereign debt: Risk weights vs large exposure limits. *VOX CEPR's Policy Portal*, March 2, <http://www.voxeu.org/article/regulatory-treatment-sovereign-debt-0> (accessed July 10, 2016).

Grieco, J. M. (1988). Realist theory and the problem of international cooperation: Analysis with an amended prisoner's dilemma model. *Journal of Politics, 50*(3), 600–24.

Grieco, J. M., Powell, R., and Snidal, D. T. (1993). The relative-gains problem for international cooperation—comment/reply. *American Political Science Review, 87*(3), 729–43.

Griffiths, J. and Todoulos, K. (2014). Conditionally yours. An analysis of the policy conditions attached to IMF loans. *European Network on Debt and Development, Report*, April.

Grittersová, J. (2014). Non-market cooperation and the variety of finance capitalism in advanced democracies. *Review of International Political Economy, 21*(2), 339–71.

Gros, D. and Alcidi, C. (2014). The case of the disappearing fiscal compact. *CEPS Commentary*, November 2, <https://www.ceps.eu/system/files/Fiscal%20Compact.pdf> (accessed July 2, 2016).

Grossman, R. S. and Rockoff, H. U. (2015). Fighting the last war: Economists on the lender of last resort. *NBER Working Paper, 20832*. Cambridge, MA: NBER.

Gruber, J. and Madrian, B. C. (2002). Health insurance, labor supply, and job mobility: A critical review of the literature. *NBER Working Paper, No. 8817*. Cambridge, MA: NBER.

Guajardo, J., Leigh, D., and Pescatori, A. (2014). Expansionary austerity? International evidence. *Journal of the European Economic Association, 12*(4), 949–68.

Hahn, F. H. (1984). Reflections on the invisible hand. In F. H. Hahn (Ed.), *Equilibrium and macroeconomics* (pp. 111–33). Oxford: Blackwell.

Hall, G. and Sargent, T. (2014). Fiscal discriminations in three wars. *Journal of Monetary Economics, 61*, 148–66.

Hall, P. A. (1989). *The political power of economic ideas: Keynesianism across nations*. Princeton, NJ: Princeton University Press.

Hall, P. A. (2012). The economics and politics of the Euro crisis. *German Politics, 21*(4), 355–71.

Hall, P. A. (2014a). Varieties of capitalism and the euro crisis. *West European Politics, 37*(6), 1223–43.

Hall, P. A. (2014b). The political sources of social solidarity. In K. Banting and W. Kymlicka (Eds), *Solidarity in Diverse Societies*. Oxford: Oxford: Oxford University Press.

Hall, P. A. and Franzese, R. J. (1998). Mixed signals: Central bank independence, coordinated wage bargaining, and European Monetary Union. *International Organization, 52*(3), 505–35.

Hall, P. A. and Soskice, D. (Eds) (2001). *Varieties of capitalism*. Oxford: Oxford University Press.

Hall, P. A. and Taylor, R. C. R. (1996). Political science and the three new institutionalisms. *Political Studies, 44*(5), 936–57.

Hallerberg, M. (2004). *Domestic budgets in a United Europe. Fiscal governance from the end of Bretton Woods to EMU*. Ithaca, NJ: Cornell University Press.

Hallerberg, M. and von Hagen, J. (1997). Electoral institutions, cabinet negotiations, and budget deficits in the European Union. *NBER Working Paper, No.6941*, December. Cambridge, MA: NBER.

Hallerberg, M., Strauch, R., and von Hagen, J. (2009). *Fiscal governance in Europe*. Cambridge: Cambridge University Press.

Hancké, B. (2013). *Unions, central banks, and EMU*. Oxford: Oxford University Press.

Hancké, B. and Rhodes, M. (2005). EMU and labor market institutions in Europe. The rise and fall of national social pacts. *Work and Occupations, 32*(2), 196–228.

Hancké, B., Rhodes, M., and Thatcher, M. (2007). Introduction: Beyond varieties of capitalism. In B. Hancké, M. Rhodes, and M. Thatcher (Eds), *Beyond varieties of capitalism* (pp. 3–38). Oxford: Oxford University Press.

Hanson, S. G., Kashyap, A. K., and Stein, J. C. (2011). A macroprudential approach to financial regulation. *Journal of Economic Perspectives 25*(1), 3–28.

Hardie, I. and Howarth, D. (Eds) (2013). *Market-based banking and the international financial crisis*. Oxford: Oxford University Press.

Hardie, I., Howarth, D., Maxfield, S., and Verdun, A. (2013). Banks and the false dichotomy in the comparative political economy of finance. *World Politics, 65*(4), 691–728.

Hardin, G. (1968). The tragedy of the commons. *Science, 162*(3859), 1243–8.

Hardin, R. (1982). *Collective action*. Baltimore, MA: Johns Hopkins University Press.

Hatton, T. J. (2014). Public opinion on immigration: Has the recession changed minds? *CEPR Discussion Paper 10008*. London: CEPR.

Heikensten, L. (2003). The Riksbank and the euro. *Speech*, June 17.

Heipertz, M. and Verdun, A. (2004). The dog that would never bite? What we can learn from the origins of the Stability and Growth Pact. In F. Torres, A. Verdun, C. Zilioli, and H. Zimmermann (Eds), *Governing EMU* (pp. 137–52). Badia Fiesole: European University Institute.

Helleiner, E. (2003). The making of national money: Territorial currencies in historical perspective. Ithaca, NY: Cornell University Press.

Helpman, E. (1988). Trade patterns under uncertainty with country specific shocks. *Econometrica, 56*(3), 645–59.

Helpman, E. and Razin, A. (1978). *A theory of international trade under uncertainty*. New York: Academic Press.

Henning, C. R. (2016). The ECB as a strategic actor: Central banking in a politically fragmented monetary union. In J. Caporaso and M. Rhodes (Eds), *The political and economic dynamics of the Eurozone crisis*. Oxford: Oxford Uiversity Press, 167–99.

Henning, C. R. (forthcoming). *Tangled governance. International regime complexity, the Ttroika, and the euro crisis*. Oxford: Oxford University Press.

Henning, C. R. and Kessler, M. (2012). Fiscal federalism: US history for architects of Europe's fiscal union. Brussels: Bruegel.

Herwig, A. (2008). The multiple understandings of conflict between trade in services and labour protection. In C. Joerges and P. F. Kjaer (Eds), *Transnational standards of social protection* (pp. 7–30). Oslo: ARENA.

Hetzel, R. L. (2013). The Treasury-Federal Reserve Accord to the mid 1960s. *Federal Reserve History*, November 22, <http://www.federalreservehistory.org/Events/DetailView/63> (accessed June 12, 2015).

Hien, J. (2013). The ordoliberalism that never was. *Contemporary Political Theory*, *12*(4), 349–58.

HM Government (2014). Review of the balance of competences between the United Kingdom and the European Union. The Single Market: Financial services and the free movement of capital, <https://www.gov.uk/review-of-the-balance-of-competences/> (accessed March 29, 2016).

Hobolt, S. B. (2009). *Europe in question: Referendums on European integration*. Oxford: Oxford University Press.

Hobza, A. and Zeugner, S. (2014a). The "imbalanced balance" and its unravelling: Current accounts and bilateral financial flows in the euro area. *European Economy Economic Papers 520*. European Commission Directorate-General for Economic and Financial Affairs (also published in *Journal of International Money and Finance*).

Hobza, A. and Zeugner, S. (2014b). Current accounts and financial flows in the euro area, <http://www.zeugner.eu/studies/finflows/> (accessed August 17, 2016).

Hodson, D. (2004). Macroeconomic co-ordination in the euro area: The scope and limits of the open method. *Journal of European Public Policy*, *11*(2), 231–48.

Hodson, D. (2009). EMU and political union: What, if anything, have we learned from the euro's first decade? *Journal of European Public Policy*, *16*(4), 508–26.

Hodson, D. (2011). *Governing the euro area in good times and bad*. Oxford: Oxford University Press.

Hoffmann, M. and Sørensen, B. (2012). Don't expect too much from EZ fiscal union—and complete the unfinished integration of European capital markets! VoxEU blog, November 9, http://www.voxeu.org/article/hedging-macroeconomic-risk-eurozone-fiscal-union-versus-capital-markets (accessed November 1, 2016).

Holmstrom, B. (1982). Moral hazard in teams. *Bell Journal of Economics*, *13*(2), 324–40.

Hopkin, J. (2015). The troubled Southern periphery: The euro experience in Spain and Italy. In M. Matthijs and M. Blyth (Eds), *The future of the euro* (pp. 161–85). Oxford: Oxford University Press.

Höpner, M. (2009). Usurpation instead of delegation: How the ECJ radicalizes Common Market integration and why it needs political control. *Working Paper*, September, revised English version of *MPIfG Discussion Paper 2008/12*.

Howarth, D. and Quaglia, L. (2013). Banking union as holy grail: Rebuilding the Single Market in financial services, stabilizing Europe's banks and "completing" economic and monetary union. *Journal of Common Market Studies, 51*, 103–23.

Howarth, D. and Quaglia, L. (2014). Economic governance and the chimera of financial system stability: The political economy of new capital requirements in the European Union. University of Edinburgh, Conference proceedings, pp. 67–85, <http://www.pol.ed.ac.uk/__data/assets/pdf_file/0019/86203/conference_proceedings.pdf>.

Howarth, D. and Quaglia, L. (2015). The political economy of the single supervisory mechanism: Squaring the "inconsistent quartet." Conference Paper, EUSA Boston, March.

Huber, P. and Tondl, G. (2012). Migration and regional convergence in the European Union. *Empirica, 39*(4), 439–60.

Huizinga, H. and Zhu, D. (2004). Domestic and international finance: How do they affect consumption smoothing? *CEPR Discussion Paper, No. 4677*. London: CEPR.

Hutchison, M. M., Noy, I., and Wang, L. (2010). Fiscal and monetary policies and the cost of sudden stops. *Journal of International Money and Finance Online*, 1–15.

IEO (2016). *The IMF and the crises in Greece, Ireland, and Portugal: An evaluation by the Independent Evaluation Office*. Washington, DC: Independent Evaluation Office of the International Monetary Fund.

Ilzetzki, E. (2014). Comment on Whelan (2014). *Economic Policy, 29*(77), 126–37.

Imbs, J. and Mauro, P. (2007). Pooling risks among countries. *IMF Working Paper, 07/132*. Washington, DC: IMF.

IMF (2012). IMF adopts institutional view on capital flows. *IMF Survey Magazine: Policy*, December 3.

IMF (2013). Dancing together? Spillovers, common shocks, and the role of financial and trade linkages. In IMF (Ed.), *World economic outlook* (pp. 81–111). Washington, DC: IMF.

IMF (2015). Factsheet: IMF conditionality, September 24, <https://www.imf.org/external/np/exr/facts/conditio.htm> (accessed January 17, 2016).

IMF (2016a). Greece. Preliminary debt sustainability analysis—updated estimates and further considerations. *IMF Country Report, No. 16/130*. Washington, DC: IMF.

IMF (2016b). Germany. Financial sector assessment report. *IMF Country Report, No.16/189*. Washington, DC: IMF.

Immervoll, H. (2009). Minimum-income benefits in OECD countries: Policy design, effectiveness and challenges. *Discussion Paper 4627*. Bonn: IZA.

Issing, O. (2002). On macroeconomic policy co-ordination in EMU. *Journal of Common Market Studies, 40*(2), 345–58.

Italianer, A. and Vanheukelen, M. (1993). Proposals for Community stabilization mechanisms: Some historical applications. *European Economy, 5*, 493–510.

Iversen, T., Soskice, D., and Hope, D. (2016). The Eurozone and political economic institutions. *Annual Review of Political Science, 19*, 10.1–10.23.

Jabko, N. (2006). *Playing the market: A political strategy for uniting Europe, 1985–2005*. Ithaca, NY: Cornell University Press.

Jabko, N. (2015). The elusive economic government and the forgotten fiscal union. In M. Matthijs and M. Blyth (Eds), *The future of the euro* (pp. 70–89). Oxford: Oxford University Press.

Jacoby, W. (2015). Europe's new German problem: The timing of politics and the politics of timing. In M. Matthijs and M. Blyth (Eds), *The future of the euro* (pp. 187–209). Oxford: Oxford University Press.

James, H. (2012). *Making the European Monetary Union*. Cambridge, MA: Harvard University Press.

Jauer, J., Liebig, T., Martin, J. P., and Puhani, P. (2014). Migration as an adjustment mechanism in the crisis? A comparison of Europe and the United States. *OECD Social, Employment and Migration Working Papers, No. 155*. Paris: OECD Publishing.

Jenkins, P. (2016). Sovereign risk system needs reforming. *Financial Times Inside Business*, May 2, <http://www.ft.com/cms/s/0/c68f7484-0df2-11e6-b41f-0beb7e589515.html#axzz4D9lmrQAb> (accessed July 2, 2016).

Jickling, M. and Murphy, E. V. (2010). Who regulates whom? An overview of U.S. financial supervision. *CRS Report for Congress, 7-5700*. Washington, DC: Congressional Research Service.

Jobst, C., Handig, M., and Holzfeind, R. (2012). Understanding TARGET 2: The Eurosystem's euro payment system from an economic and balance sheet perspective. *Monetary Policy and the Economy, Q1/12*, 81–91.

Joerges, C. and Rödl, F. (2008), On the "social deficit" of the European integration project and its perpetuation through the ECJ judgments in Viking and Laval. *RECON Online Working Paper* 2008/06. Oslo: ARENA.

John, M. and Strupczewski, J. (2014). France tests EU rules with 2015 budget, Italy also may fall short. *Reuters Business News*, October 15, 4.

Johnston, A. (2012). European Economic and Monetary Union's perverse effects on sectoral wage inflation: Negative feedback effects from institutional change? *European Union Politics, 13*(3), 345–66.

Johnston, A. (2016). *From convergence to crisis. Labor markets and the instability of the Euro*. Ithaca, NY: Cornell University Press.

Johnston, A. and Regan, A. (2016). European monetary integration and the incompatibility of national varieties of capitalism. *Journal of Common Market Studies, 54*(2), 318–36.

Jones, E. (2002). *The politics of economic and monetary union*. Lanham, MD: Rowman and Littlefield.

Jones, E. (2012). The JCMS Annual Review Lecture. European crisis, European solidarity. *Journal of Common Market Studies, 50*(2), 53–67.

Jones, E. (2013). The collapse of the Brussels–Frankfurt consensus and the future of the euro. In V. A. Schmidt and M. Thatcher (Eds), *Resilient liberalism in Europe's political economy* (pp. 145–70). Cambridge: Cambridge University Press.

Jones, E. (2015). Getting the story right: How you should choose between different interpretations of the European crisis (and why you should care). *Journal of European Integration, 37*(7), 817–32.

Jones, E. and Underhill, G. (2014). The theory of optimum financial areas: Retooling the debate on the governance of global finance. SWIFT Institute, *Working Paper No. 2013-001*.

Jones, E., Kelemen, R. D., and Meunier, S. (2016). Failing forward? The Euro crisis and the incomplete nature of European integration. *Comparative Political Studies, 49*(7), 1010–34.

Jonung, L. and Drea, E. (2009). The euro: It can't happen, it's a bad idea, it won't last. US economists on the EMU, 1989–2002. *Economic Papers, 395*, December. Brussels: European Commission.

JRC (2011). JRC report under Article 12 of Directive 94/19/EC as amended by Directive 2009/14/EC. Ispra: European Commission, Joint Research Centre, Unit G09.

Juncker, J.-C., Tusk, D., Dijsselbloem, J., Draghi, M., and Schulz, M. (2015). *Completing Europe's economic and monetary union*. Brussels: European Commission.

Kahneman, D. and A. Tversky (1979). Prospect theory: An analysis of decision under risk. *Econometrica, 47*(2), 263–92.

Kalemli-Ozcan, S., Sørensen, B., and Yosha, O. (2001). Economic integration, industrial specialization, and the asymmetry of macroeconomic fluctuations. *Journal of International Economics, 55*, 107–37.

Kalemli-Ozcan, S., Luttini, E., and Sørensen, B. (2014). Debt crises and risk-sharing: The role of markets versus sovereigns. *Scandinavian Journal of Economics, 116*(1), 253–76.

Kalemli-Ozcan, S., Sørensen, B., and Yosha, O. (2004). Asymmetric shocks and risk-sharing in a monetary union: Updated evidence and policy implications for Europe. *CEPR Discussion Paper, No. 4463*. London: CEPR.

Kang, J. S. and Shambaugh, J. (2013). The evolution of current account deficits in the euro area periphery and the Baltics: Many paths to the same endpoint. *IMF Working Paper, WP/13/169*. Washington, DC: International Monetary Fund.

Kaske, M. and Braun, M. Z. (2015). Puerto Rico's slide. *Bloomberg QuickTake Online*, December 21, <http://www.bloombergview.com/quicktake/puerto-ricos-slide> (accessed February 14, 2016).

Kawai, M. and Lombardi, D. (Eds) (2014). *Financial regionalism and the international monetary system*. Washington, DC: Brookings Institution and Asian Development Bank.

Keefer, P. and Stasavage, D. (2003). The limits of delegation: Veto players, central bank independence, and the credibility of monetary policy. *American Political Science Review, 97*(3), 407–23.

Kelemen, R. D. (2011). *Eurolegalism: The transformation of law and regulation in the European Union*. Cambridge, MA: Harvard University Press.

Kelemen, R. D. and Teo, T. K. (2014). Law, focal points, and fiscal discipline in the United States and the European Union. *American Political Science Review, 108*(2), 355–70.

Kenen, P. B. (1969). The theory of optimum currency areas: An eclectic view. In R. A. Mundell and A. Swoboda, K. (Eds), *Monetary problems of the international economy* (pp. 41–60). Chicago, IL: University of Chicago Press.

Kenen, P. B. (2000). Currency areas, policy domains, and the institutionalization of fixed exchange rates. *CEP Discussion Paper, 467*. London: London School of Economics, Centre for Economic Performance.

Kenen, P. B. (2003). Five years of the ECB. *CentrePiece*, Summer, 31–6.

Keohane, R. O. (1984). *After hegemony: Cooperation and discord in the world political economy*. Princeton, NJ: Princeton University Press.

Keohane, R. O. and Ostrom, E. (Eds) (1995). *Local commons and global interdependence: Heterogeneity and cooperation in two domains*. London: Sage Publications.

Keynes, J. M. (1936). *The general theory of employment, interest, and money*. Basingstoke: Palgrave Macmillan for the Royal Economic Society.

Kilpatrick, C. (2009a). The ECJ and labour law: A 2008 retrospective. *Industrial Law Journal, 38*(2), 180–208.

Kilpatrick, C. (2009b). *Laval*'s regulatory conundrum: Collective standard-setting and the Court's new approach to posted workers. *European Law Review, 34*(6).

Kincaid, R. and Watson, M. (2015). Avoiding another crisis in the euro area: Public and private imbalances and national policy responses. *Journal of European Integration, 37*(7), 787–801.

Kindleberger, C. P. (1973). *The world in depression, 1929–1939*. London: Allen Lane the Penguin Press.

Kindleberger, C. P. (2000). *Comparative political economy: A retrospective*. Cambridge, MA: MIT Press.

King, D. and Rueda, D. (2008). Cheap labor: The new politics of "bread and roses" in industrial democracies. *Perspectives on Politics, 6*(2), 279–97.

Kirman, A. (1989). The intrinsic limits of modern economic theory: The emperor has no clothes. *Economic Journal, 99*(395), 126–39.

Kitschelt, H., Lange, P., Marks, G., and Stephens, J. D. (Eds) (1999). *Continuity and change in contemporary capitalism*. Cambridge: Cambridge University Press.

Koning, J. (2012). The idiot's guide to the Federal Reserve Interdistrict Settlement Account. <http://www.jpkoning.blogspot.ie/2012/02/idiots-guide-to-federal-reserve.html> (accessed June 8, 2015).

Korinek, A. and Sandri, D. (2015). Capital controls or macroprudential regulation? *IMF Working Paper, No. 15/218*. Washington, DC: IMF.

Korpi, W. and Palme, J. (1998). The paradox of redistribution and strategies of equality: Welfare state institutions, inequality, and poverty in the Western countries. *American Sociological Review, 63*, 661–87.

Kose, A., Prasad, E., and Terrones, M. (2007). How does financial globalization affect risk sharing? Patterns and channels. *IZA DP*, No. 2903. Bonn: IZA.

Kose, A., Prasad, E., and Terrones, M. (2009). Does financial globalization promote risk sharing? *Journal of Development Economics, 89*(2), 258–70.

Kose, M. A., Prasad, E. S, and Terrones, M. E. (2003). Financial integration and macroeconomic volatility. *IMF Staff Papers* 50(1). Washington, DC: International Monetary Fund.

Krasner, S. D. (2013). New terrains: Sovereignty and alternative conceptions of power. In M. Finnemore and J. Goldstein (Eds), *Back to basics: State power in a contemporary world* (pp. 339–59). New York: Oxford University Press.

Krugman, P. (1979). A model of balance-of-payments crises. *Journal of Money, Credit and Banking, 11*(3), 311–25.

Krugman, P. R. (1993). Lessons of Massachusetts for EMU. In F. Torres and F. Giavazzi (Eds), *Adjustment and growth in the European Monetary Union* (pp. 241–60). Cambridge: Cambridge University Press.

Krugman, P. R. (1996). Are currency crises self-fulfilling? In B. S. Bernanke and J. J. Rotemberg (Eds), *NBER macroeconomics annual*, Vol. 11 (pp. 345–407). Cambridge, MA: NBER.

Krugman, P. R. (2013). Revenge of the optimum currency area. In D. Acemoglu, J. Parker, and M. Woodford (Eds), *NBER Macroeconomics Annual 2012*, Vol. 27 (pp. 439–48). Chicago, IL: University of Chicago Press.

Kydland, F. E. and Prescott, E. C. (1977). Rules rather than discretion: The inconsistency of optimal plans. *Journal of Political Economy, 85*(3), 473–91.

Labhard, V. and Sawicki, M. (2006). International and intranational consumption risk sharing: The evidence for the United Kingdom and OECD. *Working paper, No. 302.* London: Bank of England.

Laffan, B., O' Donnell, R., and Smith, M. (1999). *Europe's experimental union: Rethinking integration.* Milton Park, NY: Routledge.

Lannoo, K. (2015). *The great financial plumbing. From Northern Rock to banking union.* London: Rowman and Littlefield International.

Larch, M., van den Noord, P., Jonung, L. (2010). The Stability and Growth Pact: Lessons from the Great Recession. *European Economy: Economic Papers, 429.* Brussels: European Commission.

Leeper, E. M. and Nason, J. N. (2015). Bringing financial stability into monetary policy. *Sveriges Riksbank Working Paper Series, No.305*, July.

Legido-Quigley, H. and La Parra, D. (2007). The health care needs of UK pensioners living in Spain: An agenda for research. *Eurohealth, 13*(4), 14–18.

Lewis, K. K. (1996). Consumption, stock returns, and the gains from international risk-sharing. *NBER Working Paper, No. w19317.*

Lijphart, A. and Crepaz, M. M. L. (1991). Corporatism and consensus democracy in eighteen countries: Conceptual and empirical linkages. *British Journal of Political Science, 21*(2), 235–46.

Lindbeck, A. and Snower, D. (1986). Efficiency wages versus insiders and outsiders. *CEPR Discussion Paper 133.* London: CEPR.

Lohmann, S. (2003). Why do institutions matter? An audience–cost theory of institutional commitment. *Governance, 16*(1), 95–110.

Lubik, T. A. and Rhodes, K. (2012). TARGET2: Symptom, not cause, of Eurozone woes. *Economic Brief, EB 12-08.* Federal Reserve Bank of Richmond.

Lütz, S. and Kranke, M. (2010). The European rescue of the Washington consensus? EU and IMF lending to Central and Eastern European countries. *LEQS Paper No. 57/2013, No. 22.* London: London School of economics.

Lütz, S. and Kranke, M. (2014). The European rescue of the Washington consensus? EU and IMF lending to Central and Eastern European countries. *Review of International Political Economy, 21*(2), 310–38.

Lütz, S., Hilgers, S., and Schneider, S. (2015). Credit lending as two-level game: Troika-debtor negotiations in Cyprus and Portugal. Paper presented at the ECPR General Conference, Montreal, August 26–9.

Mabbett, D. (2016). The minimum wage in Germany: What brought the state in? *Journal of European Public Policy, 23*(8), 1240–58.

Mabbett, D. and Schelkle, W. (2007). Bringing macroeconomics back into the political economy of reform: the Lisbon Agenda and the "fiscal philosophy" of EMU. *Journal of Common Market Studies, 45*(1), 81–103.

Mabbett, D. and Schelkle, W. (2009). The politics of conflict management in EU regulation. *West European Politics, 32*(4), 699–718.

Mabbett, D. and Schelkle, W. (2010). Beyond the crisis—the Greek conundrum and EMU reform. *Intereconomics, 45*(April), 81–5.

Mabbett, D. and Schelkle, W. (2014). Searching under the lamppost: The evolution of fiscal surveillance. *LEQS Paper, No. 75/2014.* London: London School of Economics, European Institute.

Mabbett, D. and Schelkle, W. (2015). What difference does Euro membership make to stabilization? The political economy of international monetary systems revisited. *Review of International Political Economy, 22*(3), 508–34.

Mabbett, D. and Schelkle, W. (2016a). Searching under the lamp-post: The evolution of fiscal surveillance. In J. Caporaso and M. Rhodes (Eds), *The political and economic dynamics of the Eurozone* (pp. 122–44). Oxford: Oxford University Press.

Mabbett, D. and Schelkle, W. (2016b). Independent or lonely? Central banking with multiple veto-players. Unpublished conference paper, London.

McKinnon, R. J. (1963). Optimum currency areas. *American Economic Review, 53,* 717–25.

McNamara, K. (1998). *The currency of ideas: Monetary politics in the European Union.* Ithaca, NY: Cornell University Press.

McNamara, K. (2003). Making money: Political development, the greenback, and the euro. *Working Paper PEIF-15*, University of California, Berkeley.

McPherson, J. (2014). A brief overview of the American Civil War. Civil War Trust, <http://www.civilwar.org/education/history/civil-war-overview/overview.html>.

Maes, I. and Verdun, A. (2005). Small states and the creation of EMU: Belgium and the Netherlands, pace-setters and gate-keepers. *Journal of Common Market Studies, 43*(2), 327–48.

Mair, P. (2009). Responsible versus responsive government. *MPIfG Working Paper, 09/8.* Cologne: Max-Planck Institut für Gesellschaftsforschung.

Majone, G. (1993). *The European Community: An independent 'fourth branch of government'? EUI Working Paper, SPS No. 93/9.* Florence: European University Institute.

Majone, G. (Ed.) (1996). *Regulating Europe.* London: Routledge.

Majone, G. (2001). Two logics of delegation: Agency and fiduciary relations in EU governance. *European Union Politics, 2,* February, 103–22.

Majone, G. (2016). The limits of collective action and collective leadership. In D. Chalmers, M. Jachtenfuchs, and C. Joerges (Eds), *The end of the Eurocrats' dream. Adjusting to European diversity* (pp. 218–40). Cambridge: Cambridge University Press.

Marinheiro, C. F. (2003). Output smoothing in EMU and OECD: Can we forego government contribution? A risk sharing approach. *CESifo Working Paper, No. 1051,* October.

Marshall, T. H. (1950). *Citizenship and social class, and other essays.* Cambridge: Cambridge University Press.

Martin, L. L. (1995). Heterogeneity, linkage and commons problems. In R. O. Keohane and E. Ostrom (Eds), *Local commons and global interdependence* (pp. 71–91). London: Sage Publications.

Martin, L. L. (2001). International and domestic institutions in the EMU process and beyond. In B. Eichengreen and J. A. Frieden (Eds), *The political economy of European monetary integration* (2nd ed., pp. 131–56). Boulder, CO: Westview Press.

Matthijs, M. and Blyth, M. (Eds) (2015). *The future of the Euro*. Oxford: Oxford University Press.

Matthijs, M. and McNamara, K. (2015). The Euro crisis' theory effect: Northern saints, Southern sinners, and the demise of the Eurobond. *Journal of European Integration, 37*(2), 229–45.

Mearsheimer, J. J. (2010). The false promise of international institutions. In J. L. Goldstein and R. H. Steinberg (Eds), *International institutions* (Vol. I, pp. 391–440). London: Sage. Reprint of: Mearsheimer, J. J. (1995). The false promise of international institutions. *International security, 19*(3), 5–49.

Mélitz, J. and Zumer, F. (1999). Interregional and international risk sharing and lessons for EMU. *Carnegie-Rochester Conference Series on Public Policy, 51*, 149–88.

Merler, S. and Pisani-Ferry, J. (2012). Sudden stops in the euro area. *Bruegel Policy Contributions*. Brussels: Bruegel.

Merton, R. C. (1981). On the role of social security as a means for efficient risk-bearing in an economy where human capital is not tradeable. *NBER Working Paper 0743*. Cambridge, MA: National Bureau of Economic Research.

Meyer, T., Bridgen, P., and Andow, C. (2013). Free movement? The impact of legislation, benefit generosity and wages on the pensions of European migrants. *Population, Space and Place, 19*, 714–26.

Miller, M., Weller, P., and Williamson, J. (1989). *The stabilizing properties of target zones*. Coventry: University of Warwick.

Milne, R. and Grant, J. (2015). Iceland prepares to phase out capital controls. *Financial Times Online*, June 8.

Mody, A. and Bornhorst, F. (2012). TARGET imbalances: Financing the capital-account reversal in Europe. VoxEU blog, <http://www.voxeu.org/article/target-imbalances-financing-capital-account-reversal-europe> (accessed November 22, 2014).

Mody, A. and Sandri, D. (2012). The eurozone crisis: How banks and sovereigns came to be joined at the hip. *Economic Policy, 27*(70, April), 199–230.

Molloy, R., Smith, C. L., and Wozniak, A. (2014). Declining migration within the U.S.: The role of the labor market. *NBER Working Paper 20065*. Cambridge, MA: NBER.

Moloney, N. (2014). European banking union: Assessing its risks and resilience. *Common Market Law Review, 51*(6), 1609–70.

Monnet, J. (1976). *Mémoires*. Paris: Fayard.

Moravcsik, A. (1998). *The choice for Europe: Social purpose and state power from Messina to Maastricht*. London: UCL Press.

Moravcsik, A. (2002). Reassessing legitimacy in the European Union. *Journal of Common Market Studies, 40*(4), 603–24.

Moravcsik, A. (2012). Europe after the crisis. How to sustain a common currency. *Foreign Affairs, 91*(3), 54–64.

Mosley, L. (2003). *Global capital and national governments*. Cambridge: Cambridge University Press.

Moss, D. A. (2002). *When all else fails: Government as ultimate risk manager*. Cambridge, MA: Harvard University Press.

Moss, D. A. and Brennan, S. (2001). Managing money risk in Antebellum New York: From chartered banking to free banking and beyond. *Studies in American Political Development, 15*(Fall), 138–62.

Mourlon-Druol, E. (2012). *A Europe made of money. The emergence of the European Monetary System*. Ithaca, NY: Cornell University Press.

Mügge, D. (2010). *Widen the market, narrow the competition. Banker interests and the making of a European capital market*. Colchester: ECPR Press.

Münchau, W. (2015). Watch the presses roll as Europe scrambles to fix its banks. *Financial Times*, December 14, 13.

Münchau, W. (2016). The Eurozone cannot escape political and fiscal union. *Financial Times*, June 6, 11.

Mundell, R. (1961). A theory of optimum currency areas. *American Economic Review, 51*(4), 657–65.

Mundell, R. (1973). A plan for a European currency. In H. G. Johnson and A. Swoboda (Eds), *The economics of common currencies*. London: Allen and Unwin.

Mundell, R. (2002). Monetary unions and the problem of sovereignty. *Annals of the American Academy of Political and Social Science, 579*, Jan, 123–52.

Mundell, R. and Swoboda, A. K. (Eds) (1969). *Monetary problems of the international economy*. Chicago, IL: University of Chicago Press.

N-TV (2012). Schäuble deutet Erleichterungen an. Portugal darf hoffen. *N-TV-online*, February 10, <http://www.n-tv.de/wirtschaft/Portugal-darf-hoffen-article5459931.html> (accessed August 14, 2016).

Newman, A. (2012). Austerity and the end of the European model. *Foreign Affairs*, May 1, Snapshot.

Nicolaïdes, K. (2013). European demoicracy and its crisis. *Journal of Common Market Studies, 51*(2), 351–69.

Nichols, A. and Rehm, P. (2014). Income risk in 30 countries. *Review of Income and Wealth, 60*(S1, May), S98–S116.

Oates, W. E. (2005). Toward a second-generation theory of fiscal federalism. *International Tax and Public Finance, 12*, 349–73.

Obstfeld, M. (1984). Risk-taking, global diversification, and growth. *American Economic Review, 84*(5), 1310–29.

Obstfeld, M. (1994). Are industrial-country consumption risks globally diversified? In L. Leiderman and A. Razin (Eds), *Capital mobility: The impact of consumption, investment and growth* (pp. 13–47). New York: Cambridge University Press.

Obstfeld, M. (1996). Models of currency crises with self-fulfilling features. *European Economic Review, 40*, 1037–47.

Obstfeld, M. (2013). Finance at center stage: Some lessons of the Euro crisis. *European Economy Economic Papers, 493* (April). Brussels: European Commission.

OECD (2009). International migration and the economic crisis: Understanding the links and shaping policy responses. *International Migration Outlook 2009*. Paris: OECD.

OECD (2011). *Divided we stand: Why inequality keeps rising*. Paris: OECD.

OECD (2014a). *International migration outlook*. Paris: OECD.

OECD (2014b). *Regional outlook 2014. Regions and cities: Where policies and people meet.* Paris: OECD.

Ohlemacher, S. (2015). Republicans: Obama giving "amnesty bonuses" to immigrants. *PBS Newshour, Associated Press*, February 14. http://www.pbs.org/newshour/rundown/republicans-obama-giving-amnesty-bonuses-immigrants/ (accessed November 9, 2016).

Olson, M. (1971). *The logic of collective action: Public goods and the theory of groups*. Cambridge, MA: Harvard University Press.

Olson, M. (1982). *The rise and decline of nations: Economic growth, stagflation, and social rigidities*. New Haven, CT: Yale University Press.

Ostrom, E. (1990). *Governing the commons: The evolution of institutions for collective action*. Cambridge: Cambridge University Press.

Ozgen, C., Nijkamp, P., and Poot, J. (2010). The effect of migration on income convergence: Meta-analytic evidence. *Papers in Regional Science, 89*, 537–61.

Padoa-Schioppa, T. (2004). The euro and its central bank: Getting united after the union. Cambridge, MA: MIT Press.

Palier, B. and Thelen, K. (2010). Institutionalizing dualism: Complementarities and change in France and Germany. *Politics and Society, 38*(1), 119–48.

Parsons, C. and Matthijs, M. (2015). European integration past, present and future: Moving forward through crisis? In M. Matthijs and M. Blyth (Eds), *The future of the euro* (pp. 210–32). Oxford: Oxford University Press.

Pauly, L. W. (2009). The old and the new politics of international financial stability. *Journal of Common Market Studies, 47*(5), 955–75.

Pennings, F. (2012). EU citizenship: Access to social benefits in other EU member states. *International Journal of Comparative Labour Law and Industrial Relations*, 28(3), 307–34.

Peterson, P. E. and Rom, M. C. (1990). *Welfare magnets: A new case for a national standard*. Washington, DC: Brookings Institution Press.

Piccolo, L. (2016). The Italian troublemaker: How Renzi's European strategy is putting him at odds with Angela Merkel. *EUROPP blog*, May 9.

Pigou, A. C. (1912). *Wealth and welfare*. London: Macmillan and Co.

Piketty, T. and Saez, E. (2007). How progressive is the U.S. federal tax system? A historical and international perspective. *Journal of Economic Perspectives, 21*(1), 3–24.

Piore, M. (1979). *Birds of passage: Migrant labor and industrial societies*, New York: Cambridge University Press.

Piore, M. (1986). The shifting grounds for immigration. *Annals of the American Academy of Political and Social Science, 485*, 23–33.

Pisani-Ferry, J. (2006). Only one bed for two dreams: A critical retrospective on the debate over the economic governance of the euro area. *Journal of Common Market Studies, 44*(4), 823–44.

Pisani-Ferry, J. (2012). The euro crisis and the new impossible trinity. *Bruegel Policy Contribution, 2012/01*, January. Brussels: Bruegel.

Pisani-Ferry, J. (2013). *The euro crisis and its aftermath*. Oxford: Oxford University Press.

Pisani-Ferry, J. and Sapir, A. (2010). Banking crisis management in the EU: An early assessment. *Economic Policy, 62*, 341–74.

Pisani-Ferry, J., Sapir, A., and Wolff, G. (2013). EU-IMF assistance to euro-area countries: An early assessment. *Bruegel Blueprint series, XIX*. Brussels: Bruegel.

Pontusson, J. and Baccaro, L. (2015). Rethinking comparative political economy: Growth models and distributive dynamics. Conference paper, April. Geneva: University of Geneva.

Posner, E. (2007). Financial transformation in the European Union. In S. Meunier and K. McNamara (Eds), *Making history: European integration and institutional change at fifty* (pp. 139–56). Oxford: Oxford University Press.

Posner, E. and Véron, N. (2010). The EU and financial regulation: Power without purpose? *Journal of European Public Policy, 17*(3), 400–15.

Poterba, J. M. and von Hagen, J. (Eds) (1999). *Fiscal institutions and fiscal performance.* Chicago, IL: University of Chicago Press.

Provost, C. (2010). Another race to the bottom? Venue shopping for regulators in the American financial system. Conference paper, Third Biennial Conference of the Standing Group on Regulatory Governance, Dublin, Ireland, June 17–19.

Putnam, R. D. (1988). Diplomacy and domestic politics: The logic of two-level games. *International Organization, 42*(3), 427–60.

Putnam, R. D. and Henning, C. R. (1989). The Bonn Summit of 1978: A case study in coordination. In R. N. Cooper, B. Eichengreen, G. Holtham, R. D. Putnam, and C. R. Henning (Eds), *Can nations cooperate?* (pp. 12–140). Washington, DC: Brookings Institution.

Quaglia, L. (2008). Setting the pace? Private financial interests and European financial market integration. *British Journal of Politics and International Relations, 10*(1), 46–64.

Quaglia, L. (2010). Completing the single market in financial services: The politics of competing advocacy coalitions. *Journal of European Public Policy, 17*(7), 1007–23.

Rabin, M. and Thaler, R. H. (2001). Anomalies: Risk aversion. *Journal of Economic Perspectives, 15*(1), 219–32.

Raudla, R. (2010). Governing budgetary commons: What can we learn from Elinor Ostrom? *European Journal of Law and Economics, 30*(3), 201–21.

Regini, M. and Regalia, I. (2013). Employers, unions and the state: A resurgence of concertation in Italy? In M. Bull and M. Rhodes (Eds), *Crisis and transition in Italian politics* (pp. 210–30). Milton Park: Routledge.

Reich, N. (2008). Free movement v. social rights in an enlarged union – the *Laval* and *Viking* cases before the ECJ. *German Law Journal, 9*(2), 125–60.

Reinhart, C. M. (2010). *This time is different chartbook: Country histories on debt, default and financial crises*. Cambridge, MA: National Bureau of Economic Research.

Reinhart, C. M. and Sbrancia, M. B. (2011). The liquidation of government debt. NBER Working Paper, 16893. Cambridge, MA: NBER.

Reinhart, C. M. and Sbrancia, M. B. (2015). Debt liquidation. *Economic Policy*, April, 291–333.

Reuters (2012). France seeks 120 bln EU package, euro bonds later. *Reuters Bonds News*, June 16. <http://www.reuters.com/article/eurozone-france-idUSL5E8HG5QU20120617>.

Rey, H. (2013). The global financial cycle and monetary policy independence. *Jackson Hole Paper*, August.

Riese, H. (1989). Geldpolitik bei Preisniveaustabilität. In H.-J. Ramser and H. Riese (Eds), *Beiträge zur angewandten Wirtschaftsforschung. Gottfried Bombach zum 70. Geburtstag* (pp. 101–23). Berlin: Springer.

Ritschl, A. (2012). Does Germany owe Greece a debt? A historical perspective on the European debt crisis. Paper presented at the 40th Economics Conference, Vienna.

Robinson, K. J. (2013). Savings and loan crisis 1980–1989. *Federal Reserve History*, November 22, <http://www.federalreservehistory.org/Events/DetailView/42> (accessed June 12, 2015).

Rodden, J. and Wibbels, E. (2002). Beyond the fiction of federalism: Macroeconomic management in multitiered systems. *World Politics*, *54*(4), 494–531.

Rodden, J. and Wibbels, E. (2010). Fiscal decentralization and the business cycle: An empirical study of seven federations. *Economics and Politics*, *22*(1), 37–67.

Rodrik, D. and Zeckhauser, R. (1988). The dilemma of government responsiveness. *Journal of Policy Analysis and Management*, *7*(4), 601–20.

Romero, J. (2013). The Treasury-Federal Reserve Accord. *Federal Reserve History*, November 22, <http://www.federalreservehistory.org/Events/DetailView/30> (accessed June 12, 2015).

Rueda, D. and Pontusson, J. (2000). Wage inequality and varieties of capitalism. *World Politics*, *52*(3), 350–83.

Ruffert, M. (2011). The European debt crisis and European Union law. *Common Market Law Review*, *48*, 1777–806.

Ruhkamp, S. (2012). Schuldenkrise. Die Bundesbank fordert von der EZB bessere Sicherheiten. *faz.net*, February 29. http://www.faz.net/aktuell/wirtschaft/schuldenkrise-die-bundesbank-fordert-von-der-ezb-bessere-sicherheiten-11667413.html (accessed November 26, 2014).

Runciman, D. (2008). *Political hypocrisy: The mask of power, from Hobbes to Orwell and beyond*. Princeton, NJ: Princeton University Press.

Sachverständigenrat (2012). *Nach dem EU-Gipfel: Zeit für langfristige Lösungen nutzen*. Berlin: Sachverständigenrat zur Begutachtung der wirtschaftlichen Entwicklung.

Sadeh, T. and Verdun, A. (2009). Explaining Europe's monetary union: A survey of the literature. *International Studies Review*, *11*(2), 277–301.

Sainsbury, D. (2006). Immigrants' social rights in comparative perspective: Welfare regimes, forms of immigration and immigration policy regimes. *Journal of European Social Policy*, *16*(3), 229–44.

Saint-Paul, G. (1992). Technological choice, financial markets and economic development. *European Economic Review*, *36*(4), 763–81.

Sala-i-Martin, X. and Sachs, J. (1991). Fiscal federalism and optimum currency areas: Evidence for Europe from the United States. *Working Paper No. 3855*. Cambridge, MA: NBER.

Sandbu, M. (2015). Europe's orphan: The future of the euro and the politics of debt. Princeton, NJ: Princeton University Press.

Sargent, T. and Wallace, N. (1981). Some unpleasant monetarist arithmetic. *Federal Reserve Bank of Minneapolis Quarterly Review*, Fall, 1–17.

Savage, J. D. (2005). *Making the EMU. The politics of budgetary surveillance and the enforcement of Maastricht*. Oxford: Oxford University Press.

Sbragia, A. (2008). American federalism and intergovernmental relations. In S. A. Binder, R. A. W. Rhodes, and B. A. Rockman (Eds), *The Oxford handbook of political institutions* (pp. 240–57). Oxford: Oxford University Press.

Schäfer, D. (2016). A banking union of ideas? The impact of ordoliberalism and the vicious circle on the EU banking union. *Journal of Common Market Studies, 54*(4), 961–80.

Scharpf, F. W. (1999). *Governing in Europe: Effective and democratic?* New York: Oxford University Press.

Scharpf, F. W. (2006). The joint-decision trap revisited. *Journal of Common Market Studies, 44*(4), 845–86.

Scharpf, F. W. (2009). The double asymmetry of European integration: Or: why the EU cannot be a social market economy. *MPIfG Working Paper, 09/12*. Cologne: Max Planck Institut für Gesellschaftsforschung.

Scharpf, F. W. (2011). Monetary union, fiscal crisis and the preemption of democracy. *LEQS Annual Lecture Paper 2011*. London: European Institute, London School of Economics.

Scharpf, F. W. (2015). Political legitimacy in a non-optimal currency area. In O. Cramme and S. B. Hobolt (Eds), *Democratic politics in a European union under stress* (pp. 20–44). Oxford: Oxford University Press.

Schelkle, W. (2001). *Monetäre integration. Bestandsaufnahme und Weiterentwicklung der neueren Theorie*. Heidelberg: Physica-Verlag.

Schelkle, W. (2005). The political economy of fiscal policy co-ordination in EMU: From disciplinarian device to insurance arrangement. *Journal of Common Market Studies, 43*(2), 371–91.

Schelkle, W. (2006). The theory and practice of economic governance in EMU revisited: What have we learnt about commitment and credibility? *Journal of Common Market Studies, 44*(4), 669–85.

Schelkle, W. (2007). EU fiscal governance: Hard law in the shadow of soft law? *Columbia Journal of European Law, 13*(3), 705–32.

Schelkle, W. (2009). The contentious creation of the regulatory state in fiscal surveillance. *West European Politics, 32*(4), 829–46.

Schelkle, W. (2011). Reconfiguring welfare states in the post-industrial age: The role of trade unions. *European Journal of Industrial Relations, 17*(4), 301–14.

Schelkle, W. (2012a). Policymaking in hard times: French and German responses to economic crisis in the euro area. In N. Bermeo and J. Pontusson (Eds), *Coping with crisis. Government reactions to the Great Recession* (pp. 130–61). New York: Russell Sage.

Schelkle, W. (2012b). Good governance in crisis or a good crisis for governance? A comparison of the EU and the US. *Review of International Political Economy, 19*(1), 34–58.

Schelkle, W. (2012c). European fiscal union: From monetary back door to parliamentary main entrance. *CESifo Forum, 1*, 28–34.

Schelkle, W. (2013a). Monetary integration in crisis: How well do existing theories explain the predicament of EMU? *Transfer: European Review of Labour and Research, 19*(1), 37–48.

Schelkle, W. (2013b). The political economy of regulating longevity insurance in the EU. In U. Neergard, E. Szyszczak, J. W. van de Gronden, and M. Krajewski (Eds), *The role of social services of general interest in EU law* (pp. 433–57). The Hague: TMC Asser Press.

Schelkle, W. (2014a). Fiscal integration by default. In P. Genschel and M. Jachtenfuchs (Eds), *Beyond the regulatory polity? The European integration of core state powers* (pp. 105–23). Oxford: Oxford University Press.

Schelkle, W. (2014b). The "poundzone" is just as sub-optimal a currency area as the Eurozone. *EUROPP blog*. London: London School of Economics, <http://www.bit.ly/1s49ac3> (accessed June 27, 2016).

Schelkle, W. (2015). The insurance potential of a non-optimal currency area. In O. Cramme and S. B. Hobolt (Eds), *Democratic politics in a European union under stress* (pp. 137–54). Oxford: Oxford University Press.

Schelkle, W. (2016). Krugman's argument that the Eurozone is not an optimum currency area could easily be applied to the US. *EUROPP blog*. London: London School of economics, <http://www.bit.ly/1TgokpS> (accessed June 27, 2016).

Schelkle, W. and Hassel, A. (2013). The policy consensus ruling European political economy: The political attractions of discredited economics. *Global Policy, 3*(Supplement s1), 16–27.

Schelling, T. C. (1966). *Arms and influence*. New Haven, CT: Yale University Press.

Schelling, T. C. (1978). *Micromotives and macrobehavior*. New York: Norton.

Scheve, K. and Stasavage, D. (2015). *Taxing the rich: A history of fiscal fairness in the United States and Europe*. Princeton, NJ: Princeton University Press.

Schimmelfennig, F. (2015). Differentiated integration before and after the crisis. In O. Cramme and S. B. Hobolt (Eds), *Democratic politics in a European Union under stress* (pp. 121–36). Oxford: Oxford University Press.

Schinasi, G. J. and Teixeira, P. G. (2006). The lender of last resort in the European single financial market. *IMF Working Paper, WP/06/127*. Washington, DC: IMF.

Schiopu, R. and Siegfried, N. (2006). Determinants of workers' remittances. Evidence from the European neighbouring regions. *ECB Working Paper 688*. Frankfurt: ECB.

Schmidt, V. A. (2015). The Eurozone's crisis of democratic legitimacy: Can the EU rebuild public trust and support for European economic integration? *European Economy Discussion Paper, 015*, September. Brussels: European Commission.

Schmidt, V. A. and Thatcher, M. (Eds) (2013). *Resilient liberalism in Europe's political economy*. Cambridge: Cambridge University Press.

Schmitt, C. and Obinger, H. (2013). Spatial interdependencies and welfare state generosity in Western democracies, 1960–2000. *Journal of European Social Policy, 23*(2), 119–33.

Schoenmaker, D. (2010). Burden sharing: From theory to practice. *VOX CEPR's Policy Portal*, October 18, <http://www.voxeu.org/article/burden-sharing-eurozone> (accessed July 3, 2016).

Schoenmaker, D. and Siegmann, A. (2014). Can European bank bailouts work? *Journal of Banking and Finance, 48*, 334–49.

Schram, S. and Soss, J. (1999). The real value of welfare: Why poor families do not migrate. *Politics and Society, 27*(1), 39–66.

Schram, S., Nitz, L., and Krueger, G. (1998). Without cause or effect: Reconsidering welfare migration as a policy problem. *American Journal of Political Science, 42*(1), 210–30.

Schwartz, H. M. (2001). Round up the usual suspects! Globalization, domestic politics, and welfare state change. In P. Pierson (Ed.), *The new politics of the welfare state* (pp. 17–44). Oxford: Oxford University Press.

Shambaugh, J. C. (2012). The Euro's three crises. *Brookings Papers on Economic Activity*, Spring, 157–231.

Shiller, R. (1993). *Macro markets*. New York: Oxford University Press.

Simon, H. A. (1978). Rationality as process and as product of thought. *American Economic Review, 68*(2), 1–16.

Sims, C. (2012). Gaps in the institutional structure of the euro area. *Banque de France Financial Stability Review, 16*, April, 217–23.

Sinn, H.-W. (2012). The European balance of payments crisis: An introduction. *CESifo Forum, 13*, January, 3–10.

Sinn, H.-W. and Wollmershäuser, T. (2012). Target loans, current account balances and capital flows: The ECB's rescue facility. *International Tax and Public Finance, 19*(4), 468–508.

Skocpol, T. (1992). *Protecting soldiers and mothers: The political origins of social policy in the United States*. Cambridge, MA: Belknap Press of Harvard University Press.

Skocpol, T. (1995). *Social policy in the United States: Future possibilities in historical perspective*. Princeton, NJ: Princeton University Press.

Snidal, D. (1995). The politics of scope: Endogenous actors, heterogeneity and institutions. In R. O. Keohane and E. Ostrom (Eds), *Local commons and global interdependence* (pp. 47–70). London: Sage Publications.

Sørensen, B. and Yosha, O. (1998). International risk sharing and European monetary unification. *Journal of International Economics, 45*, 211–38.

Soskice, D. and Hope, D. (2015). The Eurozone and political economic institutions: A review article. *Annual Review of Political Science*.

Spiegel (1992). Wir waren nie so unter Druck. *Der Spiegel, 39*, 144–53.

Spiegel, P. (2014). Berlin attacks EU's easing of austerity demands. *FT blog*, February 28, <http://www.ft.com/cms/s/0/d7b79578-a000-11e3-9c65-00144feab7de.html#axzz2ui3fCfF1> (accessed March 14, 2015).

Steele, G. and Whittaker, J. (2012). Don't look to seigniorage to save the euro. *EconoMonitor blog*, August 7.

Steen, M. (2012). Weidmann isolated as ECB plan approved. *Financial Times Online*, September 6, <http://www.ft.com/cms/s/0/3651b028-f846-11e1-b0e1-00144feabdc0.html#ixzz47K4iTeYg> (accessed July 4, 2016).

Steinkamp, S. and Westermann, F. (2014). The role of creditor seniority in Europe's sovereign debt crisis. *Economic Policy, 29*(79), 495–552.

Steinmo, S. (1993). *Taxation and democracy: Swedish, British, and American approaches to financing the modern state*. New Haven, CT: Yale University Press.

Stiglitz, J. E. (1969). The effects of income, wealth, and capital gains taxation on risk taking. *Quarterly Journal of Economics, 83*, 263–83.

Stiglitz, J. E. (2016). *The Euro. How a common currency threatens the future of Europe*. New York: W. W. Norton and Company.

Svec, J. and Kondo, A. (2012). Fiscal policy cyclicality and growth within the US States. *B. E. Journal of Macroeconomics, 12*(2).

Swenson, P. (2002). *Capitalists against markets: The making of labor markets and welfare states in the United States and Sweden*. New York: Oxford University Press.

Sylla, R., Legler, J. B., and Wallis, J. J. (1987). Banks and state public finance in the new republic: The United States, 1790–1860. *Journal of Economic History, 47*(2), 391–403.

Taylor, P. (2014). Insight: European bank mergers still face hurdles post-stress tests. *Reuters*, October 12, <http://www.reuters.com/article/2014/10/12/ecb-banks-tests-idUSL6N0S23TB20141012>.

Telegraph (2012). Angela Merkel stands firm in resisting ESM bank licence. *Telegraph Online*, August 29, <http://www.telegraph.co.uk/finance/financialcrisis/9506882/Angela-Merkel-stands-firm-in-resisting-ESM-bank-licence.html>.

Tinbergen, J. (1952). *On the theory of economic policy*. Amsterdam: North Holland.

Titmuss, R. (1958). *Essays on "the welfare state."* London: University Books.

Tobin, J. (1990). On the theory of macroeconomic policy. *De Economist, 138*(1), 1–14.

Todd, W. F. (1994). Similarities and dissimilarities in the collapses of three state-chartered private deposit insurance funds. *Federal Reserve Bank of Cleveland Working Paper, No. 9411*, October.

Toniolo, G. and White, E. N. (2015). The evolution of the financial stability mandate: From its origins to the present day. *NBER Working Paper Series, No. 20844*. Cambridge, MA: NBER.

Tornell, A. and Westermann, F. (2012). Greece: The sudden stop that wasn't. *CESifo Forum, 13*, January, 102–3.

Torres, F. (2007). The long road to EMU: The economic and political reasoning behind Maastricht. *NIPE Working Paper, No. 23*. Aveira: Universidade do Minho.

Trescott, P. B. (1955). Federal-state financial relations, 1790–1860. *Journal of Economic History, 15*(3), 227–45.

Trichet, J.-C. (2009). *Interview in De Tijd and L'Echo (December)*. <http://www.ecb.int/press/key/date/2009/html/sp091210.en.html> (accessed July 14, 2013).

Tsebelis, G. (1995). Decision-making in political systems: Veto players in presidentialism, parliamentarism, multicameralism and multipartyism. *British Journal of Political Science, 25*(3), 289–325.

Tsebelis, G. (2002). *Veto-players: How political institutions work*. New York: Russell Sage.

Turner, A. (2010). *Market efficiency and rationality: Why financial markets are different*. London: London School of Economics and Political Science, <http://www.lse.ac.uk/assets/richmedia/channels/publicLecturesAndEvents/transcripts/20101012_1830_marketEfficiencyAndRationality_tr.pdf> (accessed June 9, 2015).

Ulbrich, J. and Lipponer, A. (2012). Balances in the Target2 payments system—a problem? *CESifoForum, 13*, January, 73–6.

Underhill, G. R. D. and Zhang, X. (2008). Setting the rules: Private power, political underpinnings, and legitimacy in global monetary and financial governance. *International Affairs, 84*(3), 535–54.

USNEI (2007). Recognition of foreign qualifications, U.S. Department of Education, <http://www2.ed.gov/about/offices/list/ous/international/usnei/us/edlite-visitus-forrecog.html> (accessed March 14, 2015).

Van Rompuy, H., Barroso, J. M., Juncker, J.-C., and Draghi, M. (2012). *Towards a genuine economic and monetary union*. Brussels: European Union.

Verdun, A. (2000). *European responses to globalization and financial market integration: Perceptions of economic and monetary union in Britain, France and Germany*. Basingstoke: Macmillan.

Verdun, A. (2015). A historical institutionalist explanation of the EU's responses to the euro area financial crisis. *Journal of European Public Policy, 22*(2), 219–37.

Vergote, O., Studener, W., Efthymiadis, I., and Merriman, N. (2010). Main drivers of the ECB financial accounts and ECB financial strength over the first 11 years. *Occasional Paper Series, 111*, May. Frankfurt: ECB.

Véron, N. (2014). The G20 financial reform agenda after five years. *Bruegel Policy Contribution*, 2014/11. Brussels: Bruegel.

Véron, N. (2015). *Europe's radical banking union*. Brussels: Bruegel.

von Hagen, J. (1989). Monetary targeting with exchange rate constraints: The Bundesbank in the 1980s. *Federal Reserve Bank of St. Louis Review*, September/October, 53–69.

Vroman, W. (2009). Unemployment insurance recipients and nonrecipients in the CPS. *Monthly Labour Review*, October, 44–53, <http://www.bls.gov/opub/mlr/2009/10/art4full.pdf>.

Wallis, J. J., Sylla, R. E., and Grinath, A., III. (2004). Sovereign debt and repudiation: The emerging-market debt crisis in the U.S. states, 1839–1843. *National Bureau of Economic Research Working Paper Series, No. 10753*.

Walter, S. (2008). A new approach for determining exchange-rate level preferences. *International Organization, 62*(3), 405–38.

Walters, A. (1988). A critical view of the EMS. *Cato Journal, 8*(2), 503–6.

Waysand, C., Ross, K., and De Guzman, J. C. (2010). European financial linkages: A new look at imbalances. *IMF Working Paper, No. 10/295*, December.

Weir, M. and Skocpol, T. (1985). State structures and the possibilities for "Keynesian" responses to the Great Depression in Sweden, Britain and the United States. In P. B. Evans, D. Rueschemeyer, and T. Skocpol (Eds), *Bringing the state back in* (pp. 107–63). Cambridge: Cambridge University Press.

Westermann, F. (2014). Comment on Whelan (2014). *Economic Policy, 29*(77), 117–25.

Whelan, K. (2014a). The ECB's collateral policy and its future as lender of last resort. *Note, IP/A/ECON/NT/XXX*, November. European Parliament: Policy Department A: Economic and Scientific Policy.

Whelan, K. (2014b). TARGET2 and central bank balance sheets. *Economic Policy, 29*(77), 79–137.

Whelan, K. (2014c). The monetary dialogue and accountability for the ECB. Part of the compilation PE 518.753 for the Monetary Dialogue, European Parliament.

White, E. N. (2015). Protecting financial stability in the aftermath of World War I: The Federal Reserve Bank of Atlanta's dissenting policy. *National Bureau of Economic Research Working Paper Series, No. 21341*.

White, J. (2015). Politicizing Europe: The challenge of executive discretion. In O. Cramme and S. B. Hobolt (Eds), *Democratic politics in a European Union under stress* (pp. 87–102). Oxford: Oxford University Press.

Whittaker, J. (2011). Intra-eurosystem debts. Lancaster University Management School Working Paper, <http://www.lancs.ac.uk/staff/whittaj1/eurosystem.pdf>.

Wibbels, E. (2003). Bailouts, budget constraints, and Leviathans: Comparative federalism and lessons from the early United States. *Comparative Political Studies*, *36*(5), 475–508.

Wildasin, D. E. (2002). Fiscal policy in post-EMU Europe. *European Union Politics*, *3*(2), 251–60.

Winick, S. L. (1999). A new chapter in constitutional law: Saenz v. Roe and the revival of the fourteenth amendment's privileges or immunities clause. *Hofstra Law Review*, *28* (2), 573–99.

Wolf, M. (2011). Intolerable choices for the eurozone. *Financial Times online*, May 31. http://www.ft.com/cms/s/0/1a61825a-8bb7-11e0-a725-00144feab49a.html#ixzz3L9tvwGX9 (acccessed October 29, 2016).

Woll, C. (2014). Bank rescue schemes in continental Europe: The power of collective inaction. *Government and Opposition*, *49*(3), 426–51.

Wolman, A. L. (2013). Federal Reserve interdistrict settlement. *Federal Reserve Bank of Richmond Economic Quarterly*, *99*(2), 117–41.

Wyplosz, C. (2012). The coming revolt against austerity. *VOX column*, May 2, VOX CEPR's Policy Portal.

Wyplosz, C. (2013). Europe's quest for fiscal discipline. *European Economy Economic Papers*, *498*, April. Brussels: European Commission.

Zartaloudis, S. (2014). *Europeanization through soft power in a world of neglect: The impact of the European employment strategy in Greece and Portugal*. Basingstoke: Palgrave Macmillan.

Zysman, J. (1983). *Governments, markets and growth: Financial systems and the politics of industrial change*. Oxford: Robertson.

Index

Note: Page numbers in italics denote figures and tables.

The manufacturer's authorised representative in the EU for product safety is Oxford University Press España S.A. of El Parque Empresarial San Fernando de Henares, Avenida de Castilla, 2 - 28830 Madrid (www.oup.es/en or product.safety@oup.com). OUP España S.A. also acts as importer into Spain of products made by the manufacturer.
Printed and bound by CPI Group (UK) Ltd, Croydon, CR0 4YY
14/09/2026
02216307-0003